BEST BIRD
SITES IN NORFOLK

by Neil Glenn

Dedicated to Jackie, the most perfect wife
a man could possibly dream of having.

BUCKINGHAM PRESS LTD

in association with

Published in 2006 by:
Buckingham Press Ltd
55 Thorpe Park Road, Peterborough
Cambridgeshire PE3 6LJ
United Kingdom

01733 561739
e-mail: buck.press@btinternet.com

ISBN 0 95550339 1 8
ISSN 0144-364 X

Editor: David Cromack
Design and maps: Hilary Cromack
Publisher: Hilary Cromack

Cover illustration: *Cranes at Stubb Mill* by Steve Cale

Steve began birding at the age of 13 and started sketching birds as field notes shortly after. Over 30 years, his work has become an individually recognisable style. He has birded and painted all over the world but has made his home in Norfolk where his artwork is now well known.
Contact details: tel 01328 829 589 or 07866 263 673
Email: steveshrike@aol.com

Black and white illustrations (unless otherwise stated): Ernest Leahy
Ernest is a well established professional artist who produces original watercolours and drawings of Western Palearctic birds, wildlife and country scenes. He has provided illustrations for many publications including Poysers.
Contact details: 01582 793 144
e-mail: ernest.leahy@ntlworld.com
www.wildlifewatercolours.co.uk

Printed and bound in Great Britain by:
Information Press, Eynsham, Oxford, UK.

CONTENTS

CONTENTS

INTRODUCTION

WHEN I WAS ASKED by David and Hilary Cromack to write a second edition of *Best Birdwatching Sites in Norfolk* I thought it would be a simple matter of dotting the 'i's and crossing the 't's; easy money, I thought. How wrong could I be?

Some well-known site guides have developed a reputation for making minimal changes between editions but I wanted to be thorough. It became obvious that in the three years between the first and second editions, many things on the birding scene in Norfolk had changed. After visiting site after site I found a new visitor centre here, an extra piece of boardwalk there; an increase in records of a particular species at one site while another regular site had been abandoned. It brought home to me just what an ever-changing world we live in (to quote Paul McCartney).

For this second edition, I revisited every site and have updated the information. I have also added ten new sites for you to explore. At virtually every site I found something had changed.

For instance, Rockland Broad, a simple site to cover, has been completely opened up to wheelchair users. Buckenham Fen's hide vanished overnight and by the time you read this, it should have been replaced with a new one. Many of the Broadland footpaths are being refurbished, with work due to continue for a couple of years yet. Cantley Beet Factory, the best place in the county (if not the country) to see Green and Wood Sandpipers, has been closed to casual visitors. And so I could go on but you will have to read each site page to see if your favourite reserve has altered.

As well as venues changing, so has the reliability of birds at particular sites. In the first edition, I couldn't recommend a single reliable site to see Lapland Bunting, whereas Choseley now consistently holds a handful of this species. Of course, this may yet change before Edition Three hits the presses!

Worryingly, Willow Tits are now very difficult to find in Norfolk. Only at Strumpshaw Fen and Sculthorpe Moor can one be assured of seeing this attractive species but if such a steep rate of decline continues, how long will this situation last? Black Redstarts have also failed to breed in the county for the last few years and Tree Pipits have deserted a few of their previous strongholds.

On a more upbeat note, Honey Buzzards are now easier to see. English Nature has opened up a new watchpoint at Great Ryburgh and HBs show very well from here. Montagu's Harriers are increasing in number, though no site has been opened to the public officially (listen out for RSPB announcements should it become possible to do so – there were two "secret" watchpoints opened in 2005 – let's hope they can become more widely publicised).

Major alterations are planned for NWT Cley and the Hawk & Owl Trust's Sculthorpe Moor, with new buildings being opened at WWT Welney and Whitlingham Country Park just as this book reaches the shops. I also already kno w of an NOA reserve opening in 2007/08.

So, as we all know, nothing stays the same. What species will be in decline? Which reserve

INTRODUCTION

will build a spanking new hide? No doubt I will find this out when researching Edition Three in a few years time!

I would like to say a big thank you to everyone who bought the First Edition and to the reviewers who gave it such a positive reaction. Many thanks, also, to the people who took the time to write to me or stop and tell me how much they enjoyed reading and using the book. I was particularly delighted to receive letters telling me of new species seen (sometimes one that had eluded the writer for so many years) because of my efforts. I hope this edition is as well-received and well-used as the first one.

Neil Glenn

Ed: If you would like to correspond with Neil, do so in the first instance by writing c/o Buckingham Press Ltd, 55 Thorpe Park Road, Peterborough PE3 6LJ.

ACKNOWLEDGEMENTS

I WOULD like to acknowledge the following people, without whom this book would not have been possible:

Firstly, the hard-working staff at Buckingham Press for their excellent maps and page-layouts and for asking me to write this tome in the first place;

Secondly, many friends, too numerous to mention, who have shown boundless support and enthusiasm for this project from the outset;

Thirdly, Brian of Essex for his comments on disabled access at some of the sites listed;

Fourthly, the many hard-working wardens and staff of the various management bodies who have been extremely helpful in verifying the accuracy of the site information, especially Lynette Dear from the Norfolk Wildlife Trust and Stephen Harris from *BIRDscapes* Gallery. I am also grateful for corrections provided by members of Norfolk Bird Club.

Fifthly, Ken and Maureen for use of their bungalow in Hunstanton and especially to Ken for demonstrating that my punctuation and grammar are not the worst in the world!

Finally and most importantly, my long-suffering wife who has been unconditionally supportive throughout the writing of this book and long-before I ever started work on it! She has also borne the brunt of most of the proof-reading. Maybe, after reading this material, she will have learned what a wonderful place Norfolk is!

My thanks must also go to everyone who purchased the first edition, making this second edition possible and necessary! Your kind comments made the hard work worthwhile and I hope this edition proves to be just as useful.

WHY NORFOLK IS THE TOP COUNTY FOR BIRDWATCHING

FOR the bulk of the British population, Norfolk is a sleepy tucked-away county with little to make it noteworthy but, among birdwatchers, it enjoys a reputation second to none. Why is this so? Until I began to research this book, I freely admit that I'd been content to watch the diverse bounty of birds without being particularly bothered why they were attracted to the county. However, on further reflection, this question demands some answers.

A quick glance at a map of Britain gives a simple clue to the county's importance to birds. East Anglia (of which Norfolk is the northern half) is a bulky land-mass that juts out into the North Sea, pointing towards Europe and Scandinavia. For any off-course birds migrating from these continental areas, making landfall here could be the difference between life and death.

This explains why so many rarities are discovered but many other commoner species actively choose this county as their preferred wintering or summering grounds. There must be some other attraction other than geographical positioning and that can be summed up in one word: habitat.

Many birdwatchers in Norfolk concentrate along the north coast, dominated by The Wash and large tracts of salt marsh, because this is the area with the greatest concentration of birds. The Wash is a huge estuary of mud, super-abundant in invertebrates – a crucial food supply for thousands of wintering wading birds. The 2,000 hectares of salt marsh – stretching from Holme to Salthouse – is internationally important for many breeding species and over-wintering wildfowl. For instance, up to a third of the world's population of Pink-footed Geese choose to spend the winter on these marshes. Norfolk is lucky in that most of its salt marsh has been protected from development. Similar habitat in Essex and Kent, which once supported large bird communities, has been reclaimed for housing and industrial use. As other areas of marsh disappear under housing, so the Norfolk marshes become even more important for birds.

However, it is important to remember that the interior of Norfolk contains other valuable habitats. Further south are the Norfolk Broads, a bird-rich habitat created in medieval times by people digging for peat. These waters, so beloved of boating enthusiasts, spread inland from Great Yarmouth to Wroxham and Norwich. The pure waters of The Broads attract many species of wildfowl as well as many species of insect and plant. Ironically, the activities of man are now threatening this delicate habitat through pollution, though this is being addressed by numerous conservation organisations. Most Broadland reed beds and wet woodlands (carrs) are being restored and preserved by hard-working organisations such as Norfolk Wildlife Trust, The Broads Authority and the RSPB.

Breckland is yet another important region for birds. This is an area of some 94,000 hectares, originally of sandy heathland, located around Thetford. This nutrient-poor soil was extensively planted with Scots pines in the 1940s and these are still being harvested to this day by Forest Enterprise. This harvesting creates many clearings that are inhabited by Wood Larks and Nightjars. The other important resident of The Brecks is the humble rabbit: constant nibbling of vegetation ensures the continued presence of ground-nesting species such as Stone-curlew and Wood Lark.

The Fens of East Anglia have mostly been drained and reclaimed for agricultural use, though some areas remain, most notably around The Ouse Washes. Norfolk's key site is WWT Welney and its famous wintering herds of wild swans and huge numbers of wildfowl, which find the combination of rivers, flood plains and grazing marsh to their liking. The RSPB is creating the largest wetland reserve in Britain on the Fens of Lakenheath, hoping to attract Bitterns, Bearded Tits and Marsh Harriers back to the area.

We must not forget farmland in our equation. The majority of land in Norfolk is intensively farmed and is thus inaccessible to visitors. However, it is this inaccessibility that protects some species from disturbance on farms managed sympathetically with wildlife in mind. Many of Norfolk's 100 pairs of Stone-curlews nest on farmland, free from the pressures of egg-collectors and birdwatchers. The same can be said for winter flocks of Tree Sparrows and Corn Buntings. Of course some farmers, motivated largely by EC subsidies, have much to answer for as many farms these days are completely devoid of wildlife but I feel the tide is turning.

Add gravel workings, small tracts of ancient woodland, extensive dune systems, former Victorian estates and the North Sea into the equation and the wide range of habitats in Norfolk becomes evident. There are even a couple of sea-cliffs, recently colonised by Fulmars; not bad for a "boring, flat county"!

One final thought: as Norfolk's attraction for birds became evident, more and more birdwatchers congregated in the county. Norfolk now has a large, resident population of birders, plus many more who spend their holidays there. This means that new and interesting birds are always likely to be discovered, fuelling the county's reputation as the bird capital of Britain, thus attracting more birdwatchers and so on and so forth...

WHY THIS SITE GUIDE?

THERE are several guides to Norfolk bird and wildlife sites available for you to buy, so why choose this one? I shall explain.

When I visit a bird site, particularly one I haven't visited before, I want to know:

i) Exactly what I am likely to see at the time of year I am visiting.

ii) The likelihood of seeing the birds listed in the site guide.

For instance, how many times have you been to a reserve in winter and seen Merlin on the sightings board? Lots. And how many Merlins have you seen? Not many, I bet! In this guide you will find Merlin listed for many reserves but you will also be given an idea of how likely you are to see one. This is expressed by a percentage score after the name of each target bird for each site.

The fact that Merlins zip through Titchwell once a day in winter doesn't mean you will see one and this guide makes that obvious. In this way, the visiting birdwatcher will not let their hopes rise too high but will know which birds are most likely to be encountered.

A major feature of this guide is that **sites are listed in alphabetical order**: no more struggling to find site 3.14, or reading through reams of text to find the site you want. Sites are also cross-referenced on pages for **Wheelchair Access, Partial Wheelchair Access, Public Transport Access** and **Broadland Boat Access**. If you are visiting Norfolk for a Norfolk Broads boating holiday, for instance, this feature makes it easy to look up which sites are accessible for you. You then simply turn to the site guide page for more details.

Another bugbear of many site guides is the fact they hide the most important information in masses of text. **This guide displays the most relevant facts prominently** (when to visit, grid reference of parking area, target species, likelihood of seeing your targets). More detailed background information is given in the adjoining text but the important stuff is right there up front.

Another important feature of this book is that it is up to date. I visited every site listed in 2005 (and several in 2006) and noted any changes to previous visits. Of course, things may have changed since I last visited. **This makes the Contacts section for each site an essential feature**, enabling visitors to check details of opening times, entrance fee, etc before their trip.

Complete beginners will find the **Calendar section details the seasonal comings and goings of birds in Norfolk** plus a list of birdwatching sites recommended according to the season. More experienced birders may wish to visit somewhere they have heard about but not yet visited. In either case, the reader can easily locate the relevant page, as sites are arranged in alphabetical order.

The layout for each site is designed to help you make the most of your visit. As stated above, important information (e.g. parking) is easy to find but this guide comes into its own as **the background text takes you on the walk itself**. The best areas for certain target species are described, as are tips on fieldcraft, enabling birdwatchers to make the most of their visit.

In a nutshell, this book is designed to enable any birdwatcher visiting Norfolk to confidently plan a day, weekend, or holiday seeing exactly what they want to see, when they want to see it (within reason!), no matter how experienced or inexperienced they may be.

Finally, every effort has been made to check, check and check again the details for each site. If you find that this guide is incorrect in any way, please let me know so that I can amend the details in future editions. Also, I would be extremely happy to hear from you if you have enjoyed a day out at one of the sites mentioned: it would make all my hard work worthwhile!

THE BIRDWATCHERS CODE OF CONDUCT

Around three million adults go birdwatching every year in the UK. Following *The birdwatchers' code* is good practice, common sense and will help everybody to enjoy seeing birds.

This code puts the interests of birds first and respects other people, whether or not they are interested in birds.

1. The interests of the birds come first

- Avoid going too close to birds or disturbing their habitats – if a bird flies away or makes repeated alarm calls, you're too close. If it leaves, you won't get a good view of it anyway.
- Stay on roads and paths where they exist and avoid disturbing habitat used by birds.
- Think about your fieldcraft. You might disturb a bird even if you are not very close, eg a flock of wading birds on the foreshore can be disturbed from a mile away if you stand on the seawall.
- Repeatedly playing a recording of bird song or calls to encourage a bird to respond can divert a territorial bird from other important duties, such as feeding its young.

2. Be an ambassador for birdwatching

Respond positively to questions from interested passers-by. They may not be birdwatchers yet but good view of a bird or a helpful answer may ignite a spark of interest.

Consider using local services, such as pubs, restaurants, petrol stations and public transport. Raising awareness of the benefits to local communities of trade from visiting birdwatchers may, ultimately, help the birds themselves.

3. Know the Countryside Code and follow it

Respect the wishes of local residents and landowners and don't enter private land without permission, unless it is open for public access on foot.

Follow the codes on access and the countryside for the place you're walking in. Irresponsible behaviour may cause a land manager to deny access to others (eg for important bird survey work). It may also disturb the bird or give birdwatching bad coverage in the media.

4. Law

In England, Scotland and Wales, it is a criminal offence to disturb, intentionally or recklessly, at or near the nest, a species listed on Schedule 1 of the Wildlife & Countryside Act 1981 (see www.rspb.org.uk/policy/wildbirdslaw for a full list). Disturbance could include playback of songs and calls. If you witness anyone who you suspect may be illegally disturbing or destroying wildlife or habitat, phone the police immediately (ideally, with a six-figure map reference) and report it to the RSPB.

5. Rare birds

Mobile phones, telephone and pager services and the internet mean you can now share your sightings instantly. If you discover a rare bird, please bear the following in mind.

- Consider the potential impact of spreading the news and make an effort to inform the landowner (or, on a nature reserve, the warden) first.
- On private land, always talk to the landowner first. With a little planning, access can often be arranged.
- Rare breeding birds are at risk from egg-collectors and some birds of prey from persecution. If you discover a rare breeding species that you think is vulnerable, contact the RSPB; it has considerable experience in protecting rare breeding birds. Please also report your sighting to the county bird recorder or the Rare Breeding Birds Panel. (www.rbbp.org.uk).
- Park sensibly, follow instructions and consider making a donation if requested.
- Don't get too close so that you can take a photograph – you'll incur the wrath of everyone else watching if you scare the bird away.
- Be patient if the viewing is limited, talk quietly and give others a chance to see the bird too.

6. Make your sightings count

Add to tomorrow's knowledge of birds by sending your sightings to www.birdtrack.net which allows you to input and store all of your birdwatching records and in turn helps to support species and site conservation. Your records are important for local conservation and help to build the county's ornithological history. For a list of county bird recorders, look in the County Directory of *The Yearbook*, ask at your local library, or visit www.britishbirds.co.uk/countyrecorders. You can also get involved in a UK-wide bird monitoring scheme, such as the Breeding Bird Survey and the Wetland Bird Survey (see www.bto.org for details).

YOUR BIRDING YEAR

THIS PART of the book is aimed at helping you plan your birding trips more effectively. For example, you may wish to observe wild geese: by reading the monthly summaries you will be able to find out which species will be present, the best time of year to visit and which sites to head for. Then simply turn to the site page in the main section to find out how to get to your chosen birding venue.

January's calendar is very comprehensive, covering species which occur throughout the period from October to March and is intended to be complementary to the calendars for each of those months.

Barn Owl is a familiar bird of coastal sites and Fenland farms.
By Alan Harris

JANUARY

MANY evocative sights and sounds can be experienced without much effort from the enthusiastic birdwatcher in this exciting month. What could be better than starting the day with thousands of Pink-footed Geese flying overhead on the way to their feeding grounds and ending it, by watching Hen Harriers silently drifting in to roost over a reedbed? Pure magic.

Herons and Cranes: If areas of shallow water freeze over on reserves such as Titchwell, Hickling Broad, Cley, etc, keep an eye open for Bitterns in the open, as their usual feeding areas deep in the reeds become inaccessible. One or two Little Egrets should be seen at Titchwell, no matter what the weather conditions and head for Stubb Mill to see Cranes coming into roost.

YOUR BIRDING YEAR

Geese: Huge numbers of wintering wild geese can be seen at various accessible sites. Almost half of all Britain's wintering Pink-footed Geese roost on The Wash at Snettisham. Get there early in the morning for a real avian spectacular but avoid three days either side of a full moon, when the geese will remain in the fields feeding throughout the night. During the day, flocks can be encountered anywhere along the coast and surrounding fields.

Brent Geese visit most of the salt marshes between Salthouse and Holme but try Titchwell and Cley for close views of birds on the ground. Most of the Brents will be of the dark-bellied race (*bernicla*) but it is possible to test your identification skills by trying to pick out a pale-bellied race (*hrota*) or a Black Brant (*branta*) from their commoner cousins. The Black Brant, a vagrant from America, has become an annual visitor to Norfolk, favouring sites such as Cley and Titchwell in the last couple of years. Hybrid young (*branta x bernicla*) are identified most winters to further test the keen birder!

White-fronted Geese are best viewed from Lady Anne's Drive at Holkham. Thousands of Pink-footed Geese are usually in the area and mixed in with them might be one or two Barnacle Geese, or a Lesser White-fronted Goose on rare occasions. There should also be one or two Egyptian Geese at this site along with the other two 'plastic' geese, Canada and Greylag.

The other winter goose to see in the county is the (taiga) Bean, the larger of the two races. There is a wintering flock of around 150 birds, usually to be found on Buckenham Marshes. Please call in to Strumpshaw Fen visitor centre for up-to-date sightings. A few individuals of the smaller (tundra) Bean Goose can sometimes be found with the White-fronted Geese at Holkham or the swans at Welney.

Swans: If you are looking for superb views of wild swans, then Welney is the place to head for. Most of the Bewick's and Whoopers spend the day in fields away from the reserve but return to roost in the early evening. The warden spreads grain out for the swans and ducks and the whole spectacle can be watched from the comfort of a heated hide. A small number of wild swans can sometimes be seen around Haddiscoe Marsh and occasionally in the Horsey area.

Wildfowl: Thousands of ducks make Norfolk their home in winter. These can be split into two categories: seaducks and inland ducks. Species of seaduck such as Long-tailed Duck, Common Scoter, Velvet Scoter and Red-breasted Merganser are usually best found somewhere between Hunstanton and Titchwell, though Holme seems to be the most reliable site for the former species. They can be accompanied by Red-throated, Black-throated and Great Northern Divers, or Red-necked and Slavonian Grebes. The dunes in Holkham Bay are also excellent vantage points to scan for seaduck, divers and grebes.

Species such as Wigeon, Pintail, Pochard and Mallard can be found on virtually any marsh or lake but, for the most comfortable viewing, try Welney. You can see all of the above species and many more from the comfort of the heated hide.

Also look out for Scaup and Smew around the county: neither can be guaranteed but Snettisham occasionally attracts the former species, while Tottenhill gravel pits has gained a reputation for attracting the latter.

Birds of prey: When I think of Norfolk in winter, I think of raptor roosts. There is nothing more evocative than ending a cold day's birding by watching Hen and Marsh Harriers drifting in to roost along with a lightning fast Merlin or two. My favourite site to head for is Stubb Mill, where Cranes can also be virtually guaranteed. Other raptor roosts include Roydon Common, Strumpshaw Fen and Warham Greens

Away from the traditional roost sites, raptors during January are usually just passing through. Merlin and Peregrine scour the marshes for unwary waders, so if you see a flock of ducks or waders take to the air, always look skyward for a hunting raptor.

Waders: The north Norfolk coast is an internationally important area for wintering waders and a trip to Snettisham at high tide is a must. The sight of thousands of birds coming in to roost in front of the hide is truly awe-inspiring. Never mind trying to identify the individual species, just sit and marvel at the sight and sound of Dunlin, Knot, Oystercatcher, Bar-tailed Godwit, Redshank, Ringed Plover, Sanderling, etc. as they whirl through the air, twisting and turning, seemingly at random, before landing on the beach. Magnificent!

Of course, you can see waders at many other sites in January. Hunstanton, Holme, Titchwell, Cley, etc. can be alive with commoner species but Purple Sandpipers are scarce winter visitors usually limited to Hunstanton or Titchwell.

Woodcock and Jack Snipe are by far the most elusive waders. Places to try at dusk for the former species include Titchwell, Holkham Park and Stubb Mill. Jack Snipe are very scarce in the county, the most regular site being an inaccessible area of Roydon Common, though they are occasionally seen at Surlingham Church Marshes.

Cley holds Black-tailed Godwits and maybe even an Avocet or two and Grey Plovers should grace many of the beaches on the north coast. If you feel you have to see Avocets in January, then visit Breydon Water where up to 100 can be found among the large number of commoner wader species.

Owls: One of the lasting memories of a trip to Norfolk in January – indeed any month – should be the sight of a Barn Owl silently hunting over a field or marsh. The places where I seem to have most success are Hickling, Holme, Flitcham Abbey Farm, Morston Quay and Cley, though the chances of seeing one while travelling between sites are quite good, especially if you are out and about at dawn and dusk. Short-eared Owls may be encountered on any marsh. Breydon Water is a favoured site for this owl, with one or two occasionally roosting along the north side. By day they spend their time hunting over Haddiscoe or Berney Arms Marshes. A Little Owl or two is virtually guaranteed at Flitcham Abbey or Choseley Barns.

Passerines: Small birds can seem to take a back seat at this time of year but there are plenty to see, if you have the inclination to seek them. The main target species include Twite, Snow Bunting, Lapland Bunting and Shore Lark. Numbers vary from year to year and Lapland Buntings are becoming extremely scarce, seemingly due to changes in the way the marshes are grazed. For instance, Burnham Norton used to be a reliable site for Laplands but they seem to have deserted the place in the last couple of winters. Currently, Choseley is the place to see them, where up to ten birds feed in a stubble field near the barns.

Twite spend winter on the Norfolk coast but numbers are declining. In 2006, a small flock frequented Thornham Harbour car park, though elusive. The best site for Shore Lark (in fact the *only* site in recent winters) is Holkham Dunes. Titchwell, Cley and Salthouse Beach are also traditional sites for Shore Lark in a good year but never guaranteed. In addition, Titchwell is a good bet to find Snow Buntings, though Hunstanton, Holme, Salthouse Beach, Blakeney Point and Great Yarmouth Beach are all worth searching for the mobile flocks. Holkham NNR has been the most reliable site in recent years.

Cley is virtually guaranteed to produce a handful of Water Pipits in among the Meadow Pipits and Pied Wagtails feeding to the east of the east bank. A handful of Water Pipits can also be seen at RSPB Buckenham Marshes. Large numbers of Rock Pipits spend the winter in Norfolk, the biggest flocks being on Scolt Head Island and Breydon Water. On a still day, the more colourful Bearded Tits should make an appearance at Cley, Titchwell, Welney, Gypsy Lane and Hickling.

Hawfinches should be in evidence but their numbers are declining rapidly in the county. Holkham Hall used to be a very good site but now it is best to head for Lynford Arboretum for a better chance of seeing this elusive beauty.

Buntings and finches may form large feeding flocks during the winter months, with Flitcham Abbey Farm, Choseley Barns and East Wretham Heath being prime sites. Scan any flock carefully, as it may contain one or two Bramblings or Tree Sparrows.

Rarities: Rarity-hunting can be hard work at this time of year but there are usually one or two goodies to be seen. Recent years have seen over-wintering Lesser Yellowlegs, Pine and Little Buntings, Black Brants and Arctic Redpolls, with a shorter-staying Ross's Gull. Iceland or Glaucous Gulls may be found around the county (try King's Lynn Docks or Blackborough End Tip), Mediterranean Gulls should be encountered on Great Yarmouth Beach and hardy seawatchers may be rewarded with a Pomarine Skua or two.

Waxwings may be seen during irruption years, though no single site can be recommended as they head for the nearest berry bushes, stay for a couple of days to strip them bare, then move on to another area.

A Rough-legged Buzzard is usually to be found wintering in the county but, as with Waxwings, no single site can be recommended. I have found single birds at Titchwell (1998) and Horsey (1999). In the winters of 2001 and 2002, Haddiscoe Marsh was the venue for this species but Massingham Heath seems to be the most favoured haunt (park at TF 791211).

Titchwell has gained a reputation in recent years for attracting a Penduline Tit and any feeding finch flocks encountered on your travels should be scrutinised for Common and Arctic Redpolls (Titchwell in 2002 & 2005) and Serin.

A day or weekend in Norfolk in January ensures an exciting start to the birding year for the visiting birdwatcher. For a 'sad lister' such as me, it is the ideal county to get your year-list off to a flying start!

WHAT TO LOOK FOR

FEBRUARY

THOUGH species largely mirror those detailed in January's calendar, spring migration gets under way during this month. This may seem unlikely as you stand birdwatching, dressed like Sir Ranulph Fiennes at the North Pole but it is true.

Geese: Many Pink-footed Geese will have moved on by mid-month but you should still be able to catch up with a few at Holkham NNR or Snettisham. Bean Geese usually leave Buckenham by the second week of February at the very latest, earlier if possible if the weather is mild. Egyptian Geese will already be nesting, though few of the first batch of chicks will survive if there is a prolonged freeze.

Wildfowl: Some wintering ducks will move out later in the month but there are still plenty at the sites mentioned for January.

Birds of prey: All the raptors previously mentioned in January will still be in evidence.

Waders: Avocets will return to their breeding grounds so try Cley, Breydon Water and Titchwell.

Owls: Long-eared Owls begin to breed, so listen out for hooting from suitable coniferous woods in the county (e.g. Thetford Forest and Dersingham Bog). It is a good month to call at Holkham Park to see the Tawny Owls in their traditional roost tree around the monument. Also look out for Lesser Spotted Woodpecker in this area.

Passerines: Early breeding species include Crossbill, which may start nesting in Lynford Arboretum, Holkham, Sandringham and Dersingham Bog. Bunting and finch flocks will still be around – check out sites such as Flitcham Abbey Farm, East Wretham Heath and Choseley Barns.

Apart from the above species, you should read the calendar notes for January if visiting Norfolk in February.

MARCH

SPRING migration picks up speed in March but only just. Several early-arriving species will have been recorded by the end of the month but this is usually only a tantalising taster of the mass arrival of birds in April and May.

Herons and Cranes: It is worth pausing by any large area of reeds to listen for the evocative booming of a Bittern. This is still a rare sound but is gradually increasing at places such as Strumpshaw Fen, Cley, etc. March could be the last month for a while that you catch a glimpse of Crane around the Horsey area.

Swans: Bewick's and Whooper Swans will be leaving in their droves early in the month, so watch for flying flocks. A handful of both species remain at Welney until the last week of March but after that, only injured birds unable to fly are seen here.

Geese: Brents will still be much in evidence on the coastal marshes all month. Virtually all the Pink-feet depart, though up to 1,000 can usually be found around Holkham until the end of April. All White-fronted Geese will have departed from their favoured areas (Buckenham Marshes and Holkham NNR) by mid-month.

Wildfowl: Winter ducks remain in impressive numbers, with Smew probable at Tottenhill gravel pits and Red-breasted Merganser and Common Scoter on the sea between Hunstanton and Scolt Head Island. Long-tailed Duck records are few and far between in March but Goosanders are usually still present at Barnham Cross Common (the BTO lake), Denver Sluice, etc.

Wigeon in their thousands can be seen at several sites (Welney, Buckenham Marshes, Holkham NNR, Halvergate Marshes, etc.), with numbers of Tufted Duck, Teal and Shoveler remaining stable at suitable sites such as Welney. Pochard and Pintail numbers start to dwindle as birds migrate north but many hang on to the end of the month.

Just one duck species moves in for the summer. By the end of the month, a few Garganey will have returned from Africa to breed in Norfolk. The most likely sites to encounter this attractive species are Welney, Cley, Hickling Broad and the flash at Lakenheath, though any marsh or shallow pool should be carefully checked.

Waders: Another addition to the scene will be Little Ringed Plover, usually appearing during the last third of the month at any suitable wader habitat, (e.g. Titchwell and Holme) but the most likely places are Pentney gravel pits and Welney.

Other waders to be seen include all species mentioned in January's summary. Titchwell, Cley and Welney are the main breeding centres for Avocets but you can also check out Hickling Broad, etc. High tides at Snettisham should still produce thousands of waders in the roost. Purple Sandpipers should be in residence at Hunstanton throughout the month.

Ringed Plovers move back to their breeding grounds in March and Black-tailed Godwits don their striking breeding plumage, thus becoming more conspicuous, at sites such as Cley, Breydon Water and Welney. Stone-curlews return to Norfolk during March, though the only place to see this species without disturbing them, Weeting Heath, remains closed all month to allow the birds to settle.

Birds of prey: Raptor roosts such as Roydon Common and Stubb Mill continue to attract Hen Harrier and Merlin, though numbers dwindle as the month wears on. Wintering Marsh Harriers also continue to appear at their roost sites (mainly Stubb Mill) but their numbers are augmented by migrating birds. Any north coast watchpoint should be watched for an incoming Marsh Harrier, as well as for the odd Goshawk and Buzzard. A trip to Thetford Forest should reveal a displaying Goshawk or two on mild March mornings.

Terns: A welcome reminder that warmer weather is just around the corner comes with the appearance of the first Sandwich Terns of the year, during mid to late March. Any coastal site could be the first to record this species, though Blakeney Point or Scolt Head Island are usually ahead of the rest.

Woodland species: Lesser Spotted Woodpeckers begin to display at the end of the month. Check sites such as Holkham Park, Felbrigg Hall, Upton Fen, etc. to see the fluttering display flight of this otherwise elusive species. Another species typical of a March birdwatching trip is

Wood Lark. Any clearing in The Brecks should be alive with their mournful song (try Santon Downham, East Wretham Heath, etc).

Passerines: It is a fun diversion during March to try to spot the first Swallow or House Martin of the year, though Sand Martin is more likely. Spend time at any migration watchpoint for a chance of catching these heralds of summer. Also keep an eye open for the first Wheatear, Chiffchaff and Ring Ouzel of the year: Blakeney Point or Holme are prime sites.

Any over-wintering Shore Larks and Water Pipits will be coming into their smart breeding plumage by the end of the month. Try Holkham NNR for the former species and Cley, or Buckenham Marshes, for the latter.

A visit to the Norfolk Broads on a fine, mild day in March should result in a chorus of Cetti's Warblers. They may be easier to see at this time of year, before the leaves have grown on the bushes they favour. Head for Rockland Broad, Strumpshaw Fen, etc.

After March, Hawfinches become elusive until December, so visit Lynford Arboretum before the month is out. Other finches and buntings should still be found in feeding flocks around Flitcham Abbey Farm, Choseley Barns, etc.

APRIL

SPRING is here! By the end of the April, many of Norfolk's summer visitors will have returned, though the month may start off slowly if poor weather prevails. By poor weather, I mean low pressure over Europe or strong offshore winds.

Throughout April, any site in Norfolk could produce migrants passing through or lingering for a day or two. If the weather charts show high pressure over Europe with a low pressure system over the east coast of Britain, then you should head for Winterton, Holme, Blakeney Point, Weybourne, etc. If it is raining when you arrive, do not complain as you will almost certainly discover many common migrants forced to land by these 'unpleasant' conditions.

Divers and grebes: A late Red-throated moving north at sea will be the only possible diver this month. Likewise, any wintering Red-necked and Slavonian Grebes should have moved on, though there is a slight chance of Black-necked Grebes on any suitable stretch of water: try Welney, the flashes at Lakenheath, or any of the Broads. Great Crested Grebes will be nesting on any suitable pit or lake, though the Broads is their stronghold in the county.

Geese: Of the wintering geese, only Brents will be seen in any sort of number, on any coastal marsh. A few Pink-feet may remain around Holkham but cannot be guaranteed.

Wildfowl: If you wish to catch up with Red-breasted Merganser or Goldeneye, do it early in the month but those wishing to find Pintail, Long-tailed Duck and Goosander will have to wait until next winter.

Numbers of Pochard, Gadwall, Teal and Tufted Duck greatly reduce as birds move out of the county to breed, though one or two of each species remain at traditional sites all year (Welney, Snettisham, Titchwell, etc). Eider and Common Scoter may still be found around the north coast. April is probably the best month to see Garganey, with Welney, Cley and Hickling Broad the most likely sites.

YOUR BIRDING YEAR

Birds of prey: Raptors desert their winter roost sites in March, so concentrate on watching Marsh Harriers on their breeding grounds (e.g. Hickling Broad, Cley, Titchwell, etc) or trying to find a migrating Osprey on Broadland lakes. Buzzards may also be on the move and Goshawks will still be in display flight on fine mornings in The Brecks. In late April, the first Hobbies will be arriving along with one or two Montagu's Harriers (over any watchpoint).

Gamebirds: April is a good month to locate Golden Pheasants as they are very vocal at this time of year. Visit the Wolferton Triangle, Santon Downham or Wayland Wood to hear their harsh calls.

Waders: The wader scene in Norfolk during April is a confusing mixture of returning breeding birds, lingering winter visitors and birds dropping in on migration for a quick refuelling stop.

Snettisham continues to be the centre of attraction, though numbers of birds start to dwindle. Purple Sandpipers desert their winter roost sites by mid-month but wintering Woodcock numbers begin to be augmented by migrant birds (check any coastal site for tired arrivals).

April is a good month to find species such as Green, Common and Wood Sandpipers, Whimbrel and Greenshank at any suitable marsh, scrape or gravel pit. Golden Plovers leave the county for their northern breeding grounds, while Avocets can be seen nest-building. Other waders settling down to breed include Redshank, Snipe and Lapwing on the marshes, Ringed Plover and Oystercatcher on shingle beaches and Little Ringed Plover on scrapes and gravel pits.

Weeting Heath opens its gates to visitors wishing to see Stone-curlew. This species can be particularly vocal at this time of year, especially at dawn and dusk.

Gulls and terns: Mediterranean Gulls can be virtually guaranteed on Great Yarmouth Beach while other species can be found nesting on marshes and scrapes around the county. One or two Little Gulls may be found – try Cley, Titchwell, Welney, Hickling Broad, etc.

Activity at tern colonies increases during April and, by the end of the month, most birds will have returned to sites such as Blakeney Point. Common Terns will have also returned to nesting platforms in the Broads. One or two Black Terns may be seen at the end of the month, though they are more likely in May: check out any Broadland lake or Lakenheath.

Migrants: Latest additions to the year list will be Turtle Dove, Cuckoo and Swift, all usually reported during the last week of the month at any migration point (Holme, Blakeney Point, Winterton etc). Also look out for classic spring scarcities such as Hoopoe, Wryneck and Bluethroat.

Woodpeckers: Lesser Spotted Woodpeckers may still be displaying during the first half of the month at Holkham Park, Felbrigg Hall and Ted Ellis Reserve etc.

Passerines: Wood Larks should still be singing throughout the month and several Shore Larks may linger at one or two sites (Holkham NNR for instance) with wintering flocks augmented by migrating birds. By now, this attractive species will have moulted into summer plumage and be sporting the elongated black feathers, which give it its American name, Horned Lark.

Sand Martin numbers build up during the month (Kelling Quags, Tottenhill and Pentney gravel pits, etc.) with Swallows and House Martins streaming in throughout.

Rock and Water Pipits will desert their winter quarters by the end of April. Tree Pipits return to their breeding grounds throughout the month, with migrant birds being seen on the coast from early April. This is also an excellent month to find flocks of Yellow Wagtails in any wet field. Try Kelling Quags, Cley or Salthouse Beach. Also keep an eye open for one of the rarer races of Yellow Wagtail - usually Blue-headed – among the flocks, or possibly a White Wagtail.

A trip to Norfolk in late April would not be complete without a visit to a Nightingale site such as Foulden Common or Salthouse Heath. Nightingales are easier to see now than later in the season but you may still have to settle for 'just' hearing their distinctive song.

Black Redstarts can turn up anywhere along the Norfolk coast, as can Redstart. The latter species may also be encountered at inland sites such as Felbrigg Hall and East Wretham Heath. Whinchat, Wheatear and Ring Ouzel should all be looked out for in the dunes along the coast, as well as any suitable field or hedgerow. Also keep an eye open for Fieldfare and Redwing flocks leaving the county on the way to Scandinavia.

April is an excellent month to catch a glimpse of Cetti's Warbler. Try Strumpshaw Fen, Rockland Broad and Ted Ellis Reserve. Other returning warbler species in April include Chiffchaff, Willow Warbler, Blackcap, Sedge and Reed Warblers, Whitethroat, Lesser Whitethroat, Grasshopper Warbler and maybe Garden and Wood Warblers at the end of the month. The usual migration watchpoints, such as Winterton, Blakeney Point, Holkham NNR, Wells Woods and Holme, will generally be best for warblers. Also keep an eye open at these sites, as well as Felbrigg Hall and Salthouse Heath, for Pied Flycatchers.

Bearded Tits can be quite showy at this time of year, especially on still days, as the males may already be collecting insects to feed to their sitting females. Any wintering Twite flocks will mostly be gone but one or two birds linger all month. Brambling may occasionally be seen, with some males sporting their fine breeding plumage.

In coniferous forest, listen out for the '*chip-chip*' calls of Crossbills. This species may already be feeding young and are particularly vocal at this time. Hawfinches become scarcer as the month wears on, though optimistic birders can still try their luck at sites recommended for March.

As well as the species already mentioned, common birds such as Robin, Blackbird, Song Thrush, Goldcrest, etc. can also be found in impressive numbers at migration watchpoints. In suitable weather conditions, hundreds of these common species might be forced down by fog or rain to delight the visiting birdwatcher.

MAY

WHAT a fantastic time to visit Norfolk – migrants will be streaming into all sites to set up breeding territories, so enjoy the show at migration watchpoints such as Blakeney Point, Winterton Dunes and Holme.

High pressure over Europe encourages birds to undertake the trip across the channel, only for them to hit the poor weather associated with low pressure. This inclement weather forces the migrants down at the first visible land, hopefully where you will be waiting for them. Repeat after me, "rain and fog are good......rain and fog are good........ rain and..."

By the end of the month, the enthusiastic birdwatcher will be able to watch birds from dawn until dusk. Insomniacs may wish to start the day with a woodland dawn chorus, move on to the marshes during the day, or visit The Brecks and end the day on a heathland for Nightjar and Woodcock.

Grebes: To see any grebes, venture onto inland pits and lakes where Great Cresteds will be sitting on nests. Broadland lakes sometimes turn up a Black-necked Grebe in May, by now sporting its stunning breeding plumage.

Wildfowl: A few Eider and Common Scoters may linger around the coast all month, usually around Titchwell or Holme. Other than the resident 'plastic' geese, the only species to be seen with any certainty will be Brents (Titchwell, Blakeney harbour, etc).

Terns: Replacing the ducks and divers at sea will be terns. Common, Sandwich and Little Terns will all be busy settling into their colonies (Blakeney Point, Great Yarmouth Beach, etc) and can be seen fishing anywhere along the coast. Common Terns also return to their breeding platforms at inland sites such as Hoveton Great Broad, Breydon Water and Ranworth Broad. Also look out for Arctic and Roseate Terns at Blakeney and Cley.

Black Terns used to breed on Broadland lakes but sadly they can now only be encountered on passage, May being the prime month. Try Lakenheath, Hardley Flood, etc. The first Manx Shearwaters of the year will be seen off Sheringham, Cley, Titchwell, Holme, etc. by the end of the month.

Birds of prey: Raptor enthusiasts are spoiled in May. It is an excellent time to see Honey Buzzards in the county, as a few pass over on migration. By the 20th, the Great Wood at Swanton Novers and Great Ryburgh should be occupied by this rare breeder. Marsh Harriers are likely over any marsh or reedbed.

May is a good month to scan the skies for migrating Ospreys, some dropping in on Broadland lakes for a brief fishing sortie (Ranworth Broad is the most regular stop-off site). Hobbies return during the month, causing chaos among the *hirundine* flocks at Weeting Heath, RSPB Lakenheath Fen and Hickling Broad, etc. The rarest breeding raptor in the county is Montagu's Harrier, which can sometimes be seen over any coastal watchpoint on passage, so stay alert.

Waders: Snettisham still attracts good numbers of waders to its roost and several attractive species can be seen on breeding grounds. Avocets can be seen on virtually any marsh or pit and stunning Black-tailed Godwits should be sought out at Holme and Welney etc.

If you are walking on any shingle beach, you should be careful not to disturb Ringed Plovers and Oystercatchers from their nests. Little Ringed Plover can be seen well at Welney and more distantly at Pentney gravel pits. Stone-curlews will be raising young at Weeting, with Wood Larks also showing well here in front of the hides.

WHAT TO LOOK FOR

This is a good month to find scarce and rare waders throughout the county. Regular species include Red-necked Phalarope and Temminck's Stint at Cley, with Kentish Plover and Temminck's Stint sometimes at Breydon Water.

Heathland species: From late May you can make a dusk visit to a Nightjar site (Roydon Common, Buxton Heath, Santon Downham, Salthouse Heath, Dersingham Bog). While waiting for the Nightjars to appear, you should see roding Woodcock and hear young Tawny Owls begging for food (listen out for a sound like an asthmatic smoker sprinting for a bus on a smoggy morning). Also keep an ear open for the begging squeaks of young Long-eared Owls.

Passerines: Swifts arrive from early to mid-month, as do most Turtle Doves. Listen for the latter's evocative purring calls especially at Flitcham Abbey Farm and Santon Downham. Another species that gives itself away by its song in May is Tree Pipit. Breckland is a stronghold of this species but it can also be heard at Dersingham Bog, Roydon Common and Kelling Heath as well. Wood Larks will also still be singing over any suitable clearing in the Brecks (Barnham Cross Common, Santon Downham, etc).

On the subject of calling birds, seemingly every patch of woodland, heath and reedbed in Norfolk will have a Cuckoo in residence by the end of the month, on the lookout for a suitable nest in which to lay its single egg.

May is a good month to scan any suitable wetland for Yellow Wagtails. Cley is a favoured haunt but also try Buckenham Marsh, Surlingham Church Marsh, etc. This is a prime month to find scarce sub-species such as Blue-headed and White among the commoner Yellows and Pieds.

May is a good time to see Bearded Tits in any expanse of reedbed (Hickling Broad, Cley, Titchwell, Gypsy Lane, etc.). From mid-month, I strongly suggest you pay a visit to Lakenheath to try to catch a glimpse of Golden Oriole. You will almost certainly hear them from the poplars but seeing one might involve much patience!

Migrants: Migrants to watch out for include Bluethroat (Blakeney Point, Holme Dunes, etc), Redstart and Wood Warbler (Salthouse Heath, Felbrigg Hall, East Wretham Heath, etc.) and Pied Flycatcher (Stiffkey, Wells Woods, etc). Black Redstarts used to breed around the power station and industrial units of Great Yarmouth but have been absent for a couple of years. It is still worth listening out for them as this species is notoriously unpredictable in its breeding habits. Wryneck may be found skulking in any suitable dune system (Winterton, Holme Dunes, etc), where you should also keep an eye open for Red-backed Shrike. Early in the month is a good time to listen for Nightingale at such sites as Foulden Common and Salthouse Heath.

May is definitely a warbler month! As the days tick by, Sedge, Reed, Garden and Willow Warblers all arrive en masse, as well as Whitethroat, Lesser Whitethroat, Blackcap and Chiffchaff. Grasshopper Warblers may well be heard 'reeling' from suitable habitat (Wells Woods, Winterton Dunes, Horsey, etc.) and rarer visitors could include Icterine and Savi's Warblers. A visit to a large wood at dawn is a must during May, so try Ken Hill Wood, Sandringham or Santon Downham.

Spotted Flycatcher is one of the latest summer arrivals but a handful will be at breeding sites late in the month (Weeting Heath, Holkham NNR).

Rarities: Rarity hunters will find themselves spoiled for choice. Regular rarities include Red-footed falcon, Caspian Tern, Purple Heron and Broad-billed Sandpiper as well as scarcities such as Temminck's Stint, Red-necked Phalarope, Spoonbill, Wryneck and Bluethroat. There should be at least one national rarity to see in Norfolk during the month, so good hunting.

JUNE

THOUGH June is probably the quietest month for birds in Norfolk, there is still plenty to see. As migration is at its lowest level of the year, the main interest is in watching breeding birds go about the business of raising a family.

Wildfowl: Any wildfowl in the county will probably be elusive as they tend to hide while sitting on nests. Noisy Egyptian Geese will be waddling around their chosen breeding sites with large young in tow (Flitcham Abbey Farm, Holkham NNR, Pentney gravel pits, Norfolk Broads, etc).

Birds of prey: Many visitors to Norfolk will be enthralled by Marsh Harriers in June, as they drift over any suitable marsh or reedbed. If you are lucky, you will witness the aerobatics of a food-passing manoeuvre by these wonderful birds.

Honey Buzzard and Montagu's Harrier tend to be elusive during June but Hobbies are regularly seen at Hickling Broad, Lakenheath Fen and Weeting Heath throughout the month.

Waders: Wader species will be on nests, the star attractions being Avocets at Titchwell, Cley and Welney. Common waders such as Redshank, Lapwing and Snipe nest at a few sites but can be hard to locate (try Buckenham Marshes and Welney). Little Ringed Plover, a scarce Norfolk breeder, is best viewed from the main hide at Welney. The Stone-curlews at Weeting will have large young by now but viewing them through the heat-haze can be frustrating.

Terns and seabirds: A few Manx Shearwaters may be seen off seawatching points but tern activity is usually restricted to colonies such as Blakeney Point and Great Yarmouth Beach. Common Terns will be seen on any suitable river or pit, especially those with breeding platforms or islands. Noisy Black-headed Gulls are not hard to locate but Kelling Quags is the best site for good views of them at the nest.

Heathland species: One species that shows well throughout the month is Nightjar. Balmy June evenings are perfect to watch these moth-like creatures at such places as Dersingham Bog, Winterton Dunes and Sandringham. At Salthouse Heath, you can combine a Nightjar search with a Nightingale chorus, while at Winterton Dunes, you may also listen to the reeling of Grasshopper Warblers and the croaking of natterjack toads.

Passerines: Warblers will still be in full song throughout the month but towards the end of the month many species become more elusive after the initial explosive start to the day, so catch a dawn chorus sooner rather than later.

Bushes around any marsh, river or pit will be alive with the scratchy song of Sedge Warblers and the grumpy-sounding song of Reed Warblers will be emanating from every patch of reedbed. Cetti's Warblers should still be singing intermittently from deep cover around their Broadland strongholds but you will probably not see one!

June is the prime month for Marsh Warbler to appear, so pay attention to any strange song you may hear. The last one I saw in Norfolk was singing by a very well used footpath next to a school in King's Lynn, so be alert in any location.

Golden Orioles will still be whistling from poplars around Lakenheath and Fordham during the early part of the month but then become very difficult to locate, until the young are out and about in late August.

JULY

WHILE you stand sweating on the footpath at Titchwell, watching Avocet chicks waddle after their parents, it is hard to believe that autumn migration is under way. Many non-breeding waders return to Norfolk from Scandinavia during July, so it can be an interesting diversion at the end of the month to attempt to match the number of wader species to the date (i.e. 28 species of wader on July 28 and so on).

Seabirds: Seawatching picks up slightly during July, with increased numbers of Manx Shearwaters being seen and maybe one or two Balearic Shearwaters.

Spoonbills: A touch of the exotic may come in the form of a Spoonbill or two, Holkham NNR seems to be the favoured site.

Wildfowl: Duck-watching becomes very dull in July, as the drakes moult into their dowdy 'eclipse' plumage.

Birds of prey: Rare breeding raptors show more often as the month wears on. Honey Buzzards should be showing well at Great Ryburgh and to a lesser extent, Swanton Novers. Listen out for any RSPB Montagu's Harrier watchpoints that may be set up to see this much sought-after species. Marsh Harriers will be much in evidence over reeds and marshes across the county (Hickling Broad, Titchwell, Cley, etc), making it hard to believe they were faced with extinction as a British breeding bird just a few years ago. Hobbies will become more obvious as they take advantage of new prey, dragonflies.

Quail: While driving around the county, it may be worth stopping at the side of any barley field to listen for the *'wet-my-lips'* call of Quail. They turn up anywhere and are almost impossible to see. Remember, it is illegal to tape-lure this species and you should never enter fields to try to flush one into view!

Waders: Young birds will be prominent and many a sigh of 'aahhh' has gone up from admiring birders at the sight of a young Lapwing/Avocet chick trotting along after its parents, only to be followed by gasps of horror as a Herring or Great Black-backed Gull swoops down and swallows the poor thing whole. Life is tough! Visit sites such as Welney, Titchwell and Cley to see nature in all its gory splendour.

By the end of July, waders such as Knot, Dunlin and Sanderling. will be returning from their breeding grounds. The roost at Snettisham once again begins to attract many birds, though not as numerous as in winter. Female Red-necked Phalaropes sometimes appear at Cley or Titchwell to sun themselves after leaving the hapless males to rear their young in the bleak northern breeding grounds.

Welney is a good place to visit in July to obtain superb views of baby Little Ringed Plovers, complete with tiny yellow eye-rings. Adult and almost fully grown Stone-curlews should be showing well on Weeting Heath.

Gulls and terns: Yellow-legged Gull is a summer feature of Norfolk, prime sites being Blackborough End Tip, Cley, King's Lynn Docks and Hickling Broad. Black-headed Gull colonies become even noisier as the youngsters beg for food from harassed adults.

July is the best month to visit a tern colony. A boat trip out to Blakeney Point at this time of year is a real treat. Many a happy hour can be spent at Little Tern colonies (Great Yarmouth Beach, Winterton Dunes, etc.) watching chicks run to their parents as they land close by.

Heathland species: Nightjars will be churring at dusk throughout the month at sites such as Roydon Common, Buxton Heath, Winterton Dunes, Sandringham and Dersingham Bog. Insect repellent may be advisable if waiting any length of time for the Nightjars to appear.

Passerines: The majority of warblers and woodland birds will become more elusive as the month wears on and the heat builds up. Many species will be hiding away, quietly moulting out of the reach of predators. Even more unsportingly, they stop singing, so you can't even locate them that way.

Alternatives: If things appear to be a little quiet on the birding front, don't forget that there are always plenty of plants, butterflies and dragonflies to be seen, making Norfolk an exciting place to be, even during a supposedly quiet month like July.

AUGUST

IN BIRDING terms, August heralds the onset of winter with many south-bound species stopping off. Lots of young birds can still be seen, most making very unfamiliar noises that often fool even the most ardent bird-call fanatic. Because there are so many youngsters around, this is a bumper time for raptors too.

Seabirds: August is the real start of the seawatching season. Manx Shearwaters pass watchpoints in impressive numbers in some years, often joined by Balearic or Sooty Shearwaters, or maybe something rarer such as Cory's or Great Shearwaters. Many watchpoints, such as Holme Observatory, Cley and Sheringham will be crowded with birders hoping for the 'biggie' to come past, especially if there is a stiff north wind blowing. However, Gannets and Kittiwakes are much more likely. Tern activity will be at a peak at sea, as adults are joined by scruffy-looking juveniles learning how to fish.

All four skua species should be recorded off seawatching points (Holme Observatory, Cley, Sheringham, etc.) throughout the month but concentrate your efforts if the wind is coming from the north or north-west. Auk species may also pass watchpoints in reasonable numbers.

Wildfowl: Wigeon numbers will be gradually building on the marshes, along with Teal. By the end of the month, the first returning Pintail will have been noted. Garganey begin to show again, after hiding the whole summer, with juveniles testing the identification skills of birders at Cley, Welney and Hickling Broad among others. The bad news is that male ducks will still be in their dull 'eclipse' plumage.

Birds of prey: Raptors to be seen in Norfolk during August include the first returning Merlin (maybe Blakeney Point) and the pair of Honey Buzzards at Swanton Novers or Great Ryburgh, possibly accompanied by their young: catch them while you can as they usually depart late in the month. Montagu's Harriers roam far and wide during August and may be encountered anywhere. This is probably the best month to see a Hobby as the youngsters are on the wing learning how to catch Swallows, House Martins and dragonflies at sites such as Upton Fen or Weeting Heath. As ever, Marsh Harriers will be seen over any marsh or reedbed, sometimes food-passing in mid-air.

Crakes and gamebirds: August is a prime month to find a Spotted Crake. Any marsh may be graced by this elusive species, though Titchwell seems to be the favourite site. Any Quail in the county should still be calling so check bird newslines to find out this year's best location

Waders: A fine selection will be on show. You may wish to visit the Snettisham roost or concentrate on finding passage birds on any suitable pool or marsh. Greenshank, Green Sandpiper, Wood Sandpiper and Common Sandpiper are guaranteed during August, the best sites being Cley, Redwell Marsh, Welney and Breydon Water. The latter site also sees a build-up in number of Avocets during the month. Cantley Beet Factory is the best site to see Green, Wood and Common Sandpipers in the autumn, though access is now tricky. If you want permission to visit this site regularly, please write to: The Site Manager, British Sugar plc, Cantley Sugar Factory, Norwich NR13 3ST (Tel: 01493-700351) as a casual visit is not now possible.

In general, many species of wader (Whimbrel, Ruff, Little Ringed Plover, Spotted Redshank, Little Stint, Temminck's Stint, etc) can turn up anywhere, so check any suitable-looking patch of marsh, wetland or pool and find your own.

Stone-curlews will be gathering in small flocks by the end of the month, with more than 30 being counted at Weeting Heath in some years.

Gulls and terns: Gull colonies will still be boisterous and Yellow-legged Gull numbers at King's Lynn Docks or Cley can reach double figures. Terns will show well in good numbers throughout the month. Keep an eye open for migrating Black Terns at any seawatching point.

Nightjars: If you want to hear Nightjar in August, visit your chosen site (Winterton, Buxton Heath, Roydon Common, etc.) sooner rather than later. On cooler evenings, Nightjars may not churr at all and, by the end of the month, most visits will be silent.

Migrants: The number of Turtle Doves, Cuckoos, Sand Martins and Swifts reported start to dwindle as the days tick by but Swallows and House Martins should still be swarming over any area of water, often pursued by a Hobby or two. Listen and look out for Tree Pipits at any migration watchpoint as they begin to move out of their breeding areas.

Heart-rates of migrant hunters begin to rise as August wears on. Common early drop-ins at watchpoints (Winterton Dunes, Blakeney Point, Holme, etc.) include Redstart, Whinchat, Wheatear, Ring Ouzel, Spotted Flycatcher and Pied Flycatcher. By the end of the month, the first Red-backed Shrike should have been reported.

If easterly winds are forecast, it may be worth a walk to Blakeney Point for such classic species as Greenish and Barred Warblers. The trickle of migrants in August is just a taster of things to come in September and October.

SEPTEMBER

SEPTEMBER can be an amazing month in Norfolk. If strong winds blow in from the north, seawatchers come out in their droves. If easterly winds prevail, places such as Blakeney Point, Warham Greens and Holme can be full of birders looking for tasty treats such as Barred Warbler and Red-backed Shrike. If conditions are perfect (high pressure over Scandinavia and the east, with low pressure over Britain and strong easterly winds), anything can turn up.

Seabirds: Throughout the month, seawatching enthusiasts will be out and about at such sites as Sheringham and Holme Observatory, searching the swell for shearwaters, skuas and petrels. Common passage birds during the month include Gannet and Kittiwake in good numbers.

The fun really starts when a prolonged period of north or north-westerly winds is experienced. If this happens, seawatching can be extremely exciting (yes, trust me, it can)! Spending a whole morning watching hundreds of terns passing your vantage point is exciting enough but add up to four species of skua occasionally pursuing them and Manx, Balearic and Sooty Shearwaters gliding just above the surface of the sea and you have the recipe for an exceptional day's birding.

Wildfowl: Duck numbers build up on marshes and pools, as winter migration gathers apace. Garganey can still be seen at Cley but still in drab eclipse or immature plumage. Make sure you catch up with this species early in the month. At the very end of September you can expect to find the first Goldeneyes and Red-breasted Mergansers of winter, though predicting where they will occur is more difficult.

A few Brent Geese will be returning to their regular haunts by mid-month (Blakeney, Brancaster, etc.) as will Pink-footed Geese (Holkham).

Birds of prey: Honey Buzzard, Montagu's Harrier and Hobby all depart for warmer climes during September and can turn up at any migration watchpoint, or indeed over any other site in Norfolk. Osprey may also pass through on the way to Africa. Peregrines arrive at their wintering grounds during early September and reports of Merlin increase as the month progresses.

Waders: September is another exciting wader month in the county. Any area and I do mean *any* area, of marsh or water with a muddy edge should be scanned thoroughly for passage birds. Common, Wood and Green Sandpipers are classic September birds, with Cley and Redwell Marsh being favoured sites.

I feel this is the best month in which to see Curlew Sandpiper. They tend to show particularly well at Titchwell but don't expect any gaudy red birds, as most will be juveniles. Other species which should be in evidence include Ruff, Whimbrel, Spotted Redshank and Little Stint among the common species. Wader rarities in September can include such goodies as Pectoral and Buff-breasted Sandpipers and, while on the marsh, keep an eye open for a Spotted Crake creeping at the edge of the reeds (try Titchwell).

A feature of September in The Brecks is the flocking of juvenile Stone-curlews before they migrate south. In some years, more than 30 birds can be seen together at Weeting but scan any field in the area for the chance of a wonderful discovery. Up to 60 birds together have been reported on Norfolk farmland in some years.

Migrants: The majority of *hirundines* leave the county by the end of the month but early on, it may be worth watching reedbeds at dusk for roosting birds (Martham Broad, Cley, etc).

September is a superb time to find your own birds. Depending on weather conditions, numbers of migrants at coastal watchpoints can be staggering. Common species such as Robin, Chiffchaff and Goldcrest can be forced down by fog or rain. Summer warblers such as Whitethroat, Lesser Whitethroat, Garden Warbler and Blackcap should all be encountered on the coast and hiding among them, might be something a bit special.

Other common migrants at this time should include Wheatear, Whinchat and maybe a few Ring Ouzel. Redstart and Pied Flycatcher are also recorded in good numbers each September. Scarce species regularly recorded this month include Wryneck, Richard's Pipit, Red-backed Shrike, Common Rosefinch, Firecrest, Ortolan and Barred Warbler (Holme, Winterton, Blakeney Point).

Any site – and any bush! – on the coast should be checked thoroughly, though hot-spots such as Blakeney Point, NWT Holme Dunes, NOA Holme Observatory, Great Yarmouth Cemetery and Warham Greens are the most visited. Migrant-hunters will be hoping for something a bit rarer (such as Lanceolated Warbler and Pechora Pipit) for their efforts.

Passerines: In my experience, September is the best month to see Bearded Tit. Family parties are very noisy and active and usually show very well at sites such as Titchwell (around the first hide), Hickling Broad, Gypsy Lane and Brancaster Marsh. Instead of the usual fleeting flight glimpse, at this time of year the patient birdwatcher can obtain very close and prolonged views.

OCTOBER

EXCITEMENT among birders remains high this month. Not only do rarities abound, but common winter visitors arrive seemingly unnoticed. Swans, geese and ducks return in decent numbers and raptor roosts begin to attract Hen Harriers once more. Winter has arrived!

Seabirds: As in September, keep an eye on weather forecasts for northerly winds. Head for seawatching watchpoints in these conditions as skuas, shearwaters, Gannets and Kittiwakes should be seen in reasonable numbers.

October seems to be the most likely month to encounter the exquisite Sabine's Gull off the Norfolk coast but beware of confusion with immature Kittiwake (a common error).

Numbers of divers, grebes and seaduck build during the month, adding to the excitement of any seawatch.

Wildfowl: Wild swans gradually return to their traditional wintering grounds during the middle of the month. Pink-footed and Brent Goose numbers also build up throughout October (Holkham NNR, Snettisham) and one or two White-fronted Geese may have been recorded by the end of the month, though most return in November. The steady influx of wintering ducks which began in September continues throughout October. Welney and other wetland sites will hold thousands of Wigeon, Teal, Pintail, Pochard, etc, by the end of the month.

Birds of prey: As mentioned before, Hen Harriers return to their traditional roosts, as do Merlins. Numbers may be small but birds should be present during the second half of the month. Peregrines slowly return to their wintering grounds and migration watchpoints may record Buzzard and Marsh Harrier, as they leave the county for the winter. Some Marsh Harriers do remain in Norfolk and can be seen over any marsh or reedbed (Cley, Horsey, etc).

Waders: Many passage waders such as Greenshank, Little Stint, Ruff, Green Sandpiper and Curlew Sandpiper will remain on muddy-edged pools and pits such as Pentney, Rush Hill scrape (Hickling) and Redwell Marsh.

Thousands of common waders continue to arrive for the winter, augmenting the earlier arrivals. The roost at Snettisham attracts thousands of birds at high tide. Any beach or marsh, such as Holme Dunes, Titchwell and Cley, can hold common wader species. Any Spotted Crakes that turned up in late summer may still be in residence (try Titchwell).

Terns: Numbers drop to a trickle by the end of October but Sandwich, Common, Little and Arctic Terns are all reported regularly.

Migrants: October is a fantastic month for finding your own migrant birds in Norfolk. Handfuls of Swallows, Swifts, Sand and House Martins pass over watchpoints all month and winter thrushes begin to trickle in. This trickle may become a flood if a high pressure system over Scandinavia combines with strong easterly winds and rain or fog over East Anglia. Sites such as Blakeney Point and Holme should be visited if these conditions prevail.

Experienced birdwatchers will expect something more exciting to turn up in these conditions, with such classic species as Short-toed Lark, Barred Warbler, Richard's Pipit and Red-backed Shrike all possibilities. Dune systems along the coast (Holme, Winterton, etc.) may also hide exhausted Short or Long-eared Owls, Woodcock or even a Corn Crake.

Warbler numbers at migration watchpoints can be impressive in October, as birds pause on the coast to feed up or await perfect conditions before heading south. Wells Woods, Holkham NNR, Warham Greens and Stiffkey can produce many species, including Garden Warbler, Willow Warbler, Lesser Whitethroat, Whitethroat, Chiffchaff and Blackcap. Among these commoner species may be Firecrest, Red-breasted Flycatcher, Yellow-browed Warbler or Barred Warbler. Any feeding flock should be scanned thoroughly, as scarce and rare birds often latch onto such flocks: every bird should be scrutinised.

Reed Warblers can sometimes turn up in strange habitat at this time, occasionally confusing unwary birders. Many a time I have witnessed over-eager rarity hunters mistake a Reed Warbler for some unlikely species (for instance, Red-breasted Flycatcher!), simply because it was hopping about in a tree or bush and not in reeds.

Expect to see Whinchat, Wheatear, Pied Flycatcher and Redstart, with common species such as Robin, Song Thrush and Goldcrest, sometimes appearing in their hundreds. Though Lapland Bunting is now a scarce over-wintering species in the county, one or two very occasionally drop in at Salthouse Beach (Little Eye) or Cley (Eye Field) in October.

NOVEMBER

MANY birdwatchers regard November migration as quieter than that of September and October, usually because rare species can be thin on the ground. However, common summer visitors often linger until the first half of the month and, at the same time, winter visitors stream in from Scandinavia and further north to settle until next spring. And the rarities that do show up are usually very sought-after species indeed. You cannot afford to relax just yet.

Seabirds: Divers, grebes and winter seaduck return to the seas of Norfolk during the month as winter takes a hold. Red-throated Diver is common off such places as Titchwell, Holme and Cley. Long-tailed Duck should be seen off Holme, though numbers are small (usually only up to 30). November also seems a good month to connect with Red-necked Grebe (try Titchwell).

The tiny Little Auks should be seen on most days if conditions are favourable, with strong northerly winds. Any flock of Starlings coming in off the sea should be scrutinised thoroughly, as Little Auks sometimes tag on to the end of such flocks and follow them inland. Sometimes, exhausted Little Auk are discovered on inland waters. Recent sites have included Snettisham and Wells boating lake.

Wildfowl: Inland duck species return in force, with Wigeon being the most obvious arrival on most coastal marshes. The only wildfowl species leaving us, Garganey, will be gone by the second week of the month.

Bewick's and Whooper Swan numbers build up at Welney along with those of common ducks, while White-fronted Geese return to Holkham and Buckenham Marshes. If visiting Buckenham, I recommend you wait until the latter half of the month by which time the (taiga) Bean Geese should have arrived, though they sometimes don't turn up until December.

Birds of prey: Hen Harrier numbers increase at their traditional roost sites (Stubb Mill, etc.) as do Merlin records. Marsh Harriers become scarcer, though a few remain in the county during winter (Stubb Mill, Horsey, etc). Short-eared Owl and Peregrine are recorded daily, though can turn up on any marsh at any time (try Haddiscoe Marsh).

Waders: The majority of winter waders have returned to the county by now, including the small flock of Purple Sandpipers at Hunstanton. Breydon Water supports up to 100 Avocets throughout the winter, the only place to see them during this time.

Snettisham is well worth a visit at high tide for the spectacular wader roost. Common species present include thousands of Dunlin, Golden Plover, Knot, Bar-tailed Godwit, Turnstone, Ringed Plover and Oystercatcher along with smaller numbers of Grey Plover, Snipe, Sanderling, etc.

Most of the passage waders (Green Sandpiper, Greenshank, Little Stint, etc.) will have departed, though a few linger throughout the month. November seems to be a good month to see Grey Phalarope, usually from seawatching sites such as Sheringham during northerly winds.

Please read January's Calendar for a more detailed run-down of waders in the county in November.

Passerines: A tiny number of Swallows and House Martins continue to be recorded throughout November, usually at coastal sites. Any Swift seen should be studied very carefully indeed, as recent Novembers have turned up about ten Pallid Swifts. Chimney Swift is not out of the question either.

Similarly, any November Wheatear should be scrutinised to make sure it is not of the Desert or Black-eared variety. November is the prime month for records of Pallas's and Dusky Warblers and Olive-backed Pipit, with Wells Woods being as good a place as any to find one.

Shore Larks, Snow Buntings and Twite return to the marshes and saltings of Norfolk during the month and usually remain until April. Please do not harass these birds at this time (or ever) as they need time to settle down into their chosen winter home.

Woodland birds now become easier to see as the trees lose their leaves: a trip to Holkham Park, Ken Hill Wood or Sandringham may prove to be very productive. The former site should provide you with good views of Tawny Owls in their traditional roost tree by the monument.

By the end of the month, winter will have arrived. Read January's Calendar section for further details of birds to be seen.

DECEMBER

THIS MONTH'S calendar is basically the same as January's, with one or two minor alterations. In my experience, December is the best month to catch up with Hawfinch. Lynford Arboretum seems to have become the prime site for this secretive species in recent winters.

All in all, December provides the opportunity to catch up with winter species you may have missed earlier in the year. Also, there are plenty of bracing walks to help you walk-off your Christmas turkey dinner.

HOW TO USE THIS BOOK

HERE is a typical layout of the site guide pages. Once familiar with the layout, you will be able to extract the information you need quickly and painlessly.

Title of site. Sites are listed in alphabetical order and numbered.

Key points: Opening times, terrain, suitability for wheelchair users and other useful tips. ALWAYS check opening times before you visit.

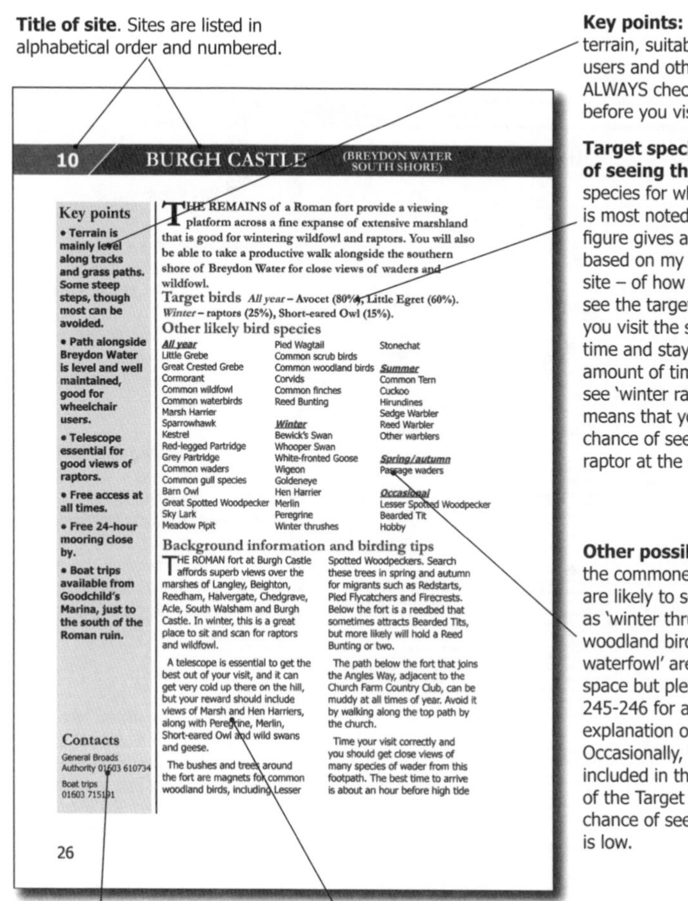

10 BURGH CASTLE (BREYDON WATER SOUTH SHORE)

Key points

- **Terrain is mainly level along tracks and grass paths. Some steep steps, though most can be avoided.**
- **Path alongside Breydon Water is level and well maintained, good for wheelchair users.**
- **Telescope essential for good views of raptors.**
- **Free access at all times.**
- **Free 24-hour mooring close by.**
- **Boat trips available from Goodchild's Marina, just to the south of the Roman ruin.**

Contacts

General Broads Authority 01603 610734

Boat trips 01603 715191

THE REMAINS of a Roman fort provide a viewing platform across a fine expanse of extensive marshland that is good for wintering wildfowl and raptors. You will also be able to take a productive walk alongside the southern shore of Breydon Water for close views of waders and wildfowl.

Target birds ***All year*** **– Avocet (80%), Little Egret (60%).** ***Winter*** **– raptors (25%), Short-eared Owl (15%).**

Other likely bird species

All year
Little Grebe
Great Crested Grebe
Cormorant
Common wildfowl
Common waterbirds
Marsh Harrier
Sparrowhawk
Kestrel
Red-legged Partridge
Grey Partridge
Common waders
Common gull species
Barn Owl
Great Spotted Woodpecker
Sky Lark
Meadow Pipit
Pied Wagtail
Common scrub birds
Common woodland birds
Corvids
Common finches
Reed Bunting
Stonechat

Winter
Bewick's Swan
Whooper Swan
White-fronted Goose
Wigeon
Goldeneye
Hen Harrier
Merlin
Peregrine
Winter thrushes

Summer
Common Tern
Cuckoo
Hirundines
Sedge Warbler
Reed Warbler
Other warblers

Spring/autumn
Passage waders

Occasional
Lesser Spotted Woodpecker
Bearded Tit
Hobby

Background information and birding tips

THE ROMAN fort at Burgh Castle affords superb views over the marshes of Langley, Beighton, Reedham, Halvergate, Chedgrave, Acle, South Walsham and Burgh Castle. In winter, this is a great place to sit and scan for raptors and wildfowl.

A telescope is essential to get the best out of your visit, and it can get very cold up there on the hill, but your reward should include views of Marsh and Hen Harriers, along with Peregrine, Merlin, Short-eared Owl and wild swans and geese.

The bushes and trees around the fort are magnets for common woodland birds, including Lesser Spotted Woodpeckers. Search these trees in spring and autumn for migrants such as Redstarts, Pied Flycatchers and Firecrests. Below the fort is a reedbed that sometimes attracts Bearded Tits, but more likely will hold a Reed Bunting or two.

The path below the fort that joins the Angles Way, adjacent to the Church Farm Country Club, can be muddy at all times of year. Avoid it by walking along the top path by the church.

Time your visit correctly and you should get close views of many species of wader from this footpath. The best time to arrive is about an hour before high tide

26

Target species and likelihood of seeing them: Lists the species for which the reserve is most noted. The percentage figure gives a rough idea – based on my experiences at the site – of how likely you are to see the target species, provided you visit the site at the correct time and stay for a reasonable amount of time. Where you see 'winter raptors (25%)' this means that you have a 25% chance of seeing each species of raptor at the site.

Other possible species: Lists the commoner species you are likely to see. Phrases such as 'winter thrushes', 'common woodland birds', 'common waterfowl' are used to save space but please see pages 245-246 for a more detailed explanation of what is included. Occasionally, 'good' species are included in this section instead of the Target section if the chance of seeing that species is low.

Useful contacts: Phone numbers to confirm access details etc.

Background information: Generally, this section will take you through the walk, with details of the birds that you might see and handy tips to help you see them. It might contain more information on points which have been briefly mentioned in previous sections, e.g. more extensive bird lists, more detailed information about terrain etc.

HOW TO USE THIS BOOK

Best time of year to visit. There may be things to see at other times of year but this season is likely to produce the best results.

OS Landranger map number

Grid reference(s) of parking area(s) giving easiest access to site.

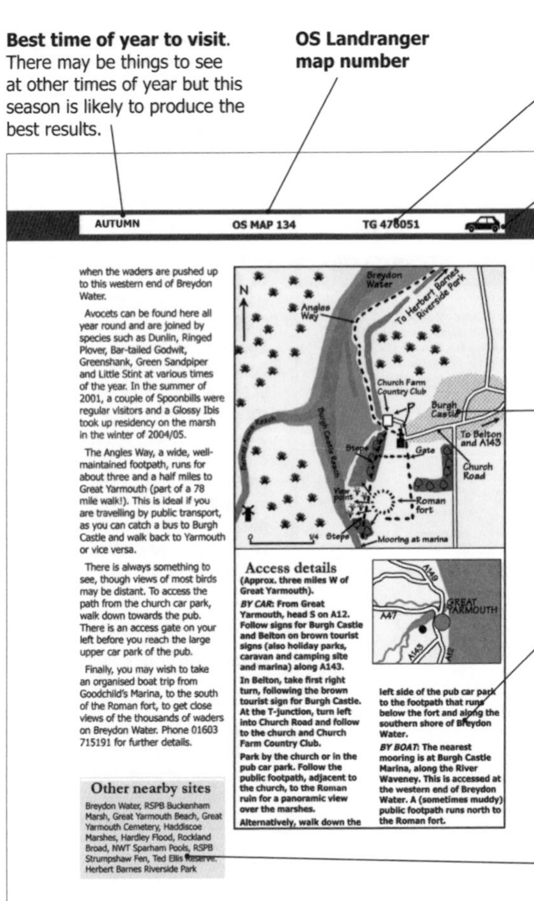

AUTUMN | OS MAP 134 | TG 478051

when the waders are pushed up to this western end of Breydon Water.

Avocets can be found here all year round and are joined by species such as Dunlin, Ringed Plover, Bar-tailed Godwit, Greenshank, Green Sandpiper and Little Stint at various times of the year. In the summer of 2001, a couple of Spoonbills were regular visitors and a Glossy Ibis took up residency on the marsh in the winter of 2004/05.

The Angles Way, a wide, well-maintained footpath, runs for about three and a half miles to Great Yarmouth (part of a 78 mile walk!). This is ideal if you are travelling by public transport, as you can catch a bus to Burgh Castle and walk back to Yarmouth or vice versa.

There is always something to see, though views of most birds may be distant. To access the path from the church car park, walk down towards the pub. There is an access gate on your left before you reach the large upper car park of the pub.

Finally, you may wish to take an organised boat trip from Goodchild's Marina, to the south of the Roman fort, to get close views of the thousands of waders on Breydon Water. Phone 01603 715191 for further details.

Access details

(Approx. three miles W of Great Yarmouth).

BY CAR: From Great Yarmouth, head S on A12. Follow signs for Burgh Castle and Belton on brown tourist signs (also holiday parks, caravan and camping site and marina) along A143.

In Belton, take first right turn, following the brown tourist sign for Burgh Castle. At the T-junction, turn left into Church Road and follow to the church and Church Farm Country Club.

Park by the church or in the pub car park. Follow the public footpath, adjacent to the church, to the Roman ruin for a panoramic view over the marshes.

Alternatively, walk down the left side of the pub car park to the footpath that runs below the fort and along the southern shore of Breydon Water.

BY BOAT: The nearest mooring is at Burgh Castle Marina, along the River Waveney. This is accessed at the western end of Breydon Water. A (sometimes muddy) public footpath runs north to the Roman fort.

Other nearby sites

Breydon Water, RSPB Buckenham Marsh, Great Yarmouth Beach, Great Yarmouth Cemetery, Haddiscoe Marshes, Hardley Flood, Rockland Broad, NWT Sparham Pools, RSPB Strumpshaw Fen, Ted Ellis Reserve, Herbert Barnes Riverside Park

27

Site facility symbols:

- £ Payment required
- Parking available
- Visitor centre
- Refreshments available
- Toilets
- Wheelchair access

Maps: The larger, more detailed map shows trails, hides and other key features for the reserve. (See key to symbols below). The small thumbnail map shows the reserve's position within Norfolk.

Access: Detailed directions to the parking area(s) or reserve entrance (the harder a site is to find, the more detailed the description). For some sites, I have detailed the most straightforward route, for those unfamiliar with the area, not necessarily the quickest.

Other nearby sites: Not comprehensive but a selection of ideas for sites to visit in the general area of the reserve you have chosen. Refer to the Norfolk map for a complete list of sites in the area.

Key to map symbols

FEATURED SITES IN NORFOLK

Today one would be unlucky not to see the once-rare Avocet on a visit to the Norfolk coast.

1 NWT ALDERFEN BROAD

Key points

- **Site is a designated SSSI.**
- **Free access at all times.**
- **Level terrain along muddy grass paths.**
- **Observation blind, no seating.**
- **No dogs.**
- **Keep to colour-marked trails at all times.**
- **Information board in car park.**
- **Use insect repellent in summer.**

Contacts

Norfolk Wildlife Trust
01603 625540

SMALL AND SECLUDED, this Norfolk Wildlife Trust reserve on the edge of the Broads is well worth visiting at any time of year. NWT Alderfen Broad is excellent for many common birds species, plus several scarce insects and plants – truly a site for the all-round naturalist.

Target birds

All year – **Common wildfowl (100%), Cetti's Warbler (hear 50%, see 10%).** *Summer* – **Common Tern (80%).**

Other possible bird species

All year
Great Crested Grebe
Cormorant
Common waterbirds
Sparrowhawk
Common gull species
Tawny Owl
Green Woodpecker
Great Spotted Woodpecker
Kingfisher
Marsh Tit
Pied Wagtail
Common scrub birds
Common woodland birds
Siskin
Redpoll
Other finches

Summer
Cuckoo
Hirundines
Sedge Warbler
Reed Warbler
Grasshopper Warbler
Other warblers

Occasional
Bittern (winter)
Osprey (passage)
Lesser Spotted Woodpecker

Background information and birding tips

SECLUSION is the chief attribute of NWT Alderfen Broad, which isn't to imply there are no birds or other wildlife to see, just that it lacks the drama of the top Norfolk birding sites.

The major plus-point is that I can almost guarantee you will be on your own as you wait patiently for that elusive Cetti's Warbler in the dense undergrowth to show itself, or scan the Broad to find Britain's first Cinnamon Teal!

There are two colour-marked trails from the car park. The one off to your right (as you face the info board in the car park) is along an uneven grass path and runs alongside a creek (good for dragonflies in summer) to an area of dense cover (ideal for Cetti's Warblers) and a wood (common scrub birds and warblers). This trail is 0.8km long.

Immediately you join this path from the car park, there is a narrower grass path off to your left, leading down to a wooden screen.

The screen overlooks the 5.4 hectare broad, where Common Terns and hirundines can be seen in summer. The reeds opposite the screen hold Reed Warblers in summer and a Bittern can sometimes be seen here in winter. Common waterbirds, Kingfishers and wildfowl frequent the broad throughout the year and an Osprey often drops in on passage.

A colour-marked trail also runs from the left of the car park and then turns immediately right, down a grassy path, to run in a loop through the reserve (1.7km long). Boots are recommended for this route, which remains boggy at all times of year.

This trail takes you through a reedbed where it is worth pausing to see what you can see and hear (good for swallowtail butterflies

here in summer). It opens out into a clearing where a Grasshopper Warbler or two may be heard reeling.

A short, muddy path through a small wood starts from the left of the car park. This wood can be alive with many common bird species such as Dunnock, Long-tailed and Marsh Tits, Robin, Blackbird, etc, etc. The path leads to some fields where you may see winter thrushes and buntings.

In summer, the resident birds are joined by Willow Warblers, Chiffchaffs, Blackcaps, Whitethroats and Garden Warblers.

There is a slim chance of Lesser Spotted Woodpecker anywhere on the reserve and the whole place is packed with rare and scarce wildlife (swallowtail butterfly, royal fern, hairy dragonfly, etc, etc). An all-round naturalist could spend a whole day exploring the 23 hectares of habitats here, while a bird specialist would only spend a couple of hours on site.

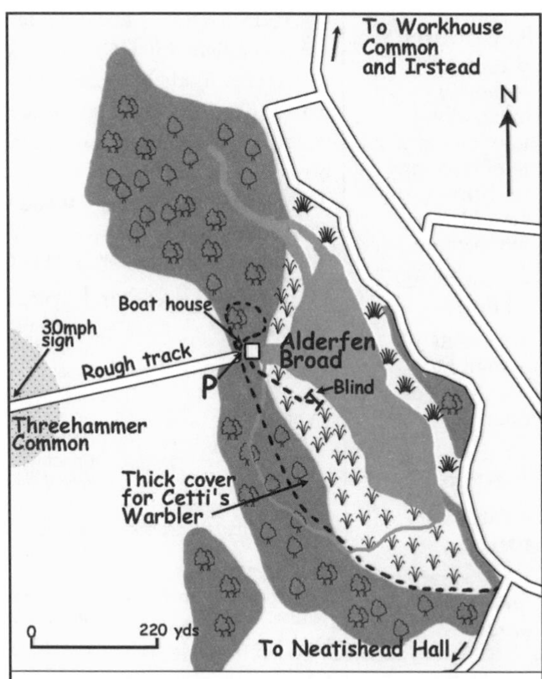

Access details

(Approx. ten miles NE of Norwich)

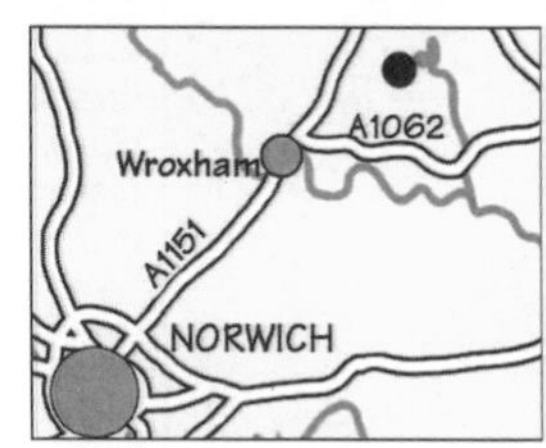

At Wroxham, NE of Norwich on the A1151, turn onto A1062 to Horning. In village turn left to Neatishead. At the crossroads, turn right, go past the Radar Museum and take the next left, sign-posted 'Threehammer Common'. Go into the village and just before 30mph speed limit sign, turn right along a track by the side of a house. Follow this very bumpy track to the NWT car park at the end.

Other nearby sites

NWT Barton Broad, Breydon Water, Burgh Castle Marshes, Buxton Heath, NWT Cockshoot Broad, How Hill NNR, NWT Ranworth Broad, NWT Sparham Pools, RSPB Surlingham Church Marshes, Ted Ellis Reserve.

BARNHAM CROSS COMMON

Key points

- **Terrain is mostly level, along uneven paths. Muddy/boggy in winter (not suitable for wheelchairs).**
- **Free access at all times.**
- **An SSSI owned by Thetford Town Council.**
- **Facilities in Thetford.**
- **Large car park.**
- **Information boards in car parks.**

Contacts

British Trust for Ornithology 01842 750050

Forest Enterprise, 01842 810271

High Lodge Forest Centre 01842 815434

Thetford Town Council 01842 754247 www.brecks.org

THIS AREA of common land covered by scrub has established itself as the second best site in the county to see Hawfinches. It can be hard work to cover but is well worth the effort. Nunnery Lake, a small body of water, is visible from the Common where you may see familiar water birds.

Target birds

Spring – **Wood Lark (late February to mid-June 80%), Nightingale (late April to early June, hear 75%, see 20%).** *Winter* – **Goosander (80%), Hawfinch (15%).**

Other possible bird species

All year
Little Grebe
Common wildfowl
Sparrowhawk
Kestrel
Lapwing
Snipe
Kingfisher
Green Woodpecker
Great Spotted Woodpecker
Sky Lark
Pied Wagtail
Common scrub birds
Mistle Thrush
Long-tailed Tit
Blue Tit
Great Tit
Treecreeper
Jay
Corvids
Linnet
Yellowhammer

Spring
Turtle Dove
Cuckoo
Hirundines
Grasshopper Warbler
Lesser Whitethroat
Whitethroat
Blackcap
Chiffchaff
Willow Warbler

Winter
Winter thrushes

Occasional (Spring)
Hobby
Yellow Wagtail

Background information and birding tips

BARNHAM CROSS COMMON is a large (65ha) expanse of grass heathland that attracts many dogwalkers and joggers. For this reason, I prefer to visit early in the morning when the birding tends to be at its best.

A maze of small paths gives excellent access to all the birds without disturbing them. Access is very difficult for wheelchair users, due to boggy tracks but some areas can be viewed from the road.

During recent winters the Common has become one of the best places to see Hawfinches in Norfolk, following the decline of the Holkham Park colony. These handsome finches can prove very elusive but if you are familiar with their call (a subtle but far-carrying '*tick, tick*') you should eventually locate the small flock. Numbers vary from winter to winter (2004 was a good year, 2005 a poor one).

The Hawfinches tend to be seen in and around the large trees in the vicinity of the pumping station. To reach here from the large car park, carefully cross the busy A134 and walk back towards Thetford. When you reach the 30mph sign, turn right down a wide sandy track and walk 300 yards to the pumping station (this track is gated but you can walk around the gate. When the gate is open, wheelchairs can gain access).

From late February to mid-June you should hear the mournful song of Wood Lark at Barnham Cross. The best area is across the A134 from the car park and about 300

yards south (just south of the Nunnery compound). When they are not in song flight, Wood Larks like to perch in the tops of the isolated bushes and trees dotted around the Common.

Nightingales return to the Common in late April and sing from thick cover adjacent to the playing field. They can be extremely difficult to see here – even more so than at other sites, if that is possible! Bear in mind that they stay very close to the ground most of the time and you might stand a chance.

Other birds include Jays and Green Woodpeckers which will usually be heard before you pick them out, normally flying from bush to bush. In winter, thrushes including Redwings and Fieldfares, are readily seen. Finch flocks will feed noisily in the bushes.

From the east side of the Common you can look into the compound of The Nunnery, headquarters of the British Trust for Ornithology. The small lake in winter is possibly the most reliable site for Goosander in Norfolk. Common ducks, grebes and geese should also be seen on the lake.

Lapwings are present all year, with maybe a Snipe or two in winter. Also on the east side of the Common, behind Nunnery Lake, is the Little Ouse River that usually holds a Kingfisher somewhere along its length.

In summer, the resident birds are joined by several warbler species including Whitethroat, Lesser Whitethroat, Blackcap, Garden Warbler, Willow Warbler and Chiffchaff. Cuckoos may also show well here in early May.

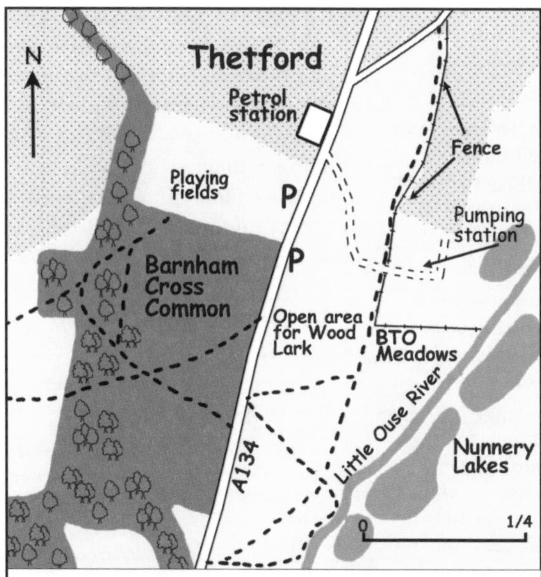

Access details

(Approx. one mile S of Thetford town centre)

Head S from Thetford on A134 (sign-posted Bury St. Edmunds) over new mini-roundabout and through traffic lights until you are out of the housing area. Beyond a petrol station on the right the vista opens out to wide grassy areas either side of the road. Park on the right and walk across the playing field to the trees and bushes.

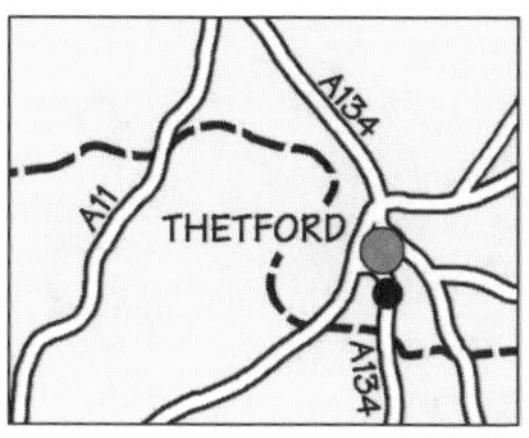

The Common also continues across the road from the car park where you can view the BTO's Nunnery Lake.

The telephone wires on the south-west side of this site are a favoured perch of Turtle Doves from the end of April until July, given away by their gentle purring call.

Barnham Cross Common provides an hour or so's gentle birding, especially useful if you have made Thetford your base for a birding break.

Other nearby sites

NWT East Wretham Heath, Fordham, NWT Foulden Common, RSPB Lakenheath, Lynford Arboretum, Santon Downham, Wayland Wood, NWT Weeting Heath.

3 NWT BARTON BROAD NNR

Key points

- **Reserve is a designated SSSI.**
- **Terrain level along gravel footpaths and boardwalks.**
- **Toilet block at car park.**
- **Food, etc available in Neatishead village.**
- **Boat runs from Gay's Staithe, signed from the car park. Wheelchair accessible.**
- **Disabled parking at Heron's Carr.**
- **Free 24-hour mooring available.**
- **No dogs on boardwalk.**
- **No cycling on boardwalk but bike rails situated at Heron's Carr.**
- **Caution! Boardwalk can be slippery when wet.**

Contacts

Norfolk Wildlife Trust
01603 625540

General Broads Authority
01603 610734

THIS IS THE second largest of all the broads, covering 164 hectares. Extensive work by the Broads Authority and Norfolk Wildlife Trust has opened this previously difficult-to-visit site to birdwatchers. A boardwalk to a viewpoint over NWT Barton Broad has been constructed, along with a new car park, toilet block and footpath. As improvements to water quality begin to take effect, the variety and quantity of wildlife should also improve. Please reward all this hard work by paying the reserve a visit soon.

Target birds

All year – **Common wildfowl (100%), Cetti's Warbler (hear 60%, see 10%).**

Other possible bird species

All year
Great Crested Grebe
Cormorant
Egyptian Goose
Common waterbirds
Sparrowhawk
Kestrel
Common gull species
Kingfisher
Green Woodpecker
Great Spotted Woodpecker
Pied Wagtail
Common scrub birds
Common woodland birds
Common finches

Summer
Common Tern
Hirundines
Summer warblers

Winter
Goldeneye
Winter thrushes

Occasional
Lesser Spotted Woodpecker
Marsh Harrier

Background information and birding tips

PREVIOUSLY, NWT Barton Broad could only be viewed from a boat but thanks to some incredibly hard work by Norfolk Wildlife Trust and the Broads Authority, all birders should be able to enjoy the delights of this site.

There is an easy-access path from the large car park, which runs alongside the trees you can see to your right, as you enter the parking area. It passes through fields (check for hirundines in summer as well as partridges) and along a narrow road (beware of traffic) to the entrance to the boardwalk, marked by three wooden posts with red tops.

The boardwalk winds through a wet woodland and reaches a viewing platform overlooking Barton Broad. There are benches here where you can spend as long as you wish scanning the water for common wildfowl. Common Terns nest on the platforms and you can spend a leisurely hour watching the comings and goings of the colony.

An alternative way of seeing the broad is from the electric boat (*Ra*) that runs from the staithe near the car park. The boat trip lasts an hour and a quarter and takes you along the River Ant to Barton Broad (£4.50 adults, £3.50 children, £10 family in 2005) with a commentary by a warden all the way around. *Ra* is accessible to wheelchair users. Booking is advisable on 01603 782281. You can also view some of the broad from your own holiday boat.

So what can the visiting birdwatcher expect to see? Cetti's Warblers inhabit the wet woodland but can be tricky to see. The wood is also a good place to see common woodland birds such as Marsh Tit and Great Spotted Woodpecker and, if you are lucky, a Lesser Spotted Woodpecker. The carr is also alive with warblers in summer.

The broad holds good numbers of Great Crested Grebes, Cormorants and Egyptian Geese among the common wildfowl, joined by Goldeneyes in winter as well as the occasional Smew and rarer grebe. Ospreys sometimes pass through in spring and autumn.

If you wish to know more about Barton, there is an information pack available from Broads Authority offices (see Contacts section on page 249 for a full list of all offices). Visitors may borrow the pack for up to three weeks (£5) and it is also available in large print and braille editions or as a CD or audio cassette.

The hard work of NWT and BA ensures that NWT Barton Broad is one to watch in the future. I suggest you reward their hard work by paying Heron's Carr a visit as soon as you can and inject a little cash into the local economy. This may have the effect of damping down some local objections to the development of the reserve.

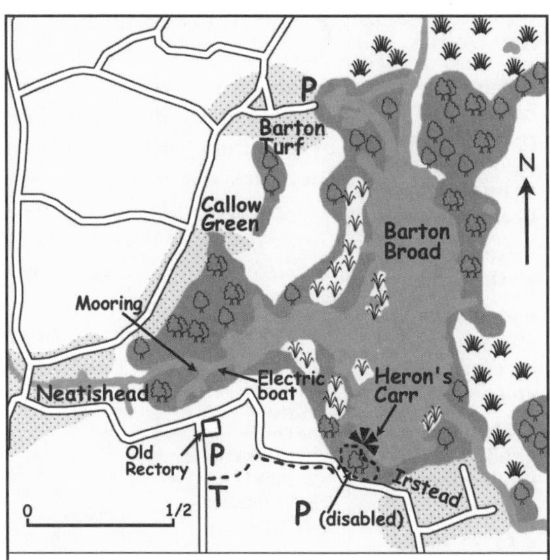

Access details

(Approx. 10.5 miles NE of Norwich).

BY CAR: **In Wroxham, follow signs to Stalham/Yarmouth/Cromer/N.Walsham (along A1151). Two miles N of roundabout at junction with A1062, turn right at signs to 'Rose Centre'/Neatishead/Duck Boardwalk. Continue into Neatishead village and turn right at Ye Olde Saddlery public house and B&B (sign-posted to Irstead and Duck Boardwalk).**

After 0.7 miles, turn right at the Old Rectory, still following the brown duck signs. The car park entrance is 75 yards on the left. Take the gravel path from the top of the car park (starts near the entrance to the car park) for 500 yards to Heron's Carr. Wheelchair users should ignore this car park and continue past the Old Rectory to Heron's Carr (TG 358207) where there is disabled parking only.

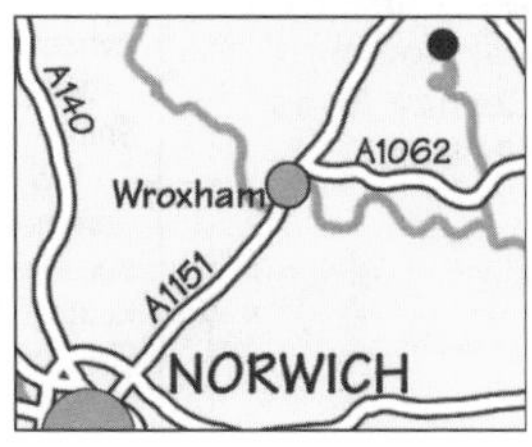

BY BOAT: **NWT Barton Broad is situated along the River Ant, one day's sail from Wroxham. Mooring for reserve is at Lime Kiln Dyke.**

Mooring with facilities is available at Neatishead, at the end of Lime Kiln Dyke, or further N at Barton Turf, though this does not give access to Heron's Carr. The whole of Barton Broad can also be seen from your boat.

The electric boat is signposted from the car park. Walk down the access road, turn right then immediately left to Gay's Staithe. A warden offers a commentary during each trip.

Other nearby sites

NWT Alderfen Broad, Buxton Heath, NWT Hickling Broad, How Hill NNR, Hoveton Great Broad, NWT Martham Broad, NWT Ranworth Broad, Sparham Pools, NWT Upton Fen, Winterton Dunes.

RSPB BERNEY MARSHES

Key points

- **Berney Arms can only be reached by train (request-stop), or by foot from Great Yarmouth.**
- **Free access at all times.**
- **Plan your journey carefully before you set off.**
- **Walking boots needed at least, Wellingtons in winter.**
- **£1.70 single train fare from Yarmouth to Berney Arms (2006).**

Contacts

Warden
01493 700645
General Broads Authority 01603 610734

RSPB Mid-Yare Office
01603 715191

http://web.ukonline.co.uk/berneyarms/index.htm

CLOSE VIEWS of several species of raptor, normally only seen at a distance at other sites, will be a possible reward for your efforts to reach this area of marshland adjacent to Breydon Water. Berney Marsh can be reached by train from Yarmouth or by an exposed walk alongside Breydon Water or across Halvergate Marshes.

Target birds *All Year* – **Marsh Harrier (50%), Bearded Tit (10%).** *Winter* – **Winter raptors inc. Short-eared Owl (25%).** *Spring/autumn* – **Passage waders (100%).** *Summer* – **Breeding waders (100%).**

Other possible bird species

All Year
Cormorant
Grey Heron
Little Egret
Common wildfowl
Red-legged Partridge
Grey Partridge
Sparrowhawk
Kestrel
Water Rail
Avocet
Lapwing
Snipe
Curlew
Common gull species
Barn Owl
Kingfisher
Sky Lark
Meadow Pipit
Common scrub birds
Corvids
Common finches
Reed Bunting

Winter
Wigeon
Teal
Pintail
Golden Plover
Rock Pipit
Winter thrushes
Stonechat

Spring/autumn
Garganey
Hobby
Curlew Sandpiper
Little Stint
Ruff
Whimbrel
Greenshank
Green Sandpiper
Wood Sandpiper
Common Sandpiper
Other common waders
Hirundines
Yellow Wagtail
Wheatear
Whinchat

Summer
Hobby
Little Ringed Plover
Hirundines
Yellow Wagtail
Sedge Warbler
Reed Warbler

Occasional
Bewick's Swan
Whooper Swan
White-fronted Goose
Pink-footed Goose
Mediterranean Gull
Yellow-legged Gull
Twite
Snow Bunting
Lapland Bunting

Background information and birding tips

THE RSPB RESERVE at Berney Arms covers 366 hectares of the vast Halvergate Marshes complex. The RSPB deliberately floods the reserve in winter to attract thousands of wildfowl. For the rest of the year the pool remains muddy, attracting passage and breeding waders.

Your first task is to actually get to the reserve. Full details can be found in the Access Section but you have several choices. There is a train from Great Yarmouth or you may walk from Yarmouth, Halvergate, Wickhampton and Reedham. For those birders holidaying on a Broadland boat, there is mooring (and facilities) at the Berney Arms public house. My favourite route is to take the train from Yarmouth, walk to the reserve and then return to the town, via the Weaver's Way footpath along the north shore of Breydon Water. Whichever way you approach it there is usually something to see.

From Berney Arms Station,

Access details

(On eastern outskirts of Great Yarmouth).

BY TRAIN: **Purchase ticket from Yarmouth station (£1.70 in 2006). You must ask the train driver to stop at Berney Arms Station (5 mins – TG 460053), as this is a request stop only. Follow signs to Berney Arms Mill from Berney Arms Station.**

BY FOOT: **From Yarmouth, follow the Weaver's Way footpath (past Asda and the train station) along the north shore of Breydon Water to the RSPB reserve (4 miles). Footpaths also lead from Wickhampton and Reedham.**

BY CAR: **Park in Asda (3 hr limit) or train station car park in Great Yarmouth. (See Breydon Water page for directions). Follow directions for foot or train access above.**

Or

Park in Halvergate at TG 434066. Turn right off the Acle to Yarmouth (A47) road, 2.2 miles from the large Acle roundabout (signed to Halvergate, opposite The Pontiac Roadhouse just after the suggested 40mph speed limit. Be aware that this is an extremely dangerous road!). After 1.4 miles, the main road bends sharp right but you need to turn left down Stone Rd. Park sensibly (very busy with farm vehicles so don't block access!). One small lay-by on right, room for 2 cars, or alternatively park sensibly on main road and walk back along Stone Rd. At end of Stone Rd, follow the sign posts to Weaver's Way footpath (you take the path on the right), which takes you across rough, muddy fields to Berney Arms Station (1hr walk).

BY BOAT: **Moor at the Berney Arms public house on the River Yare (free) and follow signs to RSPB reserve (down the seawall).**

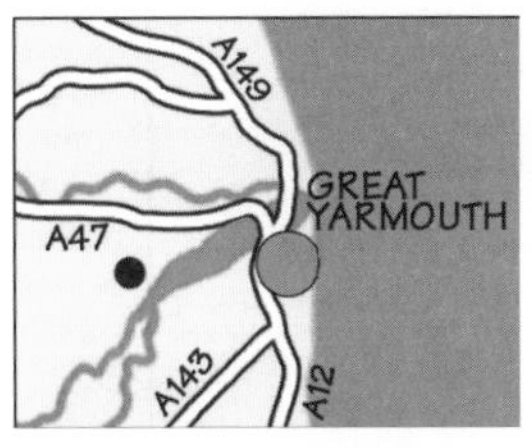

carefully cross the railway line via the obvious wooden crossing (following the exit sign). The train platform is an ideal perch to sit and scan the marshes towards Halvergate. When the exit path reaches the Weaver's Way footpath, turn left (south-east) towards the black and white mill (no sails). There is an RSPB information board and map near the station.

Follow the footpath to the mill. There is another RSPB information board by the mill and a donations box. There are also picnic tables. You may either walk left along the seawall towards the public house (there are some benches here for you to sit and scan the fields and pools to your left, though distant, and the river) or go through a gate along an obvious gravel path before you reach the mill. Either way, you can get to the RSPB viewing screen. From the pub, go down the seawall steps, cross a track and follow the sign to 'reed screen' down a grassy path. The gravel path joins

Key points

- **Several stiles to negotiate.**
- **Well-marked footpath across very muddy, wet fields.**
- **Donations asked for.**
- **Viewing screen with seat.**
- **Telesccope useful.**

the 'reed screen' path at the back of the pub. The screen overlooks Seago's Marsh. Wildfowl may be close in winter but birds may be distant at other times of year.

It is possible to follow the main track eastwards (scanning pools and fields on your left as you go) to where it rejoins the Weaver's Way path. From here you can walk to Yarmouth or take the loop to your left back to Halvergate and Berney Arms Station.

In winter, the flooded fields are home to thousands of wildfowl such as Wigeon, Teal, Pochard, Pintail, Tufted Duck, etc, etc, sometimes joined by wild swans and geese (Bewick's, Whoopers, Pink-footed and White-fronted) roosting on the flood. The surrounding marshes are patrolled by Hen and Marsh Harriers, Peregrine, Merlin, Barn and Short-eared Owls plus the usual Kestrels and Sparrowhawks.

The marshes are also a winter home for Rock and Meadow Pipits, occasionally joined by Snow and Lapland Buntings and Twite. Because this is such a huge area, species may be difficult to locate but the longer you stay on site, the more you will see.

In spring and autumn, the shallow pools attract many species of wader. Whimbrel, Curlew Sandpiper, Temminck's and Little Stints, Green, Wood and Common Sandpipers are all regular passage visitors along with the expected Black-tailed Godwit, Avocet, Ruff, Redshank, Oystercatcher, Dunlin, Lapwing, Snipe, Curlew, Ringed Plover, etc, etc. Garganey is another expected passage migrant. The best time to see waders is when there is a high tide on Breydon Water.

The reedbed and bushes around the main pool holds resident Bearded Tits, joined by Reed and Sedge Warblers in summer. Yellow Wagtails may be seen throughout the spring and summer. Wheatears and Whinchats may drop in on passage also.

The marsh is home to many cows (in fact, if you are nervous of these inquisitive animals, I suggest you avoid the public footpath from Halvergate village to the reserve!), which in turn attract flies. These annoying insects are hunted by hundreds of hirundines, which are occasionally attacked by a Hobby!

Visitors shouldn't forget to check the River Yare when they are at Berney. Approach the seawall carefully and you may get close views of waders and a Little Egret or two on the muddy edges of Berney Arms Reach.

Because of its remoteness, Berney Arms Marsh is an under-watched site. There is a strong possibility that you'll be alone to enjoy the birds and you may even find something out of the ordinary. Previous finds include Kentish Plover, Great Reed Warbler, Terek Sandpiper and American Wigeon among an impressive list of rarities.

Other nearby sites

Breydon Water, RSPB Buckenham Marshes, Burgh Castle Marsh, Great Yarmouth Beach, Haddiscoe Marshes, Hardley Flood, Herbert Barnes Riverside Park, NWT Hickling Broad, RSPB Strumpshaw Fen, NWT Stubb Mill.

BLACKBOROUGH END TIP

BLACKBOROUGH END Tip is gaining a strong reputation for attracting white-winged gulls in winter. It isn't the most attractive of birding sites but gull-lovers will have the time of their lives sorting through the throng.

Target birds

All year – **Yellow-legged Gull – including Caspian (40%).** *Winter* – **Glaucous Gull (25%), Iceland Gull (25%).**

Other possible bird species

Resident
Great Crested Grebe
Little Grebe
Cormorant
Grey Heron
Common waterbirds
Common wildfowl
Egyptian Goose
Sparrowhawk
Kestrel
Lapwing
Common gull species
Green Woodpecker
Great Spotted Woodpecker
Stock Dove
Sky Lark
Meadow Pipit
Pied Wagtail
Common scrub birds
Goldcrest
Corvids
Marsh Tit
Common finches
Reed Bunting
Yellowhammer

Summer
Hobby
Common Tern
Turtle Dove
Hirundines
Kingfisher
Yellow Wagtail
Summer warblers

Winter
Redshank
Grey Wagtail
Winter thrushes

Passage
Passage waders

Background information and birding tips

BLACKBOROUGH END Tip is a working household waste centre (a.k.a. rubbish tip!) and quarry. The foul-smelling waste is a magnet for thousands of gulls at all times of year (all common species are recorded in impressive numbers). In winter, these may be joined by one or two Iceland and Glaucous Gulls. In 2005, there were at least two of each species present but they were scarcer in 2006.

When arriving on site, please be sure to park your vehicle away from the bend on the main road, as large lorries need space to swing in and out of the track. The site manager is a friendly chap who is pleased that his tip attracts rare birds but he has asked me to ask you all for your co-operation in leaving clear access for his trucks.

Follow the sandy track away from the road (signed 'bridleway'). After approximately 200 yards, the bridleway takes a sharp turn right but ignore this unless you want to view the fishing lake. Gulls bathe on this lake and there are usually a few common wildfowl species to be seen here. The conifers on the left of this diversion are good for Goldcrest and Coal Tit.

Carry on along the wide sandy track. You will pass a sign reading 'caution gate locked ahead', then a large house on your right. The path bends, then opens out so you can see the mound of rubbish on your left (about half a mile from the car park). Go a few yards further and there are a couple of raised grass banks by the path that are ideal platforms to view the area.

In my experience, it is advisable to be on site early in the morning. The white-winged gulls tend to

Key points

- **Access track is used by quarry lorries, so take extra care on site.**
- **Level terrain but can be muddy with large puddles.**
- **Arrive early before gulls disperse.**
- **Free access at all times.**
- **Park sensibly. Do not block lorry access.**

Contacts

None.

ALL YEAR | **OS MAP 132** | **TF 673143**

loaf on the banks of the tip or bathe in the two pools visible from the path before heading off at around 9.00am. Sightings of Glaucs and Icelands become very sporadic throughout the day from that point onwards.

The pools by the path hold bathing gulls. If the white-winged species get on here they allow very good views indeed. I have also seen Redshank and Grey and Pied Wagtails on this pool and it should also be attractive to passage waders such as Green and Common Sandpipers.

The surrounding bushes hide many species of common birds such as Bullfinch, Long-tailed Tit, Blackbird, Dunnock, Wren, Robin, Song Thrush, Yellowhammer, etc, etc, joined by Redwing and Fieldfare in winter.

A summer visit can be unproductive, unless you like scanning through gull flocks to find a Yellow-legged Gull. Several Caspian Gulls were reported from here in the summer of 2005 so someone was having fun!

The bushes and trees along the track attract several species of warbler in spring and summer. Whitethroats, Lesser Whitethroats, Willow Warblers and Chiffchaffs all visit, as do Turtle Doves.

The fishing lake usually has a swarm of hirundines hunting insects over it and one or two Common Terns drop in occasionally. Egyptian Geese are ever-present on the lake.

Blackborough End Tip makes for a bracing start to a winter day's birding in Norfolk. Start here, then head for the coastal hotspots for waders, geese and ducks then end the day at a raptor roost. Does a day's entertainment come any more exciting than that?!

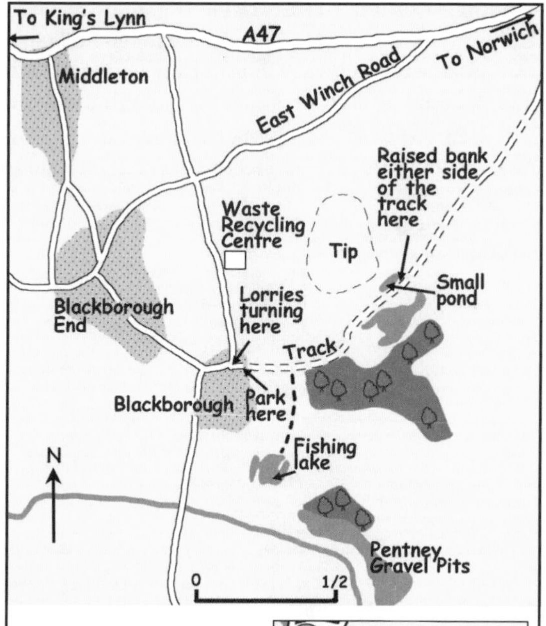

Access details

(Approx 5 miles from King's Lynn)

From King's Lynn, take the A47 signed to Norwich (ignoring brown signs for 'Pentney Lakes'). After approx. 3 miles take East Winch Road, signed to the Waste Disposal Tip. After 1 mile, take the first left (signposted 'Waste Recycling Centre', immediately before 7.5 tonne restriction sign). Go down the hill for 0.7 miles, (past the recycling centre) and at the sharp right bend at the bottom of the hill turn sharp left onto a wide sandy track. Do not park on the bend (because lorries come down the hill and need room to turn onto this track) but go a little way down the track to park.

Other nearby sites

Pentney Gravel Pits, NWT Roydon Common, Snettisham RSPB, Ken Hill Wood, Sandringham House, Wolferton Triangle, Dersingham Bog, Hunstanton, north coast sites, King's Lynn Docks.

BLAKENEY POINT

FAMOUS WITH birders and non-birders alike as a great place to view tern and seal colonies in summer, Blakeney Point attracts many common, scarce and rare migrants in spring and autumn. However, unless you take a boat to The Point you have to undertake an arduous eight mile round trek along a shingle bank to see them! In winter thousands of waders roost on The Point.

Target birds

Summer – Nesting terns (100%), Mediterranean Gull (10%). *Spring/autumn* – Passage seabirds, passage migrants. *Winter* – Waders (100%), raptors (20%).

Other possible bird species

All year
Cormorant
Shelduck
Other common wildfowl
Kestrel
Red-legged Partridge
Common waders
Common gull species
Sky Lark
Meadow Pipit
Pied Wagtail
Corvids
Common finches
Reed Bunting

Spring/autumn
Shearwaters
Gannet
Whimbrel
Skuas
Hirundines
Yellow Wagtail
Ring Ouzel
Bluethroat
Whinchat
Wheatear
Black Redstart
Grasshopper Warbler
Goldcrest

Winter
Brent Goose
Wigeon
Grey Plover
Rock Pipit
Winter thrushes

Occasional
Hen Harrier
Merlin
Peregrine
Short-eared Owl
Richard's Pipit

Possible migrants
Wryneck
Richard's Pipit
Ortolan Bunting

Background information and birding tips

A VISIT to Blakeney Point in ideal migrant conditions (fog, drizzle, onshore winds) can seem a very bleak experience. Visit in spring and summer sunshine for the tern and seal colonies and it can seem like a naturalist's paradise.

Summer boat trips are popular with tourists interested in seeing common and grey seals on The Point but also they provide superb for obtaining close views of Sandwich, Common, Little and Arctic Terns busily going about the business of raising chicks. Sharp-eyed birders will manage to pick out a Roseate Tern or Mediterranean Gull.

Along Blakeney Channel you will see many common waders on the mud banks and see terns as they fish the large inlet. At most times, the trip takes about one hour and you do not land on The Point. However, if the tide is right, the boat does land, extending the round trip to two hours. Booking boat trips is essential, especially in school holidays. In 2005 the trip cost £7 for adults and £4 for children.

Birdwatchers on the look-out for migrants in spring and autumn, should endeavour to walk the whole length of Blakeney Point from Cley beach car park. This

Key points

- **A National Trust reserve.**
- **Dogs must be kept under control.**
- **No foot access to western tip between April and the end of July, to protect terns from disturbance.**
- **Phone boat company for sailing times.**
- **Facilities at parking places (Cley, Morston and Blakeney) can be closed off-peak.**
- **Keep to boardwalks around the visitor centre.**
- **Avoid roped-off areas.**
- **Visitor centre has disabled toilets and sells drinks and snacks. Opening times unpredictable so go prepared! Usually open April – end September.**

ALL YEAR	OS MAP 133	TG 048452 (then walk) TG 006443, TG 027441 (boats)	£ £

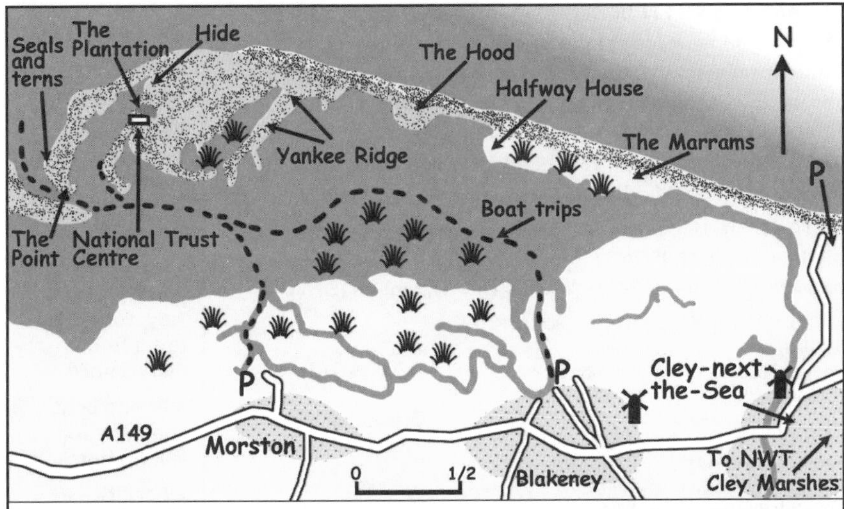

Access details

(Approx. 11 miles W of Cromer.)

You can tackle Blakeney Point the hard way or the easy way. The easy way is to travel by boat from either Morston Quay or Blakeney Harbour. Call contact numbers for sailing times, as these depend on tides. Boats run throughout the year, though tide times dictate whether you are able to land on The Point or not.

Morston is about two miles W of Blakeney village, both connected by A149. Obtain boat tickets where the chalk boards advertise 'Boat Trips' by The Anchor pub on A149. Morston Quay is sign-posted on a brown tourist sign. Follow this rough track to a pay and display car park.

Blakeney Harbour is sign-posted off the A149 down Westgate Street. Follow the road to the quay car park and the moorings for the seal and bird trips are very obvious.

If you want a challenge in spring and autumn, the best way to find the birds is by walking from Cley beach car park, out of the village

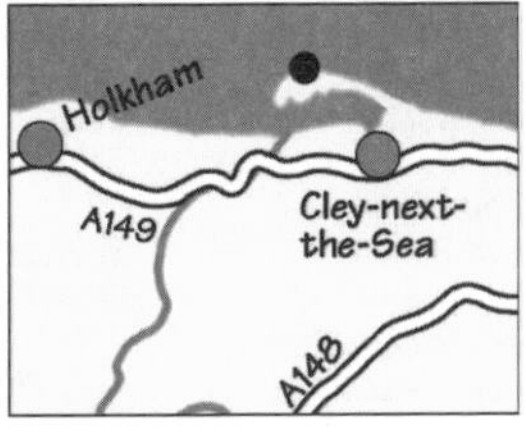

towards Sheringham, then turn left at the sign for 'Beach'. Walk W along the shingle bank for four miles. The going may be easier if the tide is out as you can walk on hard sand.

is an arduous walk along a shingle sea wall and, at the end of the eight mile trek (four miles each way), your calf muscles will be complaining bitterly! If you are lucky, the tide will be out, enabling you to walk on hard sand. Please keep clear of Oystercatchers and Ringed Plovers in spring as they will be trying to nest on the shingle.

For the first mile you will have the sea on your right and a marsh on your left. Scan both at regular intervals for passing seabirds over the former and geese, ducks and raptors over the latter. The shingle then opens out to an area of stubby vegetation, known as The Marrams. Wait here awhile as the dense plants can hold various species but they do tend to hide.

Wheatears are common here on passage and look out for thrushes, warblers, Goldcrests, finches etc as they make their first landing from the continent. Such tired, small birds attract the attention of raptors so keep one eye on the skies!

A mile further on, you reach Halfway House. Don't let the name fool you: this is only Quarterway or Three-quarterway House depending if you are on your way to The Point or on your way back. Either way, it will feel good to get your feet on solid ground for a few moments after sand and shingle. The bushes around Halfway House are excellent migrant traps.

After a further half a mile, you reach a dune system, known as The Hood, which is good for migrant pipits, chats, thrushes etc. Search the area thoroughly before continuing your journey.

Eventually, you will reach an odd-shaped blue building, which was the old lifeboat station but now houses the National Trust visitor centre. The area here has three trees, known optimistically as The Plantation and, in this barren landscape, they do act as magnets for birds on passage!

The area around the lifeboat station and chalets is excellent for Wheatears, Whinchats, thrushes, etc. in spring and autumn. There is also a seat here where you can look over Blakeney Channel and marsh. When the tide permits, Grey Plovers, Curlew, Dunlin, Bar-tailed Godwits, Ringed Plovers, etc can be seen and Brent Geese are present on the marsh until May.

Terns fish the channel from April onwards but the nesting area is another half a mile from here, at the western tip of The Point. There is no access by foot to the tern colony between April and July.

A boardwalk runs from behind the visitor centre to a hide overlooking a channel. This is good for fishing terns in summer when the tide is in and geese and waders in winter, when the mud is exposed. A telescope is useful.

The boardwalk also leads to the beach. This can be a spectacular place when the wind is blowing strongly onshore. Skuas and shearwaters seem to pass closer here than at any other seawatching site in Norfolk (with the possible exception of Sheringham), though there is no shelter.

Blakeney Point also boasts a disabled toilet. The most baffling thing is exactly how the National Trust expects wheelchair users to get to it, as a steep step from the sand onto a boardwalk has to be negotiated. If you have mobility problems, I would phone the warden to clarify things first!

As mentioned before, Blakeney Point is famous for its seal colony. More than 400 animals can be seen here, most of them common seals. The seals and terns provide a noisy spectacle on the boat trips and I thoroughly recommend it to you, even if you are prone to queasiness on boats.

Usually I feel ill at the slightest sea-swell but this trip is a breeze. I am usually more concerned with sorting out the terns ('was that a Roseate which just flew over my head?') and cooing at the baby seals!

In truth, the walk from Cley is usually only undertaken by hardened birdwatchers trying to find rare migrants in spring and autumn. Hardy, persistent searchers can turn up anything. The list of rare and scarce birds seen on Blakeney are too numerous to mention but Pallas's Grasshopper Warbler, Thrush Nightingale, Desert Warbler, etc should get your mouth watering!

Key points

- **No bikes or wheeled vehicles.**
- **If walking, the terrain is tough.**
- **Difficult wheelchair access. Please phone the warden.**
- **Hearing loop installed for 'sea and bird sounds atmosphere'.**

Contacts

The Warden, Cornfield, Langham, Holt, Norfolk NR25 7DQ.

01263 740480 (April – Sept)

01328 830401 (Oct – March)

Winter warden: 01263 740241

The National Trust, East Anglia Regional Office 01263 733471 www.nationaltrust.org.uk/regions/eastanglia/

Blakeney boats:
Graham Bean 01263 740505

Colin Bishop 01263 740753

Roy Moreton 01328 830394

Morston boats:
John Bean 01263 740038

Jim Temple 01263 740791

7 BLICKLING HALL

Key points

- **Park open all year, dawn to dusk.**
- **Free parking.**
- **Restaurant & shop when hall open (check before you travel).**
- **Dogs on leads.**
- **Blue trail is 5 miles long, brown trail is 2.25 miles, lakeside trail is 2.25 miles.**
- **Owned by the National Trust.**
- **Leaflet available + info boards.**
- **Level terrain, mostly along muddy(ish) paths.**

BLICKLING HALL and grounds contains a mixture of habitats including 600 acres of ancient woodland, 800 acres of pasture and an artificial lake. It is an ideal site for non-birdwatching members of the family as they can look round the house and gardens.

Target birds

All year – **Lesser Spotted Woodpecker (15%), common woodland and parkland birds.**

Other possible bird species

All Year
Little Grebe
Great Crested Grebe
Common waterbirds and wildfowl
Egyptian Goose
Sparrowhawk
Kestrel
Common gull species
Stock Dove
Barn Owl
Little Owl
Tawny Owl
Green Woodpecker
Great Spotted Woodpecker
Lesser Spotted Woodpecker
Kingfisher
Sky Lark
Pied Wagtail
Meadow Pipit
Common scrub birds
Goldcrest
Common woodland birds
Nuthatch
Treecreeper
Jay
Other corvids
Common finches
Reed Bunting
Yellowhammer

Winter
Goldeneye
Goosander
Lapwing
Grey Wagtail
Winter thrushes

Summer
Hobby
Common Tern
Cuckoo
Turtle Dove
Sand Martin
Other hirundines
Reed Warbler
Sedge Warbler
Other summer warblers
Spotted Flycatcher

Occasional
Buzzard
Yellow Wagtail
Crossbill

Background information and birding tips

FROM THE main car park, follow signs for the Lakeside Walk. Go past some beautiful cottages and through the park gates. Almost immediately, you can turn right through a small wooden gate onto a grass footpath (if you head left along the main track you reach the Great Wood). This takes you to the lake through some mature trees. Spend time in the area as this is a good place for woodpeckers all year round and summer warblers. There may be Spotted Flycatchers here in summer and one or two migrants such as Pied Flycatcher, Redstart and Wood Warbler may be found at passage times.

The path reaches the lake where you will see many common waterbirds at any time of year. Expect to see Great Crested Grebe, Coot, Moorhen, Egyptian Goose, Tufted Duck, Gadwall, etc. In winter, these are joined by Goosander, Pochard, Shoveler, Goldeneye, etc and maybe even one of the rarer grebes. The path encircles the whole lake, taking you back around the hall to the car park.

The reeds around the edge of the large lake has breeding Reed Warblers in summer but you will be lucky to see one of the resident Water Rails. There are a few muddy edges to the lake so be watchful for waders at passage time (again, visit before the general public are out and about). A walk early in the morning will produce the best birding as the

lake area is popular with general visitors during the day.

At the northern end of the lake, you can walk around the other bank to another wood or you can turn left, following the brown trail. The wood is probably the best place to see Lesser Spotted Woodpeckers, though they are very elusive. There is a water tower in the wood and this seems to be the most likely spot for the Lessers (especially in early March when they are displaying).

The trail linking the lake with the Great Wood is quiet as far as birds go but keep your eyes open for Little Owls, perched on fence posts and isolated trees and Barn Owls hunting over the fields at dawn and dusk (they breed in the park).

Before you get to the Great Wood, you pass a smaller wood, including some larch trees. Crossbills have been seen here but Siskin and Redpoll are more likely. This wood can be surprisingly devoid of people, making it ideal for birdwatchers to wait patiently to see what shows itself.

Many common woodland species inhabit the wood, so expect to see Coal and Long-tailed Tits, Nuthatch, Treecreeper, Spotted Flycatcher, Willow Warbler, Chiffchaff, etc. It will be hard to avoid seeing a Great Spotted Woodpecker! The footpath affords excellent overviews of several woods and it may be worth regularly scanning for birds of prey when you reach a suitable vantage point.

If you don't fancy walking all the way to the wood from the main car park, there is also a car park

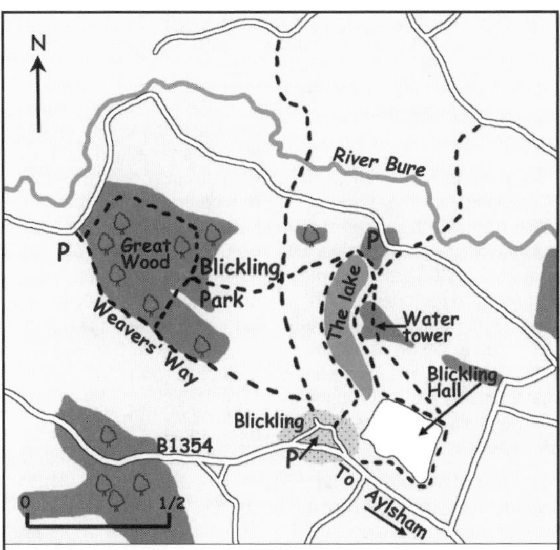

Access Details

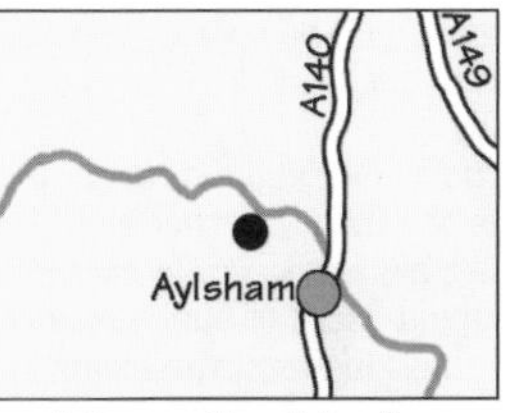

(15 miles north of Norwich, 1.25 miles north west of Aylsham).

On the A140 Norwich to Cromer road turn off at the roundabout (signed Aylsham). Follow the road through Aylsham where you pick up brown tourist signs for Blickling Hall. Then choose your route from below:

***LAKE:* After passing through Aylsham, take the second right turn to Ingworth, (1.6 miles from the A140 roundabout). Turn left at signs for Ingworth and Blickling Lake, then after 0.7 miles turn left into the lake car park (this gives quick access to the lake and wood on the eastern side of the lake). TG 180295.**

***GREAT WOOD:* The Woodgate car park is reached by continuing along the road from the lake car park for another 1.7 miles and turning left (opposite a house where the road bends sharply right) onto what looks like a farm track. TG 162297.**

***HALL:* If you want the main car park, continue on the B1149 through Aylsham and the hall is 2.2 miles along (from the A140 roundabout). The Common car park is on your right, 1.4 miles past the hall car park (immediately past a brown tourist sign for Mannington Hall/Tudor Tour and just before the turn off for Cawston). TG 157289.**

Disabled badge holders may park at the hall itself.

here (see access section). This is ideal if you haven't got lots of time to spend in the park as you can easily access different habitats from different car parks.

You eventually reach The Mausoleum, another good place from which to scan the surrounding area. The trails split about 500 yards past the Mausoleum, red goes left, the blue bears right. The blue trail leads you to Great Wood and Woodgate car park. There are many smaller paths through the trees, so explore as much as you desire!

The rest of the trail can be quiet for birds but if you have walked this far you may as well carry on. It is generally well-signed on colour-marked posts but if one is missing you may get a bit lost. There is usually a large dung heap by the tower/folly further along the trail, a magnet for winter feeding flocks of buntings and finches. Just past the tower is a pine wood, a good place to see Coal Tit, Goldcrest, Treecreeper and occasional Crossbills. At other times it can seem very dead in here!

At the end of this wood, the trail takes you across a busy road then bears left through more trees. It passes an old kiln and joins another road, where you may see Whitethroat and Bullfinch, etc, etc in the hedgerows. Just before you reach a large farm, turn left (it looks as if you are entering a field) then immediately right to follow the footpath along the edge of this field. The footpath here is very rough and narrow so watch your footing while scanning the hedgerows!

The path takes you across two stiles and a very muddy field. Scan the field for Yellow Wagtails in spring (they love to feed around the cows' hooves) and Redwings and Fieldfares in winter. You finally emerge onto a road through a tiny gap in a tall hedge. Turn left and then left again at the T-junction with the busy main road back to the car park.

If I am honest, there are only three areas of great interest to birdwatchers: the lake; the wood at the back of the lake; the Great Wood. All of these have their own car parks so you can move between each site without having to bother with the less interesting bits in between. If you have a bike, there is a marked cycle route around the park (cycles are available for hire at the hall at certain times). You may want to spend the whole day in the park birding, visiting the hall, picnicking, etc but if you wish to tour the hall I suggest you phone to check it is open beforehand – I have lost count of the number of people who turn up to find it is closed!

Sand Martins nesting nearby hunt for insects over the lake.

Other nearby sites

NWT Buxton Heath, Felbrigg Hall, NWT Sparham Pools, Hoveton Great Broad, RSPB Surlingham Church Marshes, Rockland Broad.

BRANCASTER MARSH 8

ENJOY this typical North Norfolk marsh, complete with typical marsh birds, without crowds of other birdwatchers. Situated within walking distance of the RSPB Titchwell Marsh reserve along the beach, it can be a productive place, especially in winter.

Target birds

Resident – **Little Egret (85%), Bearded Tit (70%), Barn Owl (40%).** *Winter* – **Brent Goose (95%), Seaduck (40%), Raptors (25%).** *Summer* – **Marsh Harrier (90%).** *Spring/ autumn* – **Passage migrants.**

Other possible bird species

All year
Cormorant
Shelduck
Kestrel
Common waders
Common gull species
Green Woodpecker
Sky Lark
Meadow Pipit
Pied Wagtail
Bullfinch
Reed Bunting

Summer
Terns
Hirundines
Sedge Warbler
Reed Warbler
Whitethroat
Blackcap
Chiffchaff
Willow Warbler

Winter
Red-throated Diver
Wigeon
Teal
Long-tailed Duck
Common Scoter
Goldeneye
Red-breasted Merganser
Hen Harrier
Merlin
Peregrine
Grey Plover
Short-eared Owl
Stonechat
Winter thrushes
Twite
Snow Bunting

Spring/autumn
Shearwaters
Gannet
Garganey
Hobby
Whimbrel
Skuas
Wryneck
Yellow Wagtail
Redstart
Whinchat
Wheatear
Ring Ouzel
Winter thrushes
Barred Warbler
Yellow-browed Warbler
Firecrest
Pied Flycatcher

Background information and birding tips

BRANCASTER MARSH is another coastal site neglected by birders, making it ideal for those wishing to birdwatch on their own. It is an extension of the Gypsy Lane walk to the west.

Close to the small lay-by along the road, listen out for the '*ping-ping*' calls of Bearded Tits in the surrounding reedbed: they can show well here. The start of the track is marked by a National Trust ("Norfolk Coastal Path – Brancaster Manor") sign about 75 yards back towards the village from the small lay-by.

The path starts off along a rough track through a small reedbed. This is frequented by Reed Warblers in summer. The trees and bushes around the start of the track are alive with species such as Goldfinch, Greenfinch, Reed Bunting and other common birds.

The path narrows and continues east until it reaches a stile from where you start to get a great overview of the marsh. This is also a good place to watch for Sedge Warblers. Until this point, the vertically-challenged among us will have seen very little of the marsh over the reeds!

Key points

- **National Trust site – free access.**
- **£3 beach car park, £2 after 4.00pm (NT members must also pay).**
- **Road to car park may flood at high tide.**
- **Toilet block near main car park.**
- **Access trail consists of railway sleepers.**
- **Wheelchair users restricted to beach road.**
- **Terrain is level but at least one stile to negotiate.**
- **Insect repellent advisable in summer.**
- **Telescope advisable.**

Contacts

None.

All along this section there are bushes to scan for common birds and migrants in spring and autumn. There is a distinct possibility of the occasional Redstart, Pied Flycatcher, Barred Warbler or Firecrest turning up here in May or, more likely, in September/October.

After the stile, the path consists of two railway sleepers side by side (quite narrow when passing other walkers, especially those clad in winter woollies). The whole path gives excellent views over the marsh. In winter, expect Hen Harriers and maybe a Merlin with a distinct possibility of a Barn or Short-eared Owl. Flying in and out of the marsh will be small flocks of Brent Geese and Wigeon. Little Egrets are resident but can be hidden in the channels.

The marsh is quieter in summer but you should obtain reasonable views of a Marsh Harrier or two. Hirundines should be seen overhead, sometimes being pursued by a Hobby.

The path reaches a beautiful cottage with views over the marsh and, if I win the lottery, I shall be knocking on the owner's door to make them an offer they can't refuse! Just after this cottage, you come across a creek, which is a good place to scan for waders when the tide is out.

From here the path continues with good views over the marsh to your left and bushes to your right. The longer you walk along towards Holkham, the more birds you are likely to see, especially in winter.

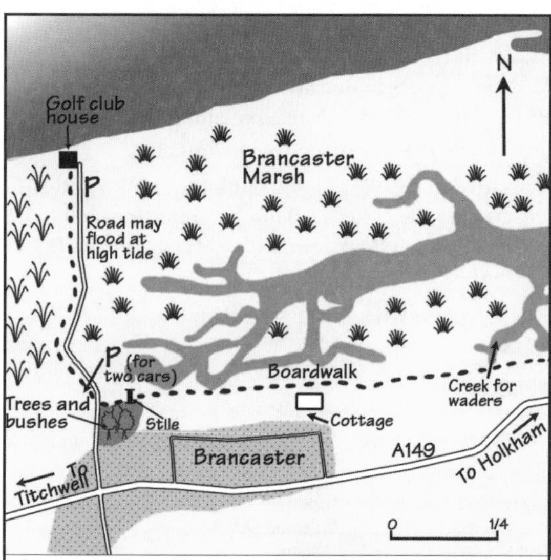

Access details

(Approx. 6.5 miles E of Hunstanton).

Enter Brancaster village on A149 Norfolk coast road and take Broad Lane, sign-posted 'The Beach'.

There is a small pull-in on the left with room for two cars at the point where the road splits the reedbed. If this is full, follow the road to the car park (you may have to pay the attendant, depending on time of year).

The footpath is 75 yards back towards the village from the small lay-by. Turn left along a track in the reeds and follow for as far as you like (this path is part of The Peddar's Way long distance footpath).

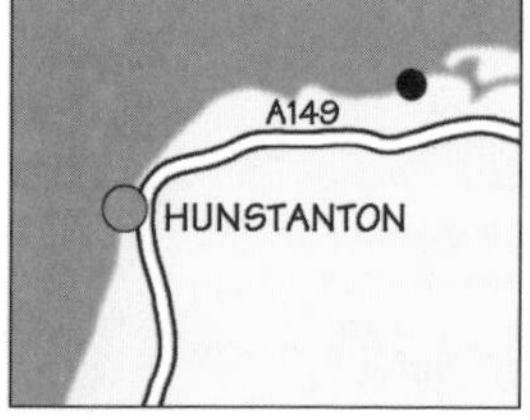

If you wish to partake in a spot of seawatching, you should park in the beach car park and view the sea from the beach. In winter, you should be rewarded with views of divers, grebes and waders, with shearwaters and skuas in autumn and terns in summer.

If you fancy walking along the beach to Titchwell, only attempt it at low tide: There is a deep channel in between the two reserves!

Visitors can expect some disturbance at this site in the future, as a new sea wall is being constructed to protect the marsh and reeds from flooding. Work is planned to start in 2006.

BREYDON WATER (NORTH SHORE) 9

BREYDON comprises more than a thousand hectares of marsh and water or, when the tide is out, mud. It is best viewed from the hide or footpath along the north-east corner, though you may wish to walk the whole area to maximise your chances of seeing everything of interest. An hour before high tide is best for viewing the waders. A highly recommended way of seeing birds up close, is to have a trip on an organised boat tour (see Contacts section below).

Target birds

Winter – Avocet (90%), Rock Pipit (50%), Short-eared Owl (25%). *Spring/summer* – Avocet (90%), Little Gull (50%), Roseate Tern (10%). *Spring/autumn* – Passage waders, Little Gull (60%).

Other possible bird species

All year
Cormorant
Little Egret
Shelduck
Common wildfowl
Marsh Harrier
Sparrowhawk
Kestrel
Grey Partridge
Red-legged Partridge
Common waders
Gull species
Barn Owl
Pied Wagtail

Winter
Bewick's Swan
Whooper Swan
Pink-footed Goose
Wigeon
Pintail
Goldeneye
Golden Plover
Grey Plover
Knot
Bar-tailed Godwit

Spring/summer
Garganey
Sandwich Tern
Common Tern
Little Tern

Passage
Ruff
Little Stint
Curlew Sandpiper
Black-tailed Godwit
Whimbrel
Greenshank
Spotted Redshank
Green Sandpiper
Wood Sandpiper
Common Sandpiper
Black Tern
Arctic Tern
Hirundines

Occasional
White-fronted Goose
Marsh Harrier
Hen Harrier (winter)
Merlin
Peregrine
Little Tern
Mediterranean Gull

Background information and birding tips

BREYDON WATER is at the confluence of the Rivers Bure, Waveney and Yare. It forms the only tidal flats on the east coast of Norfolk and is internationally important for wintering waterbirds.

Such a huge area can seem a very daunting place to watch birds but getting there at the right time makes this an accessible place, as the tide will do all your hard work for you. The north-east area is the last to be covered by the tide, so if you reach here about 60 or 90 minutes before high tide, all the waders and roosting terns will have been pushed towards you.

Breydon is the only reliable place to see wintering Avocets in Norfolk. There may be one or two at other sites in the county but more than 50 stay here from October to March. These are joined by others in summer, with numbers reaching up to 300 in July and August. Dotted among the Avocets you

Key points

- **Not accessible for wheelchair users.**
- **Free access at all times.**
- **Terrain is level along a narrow, muddy path.**
- **One hide overlooks Breydon Water (accessed up steep steps).**
- **Excellent views available from raised 'sea-wall'.**
- **Telescope essential.**
- **Best viewed an hour before high tide when birds are pushed into NE corner.**
- **Morning 2hr boat trips run throughout the year (£6 adults, £4 children in 2006) from Burgh Castle. Booking essential.**
- **Car parking restrictions (see access details).**

Contacts

General Broads Authority
01603 610734

Boat trips across Breydon Water
01603 715191

should see one or two Grey Plovers and Bar-tailed Godwits, along with other species of commoner waders and a Little Egret or two.

If you follow the path from the Asda car park along the north shore, passing the hide, you are able to look out over Acle Marshes on your right. In winter Hen Harriers are sometimes seen, while Merlins are even more infrequent. This area is probably the most reliable site in the county for Short-eared Owls, as up to three birds may roost here in winter. Barn Owl is also possible.

The marshes around Breydon also hold varying numbers of wintering wildfowl. White-fronted Geese numbers seem to be declining here but Wigeon are numerous and you might pick out a few Bewick's or Whooper Swans in the fields. You should also find one or two Rock Pipits as 100 or so over-winter.

Common waders will be joined by several more exciting species at passage times in spring and autumn. These can include Whimbrel, Spotted Redshank, Little Stint, Ruff and Green, Common, Wood and Curlew Sandpipers. Numbers are usually better in autumn. Also look out for Black and Arctic Terns at these times.

In summer, Breydon is frequented by several species of roosting tern. Sandwich and Common Terns are the most numerous but watch out for Little and Roseate Terns among them. The hide overlooks the tern nesting platforms.

If you wish, you can continue along the north shore path across the Halvergate Marshes to Halvergate village, a distance of seven miles. There is an infrequent bus service back to Yarmouth from Halvergate but check times first.

If you are visiting The Broads area by boat, you can get excellent views of Breydon Water's birds from your vessel. Alternatively, the RSPB organise two hour boat trips across Breydon. The boat runs from Goodchild Marina, Burgh Castle. It is essential to book in advance as the boat only holds 12 people (see Contacts).

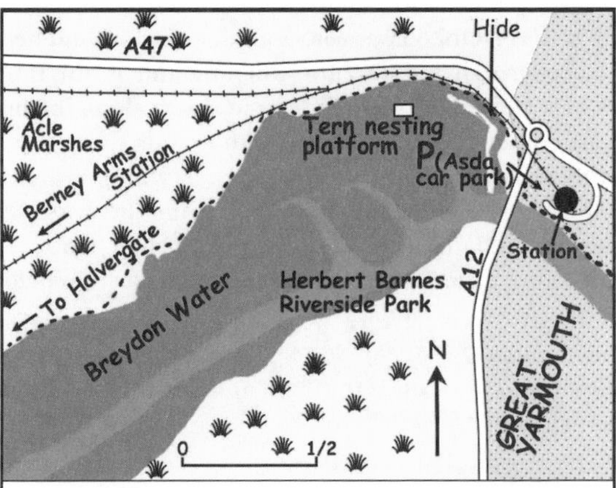

Access details

(On outskirts of Great Yarmouth).

***BY CAR:* Take A47 into Great Yarmouth, heading straight over the first roundabout (junction with A12) towards the town centre. Move immediately into the right hand lane and turn right at the traffic lights (50 yards after the A12 island) signed to the train station. Go past the station and park in the left hand side of the Asda car park, by the raised 'sea-wall' (be careful, there is only a 3 hr waiting limit here). Walking adjacent to the wall, continue to the information board. The Weavers Way footpath starts here, going under the road bridge and following the north shore of Breydon Water to the hide and beyond to Berney Marshes.**

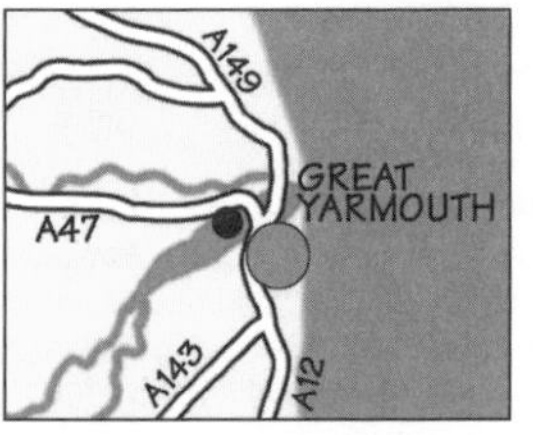

***BY BOAT:* There is free 24hr mooring on the River Bure at Great Yarmouth, near the tourist information centre at TG 521083. Walk south and cross A47 road bridge to the train station and Asda supermarket. Follow directions above. Alternatively be 'green' and catch a train to Great Yarmouth or Berney Arms.**

10 RSPB BUCKENHAM MARSHES

Key points

- **Call in at the Strumpshaw Fen reception for details of where the Bean Geese are currently showing.**
- **Free parking.**
- **Access via a rough track that may be wet at all times of year. Boots or wellies recommended.**
- **Telescope essential as target species are invariably distant.**
- **Please leave sightings information in hide.**

Contacts

RSPB Mid Yare Office
01603 715191

RSPB East Anglia Office
01603 661662

RENOWNED for its wintering flock of Bean Geese, Buckenham also attracts a large number of Wigeon and Teal. In summer, several nationally declining breeding species raise their young on the marshes, making this a very important bird reserve. This site incorporates RSPB Cantley Marsh.

Target birds

All year – **Marsh Harrier (65%).** *Winter* – **(Taiga) Bean Goose (85%), White-fronted Goose (85%), Water Pipit (60%).** *Summer* – **Breeding waders, Hobby (40%).**

Other possible bird species

Winter
Wigeon
Teal
Pintail
Other wildfowl
Common waterbirds
Winter raptors
Golden Plover
Common gull species
Barn Owl
Short-eared Owl
Winter thrushes
Corvids

Summer
Egyptian Goose
Gadwall
Shoveler
Oystercatcher
Avocet
Lapwing
Snipe
Curlew
Redshank
Black-headed Gull
Yellow Wagtail

Spring/autumn
Garganey
Passage waders
Little Gull

Background information and birding tips

ENGLAND'S only regular wintering flock of Bean Geese has made the RSPB's Buckenham Marshes famous. These birds are usually present from November through to the end of January. They sometimes linger until mid-February but I recommend you visit earlier in the year to be sure of connecting with this scarce species. A small flock of White-fronted Geese also over-winters on the marsh.

Visiting birdwatchers wanting to see Bean Geese should call in at the RSPB Strumpshaw Fen reception hide (see page 184 for instructions) before continuing to Buckenham Marsh. They can then find out the best place to view the flock on that day, as the geese can roam over a wide area.

There is a hide overlooking Buckenham Marsh. To reach this, cross the manned level crossing at Strumpshaw and follow the road/track to the parking area, next to the river. Walk to the hide by the derelict windmill. Alternatively, park at Buckenham Station (TG 351056) and cross the railway line on foot to the access track.

In winter, as well as Bean and White-fronted Geese, you will also see thousands of Wigeon and Teal. These birds allow you superb views, generally taking no notice while you walk along the access track, as they are too busy feeding. In recent winters, the Teal flock has been joined by a Green-winged Teal. Scan the marshes either side of the access track for waders such as Redshank, Curlew and Ruff.

Raptors and owls regularly patrol the fields in winter, Peregrine being the most regularly noted. Barn Owls can be encountered at most

ALL YEAR **OS MAP 134** **TG 349050 TG 351056** 

times of year but I have never been very lucky at this site. Up to half a dozen Water Pipits can usually be found around the pools near the hide, though they are elusive at times.

At dusk in winter an enormous corvid roost of many thousands of birds provides one of the best bird spectacles in the Broads. They arrive in groups of 100-500, from all over the area, to roost in the carrs to the north of Buckenham and act as a timely reminder to those working in the reedbeds that it is time for home.

In summer, Buckenham is an important breeding area for several species that are declining rapidly on the national stage. These include Sky Lark, Yellow Wagtail, Redshank, Snipe, Shoveler and Lapwing. Egyptian and Greylag Geese also breed, as does Meadow Pipit. Marsh Harriers and Hobbies frequently cause panic as they hunt over the marsh. One or two Avocets are seen occasionally.

In spring and autumn, the site attracts several species of passage wader. Ruff, Black-tailed Godwit, Green and Wood Sandpipers and Little Stint are the most regular species but anything can turn up. Recent rarities include Pacific Golden Plover and Pectoral Sandpiper (and a White Pelican but we can safely ignore that one). Little Gull and Garganey are recorded regularly on passage.

This is an important reserve for birds, both for wintering wildfowl and breeding waders. The birds can be distant and elusive but patience will be rewarded with sightings of several rare and scarce species and close views of normally shy common wildfowl.

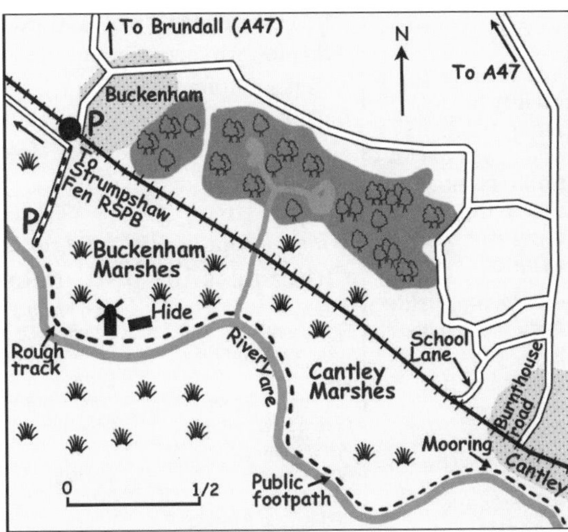

Access details

(General area: approx. seven miles E of Norwich)

From Norwich take A47 east to roundabout sign-posted to Brundall. Continue on minor road for 0.4 miles and bear left at the sharp bend onto The Street (sign-posted Brundall Station). Follow the road around mini-roundabouts and across the traffic-calmed area.

After 1.1 miles you go under a railway bridge, then reach a sign for Strumpshaw Fen RSPB (follow the RSPB signs if you want information on where to see the Bean Geese). Turn right (Stone Road) and follow signs for the Household Waste Disposal Centre. Go past this centre, then turn right after 0.7 miles, sign-posted to Buckenham Station (Station Road). After half a mile, park in gravel car park by the old railway station. Carefully cross the railway line and head left for the derelict windmill along the wide, rough track.

NORWICH
A47
A140
A146

There is no boat mooring facility at Buckenham, though you may moor at Cantley and walk back along the River Yare footpath to the reserve, a distance of about two miles.

Other nearby sites

Breydon Water, Burgh Castle, Great Yarmouth Beach, Hardley Flood, Rockland Broad, NWT Sparham Pools, RSPB Strumpshaw Fen, RSPB Surlingham Church Marshes, Ted Ellis Reserve.

11 BURGH CASTLE (BREYDON WATER SOUTH SHORE)

Key points

- **Terrain is mainly level along tracks and grass paths. Some steep steps, though most can be avoided.**
- **Path alongside Breydon Water is level and well maintained, good for wheelchair users.**
- **Telescope essential for good views of raptors.**
- **Free access at all times.**
- **Free 24-hour mooring close by.**
- **Boat trips available from Goodchild's Marina, just to the south of the Roman ruin.**

Contacts

General Broads Authority
01603 610734

Boat trips
01603 715191

THE REMAINS of a Roman fort provide a viewing platform across a fine expanse of extensive marshland that is good for wintering wildfowl and raptors. You will also be able to take a productive walk alongside the southern shore of Breydon Water for close views of waders and wildfowl.

Target birds

All year – **Avocet (80%), Little Egret (60%).** *Winter* – **Raptors (25%), Short-eared Owl (25%).**

Other possible bird species

All year
Little Grebe
Great Crested Grebe
Cormorant
Common wildfowl
Common waterbirds
Marsh Harrier
Sparrowhawk
Kestrel
Red-legged Partridge
Grey Partridge
Common waders
Common gull species
Barn Owl
Great Spotted Woodpecker
Sky Lark
Meadow Pipit
Pied Wagtail
Common scrub birds
Common woodland birds
Corvids
Common finches
Reed Bunting
Stonechat

Winter
Bewick's Swan
Whooper Swan
White-fronted Goose
Wigeon
Goldeneye
Hen Harrier
Merlin
Peregrine
Winter thrushes

Summer
Common Tern
Cuckoo
Hirundines
Sedge Warbler
Reed Warbler
Other warblers

Spring/autumn
Passage waders

Occasional
Lesser Spotted Woodpecker
Bearded Tit
Hobby

Background information and birding tips

THE ROMAN fort at Burgh Castle affords superb views over the marshes of Langley, Beighton, Reedham, Halvergate, Chedgrave, Acle, South Walsham and Burgh Castle. In winter, this is a great place to sit and scan for raptors and wildfowl.

A telescope is essential to get the best out of your visit and it can get very cold up there on the hill but your reward should include views of Marsh and Hen Harriers, along with Peregrine, Merlin, Short-eared Owl and wild swans and geese.

The bushes and trees around the fort are magnets for common woodland birds, including Lesser Spotted Woodpeckers. Search these trees in spring and autumn for migrants such as Redstarts, Pied Flycatchers and Firecrests. Below the fort is a reedbed that sometimes attracts Bearded Tits but more likely will hold a Reed Bunting or two.

The path below the fort that joins the Angles Way, adjacent to the Church Farm Country Club, can be muddy at all times of year. Avoid it by walking along the top path by the church.

Time your visit correctly and you should get close views of many species of wader from this footpath. The best time to arrive is about an hour before high tide when the waders are pushed up to this western end of Breydon Water.

Avocets can be found here all year round and are joined by

species such as Dunlin, Ringed Plover, Bar-tailed Godwit, Greenshank, Green Sandpiper and Little Stint at various times of the year. In the summer of 2001, a couple of Spoonbills were regular visitors and a Glossy Ibis took up residency on the marsh in the winter of 2004/05.

The Angles Way, a wide, well-maintained footpath, runs for about three and a half miles to Great Yarmouth (part of a 78 mile walk!). This is ideal if you are travelling by public transport, as you can catch a bus to Burgh Castle and walk back to Yarmouth or vice versa.

There is always something to see, though views of most birds may be distant. To access the path from the church car park, walk down towards the pub. There is an access gate on your left before you reach the large upper car park of the pub.

Finally, you may wish to take an organised boat trip from Goodchild's Marina, to the south of the Roman fort, to get close views of the thousands of waders on Breydon Water. Phone 01603 715191 for further details.

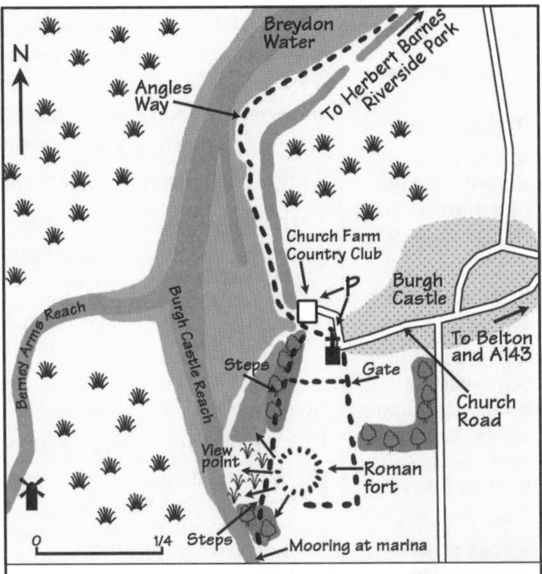

Access details

(Approx. three miles W of Great Yarmouth).

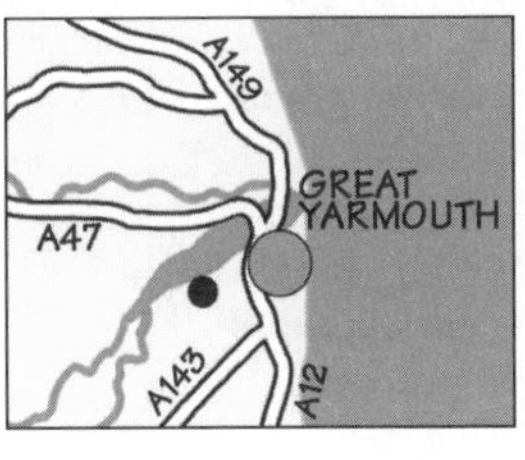

***BY CAR:* From Great Yarmouth, head S on A12. Follow signs for Burgh Castle and Belton on brown tourist signs (also holiday parks, caravan and camping site and marina) along A143.**

In Belton, take first right turn, following the brown tourist sign for Burgh Castle. At the T-junction, turn left into Church Road and follow to the church and Church Farm Country Club.

Park by the church or in the pub car park. Follow the public footpath, adjacent to the church, to the Roman ruin for a panoramic view over the marshes.

Alternatively, walk down the left side of the pub car park to the footpath that runs below the fort and along the southern shore of Breydon Water.

***BY BOAT:* The nearest mooring is at Burgh Castle Marina, along the River Waveney. This is accessed at the western end of Breydon Water. A (sometimes muddy) public footpath runs north to the Roman fort.**

Other nearby sites

Breydon Water, RSPB Buckenham Marsh, Great Yarmouth Beach, Great Yarmouth Cemetery, Haddiscoe Marshes, Hardley Flood, Rockland Broad, NWT Sparham Pools, RSPB Strumpshaw Fen, Ted Ellis Reserve, Herbert Barnes Riverside Park.

NWT BUXTON HEATH

Key points

- **No facilities other than a car park.**
- **A torch is essential when nightjarring (to find your way back).**
- **Insect repellent advised.**
- **Level terrain but paths can be muddy so wear boots, especially early in the season (May).**
- **Stay on the tracks at all times as there are many delicate plants on site.**
- **Managed by Norfolk Wildlife Trust on behalf of the Buxton Trustees.**

Contacts

Norfolk Wildlife Trust
01603 625540

SEVERAL PAIRS of Nightjar traditionally occupy this expanse of heath but it is rarely visited by birdwatchers. A maze of footpaths criss-cross the heath, so only explore if you have a good sense of direction! Woodcock show better here than anywhere else I've visited in Norfolk.

Target birds *Summer* – Woodcock (99%), Nightjar (90%).

Other possible bird species

Summer
Sparrowhawk
Kestrel
Hobby
Turtle Dove
Cuckoo
Tawny Owl
Green Woodpecker
Great Spotted Woodpecker
Sky Lark
Hirundines
Common scrub birds
Lesser Whitethroat
Whitethroat
Grasshopper Warbler
Reed Warbler
Sedge Warbler
Goldcrest
Jay
Common finches
Yellowhammer
Reed Bunting

Background information and birding tips

BUXTON HEATH is a handy site for Nightjars if you are staying in Norwich or Wroxham. The Norfolk Wildlife Trust has cleared bracken from large areas of the heath, thus Nightjars are increasing in number at this site.

To find the best Nightjar location follow the path at the end of the car park through the trees (many common woodland and scrub birds frequent this area). This track wends its way up to the reserve boundary, back into the wood, then into a cleared patch of heathland. The muddy path widens and now becomes a sandy track. You may wish to walk up a slight incline, following the track as it runs parallel to a mature wood, to where another track joins the main one on your right. All these areas attract Nightjars.

If you arrive early, it is worth exploring the track that runs from the right of the car park. Go over the cattle grid and follow the muddy path until it overlooks a reedbed. This is still establishing itself but you should see Reed Warblers and Reed Buntings and hear Grasshopper Warblers in the surrounding scrub (very difficult to see). You may also wish to explore the Great Wood to the north of the reserve, accessed through a metal gate along the wide, sandy track.

Once you have found the right area, wait for dusk when the Nightjars become active. While waiting for Nightjars to appear, you should get excellent flight views of one or two roding Woodcock. They seem to come out much earlier here than at other sites, perhaps to make up for the tardy Nightjars.

You should also hear Tawny Owls hooting and may see Green Woodpecker, Jay, Yellowhammer, Turtle Dove, Stock Dove, Sparrowhawk or Kestrel along with common woodland and scrub birds. Overhead, Swallows, Swifts and House Martins help keep the midges away from you but they may fall prey to a dashing Hobby.

The Nightjars here seem to like a lie-in as they always start 'churring' later than at other sites. In fact, they sometimes fail to 'churr' at

all and the first you will know of their presence is when something silently flaps, ghost-like, past your ear. You will have just become accustomed to the owl hooting, the pipistrelle bats fluttering overhead and the Woodcocks squeaking and honking, when a suggestion of a dark shape startles you. Eerie but strangely tranquil!

I can personally guarantee that the midges will love you for your effort, especially if you forget your insect repellent but, with luck, you may also find one or two glow worms on your way back.

As a postscript, the habitat looks good for Wood Lark, Tree Pipit, Crossbill and Nightingale but I have never seen or heard any of them here. Please let me know if you have any success at this site with these four sought-after species.

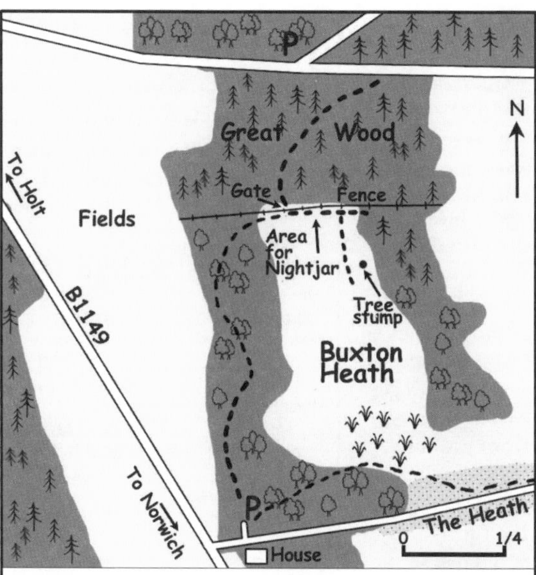

Access details

(Approx. 7.5 miles N of Norwich).

From Norwich, head N on A140 (to Aylsham/Cromer), then left along B1149 (sign-posted to Horsford). After about five miles, turn right into The Heath sign-posted 'Buxton Heath' on a white wooden road sign (third minor road right after Horsford village).

Look for a track on the left, sign-posted 'Buxton Heath' on a white wooden signpost, opposite the first house on the right. Park in the small car park at the bottom of the track (75 yards from the road).

The footpath to the right (as you go down the access track) takes you through a squeaky metal gate and over a cattle grid. The path overlooks a large reedbed plus you may see Nightjars in this area too.

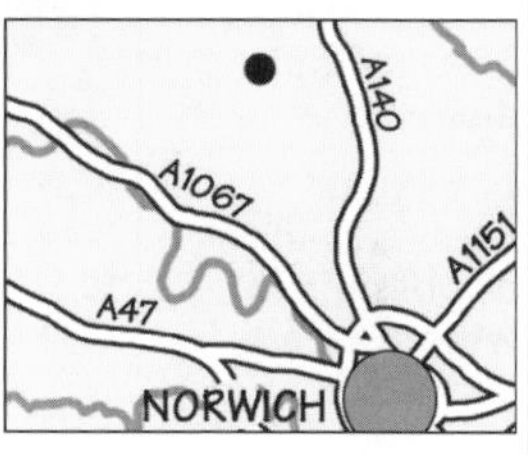

The best area for Nightjars is straight ahead from the car park (as if continuing along the access track). Follow the narrow path for 50 yards to a metal gate. Go through the gate and follow the wide path that meanders through the trees until it opens out into a cleared area and finally onto a sandy track. The whole of this cleared area is excellent for Nightjars. Explore the tracks but do not stray off them.

Other nearby sites

Breydon Water, NWT Cockshoot Broad, Great Yarmouth Beach, NWT Hickling Broad, Horsey, NWT Ranworth Broad, NWT Sparham Pools, Swanton Novers, NWT Martham Broad, Ted Ellis Reserve, NWT Upton Fen.

13 CHOSELEY BARNS

Key points

- **Open access at all times.**
- **Best views in early mornings and evenings when birds not disturbed by farm traffic.**
- **Level terrain along an uneven, grass path.**
- **The farmyard can be viewed from the road.**
- **Birds are easily disturbed in the farmyard, so please be quiet and keep a respectable distance.**

Birds need to feed as much as possible in winter, so any disturbance could literally mean the difference between life and death at this critical time.

Contacts

None

JUST A SHORT drive from RSPB Titchwell Marsh reserve, this farmyard attracts Corn Buntings and Yellowhammers throughout the year. It is bordered by a hedge-lined track which attracts migrants in spring and autumn.

Target birds

All year – **Corn Bunting (95%), Little Owl (40%), Tree Sparrow (20%).** *Spring/autumn* – **Passage migrants.** *Winter* – **Lapland Bunting, Snow Bunting (both 80% in recent years).**

Other possible bird species

All year
Sparrowhawk
Kestrel
Red-legged Partridge
Grey Partridge
Stock Dove
Sky Lark
Common scrub birds
Corvids
Common finches
Yellowhammer

Summer
Quail
Hirundines
Whitethroat
Blackcap
Yellow Wagtail
Turtle Dove

Spring/autumn
Redstart
Whinchat
Wheatear
Winter thrushes
Ring Ouzel
Goldcrest
Pied Flycatcher

Winter
Pink-footed Goose
Hen Harrier
Peregrine
Merlin
Reed Bunting

Occasional
Barn Owl
Brambling

Background information and birding tips

CHOSELEY BARNS is an unlikely looking site to go birdwatching but it is the best place in Norfolk to see Corn Buntings. They usually feed around the large drying barn just off the minor road near the RSPB Titchwell Marsh reserve.

They are usually joined by many Yellowhammers and a variety of finches and other common birds. Tree Sparrows are also occasionally seen among the mixed flocks feeding on the spilt grain and it is worth keeping an eye open for rarities: a Pine Bunting joined the throng in February 2004!

I suggest you sit quietly in your car by the barn and it won't be long before several of the above species hop into view. Birds can be present throughout the day, though early mornings and evenings are best because farm traffic is less frequent at these times.

The public footpath running west from the barn is bordered by tall hedges. These (and the ones bordering the access road from the A149) may attract migrants in spring and autumn, so should be checked thoroughly from late April to late May and from mid September to early November.

Anything can turn up here, due to its ideal position close to the coast. The mature, ivy-covered trees in the hedgerow are home to a pair of Little Owls, though they can be elusive.

In recent winters, the second field on the right, down the public footpath, has held feeding flocks of Snow (up to 100) and Lapland Buntings (a dozen), as well as Sky

Larks and Meadow Pipits. They may also feed in any stubble field where they are impossible to see until they fly up and perch on wires. In turn, these small birds may attract raptors such as Sparrowhawk, Kestrel, Peregrine or Merlin. Hen Harriers are occasionally seen in winter and Marsh Harriers can turn up at any time of year.

If you stand on the footpath at the RSPB Titchwell Marsh reserve and look inland, you will see the communications mast and hedge on the hill, demonstrating what an irresistible magnet the area makes for tired migrants. Everything from the humble Goldcrest to the mega-rare Pied Wheatear has been recorded here!

Records of Ring Ouzel in April have become regular in recent years and many other species make this hedge a feeding stop-off in spring and autumn.

In summer, look out for Blackcap, Whitethroat and Yellow Wagtail, which return to breed in May. One or two Quails have been heard in recent summers ('*wet-my-lips*') but you won't see one: PLEASE NOTE THAT IT IS ILLEGAL TO TAPE LURE THIS SPECIES!

Summing up, Choseley Barns makes an ideal quick call-in spot as you travel between more well known places along the Norfolk coast.

The public footpath runs past the barn but do not use it, as you will frighten away all the birds!

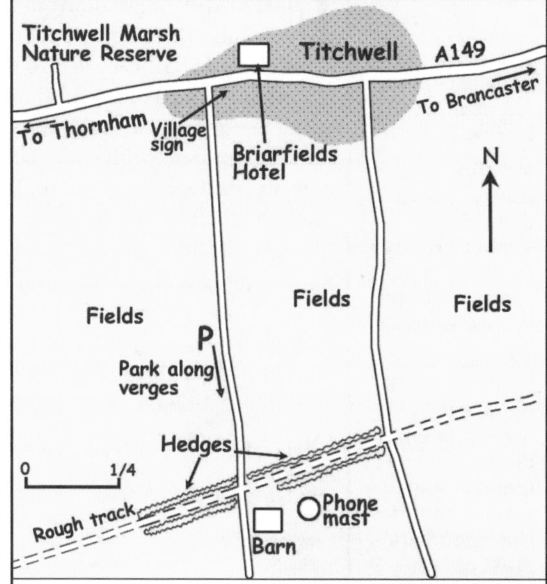

Access details

(Approx. six miles E of Hunstanton).

From the entrance to RSPB Titchwell Marsh on A149, head E to Titchwell village. After 0.4 miles, take the first right turn (where the Titchwell village post is situated on a small green, by the farm. If you reach the Briarfields Hotel you have gone too far).

Keep on this minor road up the hill for one mile. Park sensibly on the verges: DO

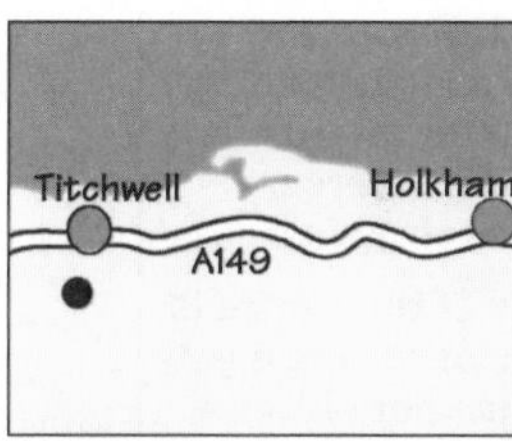

NOT BLOCK FARM ACCESS. Scan the farmyard for birds, plus walk west (away from the barn) down the footpath to view the fields and hedgerows.

Other nearby sites

Brancaster Marsh, Gypsy Lane, NOA Holme Observatory, NWT Holme Dunes, Hunstanton, NOA Redwell Marsh, Sandringham, RSPB Titchwell Marsh, Wolferton Triangle.

NWT CLEY MARSHES

Key points

- **Reserve open daily except Christmas and Boxing Day.**
- **Visitor centre is open daily. Easter – mid December. (10am – 5pm) summer (10am - 4pm) winter.**
- **Permit required. NWT members access dawn to dusk but carry membership card at all times. Non-members must obtain permit from visitor centre (£3.75 in 2006) and can access the reserve 10am - dusk.**
- **If the centre is closed (i.e. if you cannot obtain a permit) there is no access to the reserve for non-members.**
- **Permit is half price for public transport users (bus stop outside visitor centre).**
- **Free access to East Bank and shingle sea wall.**

FOR MANY generations this site has enjoyed a worldwide reputation as a superb centre for watching birds and is a designated SSSI. Cley is also the quintessential Norfolk reserve: paintings of its windmill with the reserve's reedbed in the foreground are legion! As there is nearly always something to see, with easy access points, this coastal reserve pulls in crowds all year round. If NWT Cley Marshes reserve was a violin, it would definitely be a Stradivarius!

Target birds

All year – **Bearded Tit (75%), Barn Owl (50%), Bittern (10%).** *Winter* – **Water Pipit (50%), winter raptors (25%).** *Spring* – **Avocet (99%), Marsh Harrier (95%), Garganey (75%), Red-necked Phalarope (15%), Temminck's Stint (15%).** *Summer* – **Avocet (99%), Marsh Harrier (95%), Garganey (60%), Roseate Tern (15%).** *Autumn* – **Passage seabirds, passage waders.**

Other possible bird species

All year
Little Grebe
Cormorant
Egyptian Goose
Shelduck
Other common wildfowl
Sparrowhawk
Kestrel
Water Rail
Black-tailed Godwit
Other common waders
Common gull species
Guillemot (at sea)
Razorbill (at sea)
Kingfisher
Sky Lark
Meadow Pipit
Pied Wagtail
Common scrub birds
Corvids
Common finches
Reed Bunting

Winter
Divers
Grebes
Brent Goose
Wigeon
Pintail
Goldeneye
Red-breasted Merganser
Hen Harrier
Merlin
Peregrine
Golden Plover
Bar-tailed Godwit
Rock Pipit
Stonechat
Winter thrushes

Spring
Little Ringed Plover
Whimbrel
Greenshank
Arctic Tern
Yellow Wagtail
Whinchat
Wheatear
Ring Ouzel

Summer
Yellow-legged Gull
Sandwich Tern
Common Tern
Little Tern
Hirundines
Sedge Warbler
Reed Warbler

Autumn
Fulmar
Manx Shearwater
Balearic Shearwater
Gannet
Whimbrel
Little Stint
Curlew Sandpiper
Ruff
Spotted Redshank
Greenshank
Green Sandpiper
Wood Sandpiper
Common Sandpiper
Skuas
Kittiwake
Whinchat
Wheatear
Lapland Bunting

Occasional
Jack Snipe
Short-eared Owl
Shore Lark
Twite
Snow Bunting

ALL YEAR **OS MAP 133** **TG 053441**

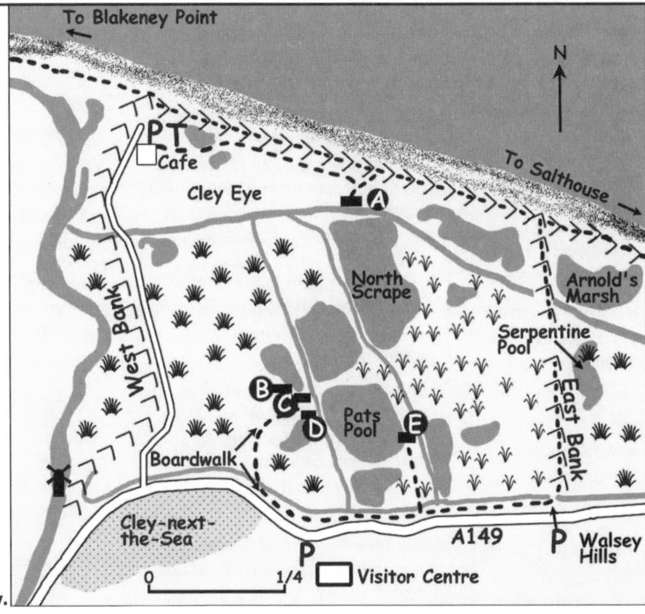

Key

A North Hide
B Avocet Hide
C Dauke's Hide
D Teal Hide
E Bishop's Hide

Access details

(Approx. 10.5 miles W of Cromer).

MAIN VISITOR CAR PARK (TG 053441): **The main (free) car park is sign-posted off A149 half a mile E of Cley-Next-The-Sea village (car park is landward side of the road). The visitor centre is open from Easter to mid-December. From here, a boardwalk ensures easy access to Dawke's and Teal hides overlooking Dawke's Pool and Pat's Pool respectively.**

BEACH ROAD CAR PARK (TG 048452): **This is sign-posted 'Beach' off A149 just E of Cley village. £1 fee payable for car parking. There is a toilet block here and a café, which is open from Easter until around the end of August.**

EAST BANK CAR PARK (TG 059442): **This rough-surface car park is on the seaward side of A149. Heading E from Cley village, go past the visitor centre car park for about 300 yards. If you reach the Walsey Hills 'NOA Watchpoint' sign-post you have gone too far. This car park gives easiest access to the East Bank area of the reserve.**

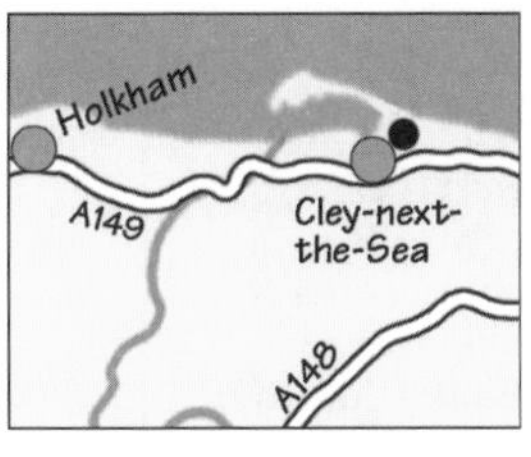

Background information and birding tips

THIS NORFOLK Wildlife Trust reserve is a large area to cover but there are three access points to ease the way. The main entrance is at the visitor centre. Disabled visitors are able to park at the centre itself, whereas able-bodied visitors must park below in the large car park.

Before entering the reserve you must obtain a permit from the visitor centre. Norfolk Wildlife Trust members should obtain a permit from the centre when open, or carry their membership cards at all times if the centre is closed. Non-members are not allowed on the reserve until they have obtained a permit. Access along the East Bank to the beach is free at all times.

After obtaining your permit, cross the busy coast road and follow the boardwalk left to the three hides. This is the site's only wheelchair-friendly trail but it can be very productive. The wide channel running adjacent to the road should be scanned for Kingfisher and Little Grebe and the fields behind usually hold Wigeon and

Key points

- **Visitor centre stocks an extensive range of bird books, bird food, etc.**
- **Toilets (including disabled) at visitor centre.**
- **Toilets (not wheelchair friendly) and café at beach car park.**
- **Wheelchair access to Avocet, Dawke's and Teal Hides along a boardwalk. Take care crossing coast road.**
- **Terrain is level (though access to the visitor centre is up a steep concrete slope). East Bank is narrow. Some paths on the reserve itself may be muddy.**
- **No dogs or cycles.**
- **Beach car park £1.60 in 2005.**

Teal all year (with larger numbers present in winter). The flooded fields around here are a favoured haunt of Rock Pipits in winter.

Along the boardwalk, Bearded Tits can be seen all year with Reed Warblers joining them in summer. The hides look out to wader scrapes, which are productive at any time of year. Especially look out for Red-necked Phalaropes and Temminck's Stints in May – these two migrant species have become Cley specialities, though neither is guaranteed.

The three hides (Avocet, Teal and Dauke's) are also good places to sit to watch the breeding Marsh Harriers drift over the reeds, or a Bittern lazily flap over. Keep your eyes peeled!

You now have to retrace your steps to the road, as there is no circular route from here. Instead of crossing the road to the visitor centre, keep on the path towards the East Bank. This grass path brings you to Bishop's Hide, which overlooks the same scrape (Pat's Pool) as Teal and Dauke's Hides.

In spring and summer, this is the place to see Garganey in Norfolk. Cley has a record second to none for attracting rare waders, so watch this pool in spring and autumn for migrating waders such as Greenshank, Common, Wood and Green Sandpipers and something rarer that will appeal to twitchers.

After Bishop's Hide, the path adjacent to the road brings you to the East Bank. Listen out for the resident Cetti's Warblers that sing from the bushes along this path. When you reach the East Bank, walk towards the sea wall, scanning for Bearded Tits, which should be seen all year round in the reeds. Water Pipits often feed in the field to the right from December to March.

In spring, this marshy field is a favourite haunt of Yellow Wagtails. Occasionally, the wagtail flock contains one or two of the scarcer races, such as Blue-headed and White. Also look out for the resident Barn Owl over the fields.

At all times of year, the fields and marsh to your right along East Bank will hold waders. Avocets show well here in summer and it is a favoured spot for Whimbrel and Curlew in spring and autumn. Egyptian Geese breed here also.

Closer to the sea wall, you will see Arnold's Marsh to your right. This is usually home to several species of waders, with Avocet guaranteed in spring and summer. This is also a favoured roost site of a Roseate Tern or two among the mixed tern flock but their appearance is unpredictable.

Once on the shingle sea wall, you can turn back to the visitor centre car park, left to the beach car park, or right to Salthouse. If you choose left or right, scan the sea carefully at all times of year. Cley is renowned as a prime seawatching site and if you turn up

Contacts

Visitor centre
01263 740008

Norfolk Wildlife Trust
01603 625540

Cley Bird Club:
Peter Gooden, 45 Charles Road, Holt, Norfolk, NR25 6DA
(Further reading: The Birds of Cley by SJM Gantlett) available from 'Books for Birders' 01263 741139

in favourable conditions – strong onshore winds – during September and October, you will find many telescopes set up on the shingle near the beach car park, all hoping for something special to pass.

In winter scan for grebes, divers and ducks, in summer watch out for terns. In autumn, anything can go past!

From the shingle bank, you can divert left to the North Hide, which overlooks the North Scrape. Several species of waders can be seen here at all times of year and it is another good spot to look out for the occasional flying Marsh Harrier or Bittern or a roosting Roseate Tern.

Spotted Redshanks will be coming into their dapper breeding plumage by early May.

The field by the beach car park is known as The Eye. It is home to a flock of Brent Geese in winter (joined in recent years by a Black Brant) along with many Wigeon, passage waders in spring and autumn and very occasionally a Lapland Bunting puts in an appearance (usually in autumn).

It is perfectly possible to spend the whole day at Cley, gently strolling around, stopping off at the hides, seawatching and generally feeling all is well with the world. Whichever of the car parks you start from, it is possible to take a long, circular route encompassing the whole of the reserve. And don't forget to pause awhile on the shingle sea wall to take in the famous vista of Cley windmill.

After several years of trying (and failing) to play King Canute by holding the sea back, the Norfolk Wildlife Trust has decided to change tack. It is allowing the reserve to flood but creating a channel across the marsh and through Blakeney Point to allow the floodwater to drain more easily.

This seems sensible as building a shingle wall for a short section of coastline would not work in the long term, as the sea would simply flood in from around the sides! Planning permission has also been obtained for a larger visitor centre, complete with educational facilities and a bigger car park.

Other nearby sites

Blakeney Point, Kelling Heath, Kelling Quags, Salthouse Beach, Salthouse Heath, Sheringham, Swanton Novers, NOA Walsey Hills, Warham Greens, Weybourne.

NWT COCKSHOOT BROAD

Key points

- **Site is a designated SSSI.**
- **Free access at all times.**
- **Boardwalk trail on level terrain.**
- **Free mooring at the reserve entrance.**
- **Wheelchair-accessible hide.**
- **Free parking but can get full in summer.**
- **Use insect repellent in summer.**

Contacts

Norfolk Wildlife Trust 01603 625540

English Nature 01603 620558

Broadland Conservation Centre 01603 270479

General Broads Authority 01603 610734

THIS SMALL Norfolk Wildlife Trust reserve is ideal for a stop-off during a Broadland boating holiday. Several common species of birds can be seen but this is a site for the all-round naturalist, as it is home to rare plants, butterflies and dragonflies.

Target bird *All year* – **Cetti's Warbler (hear 65%, see 20%).**

Other possible bird species

Resident
Great Crested Grebe
Common wildfowl
Egyptian Goose
Common waterbirds
Sparrowhawk
Common gull species
Kingfisher
Great Spotted Woodpecker
Common scrub birds
Marsh Tit
Common woodland birds
Siskin
Redpoll
Common finches
Reed Bunting

Summer
Common Tern
Cuckoo
Hirundines
Sedge Warbler
Reed Warbler

Occasional
Osprey
Marsh Harrier
Lesser Spotted Woodpecker

Background information and birding tips

PREVIOUSLY a privately owned shooting site, NWT Cockshoot Broad is now part of the Bure Marshes National Nature Reserve (along with Ranworth Broad and Hoveton Great Broad), managed by Norfolk Wildlife Trust. This five hectare reserve consists of open water, carr and fen. Ongoing management continues to improve water quality to benefit wildlife.

The fun starts along the approach road to the car park where you can play the little known game of 'Dodge the Dragonfly', as black-tailed skimmers love to rest on the Tarmac, only zipping away at the last minute. The site includes a pleasant, shortish, circular walk along a boardwalk (and is thus fully wheelchair accessible) through reeds and alder carr (wet woodland).

In summer, the river can be quite noisy with boat traffic and boaters enjoying themselves. Even so, this path is good for Reed Warblers, especially if you stand quietly on the first wooden bridge along the trail. On the river, to your left, you should see Great Crested Grebes, Coots and Greylag Geese. Swallows swoop overhead.

Once on the reserve itself (reached by crossing the second wooden bridge at the end of the mooring channel), the path runs adjacent to a channel where you may hear the explosive song of a Cetti's Warbler from thick cover, or catch a glimpse of a Blackcap or Garden Warbler. Marsh Tits are relatively common in the woodland.

Stay on the main path to the hide at the end, or fork left through some reeds (excellent for swallowtail butterflies in summer). Both ways can be productive and if you choose one way up to the hide, you can always return via the other route.

The hide overlooks Cockshoot Broad itself and birds seen here regularly include Kingfisher, (perched in the trees on the island) Common Tern, Shelduck, Egyptian

Goose, Grey Heron and other common waterfowl. There is a wipe-clean sightings board in the hide.

In winter, the broad holds Pochard, Teal, Shoveler, Cormorant etc. Reed Buntings are resident, as are the commoner woodland species and they are easier to see because of the lack of leaves on the trees. This is a walk for hardy souls at this time of year though. The riverside boardwalk may flood in poor weather years, so I would stick to spring and summer.

This reserve is also renowned for its dragonflies and butterflies in summer. The channel is an excellent place to see red-eyed damselflies and Norfolk hawkers while black-tailed skimmers are common along the whole length of the boardwalk. I suggest an early morning walk for the best of the bird activity followed by a search for the dragonflies as the heat of the sun brings them out.

As the water quality of Cockshoot Broad improves, the wildlife variety and quality can only improve with it. A Bittern was reported from here in June 2001, showing the potential of this quiet, picturesque place.

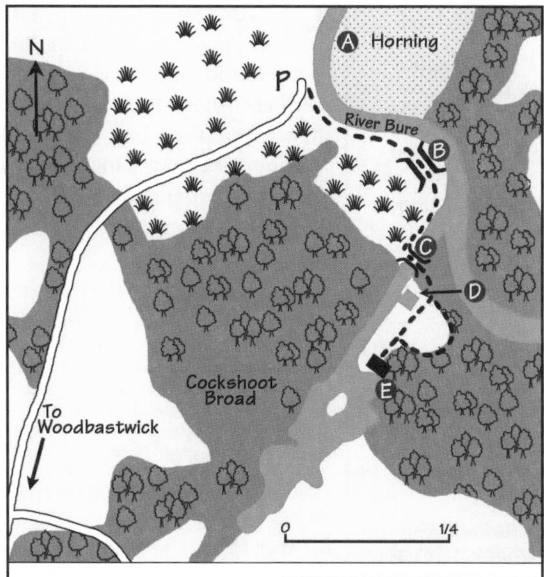

Key

A Ferry Inn
B Bridge - good for Reed Warbler
C 24hr mooring
D Dragonfly viewing platform
E Hide

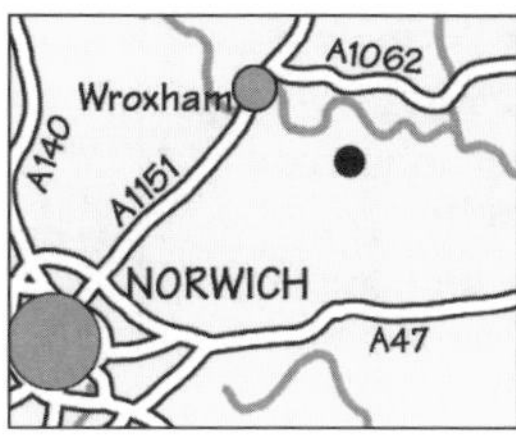

Access details

(Approx. eight miles NE of Norwich).

***BY CAR:* From B1140 (Acle to Wroxham road), turn off at the signs for Woodbastwick. In the village, head E past the church, following signs for Ranworth.**

Out of the village, the road bends sharply right but you go straight on down a narrow road sign-posted 'River Only'. It ends in a small car park at the River Bure, opposite the Ferry Inn at Horning. The path to the reserve is on the right of this car park.

***BY BOAT:* Head E from Wroxham along River Bure to Horning. In Horning, about 100 yards after the Ferry Inn on the left, there is a mooring channel on the right, 24 hours stay maximum. The path into the reserve starts at the end of this channel (TG 346160).**

Other nearby sites

Breydon Water, Buxton Heath, Great Yarmouth Beach, NWT Hickling Broad, Horsey, NWT Hoveton Great Broad, How Hill, Ranworth Broad, RSPB Strumpshaw Fen, Ted Ellis Reserve, NWT Upton Fen, Winterton Dunes.

DENVER SLUICE

Key points

- **Mill opening times:**

April 1 - October 31: Mon to Sat 10am - 5pm, Sunday 12 noon - 5pm.

November 1 - March 31: Mon to Sat 10am - 4pm, Sunday 12 noon - 4pm.

- **Free parking.**
- **Can be very bleak and birdless!**
- **Not suitable for wheelchair users.**
- **Wrap up warm!**
- **Terrain is level on an uneven path.**
- **Walking boots recommended.**

Contacts

The Borough Council of King's Lynn & West Norfolk, King's Court, Chapel Street, King's Lynn PE30 1EX. 01553 692722 www.west-norfolk.gov.uk

Denver Windmill, Denver, Downham Market PE38 0EG 01366 384009 www.denvermill.co.uk

HERE IS a site best visited in harsh weather when wintering wildfowl are forced onto the unfrozen waters of the Hundred Foot Drain – and that's bad news for fair-weather birders, because on this walk there is nowhere to shelter from the wind, rain or snow. Non-birding partners can now take refuge in the restored mill's tearoom while you brave the elements.

Target birds

Winter – **Goosander (65%), Peregrine (40%), Smew (10%).**

Other possible bird species

Winter
Winter wildfowl
Common waterfowl
Lapwing
Redshank
Curlew
Common gull species
Barn Owl
Sky Lark
Meadow Pipit
Pied Wagtail
Winter thrushes
Corvids
Starling
Common finches
Yellowhammer
Reed Bunting
Corn Bunting

Occasional
Winter raptors

Background information and birding tips

DENVER SLUICE is at its best when all other lakes and pools are frozen, because it keeps the Hundred Foot Drain free of ice even in the most hostile of conditions. In turn, this makes it the place to see Goosanders in west Norfolk.

Once you have climbed the bank near the pub, turned left and negotiated the stile, you will see the Hundred Foot Drain stretching in front of you. There is a sluice gate in the distance. The best birds are usually between Denver Sluice and the distant sluice. Walk as far as you like along this raised bank watching the water and fields for anything that moves.

On a particularly good 'Denver Day' the first thing you might see is a limping brass monkey. If you are the sort of birdwatcher who moans when your feet and hands go numb in the cold then this is not the walk for you.

Scan towards the distant sluice gate to check if there are many birds on the Drain, as this is not always the case. As you walk along the raised path keep scanning the fields for raptors such as Peregrine and Hen Harrier.

Barn Owls are seen regularly and Short-eared Owls may also be encountered. Also keep an eye on the telephone wires as they make good perches for Corn Buntings, Yellowhammers, Starlings, Linnets, Goldfinches, etc.

If the fancy takes you, you can keep going past the distant sluice gate (1.5 miles from the sluice) to WWT Welney, where a warm soup and a spell in the heated main hide goes down a treat!

A round walk from the Denver car park to Welney is about 9.5 miles and comes with this warning: there is no respite from the cold wind/snow/rain as there isn't a scrap of cover the whole way. On the other hand, on a frosty, bright morning, this can be a superbly bracing day out!

Non-birding members of the family may choose to visit the mill while you are freezing to death on the footpath! The mill was built in 1835 and has now been restored to working order. There is also a bakery and tearoom here.

The area is of little interest at other times of the year, though Turtle Doves and hirundines can usually be seen around the car park and sluice. At this time of year, you may as well go straight to Welney in your car and save yourself a long, birdless walk.

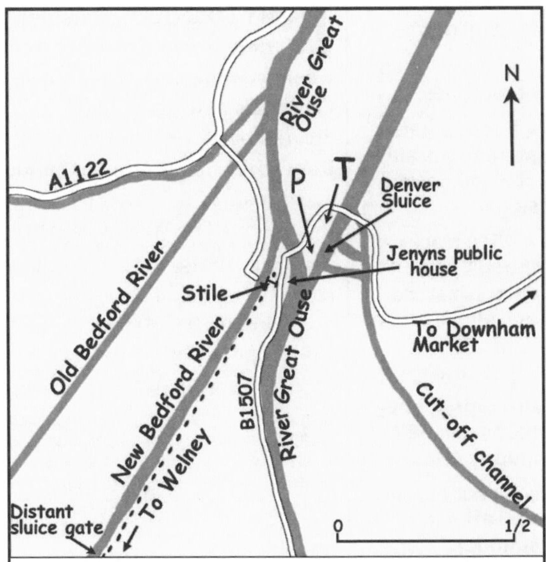

Access details

(Approx. two miles S of Downham Market).

On the A10 bypass, about one mile S of Downham Market. turn on to B1507 (sign-posted Denver/Denver Complex/Denver Mill).

Pass the recently renovated mill, following signs for Denver Sluice. Cross first bridge then park in the obvious large gravel car park on the left. There is a toilet block here but it is sometimes locked in winter.

From the car park, follow the road to a second bridge (this is Denver Sluice) and a few yards further on you will see the Jenyns Arms public house with a telephone box opposite.

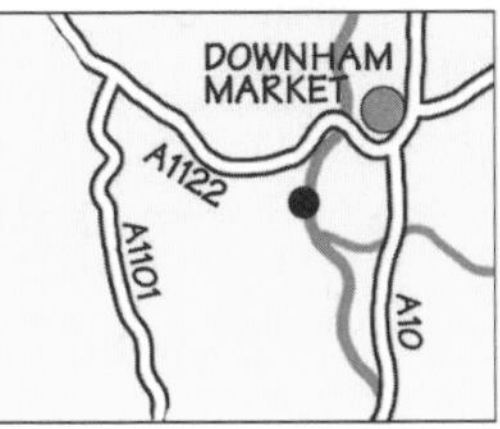

The footpath starts on the top of the bank (above the phone box) and over a stile. Turn left and walk as far as you desire, checking the channel for birds as you go.

The sluice gate you can see in the distance is 1.5 miles from the pub, WWT Welney is 5 miles away.

Other nearby sites

King's Lynn Docks, Ken Hill Wood, Roydon Common, Sandringham, RSPB Snettisham, Tottenhill, WWT Welney, Wolferton Triangle, Pentney Gravel Pits, Blackborough End Tip, Snettisham Coastal Park.

DERSINGHAM BOG NNR

Key points

- **Reserve open at all times.**
- **Keep to paths at all times and obey all no-entry signs.**
- **Wide tracks, though some steepish steps and short, steep banks.**
- **Boardwalk trail through the bog. Paths can be muddy after rain.**
- **Insect repellent essential in summer.**
- **Dogs should be kept on leads.**

Contacts

English Nature
01603 620558

Site Manager
01485 543044

IN MY OPINION, Dersingham Bog is the best place in Norfolk to see Nightjars. It is also one of the few sites where you may catch a glimpse of a Long-eared Owl and Crossbills and Wood Larks are regular visitors. 'The Cliff', created by a prehistoric sea, is an almost perfect place from which to admire the famous Norfolk orange sunsets, accompanied in winter by a few thousand Pink-footed Geese flying onto The Wash to roost.

Target birds

All year – **Golden Pheasant (20%), Crossbill (20%), Long-eared Owl (5%).** *Summer* – **Nightjar (95%), Tree Pipit (65%), Marsh Harrier (40%), Wood Lark (40%), Grasshopper Warbler (hear 60%, see 5%).**

Other possible bird species

All year
Shelduck
Sparrowhawk
Kestrel
Woodcock
Tawny Owl
Green Woodpecker
Great Spotted Woodpecker
Sky Lark
Meadow Pipit
Common scrub birds
Common woodland birds
Goldcrest
Corvids
Siskin
Redpoll

Summer
Hobby
Sand Martin
Cuckoo
Other hirundines
Summer warblers
Spotted Flycatcher

Occasional
Lesser Spotted Woodpecker
Short-eared Owl

Background information and birding tips

DERSINGHAM BOG is an area of intensively-managed heath and bog that is part of the Sandringham Estate, managed by English Nature. The reserve is not visited by a huge number of people and in winter you will find you have the whole place to yourself.

English Nature opened up another couple of miles or so of footpaths within Dersingham Bog NNR in 2006, making this an even more attractive place to visit. The main reason most birders come to the site is for Nightjars in summer. Braving the midges is well worthwhile as up to 26 Nightjars should be entertaining you and taking your mind off the annoying insects. The boardwalk area is the best place to see the birds, as they usually sit on telephone wires here, or display above your head. Magical!

From the Scissors Crossroad car park, follow the path onto the reserve (do not go up the steps to the Woodland Trail) and the habitat soon opens out to Nightjar country. Keep on the wide path to reach the boardwalk area. From the village end car park, follow the path down some steps to the boardwalk.

Woodcocks should be roding over the woods, Tawny Owls may be hooting and Long-eared Owl chicks might be begging for food from the pines. The perfect dusk chorus!

A visit on a winter morning may produce a skein or two of Pink-footed Geese overhead while you are spotting common woodland birds along the

Woodland Trail (sign-posted from both entrances). All three woodpecker species have been recorded but Great and Green Woodpecker are the two most likely. The woodland trail also offers the best chance to see the resident but shy, Golden Pheasants. You will have to walk very quietly along the path to see one, or sit patiently by a tree to see if one comes out from the rhododendron hedge. Do not leave the path!

Winter also brings Reed Buntings, Fieldfares and Redwings onto the reserve. From mid-February, listen for the mournful song of Wood Larks anywhere on the reserve. Also listen out for the moaning call of a Long-eared Owl as it establishes its territory.

Common warblers, including Blackcap, Chiffchaff, Willow and Garden Warblers arrive to breed in summer. Listen out for the display song of Tree Pipits, which breed on the reserve. Marsh Harriers occasionally quarter the heath for prey, sometimes hunting the chicks of Shelduck which breed on the reserve in good numbers (you can see them displaying on the heath at the back of the pool in spring).

The Cliff viewpoint affords superb views over The Wash. This is a peaceful place to linger at any time of year. In winter, Pink-footed Geese fly from their roost at dawn, returning at dusk hopefully silhouetted against an orange sunset. In summer, just enjoy the view and you should be joined by Woodcock and Nightjar at dusk (and, unfortunately a few midges too!). In spring and autumn, keep an eye open for birds arriving or leaving our shores (visible migration).

The newly-opened path starts from the Scissors Crossroads car park. Go through the entrance gate and immediately turn right into the wood. This is good for common woodland species such as Goldcrest,

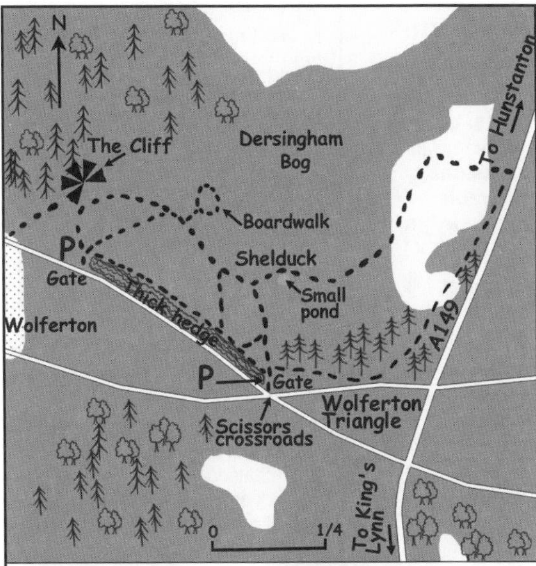

Access details

(Approx. 5.5 miles N of King's Lynn).

Take A149 N towards Hunstanton. After three miles, turn left to Wolferton. After about 300 yards this road reaches a crossroads. Park on the grass near the wooden 'No overnight parking' sign and enter reserve through a kissing gate down a narrow path from this pull-off. This is known as the Scissors Crossroads entrance.

Alternatively, at the crossroads bear right and continue for half a mile until you see a large lay-by on right. The reserve gate is visible from here and there are usually some leaflets at the gate for visitors. If you reach Wolferton village you have gone too far.

When on the reserve, follow the footpaths as sign-posted. The bog and heath habitats here are extremely fragile so stay on the paths at all times.

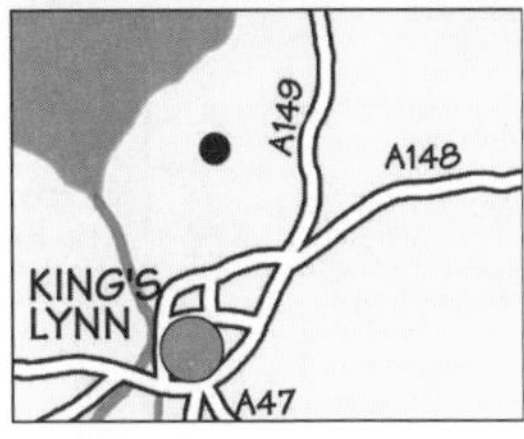

DERSINGHAM BOG NNR

Key points

- **Not suitable for wheelchair users, though Nightjars are occasionally viewable by the roadside gate (TF 663284).**
- **Leaflet available by gate.**
- **Keep to paths at all times.**

Coal Tit, Siskin, Treecreeper, etc, etc and I have seen Crossbills in these pines.

Follow the way-marked path through the trees. You come out onto a heath, where you should turn right but not before standing on the hill here to scan for raptors or flyover Crossbills, etc.

Follow the heath path with the pine wood to your right and you enter a mixed wood. Listen for the springy call of Redpoll here plus the usual woodpeckers, etc. There are one or two steep banks to negotiate in this wood.

The path drops down to another clearing and an obvious track. Turn left along the track and you will come out onto an extensive open area. Stop and scan regularly for anything interesting. The first you will know of any Crossbills in the vicinity will be their sharp "*chip, chip*" calls. In summer, also listen for Grasshopper Warblers.

You will come upon a pool on your right. I haven't seen much on here (except dragonflies) but you may be lucky to see Crossbills coming down for a drink. (The warden tells me he has seen more than 100 Pintails here and you will realise how incredible this is when you see the size of it!). Look for Shelduck beyond the pool from late winter onwards.

The track eventually brings you to the boardwalk. There are several short cuts along the way if you don't fancy the whole trek. Take any path on your left and it will lead you to the main track. Turn left when you hit the main track to get back to the car parks.

Dersingham is the best place in Norfolk to see a ghostly Nightjar.

Other nearby sites

Gypsy Lane, NWT Holme Dunes, NOA Holme Observatory, Hunstanton, Ken Hill Wood, King's Lynn Docks, NOA Redwell Marsh, Roydon Common, Sandringham, RSPB Snettisham, Snettisham Country Park, RSPB Titchwell Marsh, Wolferton Triangle.

NWT EAST WRETHAM HEATH

PLAN TO VISIT East Wretham in spring and summer when the sought-after species (Nightjar, Tree Pipit, Redstart) are in residence. In winter, this site holds large numbers of finches and buntings. The public footpath that runs along the southern edge of the reserve is one of the best birdwatching tracks in Norfolk.

Target birds

Spring/summer – **Nightjar (90%), Wood Lark (90%), Tree Pipit (80%), Redstart (30%), Crossbill (15%), Long-eared Owl (5%).**

Other possible bird species

All year
Little Grebe
Ruddy Duck
Sparrowhawk
Kestrel
Woodcock
Stock Dove
Barn Owl
Tawny Owl
Kingfisher
Woodpeckers
Nuthatch
Treecreeper
Jay
Siskin
Redpoll
Yellowhammer

Spring/autumn
Passage waders

Summer
Hobby
Cuckoo
Warblers
Spotted Flycatcher

Occasional
Goshawk
Golden Pheasant
Hawfinch

Background information and birding tips

EAST WRETHAM HEATH is a superb 143 ha reserve that holds many sought-after Breckland species. The best time to visit is on an early spring morning for Wood Lark and a late spring evening (May/June) for Nightjar. If the reserve is closed, all species can be seen from a public footpath that runs to the south of the NWT reserve.

My first walk of the year along this footpath is usually on a bright, calm, early March morning, heading west (signed to Brandon). After a short while you will get excellent views of Langmere, a lake on your right. Alternatively, there is a gate on your left, which leads to Ringmere, a smaller lake.

The water level in these meres varies greatly but Pochard, Tufted Duck, Mallard, Ruddy Duck (a scarce species in Norfolk), Gadwall and Little Grebe seem to be present at all times of year.

If water levels are low in spring and autumn, scan the muddy edges of the meres for passage waders such as Snipe, Greenshank, Green, Wood and Common Sandpipers. The changing water levels have taken their toll on the hide overlooking Langmere, making it unusable, though birds can still easily be seen from the footpaths.

Follow the track past Langmere, listening out all the time for Crossbills, Siskins and Redpolls in the trees along the path and on the reserve. After about a quarter of a mile, there is a clearing on your right, which is an excellent place to listen for Wood Lark on the reserve. You should have seen Green and Great Spotted Woodpeckers by now, as well as Coal Tit, Long-tailed Tit and Mistle Thrush.

April is a good time to watch out for displaying Sparrowhawk and Goshawk. Crossbills will be

Key points

- **Norfolk Wildlife Trust Reserve. Open daily throughout the year, 8am – dusk.**
- **Site is a designated SSSI.**
- **Free access and parking when reserve open.**
- **All species can be seen from a public footpath when reserve is closed.**
- **Public footpath terrain is flat along a wide sandy track.**
- **Can be boggy after rain.**
- **Insect repellent advisable in summer.**
- **Torch needed when walking back to car after seeing the Nightjars.**

Contacts

Norfolk Wildlife Trust
01603 625540

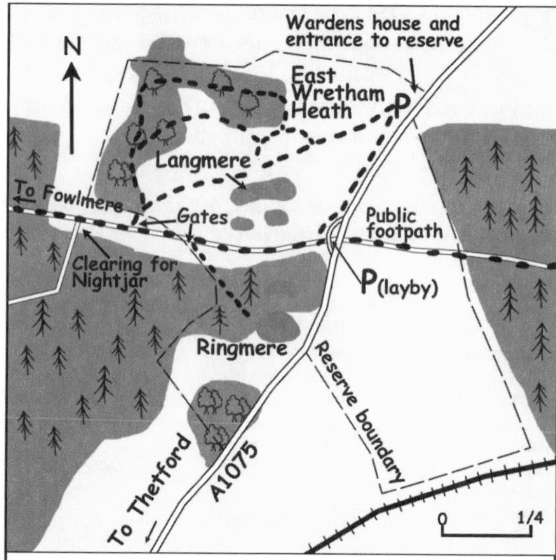

Access details

(Approx. four miles NE of Thetford).

From Thetford head E on A11 to roundabout and take A1075 (sign-posted to Watton and East Dereham). After level crossing, reserve car park is sign-posted on a brown tourist sign on left, just over two miles from the roundabout.

The reserve can be viewed from public footpath, which starts from lay-by 200 yards S of the car park. Follow directions above to the level crossing. Cross that, then there is a left-hand bend with a deer warning sign. The lay-by is on the left immediately after the sign (1.2 miles after the level crossing). Public footpath is signed to Brandon 16km and Peddars Way 2km.

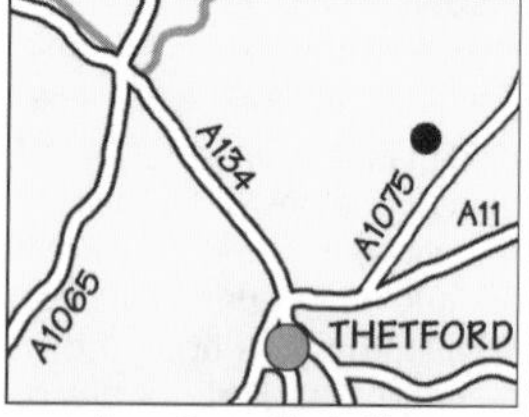

breeding by now, so listen out for their loud '*chip, chip*' calls anywhere.

From mid May, this footpath is a great place from which to see and hear Nightjars. Follow the path until you reach a wide, sandy track on your left. The land opens out here to a bracken-covered area with mature pine trees dotted around as far as the eye can see. Between mid-May and the end of August, this is a superb place to see Nightjars at dusk, especially the old beech stump by the path.

Long-eared Owl is another Wretham breeding speciality. so listen for the begging squeaks of the young at dusk in May. In summer, look out for Redstarts and Spotted Flycatchers in the trees and bushes along the whole length of this track, though the former is easier to see on East Wretham reserve itself. A little further on, the path is enclosed by mixed woodland, a good place to see Redpolls.

You can follow this track to where it joins a T-junction of two minor roads. Straight ahead leads to Fowlmere (on your right, through thick bracken and bushes) which is good for common waterfowl and wildfowl.

On the NWT reserve itself, there is a marked trail past Langmere and through mixed woodland (pick up your trail leaflet at the gate in the reserve car park). Redstarts and Crossbills breed here along with many common woodland species. Hawfinch is very occasionally seen in winter.

The open areas hold Wood Lark, Tree Pipit (check the tops of isolated hawthorn bushes) and occasional Wheatears and in winter the heath is home to large mixed feeding flocks of finches and buntings.

I have to say that the track from the lay-by to Fowlmere is the best public footpath for birds in Norfolk, with the exception of the one that cuts through the RSPB Titchwell Marsh reserve. Starting from the late February Wood Lark/Goshawk/Crossbill extravaganza through to the summer Nightjar spectacular, this is the perfect place to be.

THIS IS a six acre farmland reserve still in its infancy, set in the midst of the 2,000 acre Bayfield Estate near Glandford, south of Blakeney. The idea is to demonstrate some of the features that can be introduced to farms to benefit wildlife and birds in particular.

Target birds

All Year – **Declining farmland birds, Barn Owl (50%), Grey Wagtail (50%), Lesser Spotted Woodpecker (less than 10%).** *Summer* – **Turtle Dove (60%).**

Other possible bird species

All Year
Sparrowhawk
Kestrel
Red-legged Partridge
Grey Partridge
Lapwing
Common gull species
Stock Dove
Green Woodpecker
Great Spotted Woodpecker
Sky Lark
Pied Wagtail
Common scrub birds
Nuthatch
Treecreeper
Marsh Tit
Jay
Other corvids
House Sparrow
Bullfinch
Other common finches
Yellowhammer

Summer
Hirundines
Blackcap
Lesser Whitethroat
Whitethroat
Chiffchaff
Willow Warbler

Winter
Winter thrushes
Reed Bunting

Occasional
Marsh Harrier
Hen Harrier
Buzzard
Hobby
Brambling (winter)

Background information and birding tips

THE FARMLAND Bird Project is a six acre reserve started in 2002, created and managed jointly by Cley Spy (an optics shop) and BIRD*scapes* (a gallery specialising in bird art), in response to the decline of formerly-common and widespread countryside birds.

Located at the heart of the conservation-minded Bayfield Estate, the aim of the project is to show people some of the features that can be introduced to farmland, to help provide habitat for birds and to try to provide close-up views of some of the typical species.

On the Bayfield Estate there is a large tract of ancient wood, pasture, woodland, heathy scrubland, parkland and wet grassland alongside the River Glaven. This diversity of habitat means that the Estate has a bird list more than 130 species. From Glandford, permissive footpaths allow visitors to explore the Estate as far as Wiveton Down LNR and along the Glaven to the Wildflower Centre and Bayfield Hall on the other side of the valley.

From the car park, walk through the yard, past the converted barns and onto a track. As soon as you have left the yard you will see two small hides on your right. These hides overlook a pond and feeding area. During winter, grain is put out to attract finches, Yellowhammers, Reed Buntings and sparrows, which can be watched at close quarters.

Come summer, the resident birdlife is augmented by migrant warblers. Chiffchaff, Willow Warbler, Blackcap, Whitethroat and Lesser Whitethroat should all be seen and heard and

Key points

- **Free admission.**
- **Free use of binoculars in hide.**
- **Permissive footpaths on the estate, not public rights of way, so obey all signs and stay on footpaths!**
- **Disabled visitors may park at the hides.**
- **Dogs on leads.**
- **Bird art gallery close by.**
- **Birding equipment for sale nearby.**

Contacts

Cley Spy, Jodrell Barn, Manor Farm Barns, Glandford, Holt, Norfolk NR25 7JP
Tel. 01263 740088
E-mail: enquiries@cleyspy.co.uk
www.cleyspy.co.uk

The BIRD*scapes* Gallery, Manor Farm Barns, Glandford, Holt, Norfolk NR25 7JP
Tel. 01263 741742
www.birdscapesgallery.co.uk

you may be lucky and catch a glimpse of a Garden Warbler. Hirundines swoop over the crops and wildflower grassland to take insects. Turtle Doves can still be heard purring and occasionally seen on overhead wires. At this time of year, the reserve is vibrant with the colours of rare wildflowers that attract a profusion of butterflies.

Once past the hides, follow the farm track slightly uphill. Bear left just before a cattle grid. The track takes you alongside fields that are excellent for partridges and also offers a panoramic view over the area to scan for Barn Owl and raptors (as well as resident Sparrowhawk and Kestrel, these have included Buzzard, harriers, Hobby, Goshawk and even Red Kite). Check the fields for Wheatears at passage times and feeding flocks of buntings and finches in winter.

The track passes through a belt of trees and then bends to the left. About 200m further on, the route turns sharply left, down hill, to meet a public road. Turn left down this road for a short distance before turning off right along a steep(ish) track. The mature trees here are excellent for woodpeckers, Nuthatch, Treecreeper etc.

After a short climb, this path wends its way alongside a field with woodland on the left. At the end of the field (approx. 600yds) the path descends into a grassy valley with another pine plantation on the right and mature broadleaf trees on the left. The path continues along the valley bottom with ancient wood-pasture oaks on the left and lime trees. A public footpath joins from the right and a view opens up across the valley; check for circling raptors here. The path curves left, alongside the wood and downhill to another public road.

The whole of the woodland along these tracks is excellent for woodpeckers, Nuthatch, Treecreeper and other common woodland birds so take your time to maximise your chance of seeing them.

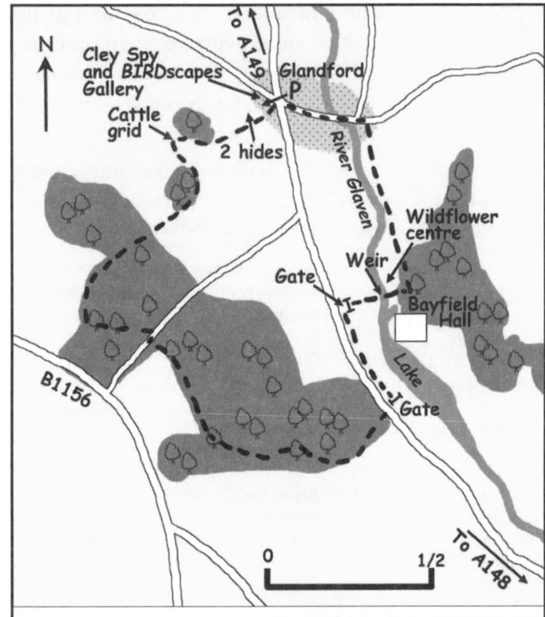

Access details

(Approx. 10 miles west of Sheringham).

From the A149 by Blakeney church, follow brown tourist signs to Cley Spy. In Wiveton village, one mile from the A149 junction in Blakeney, bear right to Holt and Glandford. After 0.8 miles you enter Glandford. Turn right into a large car park/courtyard (marked with a large pair of yellow binoculars!) where a range of small businesses includes an optics dealer and art gallery.

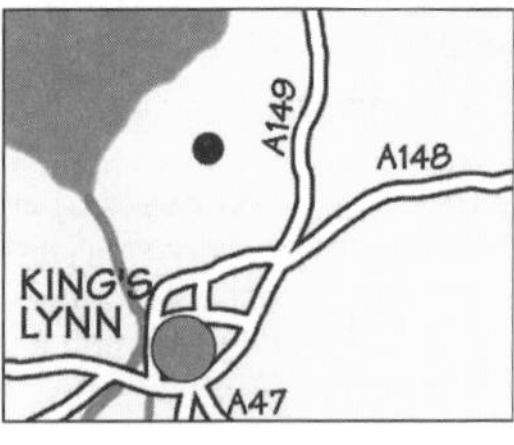

The access track to the hides is straight on (with Cley Spy optics and BIRD*scapes* Gallery to your right). The hides are on your right immediately you have left the courtyard.

Cross the road and you will see Bayfield Hall and lake in front of you. The farm gate here is ideal to lean on while you scan the lake for common wildfowl, grebes, etc.

Go through the gate and turn left to follow the course of the park wall. There is a gate at the end leading through another small wood. Turn right along the road and after 50 yards you reach a weir. This is the place to stand and wait for the resident Grey Wagtails to show and is also one of the best areas in which to see a Lesser Spotted Woodpecker (though still very scarce).

Continue up the hill and turn left through the Wildflower Centre's car park. Immediately after the car park, leave the vehicle track and go through a gate into the pasture. This narrow path runs alongside the River Glaven and a marshy field. Listen for Grasshopper Warblers in summer. The hedgerow here is excellent for scrub birds, finches, etc. Go through another gate and bear left along the road to a ford. The bridge over the ford is a good place to watch for Kingfisher, Grey Wagtail and common wildfowl. When the water level is low, the muddy edges may attract waders (a Wood Sandpiper has been recorded here!).

Follow the road past some beautiful houses and a church to a junction. Turn left and you are back at the car park/courtyard.

This is a reserve that you can drop in to while in the area visiting more famous Norfolk sites. You should see several declining bird species on this scenic, circular route, in relative solitude. And don't forget to call in at the optics shop and bird art gallery - both adjacent to the reserve - if you have money burning a hole in your pocket (or even if you don't)!

Key points

- **Map of Bayfield's paths available from Cley Spy or the BIRD*scapes* Gallery.**
- **Uneven paths, relatively undulating (for Norfolk!), can be muddy.**

Coal Tits are common in the pine woodlands on The Bayfield Estate.

Other nearby sites

Kelling Quags, Kelling Heath, Weybourne, NWT Cley, NWT Salthouse Marshes, Salthouse Heath, Stiffkey Fen, NOA Walsey Hills, Felbrigg Hall.

Key points

- **Free access to woodland and lake trails from dawn to dusk (except Christmas Day). Hall not open until 11am.**
- **Terrain is along rough tracks or across fields.**
- **Part of woodland trail is along a gravel path, quite steeply uphill.**
- **Lake trail unsuitable for wheelchairs.**
- **Free map photocopy, or buy glossy leaflet from NT shop.**
- **Some paths muddy at all times of year.**
- **Close all gates.**
- **Dog tie-up posts in courtyard with water bowls.**

Contacts

Felbrigg Hall
01263 837444

The National Trust, East Anglia Regional Office 01263 733471
www.nationaltrust.org

HEAD FOR Felbrigg if you enjoy birdwatching as part of a walk. There is a stretch of ancient woodland surrounded by parkland on this National Trust estate, plus a small lake to wander round. Non-birding members of the family can look around the house, visit the restaurant or café, or spend all your money in the Trust shop.

Target birds

All year – **Common woodland birds (100%), Lesser Spotted Woodpecker (20%).** *Spring/autumn* – **passage migrants (15%).**

Other possible bird species

All year
Little Grebe
Cormorant
Egyptian Goose
Common wildfowl
Sparrowhawk
Kestrel
Woodcock
Common gull species
Stock Dove
Barn Owl
Little Owl
Tawny Owl
Green Woodpecker
Great Spotted Woodpecker
Sky Lark
Goldcrest
Meadow Pipit
Pied Wagtail
Common scrub birds
Nuthatch
Treecreeper
Jay
Siskin
Common finches
Reed Bunting

Summer
Cuckoo
Hobby
Reed Warbler
Blackcap
Chiffchaff
Willow Warbler
Grasshopper Warbler
Spotted Flycatcher
Sand Martin
Other hirundines

Winter
Wigeon
Goosander
Brambling
Winter thrushes

Background information and birding tips

FELBRIGG HALL itself is of little interest to birdwatchers but the grounds of the 17,500 acre estate are fantastic for a leisurely stroll. There is a small lake, which holds several species of common wildfowl and waterbirds and an expanse of ancient woodland that is home to many common breeding birds. Redstart and Wood Warbler have bred here in the past.

For the lake walk, follow the signs from the car park along purple way-marked paths. Basically, you head for the small church, then diagonally right up the hill. Head for the two tall trees on the hilltop to reach a gate. Go through the gate and turn right, down the hill to the lake. The footpath circles the lake and leads back to the hall.

Scan the water for common ducks (Pochard, Mallard, Gadwall and Tufted Ducks) which are sometimes joined by one or two Goosanders in winter.

There is a small reedbed at the northern end of the lake, home to Reed Buntings all year round and Reed Warblers in summer. The marshy field adjacent to the lake is a good place for Grasshopper Warbler (and I heard several young Tawny Owls calling from the trees in the marsh in July 2005). Sand Martins nest in the muddy bank at the southern end of the lake and can be seen from late March to August. Scan the lake and adjoining fields for Egyptian Geese, joined by Wigeon in winter.

The woodland trail starts from

the entrance to the walled garden. Take the gravel path up a steepish hill, through a stand of mature trees. Fifty yards up this path, there is a paddock-type area where the trees are less densely spaced. This is the best place to look for Redstarts, Wood Warblers and Pied Flycatchers in spring and autumn. In summer, look out for Spotted Flycatchers in the woods.

Further on, the gravel track splits into several muddy grass tracks, all of which criss-cross the 500 acres of woodland. At the top of the hill is a bench around a large tree (the Victory V, planted to commemorate VE Day), an excellent place to sit and wait for the birds to come to you. From here, there is a Tarmac path leading down the hill to the estate road and back to the hall (part of the white-marked Tree Trail).

In the wood, Great Spotted Woodpeckers are usually very much in evidence but Lesser Spots can be very elusive. I have found the large trees closest to the car park to be best for the latter species, especially in late March when they give themselves away with their harsh calls, drumming and butterfly-like display flight. Occasionally, they even get in the large, lone trees in the fields towards the lake, where they show really well.

All in all, Felbrigg Hall grounds are a superb place for a stroll at any time of year. Visiting birdwatchers can spend as long as they like wandering around the woods or lake (or both) and they are likely to encounter many common species of bird along the way. Even without a map you cannot get lost on the estate, as the hall is usually in sight (if it isn't visible, walk a few hundred yards and it probably will be!).

In spring and summer, you may have the added bonus of being able to see one or two scarce breeding birds and, in autumn, who knows what may be lurking in the woods as this is a very under-watched site. Firecrest, Red-breasted Flycatcher, Yellow-browed Warbler, etc must be distinct possibilities and a Hawfinch was present in winter 2006.

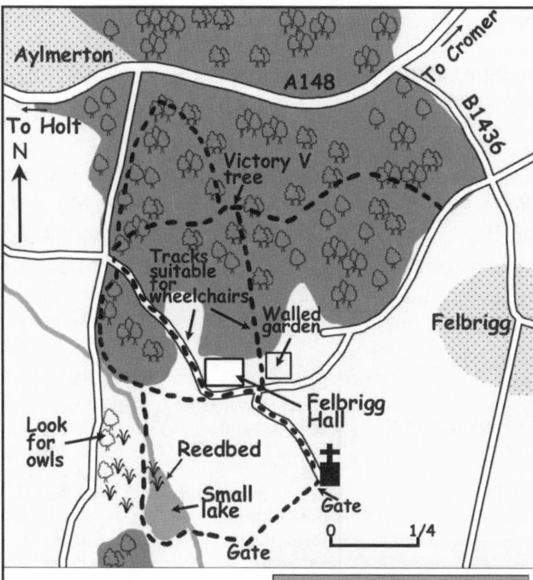

Access details

(Approx. 2.5 miles SW of Cromer).

Felbrigg Hall is extremely well sign-posted off A148 (Cromer to Holt/Fakenham road), on brown National Trust signs.

Follow these signs to the car park by the hall. From the car park, the two trails (woodland and lake) are well sign-posted.

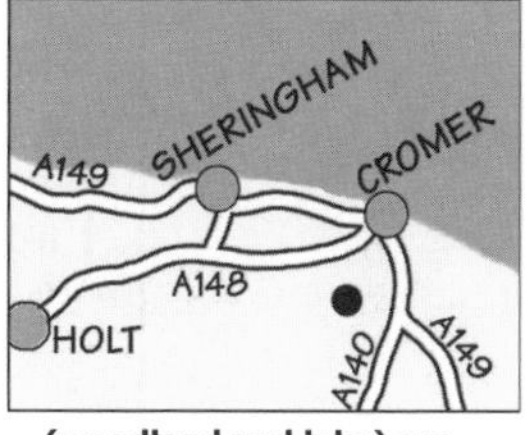

Other nearby sites

Blakeney Point, Blickling Hall, NWT Cley Marshes, Kelling Heath, NOA Kelling Quags, Salthouse Beach, Salthouse Heath, Sheringham, Swanton Novers, NOA Walsey Hills, Weybourne.

21 FLITCHAM ABBEY FARM

Key points

- **Hide is open at all times though Wednesdays can be disturbed by management work on the farm.**
- **Free car park.**
- **Wheelchair accessible hide.**
- **Log book in hide.**
- **Fieldguide in hide.**

Contacts

RS Cross & Son,
Abbey Farm,
Flitcham, Norfolk.
01485 600227

PROBABLY THE best place in Norfolk to see Little Owl, Turtle Dove and Kingfisher, with Barn Owl virtually guaranteed, this fantastic little farm reserve should not be missed. Carefully managed for wildlife, this site is good all year round.

Target birds

All year – **Marsh Harrier (70%), Little Owl (75%), Barn Owl (70%), Marsh Tit (65%), Tree Sparrow (30%).** *Winter* – **Pink-footed Goose (30%), Corn Bunting (20%).**

Other possible bird species

All year
Little Grebe
Egyptian Goose
Teal
Common wildfowl
Common waterfowl
Sparrowhawk
Buzzard
Kestrel
Red-legged Partridge
Grey Partridge
Water Rail
Lapwing
Snipe
Stock Dove
Tawny Owl
Kingfisher
Green Woodpecker
Great Spotted Woodpecker
Pied Wagtail
Corvids
Bullfinch
Other common finches
Yellowhammer
Reed Bunting

Winter
Woodcock
Grey Wagtail
Winter thrushes

Spring/autumn
Passage waders
Yellow Wagtail

Summer
Turtle Dove
Hirundines
Migrant warblers
Spotted Flycatcher

Occasional
Garganey
Hobby
Red Kite

Background information and birding tips

THIS WORKING FARM is a hidden treasure! Money provided by the Wildfowl and Wetlands Trust, DEFRA and the Countryside Stewardship Scheme goes towards managing the site as a haven for wildlife. This is how all farms could and should be but it is a sign of the times that I feel the need to praise RS Cross & Son (the owners) for their efforts.

On a winter's day, the bushes and trees around the car park can be dripping with birds. Yellowhammers and Chaffinches are present in impressive numbers (75-plus of the former and more than 100 of the latter have been recorded). Several Tree Sparrows (normally in the hedges along the road) and a few Corn Buntings are usually present, though the former seems to be declining here. Marsh Tit is a certainty in winter along with one or two Bullfinches. Pink-footed Geese sometimes feed in the large field opposite the car park in winter but be very careful not to flush them. In November 2001, this flock was joined by a Red-breasted Goose.

From the hide, Little Owls can usually be seen in the fallen oak directly in front of you, or on the large logs in the field to the left of this tree. Kingfishers regularly sit on the posts in the middle of the pool, Barn Owls breed on site and can be quite showy, while Tawny Owls also breed but are seldom seen. Several noisy Egyptian Geese are resident.

A Buzzard is sometimes seen patrolling the skies throughout

the year, while Hobbies occasionally fly over the farm from May to September (most in evidence between July and August). Marsh Harriers are reported daily during the spring and summer months and less frequently at other times of year.

Summer breeders include Whitethroats, Lesser Whitethroats, Spotted Flycatchers, Blackcaps, Willow Warblers and Chiffchaffs. This is one of the best sites in Norfolk to see Turtle Doves, which love to sit on the telephone wires running across the reserve.

In winter, pay special attention to the vegetated ditch viewable from the left side of the hide. A Water Rail regularly puts in an appearance and you may also see a Woodcock skulking in the undergrowth.

All in all, this is a cracking little place with plenty to see at all times of year. It is not unusual to see most of the target birds in a single visit. I love to drop in at Flitcham for an hour or so at the end of a hard day's birding around the Norfolk coast, just to chill out and see what is around. I am rarely disappointed.

This site is a shining example of how farming and wildlife conservation can be comfortable bedfellows. It is frightening to contrast this farm with the bird-less 'agri-deserts' so often encountered these days.

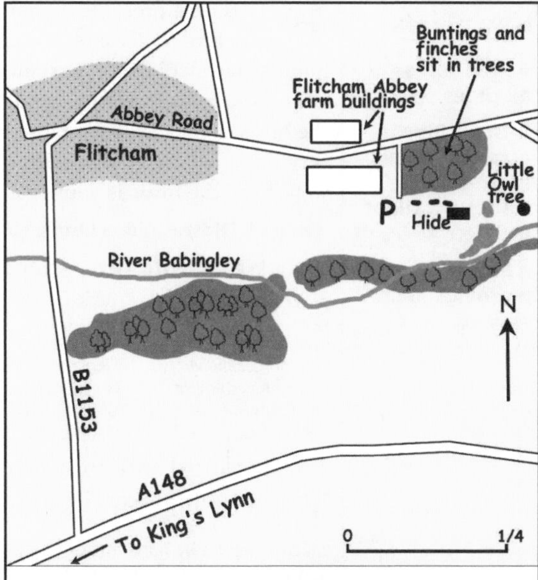

Access details

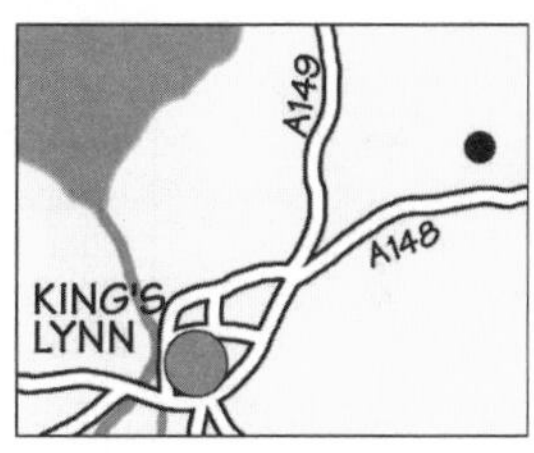

(Approx. 7.5 miles E of King's Lynn).

From King's Lynn take A148 (Cromer/Fakenham road) and then turn left onto B1153 at Hillington, sign-posted to Flitcham.

In Flitcham, turn right into Abbey Road and drive for half a mile until you have just passed the farm buildings on the right. Beyond the farmhouse, there is a small sign on the stone wall 'Abbey Farm Bird Hide' sending you down a short track.

Park at the end on the mud: the two hard-standing spaces are reserved for orange badge holders. The hide is along a short concrete path and is wheelchair friendly.

Other nearby sites

Blackborough End Tip, Dersingham Bog, Hunstanton, Ken Hill Wood, King's Lynn docks, Pentney Gravel Pits, NWT Roydon Common, Sandringham, RSPB Snettisham, Tottenhill Gravel Pits, Wolferton Triangle.

FORDHAM

Key points

- **Free access at all times.**
- **The bridge is accessed along a wide, rough track up a slight incline.**
- **Early mornings in late May are best.**

Contacts

None.

FORDHAM presents the only real chance wheelchair-using birders have of seeing Golden Orioles within the boundaries of Norfolk. Essentially, birders should stand (or sit) on the bridge over the poplar-lined channel and wait for the birds to fly across from one side to the other. This is a very sensitive site so it is essential that you ensure that the welfare of the birds is your first priority.

Target bird **Golden Oriole (15%).**

Other possible bird species

May/August
Great Crested Grebe
Cormorant
Common wildfowl
Common waterbirds
Sparrowhawk
Kestrel
Turtle Dove
Stock Dove
Hirundines
Kingfisher
Green Woodpecker
Great Spotted Woodpecker
Pied Wagtail
Common scrub birds
Common woodland birds
Whitethroat
Blackcap
Common finches

Background information and birding tips

THIS IS ANOTHER 'secret' site for Golden Orioles which is visited by hundreds of birdwatchers each year (see also Lakenheath). When Golden Oriole activity died down at Lakenheath a few years ago, I started visiting Fordham instead and obtained flight views of the Orioles every time I went. The birds also called throughout the day from mid-May to mid-June even when they didn't show themselves.

However, in recent years, I have had very few sightings and Lakenheath is now the better site again! In fact, on one trip to Fordham I didn't even hear the Goldies. The local farmer hadn't heard any either but there were apparently two pairs present. In fact, two pairs continued to breed here until 2005 at least.

More worrying was the assertion by the farmer that in 2000, birders discovered an oriole nest

The best chance of seeing a Golden Oriole at Fordham is when they fly across the canal.

in the poplars and a constant group formed to look at them, frightening the birds off the nest. If true, it is a disgraceful episode.

Birdwatchers who have the welfare of the birds as their highest priority will be content with poorish views as the Golden Orioles fly across the canal and will not approach too close. **If you see any bad behaviour at this site please report it and/or put a stop to it.**

While waiting for the orioles to appear, you will be entertained by a few common species such as Cormorant and Grey Heron flying over, while the channel should produce a Great Crested Grebe and maybe even a Kingfisher. A Hobby may flash through in pursuit of a Swallow, Swift or House Martin.

The bushes lining the Cut-off Channel are good for Whitethroats and Blackcaps and listen out for Turtle Doves 'purring' in the vicinity. Watch out for mink swimming across the water, usually pursued by an angry Moorhen or two.

One more word of warning: beware of ticking off distant Green Woodpeckers as they fly across the Channel. Many a time I have witnessed over-anxious birdwatchers count a Yaffle as a Golden Oriole and for once I am not included on that list of stringers!!

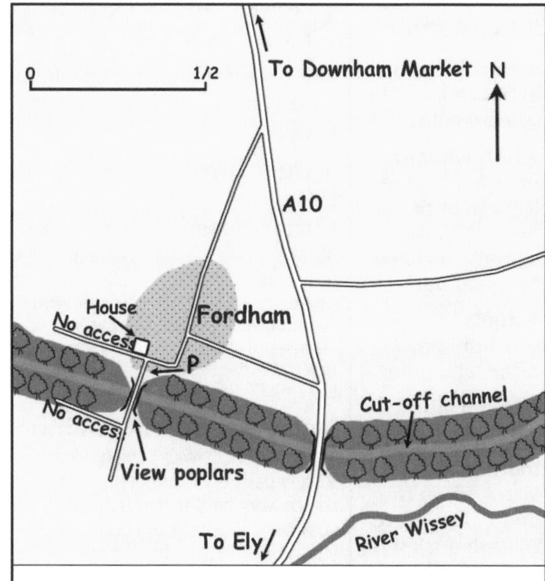

Access details

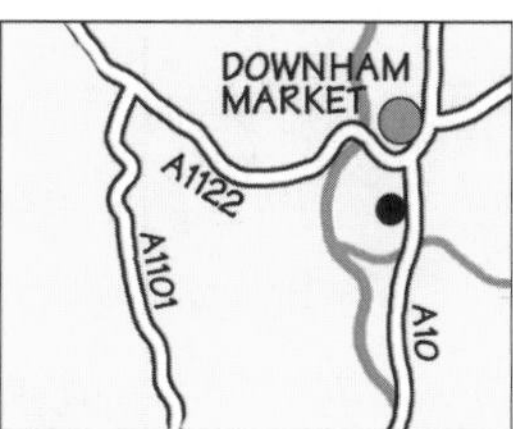

(Approx. 2.5 miles S of Downham Market).

From Downham Market follow A10 along bypass, sign-posted to Ely (do not go into Downham itself).

After about two miles, turn right at the sign to Fordham. Follow this road for half a mile, then go straight on when the 'main' road bends sharply left. After about 200 yards turn left, opposite the house, into a rough car park. Walk onto the bridge to view the poplars either side of the Cut-off Channel.

Other nearby sites

NWT East Wretham Heath, Foulden Common, RSPB Lakenheath, Lynford Arboretum, Santon Downham, Wayland Wood, NWT Weeting Heath, WWT Welney.

FOULDEN COMMON

Key points

- **Terrain is flat along rough grass tracks.**
- **Not suitable for wheelchairs, though birds can be heard and sometimes seen, from car park.**
- **Boots recommended after rain.**
- **No facilities.**
- **Early mornings from late April to the end of May best, though dusk not bad either.**

Contacts

None

SPRING MORNINGS are a joy on Foulden Common as the site will be alive with birdsong, a perfect start to a day's birding in Norfolk and, if you are lucky, you may even glimpse a Nightingale in this area of thick bushes and hedges.

Target birds *Spring/summer* – Nightingale (hear 80%, see 25%).

Other possible bird species

Spring	Hirundines	Long-tailed Tit
Sparrowhawk	Common scrub birds	Marsh Tit
Kestrel	Lesser Whitethroat	Corvids
Turtle Dove	Whitethroat	Common finches
Cuckoo	Blackcap	Yellowhammer
Green Woodpecker	Chiffchaff	Jay
Sky Lark	Willow Warbler	Other corvids

Background information and birding tips

FOULDEN COMMON still holds a few pairs of Nightingales. They can be very hard to see but, as soon as you get out of your car, you should hear them singing.

When you hear one, follow the beautiful song to the thick bush from which it is emanating. The trick now is to wait patiently for the bird to show. Do not disturb the bush to try to get a glimpse but look towards the ground for the best chance of seeing the skulking songster.

Numbers of Turtle Doves are declining in Britain but the bird is still easy to see at Foulden.

While you are waiting, you should be entertained by several commoner species of bird. Yellowhammers show well, as do Green Woodpeckers.

Cuckoos seem to show here better than at some sites; they favour the twiggy trees just inside the gate. If you get there early in the morning in mid-May you should see one or two calling from the top of one of these trees.

Turtle Doves also breed on the Common, as do Whitethroats, Lesser Whitethroats and many common species. On a fine spring morning, this place can have a deafening dawn chorus!

Park in the lay-by by the metal barrier, taking care not to block access for farm vehicles. Walk around the barrier and cross the small grassy clearing (the old car park) to the narrow kissing gate next to the farm gate

Once through the gate, head left along the obvious path to the main track. Turn right to get back to the car park. There are one or two isolated bushes along the main track which can hold Nightingales and they can be easier to see here than in the continuous bushes near the car park.

You can explore the Common further if you wish. There are several tracks zigzagging the fields but I have found that the route above gives ample opportunities to sample the rich birdlife of Foulden.

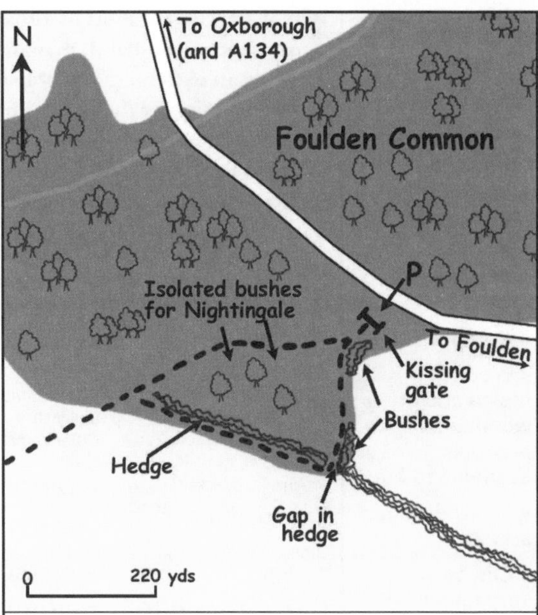

Access details

(Approx. 9.5 miles E of Downham Market).

From A134 (King's Lynn to Thetford road) turn off at Stoke Dry to Oxborough and the Iceni Village.

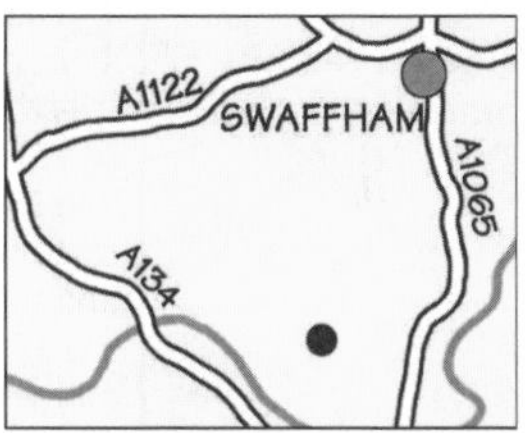

Follow minor road to Oxborough village, turning right at the church and public house (sign-posted Oxborough Hall). Follow this road (do not turn into the hall) to a sharp right hand bend sign-posted Foulden.

The road passes through a wood (start listening for Nightingale now) and the lay-by is on the right 0.6 miles from the sharp bend. Do not block access to the barrier for farm vehicles.

To enter the Common, walk around the metal barrier, through a kissing gate and follow paths homing in on the singing Nightingales.

Other nearby sites

NWT East Wretham Heath, Fordham, Ken Hill Wood, RSPB Lakenheath, Lynford Arboretum, Sandringham, RSPB Snettisham, WWT Welney, NWT Weeting Heath, Wolferton Triangle.

NWT FOXLEY WOOD

Key points

- **Free admission.**
- **Open all year round from 10am – 5pm. Closed on Thursdays.**
- **Please keep to signed trails.**
- **No dogs**
- **Woodchip mulch and other woodlands products available to buy.**
- **No wheelchair access.**
- **Can be very, very muddy all year round.**
- **Level terrain on grass paths.**

Contacts

Norfolk Wildlife Trust,
Bewick House,
22 Thorpe Road,
Norwich NR1 1RY
01603 625540

www.norfolkwildlifetrust.org.uk/

IN A COUNTY short of broad leaved forest, 300 hectares of ancient woodland, managed by the Norfolk Wildlife Trust, is an extremely valuable habitat resource. It provides an opportunity for the patient birdwatcher to see many species of common woodland birds, some of which are tricky to find in Norfolk. Foxley becomes a riot of colour in spring when spectacular numbers of bluebells bloom.

Target species

All year – **Lesser Spotted Woodpecker (25%).**

Other possible bird species

All year
Sparrowhawk
Kestrel
Stock Dove
Barn Owl
Little Owl
Tawny Owl
Green Woodpecker
Great Spotted Woodpecker
Sky Lark
Common scrub birds
Marsh Tit
Nuthatch
Treecreeper
Jay
Other corvids
Bullfinch
Other common finches

Spring/summer
Hobby
Woodcock
Cuckoo
Turtle Dove
Hirundines
Grasshopper Warbler
Other common warblers
Spotted Flycatcher

Winter
Winter thrushes
Brambling

Occasional
Buzzard
Goshawk

Background information and birding tips

FOXLEY WOOD is a quintessential English forest. It is the largest remaining stand of ancient woodland in Norfolk. The NWT is managing the wood by traditional methods (coppicing) and removing conifers planted in the 1960s along with other non-native species.

This coppicing (cutting trees close to the ground) means there are plenty of woodland products for the visitor to purchase to help fund future management.

When visiting Foxley, it is advisable to take one's time. This is a large wood and the birds may be scattered over the whole area. The more time one spends in the wood, the more species of bird will be seen.

The circular walk is well marked on posts with green arrows, with smaller paths leading into the wood for more intrepid birders. There are information boards at regular intervals to tell the visitor what they may encounter at various times of year.

All of these paths can produce birds. In winter, birds gather together in feeding flocks and roam widely in the wood. You can either stroll through the wood to find them or wait patiently for them to come to you (but always stay on the paths).

Bramblings can sometimes be seen feeding on beech mast on the floor, Siskin and Lesser Redpolls move in to feed on alders, or a flock of agitated birds may lead you to a roosting Tawny Owl.

Foxley really comes into its own in spring. The wood is bursting with bird song as the resident species are joined by a host of summer visitors. Blackcap, Whitethroat, Lesser Whitethroat, Garden Warbler, Grasshopper Warbler, Chiffchaff and Willow Warbler can all be heard along with Cuckoo and Spotted Flycatcher. At dusk, you may also hear and see a roding Woodcock.

One cautionary word: Foxley can be very busy in spring as it is a famous bluebell wood. Visitors flock from miles around to experience the spectacular rivers of blue running through the trees.

Foxley is an excellent place to see Lesser Spotted Woodpeckers all year round, though spring is the best time when the birds are displaying. It is also one of the best places in Norfolk to find Nuthatch and Treecreeper. Great Spotted and Green Woodpeckers will be hard to miss.

Spring and autumn may also produce a few passage migrants such as Redstart, Pied Flycatcher and Wood Warbler. At all times of year, you should occasionally glance upwards as Sparrowhawk, Kestrel, common gull species and Buzzard may all be seen. Goshawk has also been recorded over the wood.

In short, there is always something of interest to see in Foxley Wood. As well as the bird species, the all-round naturalist will enjoy butterflies, flowers and fungi.

And don't forget to purchase some mulch for your garden on your way out (£3.50). Tap on the office window as you exit the car park or leave a cheque (NOT CASH) in the black box at the exit gate.

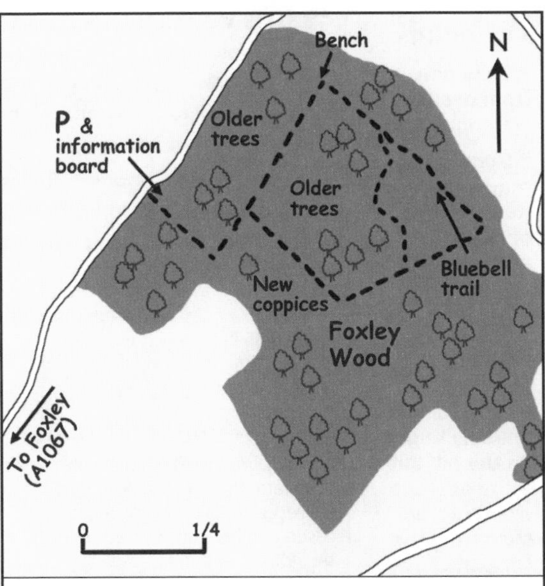

Access details

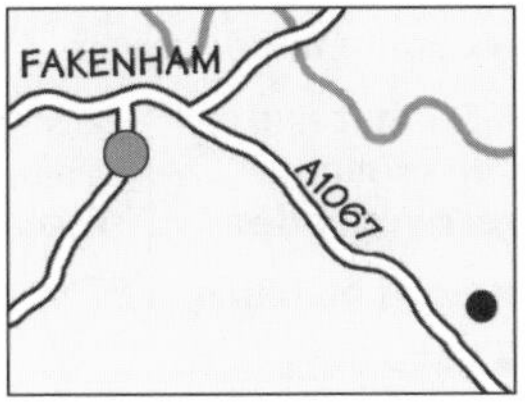

Approx 10 miles SE of Fakenham.

The reserve is signposted on brown tourist signs from the A1067 Norwich to Fakenham road, approximately one mile north of Bawdeswell, 10 miles south east of Fakenham.

Turn off A1067 (The Street) and follow the minor, narrow road through Foxley village (20mph limit) to the NWT-signed turn-in to the car park on the right (1.3 miles from main road).

Other nearby sites

NWT Sparham Pools, Pensthorpe Wildlife Park, Sculthorpe Moor, Great Ryburgh Raptor Watchpoint, Swanton Novers, north coast sites.

Key points

- **View only from designated watchpoint.**
- **Donation requested for upkeep of church at Swanton Novers.**
- **Narrow grass footpath slightly uphill.**
- **Wheelchairs unlikely to get up the hill but some of the wood can be seen from the car park.**
- **Telescope recommended.**
- **Sunhat and sun cream recommended.**
- **Dogs on leads.**
- **Take your litter home.**
- **Information leaflets in box by sightings board.**

Contacts

English Nature
01603 620558
www.english-nature.org.uk

Site Manager
01485 543044

THIS WATCHPOINT has been set up to allow birders to look over the Sennowe Estate, where a pair of Honey Buzzards takes up residence each summer. The views of the birds are generally closer and they are seen more regularly than at Swanton Novers.

Target birds *Summer* – Honey Buzzard (80%), Hobby (95%), Buzzard (95%).

Other possible bird species

Spring/summer	Sky Lark	Whitethroat
Cormorant	Hirundines	Blackcap
Shelduck	Barn Owl	Jay
Marsh Harrier	Little Owl	Other corvids
Sparrowhawk	Turtle Dove	Common finches
Kestrel	Stock Dove	Yellowhammer
Lapwing	Common scrub birds	

Background information and birding tips

SENNOWE ESTATE is a private estate, the owner feeling very privileged to have Honey Buzzards nesting on his land. And so he should!

The HBs usually arrive around the May 16 and depart at the end of August, early September. If it is raining, I wouldn't bother visiting as most of the raptors will be sheltering.

There is no access to the estate itself, so English Nature have set up a watchpoint to allow birders an uninterrupted view over the woods, thanks to Mr Cook who owns the field where the watchpoint is situated. Park only in the designated car park (a roped off section of a field) as the road is very narrow and busy with farm vehicles.

There is a donations box in the car park (by the roadside hedge) and a sightings board. Free information leaflets are available in a box by the board. Take the obvious narrow grass path up the hill for about 75 yards to view the woods. Do not enter the fields and view only from the flattened area of grass at the top of the hill, by the small trees and bushes.

Scan across the road to see any raptors. The area around the clock tower seems particularly good, especially for Honey Buzzards. I have seen six Hobbies in the air at once over the estate and the HBs will be joined by several Common Buzzards, allowing comparison of their different flight silhouette and outline.

The raptors seem to show at closer range at Ryburgh than other watchpoints in the country and they also seem to show more often. I have rarely had to wait more than an hour for a Honey Buzzard to glide into view here, whereas a wait of two to three hours was the norm at Swanton Novers.

The beauty of waiting, though, is that anything may fly into view, so keep scanning at frequent intervals. Cormorant, Shelduck, Oystercatcher and Turtle Dove are among the more common flyovers, with Marsh Harriers becoming more regular visitors. An Osprey may be seen on passage and Black Kite and Black Stork have also been recorded, so be prepared for anything!

Do not neglect the surrounding hedges and fields. Many common species of bird can be seen in the area and Little Owls are often seen sitting on the fence posts in the grounds of the estate itself or in roadside trees. The watchpoint field holds dragonflies and butterflies.

There is no shade available at the watchpoint, so if the sun is out wear a hat and smother yourself in sun cream. Wheelchair users will have difficulty getting up the hill along the grass path but some of the wood can be seen from the car park.

Please take care on the narrow roads in the area. When leaving the car park, visibility is very poor. Also note that this road forms part of the National Cycle Route so beware of being dazzled by Lycra-clad riders!

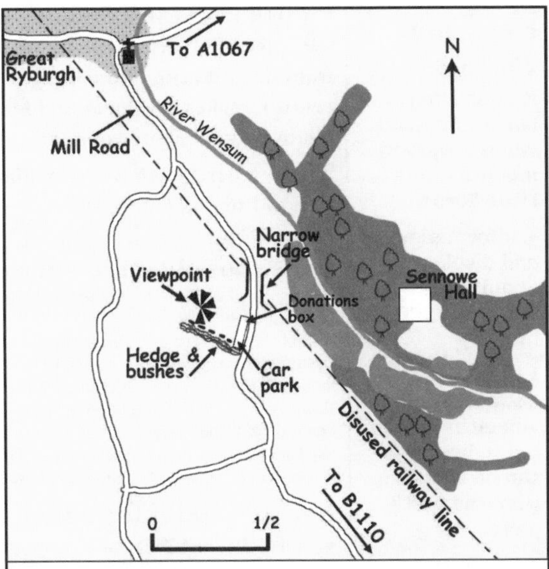

Access details

(Approx. 4 miles SE of Fakenham)

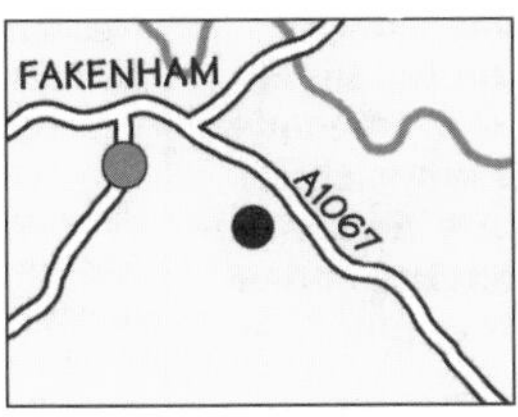

From the A148 Fakenham by-pass take the A1067 to Norwich. After approx. 3 miles, turn right, sign-posted Great Ryburgh. After 1.1 miles, turn left into Mill Road by the church and public house. Follow this road, bearing left when you reach a fork in the road after 0.5 miles (signed as a National Cycle Route), then cross the disused railway over a narrow bridge. The car park is a short distance (0.1 miles).

Other nearby sites

Swanton Novers, NWT Foxley Wood, Sculthorpe Moor, Pensthorpe Wildfowl Park, Syderstone Common, NWT Sparham Pools, north coast sites.

GREAT YARMOUTH BEACH

Key points

- The RSPB hut is open from May to August when a warden monitors the Little Terns.
- Information and display about Little Terns in RSPB hut.
- Tern colony not accessible to wheelchair users but flying birds can be viewed from the north pier.
- Mediterranean Gulls viewable from the piers and promenade for wheelchair users. Seawatch from the end of either pier.
- Many facilities in town.

RSPB East Anglia Office
01603 661662

THE POSSIBILITY of seeing scarce species (it's the best place in Norfolk to see Mediterranean Gulls just minutes from the glittering attractions of Great Yarmouth town centre), makes this location ideal for a family outing if your relatives don't share your enthusiasm for the great outdoors.

Target birds

All year – **Mediterranean Gull (95%).** *Winter* – **Snow Bunting (20%).** *Summer* – **Little Tern (100%), Roseate Tern (10%).**

Other possible bird species

All year
Cormorant
Kestrel
Oystercatcher
Ringed Plover
Turnstone
Common gull species
Sky Lark
Meadow Pipit
Common finches

Summer
Little Gull
Common Tern
Sandwich Tern

Autumn
Sooty Shearwater
Manx Shearwater
Balearic Shearwater
Gannet
Arctic Skua
Great Skua
Little Gull
Kittiwake

Background information and birding tips

YARMOUTH BEACH is the best place in Norfolk to see Mediterranean Gulls at any time of the year. Stroll along the prom between the two piers and you may see more than 40 birds of differing ages. If you cannot find any, just throw a few pieces of bread in the air and you will suddenly be joined by several 'Meds'!

In summer, there is a Little Tern colony in the North Denes area near the caravan park. The dunes are an SSSI but are heavily disturbed by holiday-makers at this time of year. Nevertheless, more than 200 pairs of Little Terns return each year and attempt to breed on the beach.

From the road, you can just see the roof of the RSPB shed poking above the dunes. From this hut, you can watch the comings and goings of the tern colony and also watch the consternation on the warden's face as the local Kestrel swoops in to take another hapless chick from the beach.

The panic this causes among the colony has to be seen and heard to be believed. To combat this predation, the RSPB has introduced sewer pipes for the terns to nest under and very cute they look in their new houses too!

From mid June, the chicks will dash up to the returning parents to collect their cargo of small fish. Running in and out of the area will be a Ringed Plover or two and flying along the shore should be Common and Sandwich Terns, plus the usual gull species. Roseate Terns are seen regularly on the beach in summer but usually only first thing in the morning before being disturbed by the ubiquitous dog walkers.

Always keep an eye on the sea as anything can pass by. I have seen passing Little Gull, Common

Scoter, Wigeon, Arctic and Great Skuas, Gannet, Kittiwake, Manx Shearwater, terns, etc from the steps of the hut.

Amazingly, Sky Lark and Meadow Pipit breed in the dunes, despite unbelievable disturbance by all and sundry. Local authorities must surely do more to protect the inhabitants of this SSSI.

In summary, this is a superb spot to sit and watch the activities of a tern colony for an hour or so. The fact that the colony is of the exquisite Little Tern makes it even more compelling viewing for the visitor.

In winter, the dunes to the north of the town hold a smallish flock of Snow Buntings but the area is large and disturbed by dog walkers. Park by Jellicoe Way and scan the extensive dune system. The buntings also get onto the beach where the Little Terns nest.

Great Yarmouth used to be a noted breeding site of Black Redstart. They could be found around the power station to the south of the town. The whole area from the power station to the industrial estate around the corner is prime Black Redstart territory, so it may still be worth checking if you are in the area.

Access details

***WINTER*: From A47 follow signs to Town Centre/ Seafront onto St. Nicholas Drive. Go over the traffic lights (the road is now called Euston Road) to the pay and display car park at the end, adjacent to the toilet block. Walk on to the beach to search for the Med Gulls, usually between the two piers.**

For Snow Buntings, park in the area described in the summer section below and search the dunes.

***SUMMER*: Follow directions as above but instead of parking, turn left (N) and follow this road for about a mile. Park on road near turn-off sign-posted to Caistor (Jellicoe Way) by The Iron Duke pub (just at the start of the caravan park).**

Walk E towards the sea through the North Denes SSSI to the RSPB hut.

Bus number 003 runs from Yarmouth along this road to the caravan site.

For Black Redstarts, follow winter directions but do not enter car park. Instead, turn right and follow the road along the seafront for about 2.5 miles. Scan the derelict buildings on the front by the power station (TG 531050) for the Black Redstarts, or continue around the corner to the industrial estate (TG 531043).

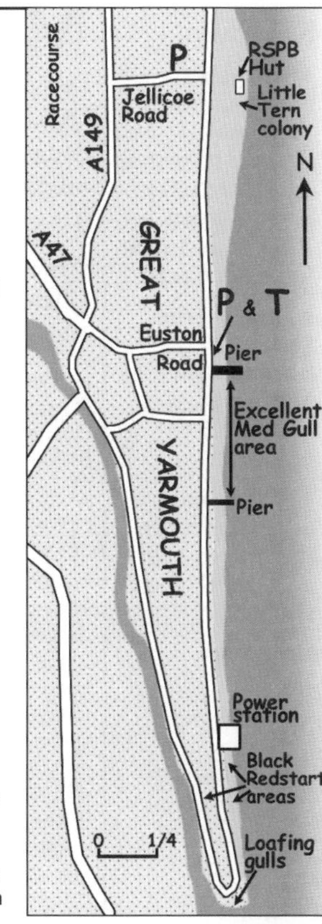

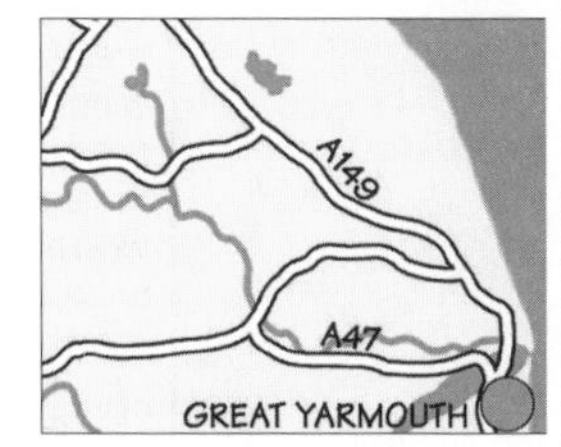

Other nearby sites

Breydon Water, RSPB Buckenham Marshes, Burgh Castle, NWT Hickling Broad, How Hill NNR, Rockland Broad, RSPB Strumpshaw Fen, Ted Ellis Reserve, Winterton Dunes.

27 GREAT YARMOUTH CEMETERY

Key points

- **The gates are open from 7.30am - 4.30pm (October 1 to March 31) and between 7.30am and 7pm for rest of year.**
- **Level terrain. Some Tarmac tracks, other paths are uneven or on grass.**
- **Please show due respect for the graves and be careful where you walk.**
- **No dogs.**

Contacts

None

MATURE TREES and a peaceful atmosphere ensures that a pleasant stroll here in spring or autumn may well produce a rare or scarce migrant. Your walk will almost certainly reveal several species of common migrants such as Song Thrush, Robin, Goldcrest, Redwing, Fieldfare, etc to brighten your day.

Target birds

Spring/autumn – **Passage migrants (anything is possible).**

Other possible bird species

Spring/autumn

Wryneck
Hirundines
Bluethroat
Black Redstart
Redstart
Whinchat
Wheatear
Ring Ouzel
Winter thrushes
Barred Warbler
Firecrest
Yellow-browed Warbler
Other warblers
Pied Flycatcher
Red-backed Shrike

Background information and birding tips

THE BUSHES and trees in the cemetery are a magnet for migrants in spring and autumn. The number of migrants is usually dictated by the weather conditions. If you are planning a migrant-hunting trip, watch the weather forecast the night before. In spring, you are looking for high pressure over southern Europe, with a low pressure system over Britain, hopefully combined with easterly winds. Better still is fog or rain on the east coast.

In autumn, look out for clear skies in Scandinavia, with low pressure over Britain. Onshore winds are a bonus. The high pressure system encourages birds to migrate, before hitting the nasty weather over Britain, which forces them to land. In Great Yarmouth cemetery, hopefully!

During both seasons, the above conditions should bring several weary travellers for you to find. Both the north and south sections of the cemetery should be searched thoroughly but care must be taken to respect non-birding visitors. Though the tradition of birders visiting the site is now well-established, please remember this is a graveyard.

On entering the cemetery, you should know whether there has been an arrival of birds by the number of Goldcrests present. A 'fall' of this species is usually a good indicator of the presence of other goodies lurking in the bushes.

Patience may be needed to see the birds as some of the cover is quite thick. The bushes can easily be reached by way of grass paths throughout the cemetery.

In spring, Ring Ouzels and Wheatears are among the earliest arrivals. Warblers making landfall should include the first Willow Warblers of the year along with Blackcaps and Chiffchaffs, which may have over-wintered in the cemetery grounds.

Later, Spotted Flycatchers may drop in, with Redstarts and Pied Flycatchers. In April 2002 a

Wryneck spent several days in the southern section.

Autumn is probably a better time to visit as virtually anything can turn up. Yellow-browed and Pallas's Warblers may be among the more regular Pied Flycatchers and Firecrests. The cemetery hosted a Red-flanked Bluetail in 1994, emphasising this site's ability to attract anything in the right conditions!

Great Yarmouth cemetery is best ignored for the rest of the year, though having said that, I found two Waxwings here in February 2001, so nothing is that certain.

In summary, this site cannot be guaranteed to produce any exciting finds but in spring and autumn the opportunity exists for an inquisitive birder to find anything – from a 'fall' of humble Robins or Goldcrests to a 'first' for Britain!

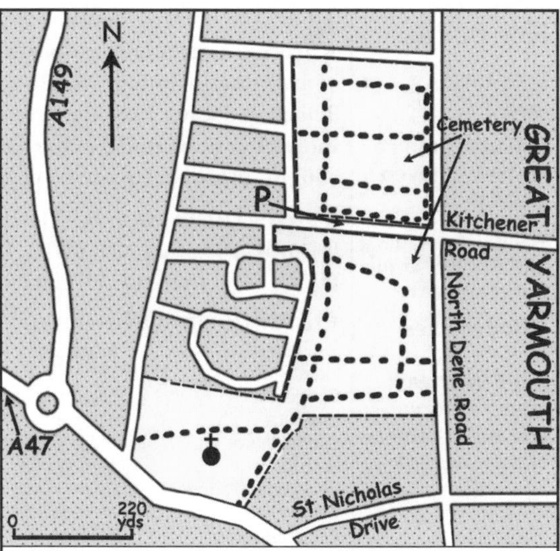

Access details

From A47, follow signs to 'Town Centre/Sea Front' to St. Nicholas Drive. Turn left at traffic lights into North Dene Road (sign-posted to coach/lorry car park). Turn left on to Kitchener Road (which is just after the coach park) and follow down to the cemetery gates, about 150 yards along. The cemetery is split into two sections, North and South and both can be accessed on foot from the road.

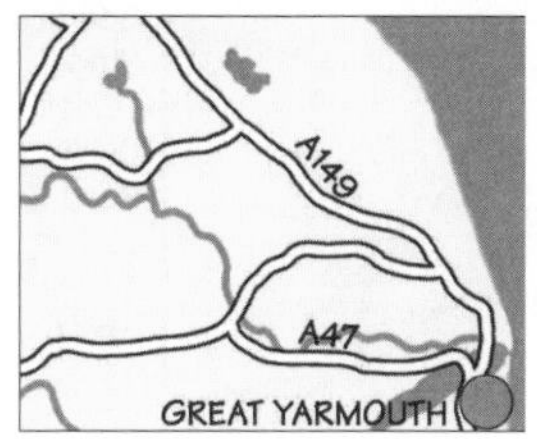

Other nearby sites

Breydon Water, Great Yarmouth Beach, Hardley Flood, NWT Hickling Broad, NWT Sparham Pools, RSPB Strumpshaw Fen, Ted Ellis Reserve, Winterton Dunes.

GYPSY LANE

Key points

- **Terrain is level.**
- **Access along a narrow, uneven grass path.**
- **Can be wet and muddy at all times of year.**
- **No facilities (toilets at RSPB Titchwell Marsh reserve and Brancaster beach car park).**

Contacts

None

SANDWICHED between Brancaster Marsh and Titchwell, this is a quiet area for birdwatchers to enjoy a variety of habitats, including marsh, reedbed, beach and sea. This site doesn't have the extensive wader scrapes of its more illustrious RSPB neighbour but close views of several sought-after species can be enjoyed in solitude.

Target birds

All year – Marsh Harrier (winter 15%, rest 90%). *Winter* – Sea duck (80%), Little Egret (80%), raptors (35%), Snow Bunting (30% on beach). *Spring* – Garganey (30%).

Other possible bird species

All year
Little Grebe
Cormorant
Shelduck
Sparrowhawk
Kestrel
Red-legged Partridge
Grey Partridge
Common waders
Sky Lark
Bearded Tit
Stonechat
Linnet
Bullfinch
Reed Bunting

Summer
Terns
Cuckoo
Hirundines
Sedge Warbler
Reed Warbler
Lesser Whitethroat
Whitethroat
Blackcap
Chiffchaff
Willow Warbler

Winter
Brent Goose
Grey Plover

Spring/autumn
Shearwaters
Gannet
Passage waders
Skuas
Passage migrants
Yellow Wagtail

Occasional
Hobby
Avocet
Water Pipit
Twite

Background information and birding tips

THIS WALK will suit people who like to do their birdwatching away from the crowds. The range of birds is similar to that encountered on RSPB Titchwell Marsh reserve, though numbers are lower because there are no wader scrapes.

It is worth remembering to use this more easterly footpath when the sun is shining in your eyes at Titchwell (in the mornings), as you can look across to the same reedbed from Gypsy Lane.

The footpath passes through trees and bushes which are excellent for commoner species joined by warblers in summer including, Lesser Whitethroat, etc and the odd migrant in autumn and spring.

After about 400 yards, the path opens out onto an extensive reedbed where you should see Marsh Harriers and Bearded Tits. Because this walk is quiet, you may get harriers flying overhead. They are present all year, though can be elusive in winter. I discovered this walk when 1993's Purple Heron dropped in, so the potential exists for you to find something really special.

Once past the reeds, the raised path crosses a marsh. One or two Little Egrets should be patrolling the channels alongside common wading species (such as Redshank) throughout the year and this is also an excellent spot for raptors, geese and ducks in winter. Garganey are regular visitors in spring and the

summer months bring Sedge and Reed Warblers to the area.

As the path bears right, look for raptors perched on old fence posts. Merlin, Peregrine, Hen Harrier, Short-eared and Barn Owls all hunt the area in winter, with the latter species present all year.

Follow the path east across a ford to the beach. In winter, all the species encountered at Titchwell on the beach and on the sea can be seen here, though there will be fewer pairs of eyes to spot things.

Waders on the beach should include Ringed Plover, Knot, Oystercatcher, Turnstone, Sanderling, Bar-tailed Godwit, Grey Plover, etc and the sea should produce Red-breasted Merganser, Goldeneye, Slavonian Grebe, Eider, Common Scoter, Long-tailed Duck, Red-throated Diver, etc.

Summer will see a similar range of waders with Little, Sandwich and Common Terns passing constantly. Be aware that the beach may be relatively crowded with summer tourists, accessing the beach from the Brancaster car park.

Autumn seawatching should produce Manx Shearwater. Keep an eye open for any of the four species of skua harassing the terns, though Arctic Skua will be the most numerous.

This walk will almost certainly not produce as many birds as the adjoining RSPB reserve but with patience, you should be rewarded with an impressive array of species. For instance, on a 30 minute power-walk one August (just to see what was around), I saw five Little Egrets, several family parties of Bearded Tits and a female and juvenile Marsh Harrier being mobbed by a pair of Sparrowhawks over my head. All this without another person in sight. Bliss!

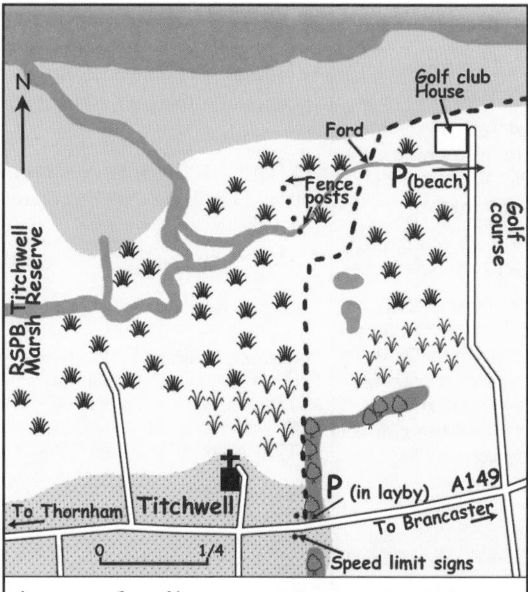

Access details

(Approx. 5.5 miles E of Hunstanton).

On entering Titchwell village on A149 from Thornham (travelling E), park in small lay-by on left, opposite the national speed limit sign. If travelling W, the lay-by will be on the right just before the 40mph signs. There is room for about four cars. Follow the public footpath N.

Alternatively, park in Brancaster Beach car park (TF 772451) and walk W along the beach to where it meets this footpath on the shore.

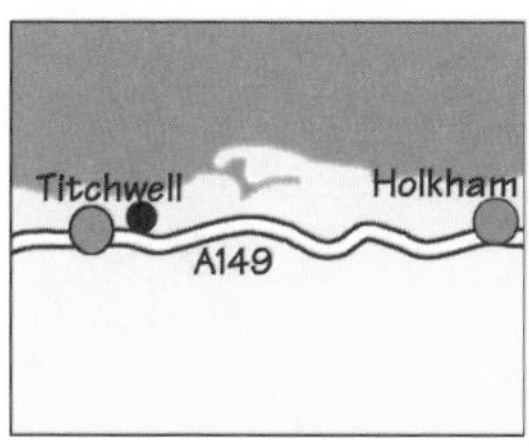

Other nearby sites

Brancaster Marsh, Choseley Barns, Dersingham Bog, NWT Holme Dunes, Holkham Hall, Holkham NNR, Ken Hill Wood, King's Lynn Docks, Sandringham, RSPB Snettisham, Swanton Novers, NOA Redwell Marsh, NWT Roydon Common, RSPB Titchwell Marsh, Wolferton Triangle.

HADDISCOE MARSHES

Key points

- **Telescope essential.**
- **Terrain is uphill on a Tarmac pavement.**
- **Very exposed, with no shelter.**
- **Excellent vantage point for wheelchair users to scan for raptors, though the bridge slope is steep.**

Contacts

None

HARDY SOULS will find this bleak marsh is excellent in winter for raptors such as Marsh and Hen Harriers and sometimes wild swans and geese. However, because there is no shelter, fair-weather birders need to choose their visiting days with care.

Target birds

Winter – **Bewick's Swan (70%), Marsh Harrier (40%), Hen Harrier (35%), Peregrine (50%), Short-eared Owl (50%).**

Other possible bird species

Winter
Cormorant
Whooper Swan
White-fronted Goose
Shelduck
Wigeon
Teal
Common waterbirds
Sparrowhawk
Kestrel
Merlin
Peregrine
Lapwing
Curlew
Common gull species
Barn Owl
Sky Lark
Meadow Pipit
Pied Wagtail
Common scrub birds
Winter thrushes
Corvids
Common finches
Reed Bunting

Background information and birding tips

THE VANTAGE point for Haddiscoe Marshes offers no shelter from the elements, so I suggest you only visit in fine weather with good visibility. In these conditions, the view of the marsh from the bridge is superb.

A wide range of raptors grace the marsh, though none can be guaranteed on any given visit. Overall, there is always something to see, though you may have to wait two or three hours to produce a decent list of desired species. By this time, your toes will no longer feel a part of your body.

Marsh Harriers, Kestrels and Sparrowhawks are the most likely raptors, though Short-eared Owls are recorded regularly. Barn Owls and Peregrines are frequent visitors to the marsh but Merlin and Hen Harrier are seen less regularly. Scan the pylons and fence posts very carefully as raptors love to use them as look-out perches.

While you are scanning for raptors and owls, you should find one or two Bewick's Swans. Whooper Swans and White-fronted Geese are less regular but not impossible. Regular visits will provide the best chance of connecting with all of the specialities. A Rough-legged Buzzard recently graced the marsh for two winters, showing the potential for anything to turn up anywhere.

The marsh also holds many common species ranging from Goldfinch, Greenfinch and Meadow Pipit, to grazing Wigeon, Teal and Mute Swan and nervous Lapwing and Curlew.

The hardy birdwatcher may wish to walk across the marsh and he or she can indeed do so. A public footpath runs along the north-east side of the canal, accessed across the A143.

In fact, you might like to walk the eight mile or so circular route, following the River Yare to Breydon Water at Berney Arms and back to

Haddiscoe alongside the River Waveney but you will have to achieve it in Wellingtons! You may also walk along the road to get a different viewpoint of the marsh but be very careful of the fast-moving traffic.

If you ask me, it is much more sensible (if standing on a high bridge in a wind-chill of –10°C can be called sensible) to scan the area from Haddiscoe bridge, from where you can dash occasionally to the car for a respite from the elements.

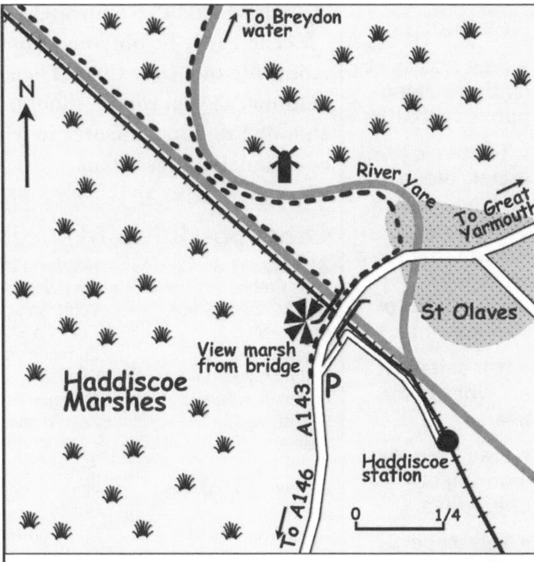

Access details

(Approx. 6.5 miles SW of Great Yarmouth).

FROM GREAT YARMOUTH: **Head S on A12 to junction with A143 (sign-posted Belton, Burgh Castle and Beccles). Continue for 5.5 miles to the village of St. Olaves. Pass through the village and after half a mile cross the steep bridge (over the canal and railway).**

At the bottom of the bridge, turn immediately left and park on the wide, Tarmac verge (sign-posted Haddiscoe Station – if you reach Haddiscoe village, you have gone too far).

Walk back to the road bridge to view the marsh on your left.

FROM NORWICH: **Leave A47 Norwich bypass on A146. Head SE for approximately 13.5 miles. Take first exit at roundabout with the junction of A143 (sign-posted Great Yarmouth). After approximately five miles, pass through the village of Haddiscoe and continue for another 1.5 miles.**

Park on the right, just before the steep bridge over the canal and railway (park by signs for Haddiscoe station).

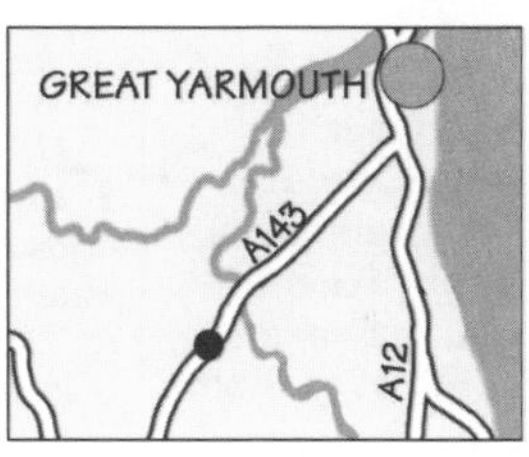

Other nearby sites

RSPB Berney Arms Marshes, Breydon Water, Burgh Castle Marshes, Great Yarmouth Beach, Hardley Flood, Herbert Barnes Riverside Park, NWT Hickling Broad, Horsey, Stubb Mill, RSPB Surlingham Church Marshes, Ted Ellis Reserve.

HARDLEY FLOOD

Key points

- Free access at all times along public footpaths.
- Terrain is level, mainly along an uneven, narrow, grass path, though there is a stretch of easy-access path to the moorings.
- Not suitable for wheelchair users.
- Free 24-hour mooring at Chedgrave.
- Telescope useful.
- Three narrow gateways to negotiate. If you are heavily built (like me!) you may need to climb over them.
- Hide accessed up a ramp.
- ID chart inside hide.
- Toilets and shops available in Chedgrave (1 mile).

Contacts

General Broads Authority
01603 610734

VIEWS OF THIS privately-owned, extensive flooded area can easily be obtained from a public footpath and hide alongside the River Chet. The site is excellent for common wildfowl all year round, though they can be distant. Regular shooting disrupts the area in winter, so be prepared for occasional birdless visits.

Target birds

All year – Common wildfowl (100%).

Other possible bird species

All year
Little Grebe
Great Crested Grebe
Cormorant
Egyptian Goose
Common wildfowl
Common waterbirds
Sparrowhawk
Kestrel
Water Rail
Common gull species
Kingfisher
Green Woodpecker
Great Spotted Woodpecker
Sky Lark
Meadow Pipit
Pied Wagtail
Common scrub birds
Cetti's Warbler
Common woodland birds
Corvids
Common finches
Reed Bunting

Summer
Marsh Harrier
Hobby
Common Tern
Cuckoo
Hirundines
Sedge Warbler
Reed Warbler
Whitethroat
Other warblers

Spring/autumn
Passage waders
Yellow Wagtail

Winter
Goldeneye
Goosander
Winter thrushes

Background information and birding tips

HARDLEY FLOOD is a privately-owned stretch of water that holds many species of common waterfowl. In winter, the large lake can be covered in Tufted Duck, Goldeneye, Wigeon, Pochard, Teal, Mallard, Gadwall, Shoveler, Shelduck and feral geese.

A large number of Coots and Great Crested Grebes congregate on the lake in winter.

One major drawback of this site for birdwatchers is the fact that this stretch of water is regularly hunted by the shooting fraternity in winter, so you may be confronted with a distressing scene. Listen out for gunfire when you get out of your car/boat to avoid a disappointing visit.

In summer, look for Reed and Sedge Warblers. Also keep an eye open for a flash of blue bulleting over the river's surface: that'll be one of the regular Kingfishers!

The footpath starts at the end of a narrow road (park sensibly) and then passes the Chedgrave mooring point, though there are no facilities here. Continue another half a mile to view Hardley Flood itself. After heavy rain, you can stand on the wooden bridge listening to the surge of water as it flows into Hardley from the river, thus demonstrating how this place got its name. Having said that, water levels may drop sufficiently to expose a few areas of mud that attract waders, especially at passage times.

At any time of year, this is a duck-watcher's paradise. This site is under-watched so I am certain many a rare duck has gone unnoticed over the years (Blue-

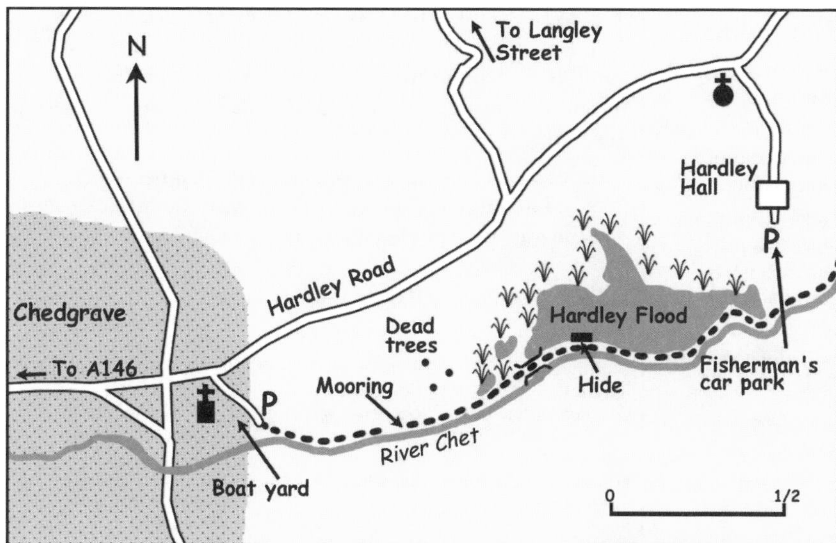

winged Teal has been recorded). In fact, it is so under-watched that I wouldn't be surprised if a Bittern hasn't remained undiscovered in the extensive reedbed on the western edge of The Flood. This reedbed also looks good for Bearded Tits, though I have never seen or heard them here.

About 100 yards past the bridge is a new hide, which you reach via a ramp. Ironically, the hide is accessible to wheelchairs but the easy-access path doesn't go as far as the hide meaning wheelchair users cannot reach it! The hide overlooks the lake and is a welcome shelter in winter.

In summer, many common ducks remain on site, joined by Common Terns. Hundreds of Swallows, Swifts and House Martins swoop over the water's surface, sometimes hunted by a Hobby. Black Terns regularly visit in spring and autumn and watch out for that Osprey dropping in!

Access details

(Approx. ten miles SE of Norwich)

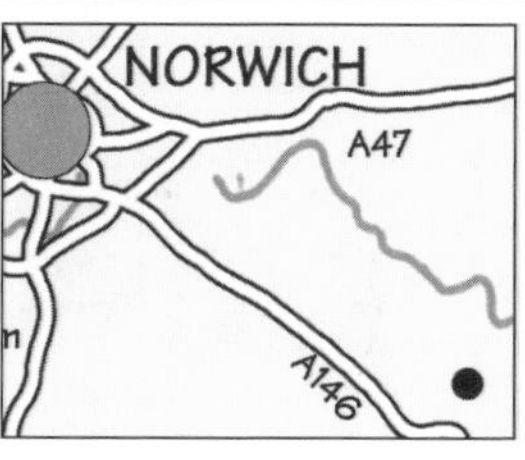

***BY CAR*: Leave A47 Norwich bypass at A146 (sign-posted to Lowestoft & Norwich). Head SE for seven miles, turning left to Chedgrave and Langley. In Chedgrave village, take the first left, sign-posted Langley. At crossroads, go straight across (Hardley Road), past the church on the right. Take next right (dead end, sign-posted 'Boatyards and Playground'). Continue for under half a mile and park by the wooden gate just before the road bears right into the boatyard. DO NOT BLOCK ACCESS.**

If there is no room here, park in the village.

Follow public footpath signs alongside the channel, then alongside the River Chet for about half a mile to view Hardley Flood on the left.

***BY BOAT*: Mooring situated along the River Chet, approximately a 30 minute sail from the junction with the River Yare. Moor at Chedgrave Common, not at the boatyards.**

Other nearby sites

RSPB Berney Arms Marshes, Breydon Water, Burgh Castle Marshes, Great Yarmouth Beach, Haddiscoe Marshes, Halvergate Marshes, Rockland Broad, RSPB Strumpshaw Fen, Ted Ellis Reserve.

Key points

- **Free access at all times.**
- **Fully wheelchair accessible.**
- **No facilities but Great Yarmouth is only a mile away.**
- **Telescope advisable.**

Contacts

Great Yarmouth Borough Council,
Town Hall, Hall Quay,
Great Yarmouth
NR30 2QF
(01493 85610)
www.great-yarmouth.gov.uk

I HAVE INCLUDED this small riverside park because it is an ideal place for wheelchair users and people with mobility difficulties to obtain superb views over Breydon Water. If you catch the tide right, waders can be very close to this park.

Target species

All Year – Avocet (90%), other waders (100%), Little Egret (75%). *Spring/autumn* – Little Gull (60%), passage waders. *Winter* – Winter raptors (30%). *Summer* – Terns.

Other possible bird species

All year
Cormorant
Little Egret
Shelduck
Common wildfowl
Marsh Harrier
Sparrowhawk
Kestrel
Grey Partridge
Red-legged Partridge
Common waders
Gull species
Barn Owl
Pied Wagtail

Winter
Bewick's Swan
Whooper Swan
Pink-footed Goose
Wigeon
Pintail
Goldeneye
Golden Plover
Grey Plover
Knot
Bar-tailed Godwit

Spring/summer
Garganey
Sandwich Tern
Common Tern
Little Tern

Passage
Ruff
Little Stint
Curlew Sandpiper
Black-tailed Godwit
Whimbrel
Greenshank
Spotted Redshank
Green Sandpiper
Wood Sandpiper
Common Sandpiper
Black Tern
Black Tern
Hirundines

Occasional
Marsh Harrier
Hen Harrier (winter)
Merlin
Peregrine

Background information and birding tips

THE HERBERT BARNES Riverside Park is named after the late councillor for Cobholm, a district of Great Yarmouth. It was previously a 'hidden gem', frequented by local birdwatchers only but came to national prominence in 2005, when a Killdeer was found in the area.

When one first arrives, the Park seems an unlikely place for birding but first impressions are misleading. The expanse of grass in the park is usually home to Meadow Pipits and Sky Larks with Pied Wagtails regularly dropping in. There are several hard-standing paths criss-crossing the area for easy access for all visitors.

The Park really comes into its own when you reach the seawall because wheelchair users can view Breydon Water from here. At certain times of the day the light can be more favourable here, than from the hide near Asda in Great Yarmouth.

The tide may also push birds closer to the Park as it fills Breydon and, if you sit quietly on the bench on the seawall, you may get very close views of waders indeed! If the tide is out you are still able to 'scope Breydon Water from this position, though birds may be distant (look right towards Yarmouth).

At all times of year you should expect to see Avocet, Redshank, Lapwing, Oystercatcher, Ringed Plover, Dunlin, Turnstone, Curlew, Shelduck and Little Egret.

In winter, you should encounter Grey and Golden Plover, Bar-tailed Godwit and Ruff and in summer Black-tailed Godwit and Little Ringed Plover. Passage waders may include Green, Wood and Common Sandpipers, Little Stint, Whimbrel and Curlew Sandpiper among others.

When the tide is in during the summer, terns fish Breydon Water, sometimes coming close to shore at The Park (the channel here is narrower than at Great Yarmouth). Common and Sandwich are the commonest species but they are joined by Little and Arctic. You may be lucky and find a Roseate Tern here and on passage you might see Black Terns patrolling the area.

Do not neglect to scan the fields across Breydon. Marsh Harriers are regularly reported all year round and in winter Peregrine, Merlin, Hen Harrier and Short-eared Owl may be expected to show occasionally.

From the Park you may wish to walk further. The footpath along the seawall forms part of Angle's Way. Head left and you reach Burgh Castle. Keep going (for 70 miles) and you reach Knettishall Heath in Suffolk but that's probably too far for one day!

Head right along the footpath and you find yourself in Great Yarmouth.

The whole walk along the southern shore is an excellent one for people who like to stretch their legs and work a bit for their birds. If you are like me however and you like the birds to come to you, this is a quiet little place to sit and see what turns up. I think Herbert Barnes would be proud such a place bears his name.

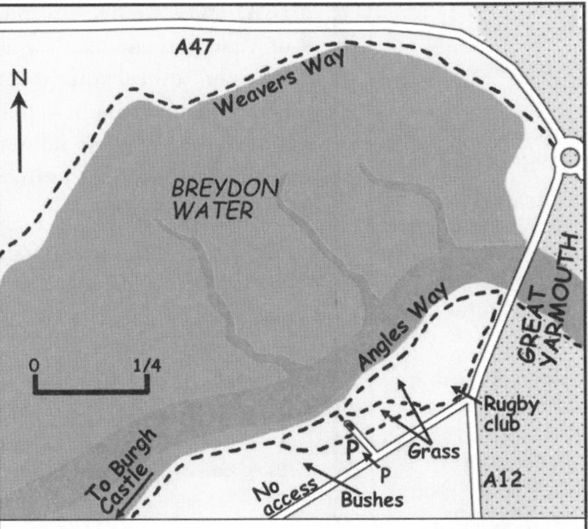

Access details

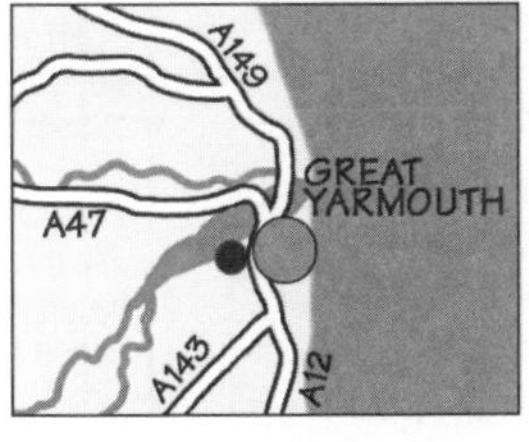

(On the edge of Great Yarmouth)

Take the A47 into Great Yarmouth. At the first roundabout, turn right onto the A12 (signposted Lowestoft). Go to the next roundabout and turn back on yourself (going back towards Yarmouth). In 0.7 miles, turn left and drive down this lane for 0.2 miles to the car park.

Other nearby sites

Breydon Water, RSPB Buckenham Marshes, Burgh Castle, Great Yarmouth, Hardley Flood, NWT Hickling Broad, How Hill NNR, Rockland Broad, RSPB Strumpshaw Fen, Ted Ellis Reserve, Winterton.

Key points

- Reserve open all year.
- Reserve is a designated SSSI.
- Access by permit (members free, £3 for non-members in 2006, under-16s free).
- Visitor centre open daily from April to September (10am-5pm).
- Refreshments available from shop (plus books etc).
- Toilets, including wheelchair access.
- Most of trail is boardwalked. Other paths can get muddy after rain.

HICKLING is a five star reserve, where, at any time of year, you can easily spend a whole day getting good views of several sought-after species. It has recently established itself as the best place to see Bittern in Norfolk, usually in flight but fairly reliable nonetheless. In summer, a trip on the electric boat to the tree tower, Swim Coots and Rush Hill Scrape is a must.

Target birds *All year* – Marsh Harrier (95%), Bearded Tit (65%), Bittern (30%), Cetti's Warbler (hear 50%, see 20%), Crane (5% on reserve, 50% in general area). *Winter* – Smew (35%), raptors (25%). *Summer* – Hobby (80%), Avocet (60%), Garganey (50%), Grasshopper Warbler (hear 45%, see 20%).

Other possible bird species

All year
Great Crested Grebe
Little Grebe
Cormorant
Common wildfowl
Sparrowhawk
Kestrel
Woodcock
Common gull species
Barn Owl
Tawny Owl
Kingfisher
Green Woodpecker
Great Spotted Woodpecker
Sky Lark
Meadow Pipit
Pied Wagtail
Marsh Tit
Jay
Other corvids
Redpoll
Common finches
Reed Bunting

Summer
Little Gull
Yellow-legged Gull
Common Tern
Turtle Dove
Cuckoo
Hirundines
Sedge Warbler
Reed Warbler
Lesser Whitethroat
Whitethroat
Garden Warbler
Blackcap
Chiffchaff
Willow Warbler

Spring/autumn
Slavonian Grebe
Black-necked Grebe
Little Ringed Plover
Ringed Plover
Little Stint
Curlew Sandpiper
Dunlin
Ruff
Greenshank
Green Sandpiper
Wood Sandpiper
Common Sandpiper
Little Gull
Black Tern
Yellow Wagtail

Winter
Goldeneye
Winter thrushes

Occasional
Savi's Warbler

Background information and birding tips

HICKLING is my favourite Broadlands reserve because it never fails to deliver a great day of nature watching.

All trails start at the visitor centre. From there you have a choice of several paths and all can produce the goods. Any patch of thick cover on the reserve may hold a Cetti's Warbler or two; listen out for their explosive song. In summer, it is worth booking a boat trip in a traditional 'reed lighter' from the visitor centre upon your arrival. This warden-guided trip explores areas not normally open to visitors and is well worth the cost. There is nothing more pleasant on a hot day than cruising along the channels with the wind rustling the reeds and your hair (if, unlike me, you have any to rustle).

My normal summer route starts along the Bittern trail, accessed

ALL YEAR | OS MAP 134 | TG 427221

Access details

(Approx. 13 miles NE of Norwich)

From Great Yarmouth head N towards North Walsham on A149. About one mile N of Potter Heigham turn right at the signpost to Hickling.

Follow to Hickling Green, then turn right at Greyhound pub (following brown tourist signs with a duck logo). Turn left about 300 yards past the pub, still following the brown duck signs. This leads down to the Norfolk Wildlife Trust's car park, about 1.5 miles from the pub.

To view Rush Hill scrape from The Weaver's Way footpath, park at Potter Heigham Church (TG 419199). This is reached by turning right (if approaching from Yarmouth) off the A149 down Station Road (sign-posted Village Hall & Church).

After 0.2 miles, turn right at the T junction (School Road and Church Road). The church is 0.4 miles on the left. Park on the grass in front of the church.

Walk up the lane, keeping the church on your right side. After 100 yards, turn right along a farm track, marked by a wooden footpath sign. After 75 yards, bear left down a wide, uneven, grassy path. At the bottom of this path is a wood. Go through the wood (over a stile), cross a wooden bridge and climb some wooden steps. This brings you onto The Weaver's Way footpath. Turn right, go through a gate after 200 yards and the public hide is about 250 yards after this gate.

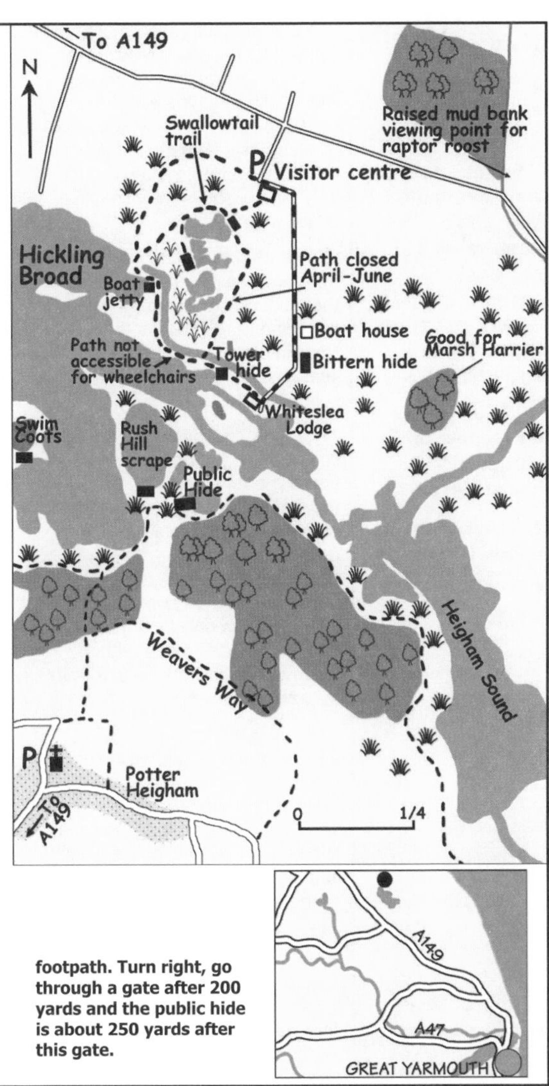

from the road immediately behind the visitor centre. It wends its way along a wide, sandy track to the Bittern hide (don't mistake the small boathouse for the hide as you will get your feet wet and see nothing)!

Along the way you should already have ticked off Reed, Sedge and Willow Warblers as well as Chiffchaff, Whitethroat and Reed Bunting and most probably Bearded Tit in the trackside reeds.

Key points

• Most hides are wheelchair-friendly.

• Summer boat trips available May 18 to September 15 but booking essential (only way of reaching Swim Coots and Rush Hill Scrape).

• Free use of binoculars on board the boat.

• A telescope would be useful.

• Close all gates.

• No dogs.

Contacts

The Warden, Hickling Broad National Nature Reserve, Stubb Road, Hickling, Norfolk NR12 0BW. 01692 598276.

Norfolk Wildlife Trust 01603 625540 www.wildlifetrusts.org.uk/norfolk

The Bittern hide (fully wheelchair-accessible) overlooks reeds that are good for Marsh Harriers, as well as Bitterns. The harriers are usually near the trees at the back of the marsh. Be patient if you definitely want to see a Bittern: they usually show every couple of hours or so!

While you are waiting, look out for dragonflies on the pond and there should be several Hobbies patrolling the sky above the dead trees in the distance (in recent years more than ten birds have been recorded).

The track continues to Whiteslea Lodge which is strictly private and is the summer home of the Cadbury family. Bear right onto a rough grass path, which runs through bushes to the Observation Tower. This path is not yet wheelchair accessible – surely it can only be a matter of time before NWT join it with the boardwalk to make a circular route for wheelchair users.

From the tower you will get a good overview of the reeds and marsh but it is impossible to sit at the windows unless your legs are less than six inches long! You will get a good overview of the reeds and marsh, excellent for Marsh Harrier and Bearded Tit.

Where the rough grass path joins the boardwalk of the Swallowtail Trail, there is a short boardwalk leading to a viewing platform complete with viewing screen, which offers a chance to scan Hickling Broad for waterfowl such as Tufted Duck, Great Crested Grebe, Mute Swan, Grey Heron, etc.

This is also a superb place to linger awhile to see what pops up. In one particular July I had a pair of Marsh Harriers food-passing, an adult Bearded Tit feeding a juvenile and a swallowtail butterfly all in the same field of view.

If you wish to go on a boat trip, they leave from a jetty near this boardwalk. This costs about £7.50 but is well worth the money. On your trip, you will visit the Tree Tower, which is a metal structure giving superb views of the whole reserve. You should see Marsh Harrier from here but sufferers of vertigo should stay on solid ground.

On the boat trip, you will next visit either Swim Coots or Rush Hill Scrape. These parts of Hickling are similar in that you reach them via narrow, reed-fringed channels, good for Reed Warblers, swallowtail butterflies, Norfolk hawker dragonflies, etc. They each have a single, thatched hide overlooking a scrape. Both are good places to see Marsh Harrier, Garganey, Teal, Avocet, Yellow-legged Gull, Little Gull, breeding Black-headed Gull, Reed Warbler, Sedge Warbler, Reed Bunting, etc.

The scrapes are also excellent places to encounter passage waders such as Little Stint and Green, Wood, Common and Curlew Sandpipers in both spring and autumn. The boat runs from mid May to mid September and in 2005 cost £7.50 for adults and £4.50 for children (with a reduction for NWT members). Check with the visitor centre for details but prior booking is strongly advised, if not essential.

Rush Hill scrape can be viewed from the Weaver's Way public footpath, accessed from Potter Heigham Church (see Access Section). A basic hide affords satisfactory views and sightings (among other things!) are sometimes chalked on the hide walls. A telescope is useful here.

Back on the main reserve, the boardwalk continues to the visitor centre, thus completing a circular route. Along the way, you may wish to visit one or both of the hides overlooking the pools (both of which are fully wheelchair-accessible) for the chance of more waders, usually the same range of species encountered on the boat trip.

Patience should reward you with views of a secretive Bearded Tit.

Alternatively, from the jetty, you could retrace your steps towards the tower, then cut across a narrow grass path off to your left (closed April-June). This cuts through the marsh back to the hides and visitor centre.

In winter, the Hickling area is renowned for its raptors. These are best seen from the Stubb Mill roost (see Stubb Mill site page 186) but may be encountered anywhere on the reserve. By day, Hen Harriers, Merlins, Marsh Harriers and Peregrines patrol the extensive marshes and dunes in the area, spreading from Sea Palling in the north to Haddiscoe Marshes to the south. This means that they can be very elusive during the day but come in to roost about an hour before dark every evening.

The summer walk described above can seem quiet in winter but Bearded Tits should still show well during windless days. Cetti's Warblers sing occasionally when it is sunny and Bitterns sometimes fly over the reeds to new feeding areas. If the pools are frozen, Bitterns may be seen feeding out in open areas and the Bittern hide is a very good place to watch from in these conditions.

Cranes are resident in the Hickling area but they are best seen at dusk from Stubb Mill or in fields around the Horsey Mere area. You may see one or two flying over Hickling reserve, usually betraying their presence by their evocative '*cronk, cronk*' calls.

In recent winters, NWT Hickling Broad has hosted one or two Smew among the common wildfowl. The Broad should be scanned for Tufted Duck, Goldeneye, Teal, Gadwall, Mallard, Pochard, Shoveler and the occasional Ruddy Duck.

If you are unlucky, this place can seem very deserted, especially in winter but patience is usually rewarded with some very good birds at all times of year.

For me this is a fantastic reserve, not only for birds but also for people and other wildlife. The whole place abounds with animals, plants and insects, making it a 'must visit' place for the all-round naturalist.

A visit to Hickling will not produce all the target species (unless you are very lucky) but there is always something to see.

Other nearby sites

NWT Barton Broad, Breydon Water, RSPB Buckenham Marshes, NWT Buxton Heath, NWT Cockshoot Broad, Great Yarmouth Beach, Great Yarmouth Cemetery, Horsey area, How Hill NNR, Rockland Broad, Stubb Mill, NWT Upton Fen, Winterton Dunes.

HOLKHAM HALL

Key points

- **Terrain is mostly level, mainly on muddy tracks. Some Tarmac roads on the estate.**
- **Deer Park is open daily 7am - 7pm in summer, (6pm in winter), closed Christmas Day.**
- **Only limited access to other parts of the grounds – remain on designated routes.**
- **Facilities on site include toilets, a pottery, a café (open from Easter) and a public house.**
- **Free parking.**
- **Wheelchair access along the estate roads. Woodland paths may be too muddy, especially in winter.**

IN THIS large country estate (25,000 acres) – just like those seen in Merchant/Ivory films – a beautiful wood surrounds a lake, which is good for waterfowl, especially in winter. There are plenty of common birds to see all year round and Holkham is the best place in the county to see Lesser Spotted Woodpecker, Tawny Owl and Nuthatch.

Target birds

All year – Tawny Owl (winter best, 80%), Lesser Spotted Woodpecker (25%), Brambling (25%).

Other possible bird species

All year
Great Crested Grebe
Little Grebe
Cormorant
Egyptian Goose
Other common wildfowl
Common waterbirds
Sparrowhawk
Kestrel
Woodcock
Red-legged Partridge
Grey Partridge
Lapwing
Common gull species
Stock Dove
Barn Owl
Green Woodpecker
Great Spotted Woodpecker
Sky Lark
Meadow Pipit
Common scrub birds
Goldcrest
Marsh Tit
Nuthatch
Treecreeper
Common woodland birds
Jay
Other corvids

Winter
Pink-footed Goose
Goldeneye
Grey Wagtail
Winter thrushes

Summer
Hobby
Cuckoo
Summer warblers
Spotted Flycatcher

Passage
Honey Buzzard
Goshawk
Redstart
Wood Warbler
Pied Flycatcher

Occasional
Hawfinch

Background information and birding tips

THIS USED to be the best site to see Hawfinches but reports of this declining species are now few and far between (one or two were reported in the winter of 2005-6). Having said that, Holkham is still an excellent place to see woodland species difficult to locate in other parts of the county.

At the north gate, before you even enter the estate grounds, you will see Blue and Great Tits, Robins, Dunnocks and Blackbirds. Stand for a few moments at the Gatekeeper's Cottage where you will almost certainly get outstanding views of a Nuthatch or two on the bird table or on the walls around the gates.

Once through the gates, walk west (right) along a muddy track, checking the gardens to your right for Marsh Tit and other more common woodland species. It shouldn't be long before a Great Spotted Woodpecker makes its presence known with its '*chick*' alarm call.

Follow this track down to the Earl Of Leicester monument (TF 884436), checking the trees and leaf litter for birds as you go. In winter, a small number of Bramblings can sometimes be found among the Chaffinches and Greenfinches rummaging about in the dead leaves below the mature trees in this wood. Careful attention to the tree trunks should produce a Treecreeper or two and

Long-tailed Tits and Goldcrests will be active in the bushes and trees.

In winter, Holkham Hall has become renowned for its roosting Tawny Owls. At the monument, the muddy track becomes a grass path. Look along this track to a large, flat-topped cedar tree a few yards down on the right. This is the roost site for the owls. They can be extremely difficult to locate but usually sit near the top just to the right of the thick branch curving off to the right. The Tawny Owls breed in the park but are difficult to locate during the breeding season.

After finding the owls, keep on the grass track to the lake. You are guaranteed to see Egyptian and Greylag Geese here, plus other common wildfowl (Tufted Duck, Pochard, Mallard etc). In winter, these are joined by Goldeneye, one or two Pink-footed Geese and maybe one of the rarer grebes if you are lucky. You can follow the path through Holkham Hall to the south.

Lesser Spotted Woodpeckers are seen regularly in the park but they are easiest to find in March when they display among the leafless trees. Listen for their drumming and watch out for their amazing, fluttering display flight. The area around the monument is particularly good. Green Woodpeckers also frequent the woods.

Woodcock are present in the park grounds in excellent numbers but seeing one involves looking over the woods at dusk. You may come across one skulking in the leaf litter but this is unlikely!

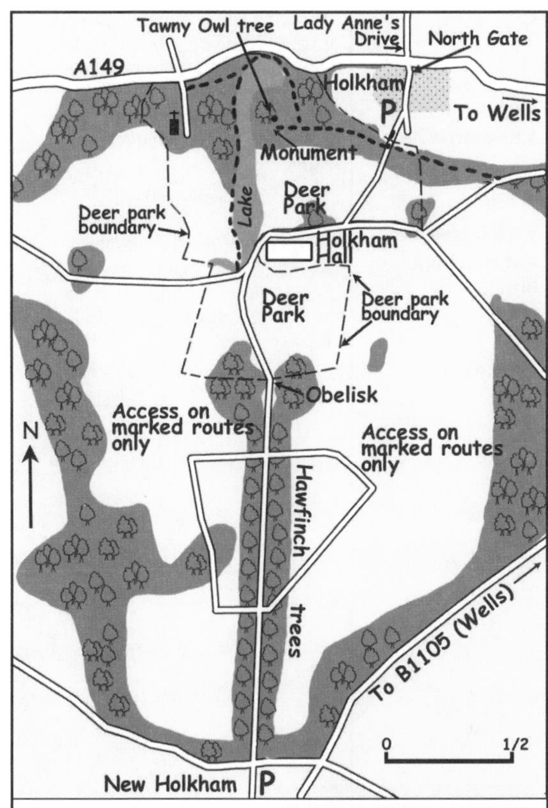

Access details

(Approx. 12 miles E of Hunstanton).

Holkham Hall's northern entrance is sign-posted off A149 between Burnham Overy Staithe and Wells-Next-The-Sea. Turn off main road to the signed car park. This is free but can be muddy in winter. Walk S (right) along access road through the estate's main gates.

My most productive walk is on the muddy track W to the lake through an area of mature woodland.

To enter the estate from the south, turn onto B1105 (sign-posted Fakenham) from A149 at western end of Wells. Take first turn-off right (after 1.1 miles) and follow for 1.7 miles to entrance gate at New Holkham. Park carefully and walk on estate roads only.

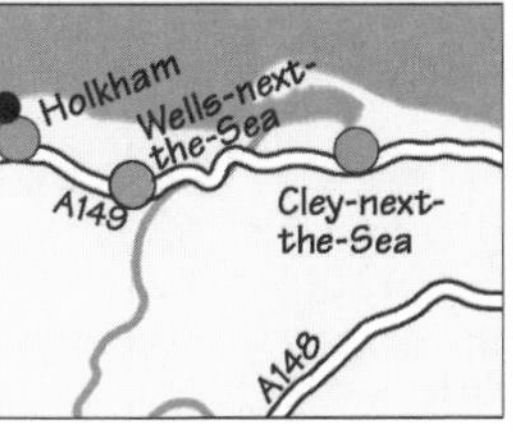

Key points

- **Can get busy with tourists in summer.**
- **Early morning is best.**
- **Also visit the ancient house and garden centre.**

Contacts

The Site Manager
Hill Farm Office
Main Road,
Holkham,
Wells-next-the-Sea,
Norfolk NR23 1AB
(01328) 711183.

Email: nature.reserve
@holkham.co.uk
www.holkham.co.uk

In spring and summer, the woods are alive with bird activity. Summer warblers join the resident species and, if you are lucky, you might find a Pied Flycatcher, Redstart or Wood Warbler during spring migration times.

Blackcap, Willow Warbler, Chiffchaff and Whitethroat all breed on site. Another delightful summer visitor to the estate is Spotted Flycatcher; listen out for their call which sounds like a squeaky wheelbarrow.

On the lake, Great Crested Grebe, Mallard, Coot, Moorhen, Greylag Goose, Tufted Duck and Egyptian Goose should all be encountered at this time of year.

The south side of the park is usually the least disturbed by people and is now the most likely area to look for Hawfinch. Most of the species mentioned above should also be in evidence. Be aware though that public access is strictly limited to connected roads in this area of the park.

Holkham Hall is a stronghold of Egyptian Goose, which is now firmly established as a British breeding bird.

Other nearby sites

Blakeney Point, NWT Cley Marshes, Holkham NNR, Kelling Quags, Kelling Heath, Salthouse Beach, Salthouse Heath, Swanton Novers, NOA Walsey Hills, Wells Woods.

HOLKHAM PINES NNR

THOUGH it is a huge site, comprising several habitats, each with its own special birds, Holkham is easy to cover. The marsh is a goose hotspot in winter, affording close encounters with White-fronted and Pink-footed Geese. The saltings are a regular site for wintering Shore Larks and Snow Buntings and several raptor species pass through on a regular basis. The pines and dunes are a migrant magnet in spring and autumn, with many scarce breeding birds present on the marsh in summer.

Target birds

All year – Little Egret (90%), Marsh Harrier (90%), Barn Owl (40%). *Winter* – Pink-footed Goose (99%), White-fronted Goose (95%), Shore Lark (80%), seaduck (80%), raptors (Hen Harrier, Merlin, Peregrine - 30%), Bearded Tit (60%), Snow Bunting (90%), divers (50%), Twite (>15%). *Spring/autumn* – Passage migrants.

Other possible bird species

All year
Little Grebe
Egyptian Goose
Shelduck
Sparrowhawk
Kestrel
Lapwing
Snipe
Woodcock
Redshank
Water Rail
Grey Partridge
Red-legged Partridge
Tawny Owl
Green Woodpecker
Great Spotted Woodpecker
Sky Lark
Treecreeper
Jay
Siskin
Redpoll
Reed Bunting

Spring/autumn
Wryneck
Bluethroat
Black Redstart
Redstart
Whinchat
Wheatear
Grasshopper Warbler
Barred Warbler
Firecrest
Red-breasted Flycatcher
Pied Flycatcher

Summer
Spoonbill
Hobby
Terns
Avocet
Common waders
Cuckoo
Hirundines
Spotted Flycatcher

Winter
Brent Goose
Wigeon
Teal
Common waders
Rock Pipit
Stonechat
Winter thrushes
Redpoll

Occasional
Bean Goose
Barnacle Goose
Crossbill

Background information and birding tips

THOUGH Holkham National Nature Reserve (owned by the Earl of Leicester and the Crown Estates and managed by English Nature and Holkham Estate) is an excellent site for all kinds of nature, it is also popular with humans too. However, once on the reserve in summer it is easy to get away from the crowds as they are more interested in the beach than the marsh, which is overlooked by a hide.

In winter, Holkham is a superb place to encounter wild geese at close range. Slowly cruise down

Key points

- **English Nature reserve, open at all times (gates close at 9pm on Fridays and Saturdays in summer).**
- **Two hides, wheelchair access to one, plus two viewing platforms on sea side of dunes.**
- **Parking fee may be charged (£3 in Jan 2006).**
- **Tracks and boardwalks are flat. Saltings only reached across a beach, wet mud and vegetation. Paths in woods can be narrow and steepish.**
- **Leaflet available from dispenser in car park.**

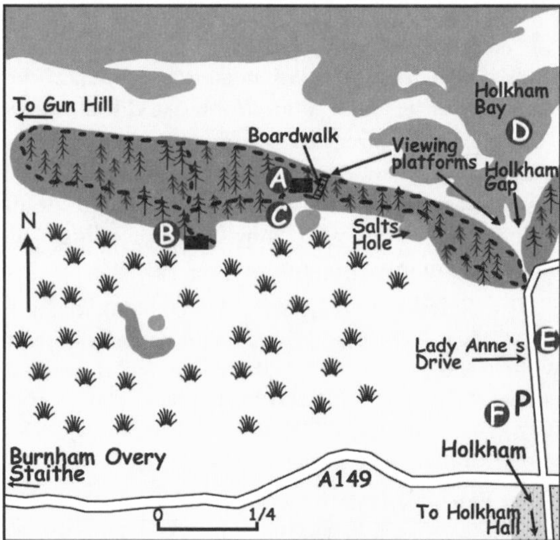

Key

A - George Washington Hide
B - Joe Jordan Hide
C - Meols House
D - Snow Bunting area at low tide.
E & F - Fields for geese

Holkham
Wells-next-the-Sea
A149
Cley-next-the-Sea
A148

Access details

(Approx. 13.5 miles E of Hunstanton).

From A149 between Burnham Overy Staithe and Wells-Next-The-Sea, turn down Lady Anne's Drive towards the sea (opposite the brown tourist sign to the Pottery and Holkham Hall). Parking is permitted all along this road, on the verges. Park at the bottom and follow the boardwalk to the Gap or turn left along a sandy track to the hides. For this guide, I have classed the sandy track to the right as Wells Woods.

Lady Anne's Drive, scanning the fields either side for geese. Pink-feet seem to prefer the first few fields, while the White-fronts seem to favour the fields at the far end. Either way, watch the birds from your car as they can easily be spooked.

Scan the goose flocks carefully, as regular interminglers include Barnacle, Bean, Greylag and Egyptian Geese, while Lesser White-fronted, small race Canada and Red-breasted are also possibilities for the alert birder. Among the geese will be large numbers of Wigeon.

For those birdwatchers who like hides, wander left at the gate at the bottom of Lady Anne's Drive. The sandy track will take you to the George Washington hide, where you can 'scope the geese and Wigeon flocks on the marsh. The pools here will also hold common ducks such as Mallard, Gadwall, Pochard, Shoveler, Teal and Tufted Duck. Also look out for common waders such as Curlew, Golden Plover, Lapwing, Snipe, Redshank etc.

At the rear of Washington Hide is a boardwalk that leads to a viewing platform. This overlooks the saltings and provides the best place for wheelchair users to sit and scan for Snow Bunting, Shore Lark and Twite.

There is always the possibility of a raptor flying over the marsh too. Regular species include Peregrine, Merlin, Hen Harrier, Kestrel and Sparrowhawk, with Barn Owl and Short-eared Owl also possible. The reeds near the hide are the haunt of Bearded Tits in winter but they can be elusive.

From the Washington hide, walk either along a boardwalk to the beach, then turn right back to Holkham Gap for the winter finches, larks and buntings (see below) or continue on past Meols House to the Joe Jordan hide.

At the point where the main track turns into a grass path, turn left down a very narrow path through the bracken, to the Jordan hide. Access is up steep steps, so it is not suitable for wheelchair users.

This hide also looks out over Holkham Marsh but at a slightly different angle. Look straight out from here and you will see a raised, grassy ridge. This is the remains of an Iron Age Fort. Beyond the ridge is a small pool with a dead tree at one end. This tree should hold several Little Egrets and Cormorants.

In recent winters Holkham Gap has become a reliable site to see Shore Larks and Snow Bunting but Twite have been very scarce. Their feeding area is reached from the car park by walking along the boardwalk straight ahead to the beach (about 300 yards). There is a viewing platform here but the birds tend to be further out in the short vegetation that is uncovered when the tide retreats.

Head right from the boardwalk along the beach/mud (you can walk as far as Wells Harbour if you wish) and scan the area. Wheelchair users may scan the saltings from this viewing platform, though the birds will almost certainly be too far away to identify! Also note that sand may have blown over the boardwalk making wheelchair access to the platform difficult.

Walking boots or Wellingtons are recommended as you may need to walk across the saltings to find the birds. I am not advocating flushing these flocks but if you wander a few yards then scan, wander and scan, then you should get good views without disturbing the birds. The Snow Buntings and Shore Larks will be so busy feeding that if you stay still they will probably edge closer to you.

Other common birds here can include Greenfinch, Goldfinch, Meadow Pipit, Sky Lark and Pied Wagtail and you should also see a Rock Pipit or two. Raptors such as Peregrine and Merlin regularly sweep across the saltings in pursuit of the feeding birds.

If you walk to the raised grassy dune at the back of the saltings you can obtain reasonable views of winter seabirds such as Red-breasted Merganser, Eider, Goldeneye, Great Crested Grebe, Slavonian Grebe, etc. In January 2002, more than 10,000 Common Scoters were seen here; 2006 produced Long-tailed Ducks, all three diver species and a couple of Red-necked Grebes. A King Eider has also overwintered. Waders such as Dunlin, Sanderling, Turnstone, etc. should also be encountered in the saltings and on the beach.

In summer, Holkham Gap is of very little interest as the area is badly disturbed by beach-loving holiday makers. I suggest you walk left along the sandy track from the car park to the hides. Along the track, you will get good views of Wren, Long-tailed Tit, Blackbird, Blackcap, Whitethroat, Willow Warbler, Chiffchaff, etc.

Always check the first pond on your left as a pair of Little Grebes is usually present. In the reeds and scrub by the hide you should see Reed and Sedge Warblers and maybe even a Bearded Tit. The pools hold breeding ducks such as Gadwall, Tufted Duck, Shoveler and Pochard as well as Coot and Moorhen.

Marsh Harriers regularly hunt over the marsh but these

Key points

- **Bike parking rails behind Washington Hide and at Holkham Gap viewing platform.**
- **Telescope very useful.**
- **Use insect repellent in summer.**
- **Do not touch any strange objects on the beach – unexploded missiles turn up occasionally.**

Contacts

English Nature
01603 620558

Site Manager
01328 711183

can give closer views from the Jordan hide. Avocets, Lapwings, Redshanks, Snipe, Shelduck, Oystercatchers, Sky Larks, Yellow Wagtails etc can all be seen on the marsh but can be distant. Large numbers of Swifts, Swallows and House Martins hunt over the pools, sometimes swooping over you along the path. Hobbies sometimes hunt here too. Holkham marsh has become a regular haunt of Spoonbills in summer though of course they cannot be guaranteed.

While non-birders are building sand castles on the pristine beach, you can watch Sandwich, Common and Little Terns fishing in the sea. The latter species sometimes nest on the beach, so watch out for any fenced-off areas. However, most seem to have moved to Gun Hill to the west, a long walk along the beach for humans but a mere minute's flight for a tern!

In spring and autumn, the woods and dunes hold the greatest attraction. These areas attract migrants freshly arrived from the continent. Regular spring arrivals include Whinchat, Wheatear, Ring Ouzel, Goldcrest and various warblers.

Autumn seems to be the best time to find Pied Flycatchers, Wood Warblers and Redstarts in the woods, along with some scarcer visitors such as Firecrest, Red-breasted Flycatcher and Yellow-browed Warbler.

This is a (if not *the*) prime site for Pallas's Warbler. These Siberian jewels usually join up with roving tit flocks. These flocks follow circuits through the woods so, rather than following the birds, stay in one place and wait for them to come to you. Meols House is a good spot.

Wrynecks are relatively frequent visitors to the dunes. Rarities include Dusky and Radde's Warblers and Britain's one and only Red-breasted Nuthatch! There is often an influx of continental Jays in autumn as well as Woodcock.

There are many paths criss-crossing the woods and dunes, which offer the visiting birdwatcher ample opportunity to find their own special birds at migration time. Please stick to these paths though, as the dunes and woods are home to other rare and scarce wildlife such as the natterjack toad.

Winter may bring an influx of Redpolls, mainly lessers, into Holkham Pines.

Other nearby sites

All year - Blakeney Point, NWT Cley Marshes, Holkham Hall, NWT Holme Dunes, NOA Holme Observatory, RSPB Titchwell Marsh, NOA Walsey Hills.

Summer - Kelling Heath, Salthouse Heath , Swanton Novers.

Spring/autumn - Wells Woods, Weybourne.

NORFOLK WILDLIFE TRUST'S Holme Dunes reserve is one of the best places in Norfolk to find your own rare, scarce and common migrants in spring and autumn. It is also the best place in the county to see Barn Owl throughout the year, Long-tailed Duck in winter and Lesser Whitethroat in summer. It could take you a whole day to cover this site properly, especially at migration times.

Key points

- Open 10am – 5pm every day except Christmas Day.
- Visitor centre open 10am – 5pm from Easter to October & weekends from Nov – March
- Permit needed (NWT members free, non-members £2.50 in 2005).
- Reserve is a designated SSSI.
- Public footpath along dunes open at all times.
- Toilets at the start of rough access track.
- The visitor centre sells books, snacks and drinks (no toilet here).
- Three hides on Holme Marsh.
- Four hides at eastern end of main reserve.

Target birds *All year* – Barn Owl (85%). *Summer* – Black-tailed Godwit (90%), Avocet (80%), Little Tern (75%), Lesser Whitethroat (60%). *Spring/autumn* – Passage migrants, passage waders. *Winter* – Long-tailed Duck (60%), Snow Bunting (50%).

Other possible bird species

All year
Little Grebe
Great Crested Grebe
Fulmar
Cormorant
Sparrowhawk
Kestrel
Oystercatcher
Little Egret
Lapwing
Ringed Plover
Turnstone
Tawny Owl
Great Spotted Woodpecker
Sky Lark
Meadow Pipit
Pied Wagtail
Goldcrest
Nuthatch
Treecreeper
Corvids
Bullfinch
Reed Bunting

Summer
Hobby
Terns
Cuckoo
Hirundines
Sedge Warbler
Reed Warbler
Whitethroat
Blackcap
Grasshopper Warbler
Other warblers
Spotted Flycatcher

Spring/autumn
Garganey
Shearwaters
Gannet
Little Ringed Plover
Little Stint
Ruff
Whimbrel
Greenshank
Green Sandpiper
Wood Sandpiper
Common Sandpiper
Skuas
Kittiwake
Terns
Auks
Long-eared Owl
Wryneck
Richard's Pipit
Tawny Pipit
Yellow Wagtail
Redstart
Whinchat
Wheatear
Ring Ouzel
Winter thrushes
Barred Warbler
Yellow-browed Warbler
Firecrest
Red-breasted Flycatcher
Pied Flycatcher
Red-backed Shrike

Winter
Divers
Grebes
Brent Goose
Wigeon
Teal
Common Scoter
Velvet Scoter
Goldeneye
Red-breasted Merganser
Merlin
Peregrine
Hen Harrier
Short-eared Owl
Golden Plover
Grey Plover
Knot
Stonechat
Winter thrushes
Siskin

Access details

(Approx. two miles NE of Hunstanton).

From Hunstanton head E and take the next left turn off A149, (sign-posted NOA Watchpoint/ NNT Reserve). After about half a mile turn right onto a rough track just before you reach the toilet block (if you need the facilities, go now as there are none on site). Travel slowly down this track or you will do irreparable damage to your trusty motor. Park on left by the visitor centre (the white house) at the end of the track. The hides are accessed by walking back past the NOA grass car park, the beach is along the footpath through the pines.

HOLME MARSH: **Heading E into Holme on A149 take last turn left before you leave the village (Eastgate Road). Along this road bear right (signed to 'Sunnymead Holiday Park'). Park carefully by the concrete bollards after about 100 yards. Take the kissing gate to your right and follow the obvious path to the three hides overlooking a pool and bushes.**

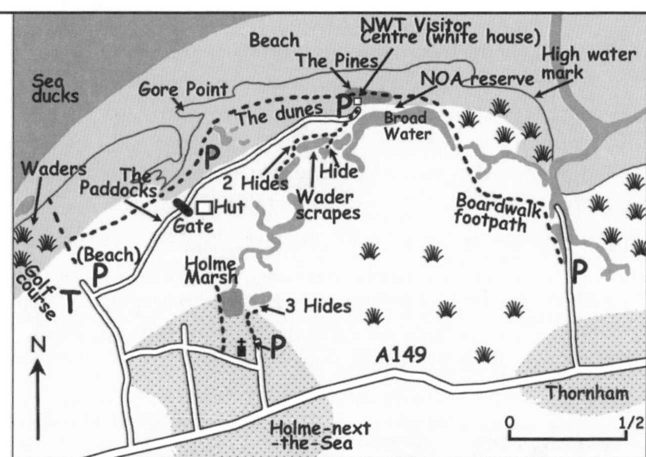

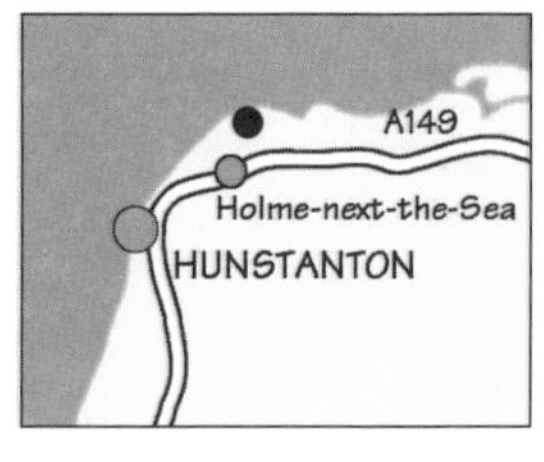

Background information and birding tips

WHERE do you start with a site as good as this? There are numerous access points to view the reserve, all of which produce good birds at most times of year. I will describe several areas including Holme Marsh, Gore Point, The Pines, The Dunes, The Paddocks and the wader scrapes.

Gore Point: This is an excellent place to see seaduck in winter, particularly at high tide. The best way to get there is to park at the toilet block in Holme (£3 in 2005), near the golf course. Walk across the golf course (watch out for stray golf balls and obey all course officials' instructions), through the dunes and onto the beach. Gore Point is to your right. Long-tailed Duck is a speciality here but there may be thousands of Common Scoter on the sea as well.

Directly to the left of the junction of the beach and golf course, a receding tide reveals a small marsh, which is a haven for waders. If you approach quietly and slowly, you will obtain stunningly close views of Knot, Dunlin, Sanderling, Bar-tailed Godwit, etc. Good fieldcraft is needed to avoid disturbing these waders as they busily feed on the saltings.

If you are lucky, you may find the small flock of Snow Buntings on the beach in winter, though these birds roam far and wide. In summer, several species of wader nest on the raised shingle bank by the beach, so take care not to disturb them. Little Terns occasionally nest here too. If they don't, you will still see them out to sea, along with Common and

Sandwich Terns. Please be aware that the tides and currents along this coast have claimed many a life.

The Paddocks: In spring and autumn, head for The Paddocks. Drive along the rough access track and park just past the warden's hut. Walk up the bank onto the dune footpath boardwalk and turn left. After about 100 yards there is a field on your left with many thick bushes scattered around.

Do not enter the Paddocks but view from the perimeter fence. Wait patiently for birds to appear out of the thick cover: possibilities include Barred Warbler, Red-backed Shrike, Redstart, Pied Flycatcher, Turtle Dove, etc. The Paddocks also attract Wheatear in spring and autumn. If you keep walking left, you reach the golf course and dunes, which may hold pipits and larks. Do not trespass onto the golf course, as the budding Tiger Woods become very grumpy.

The dunes: You may follow the boardwalk east from the beach car park all the way to the NWT visitor centre and the area of pines. If you choose to walk, scan the dunes and bushes regularly for anything that moves! Do not stray from the paths as you might trample a natterjack toad or a scarce plant or two. Alternatively, once you have scanned the paddocks, drive down the track and park by the white house at the end which is the NWT visitor centre. The roped-off grass car park on the right is for visitors to the adjoining NOA Holme Observatory site only.

The pines: These are at the back of the NWT visitor centre and attract migrants during spring and autumn. Regular drop-ins include Redstart, Pied, Red-breasted and Spotted Flycatcher, Firecrest and Crossbill. Again, check the surrounding dunes for pipits, larks and Wryneck.

The wader scrapes: These are reached by walking from the NWT visitor centre, past the NOA car park then bearing immediately left down a wheelchair-accessible track. The bushes along here hold Sedge Warblers in summer, along with common scrub birds. The first hide is wheelchair friendly but the path beyond becomes rough grass. The hides overlook a couple of scrapes made famous as the site of the first Norfolk breeding record of Black-winged Stilt.

Spring and autumn should produce a number of species including Greenshank, Whimbrel, Green Sandpiper and Ruff. In summer, you may get very close views of Avocet and Black-tailed Godwit.

Holme Marsh: This is an excellent place to see Barn Owl and Lesser Whitethroat. The three hides (with cushions!) overlook a pool surrounded by bushes, home to Whitethroat, Blackcap, Sedge Warbler and Lesser Whitethroat. The latter species tend to show well from these hides. The large tree to the left of the first hide is a favoured perch of the local Barn Owl.

If you don't see an owl here walk back to the road and follow the public footpath (a rough, wide track) to the right. The path ends at a gate (do not go over the gate) and overlooks several fields, which, with patience, are almost certain to produce a Barn Owl sighting.

Key points

- **Keep dogs on leads.**
- **Boots recommended for Holme Marsh.**
- **Terrain is mainly level along rough tracks, grass paths and boardwalks.**
- **Limited wheelchair access.**
- **Stick to paths at all times to avoid dune erosion.**
- **Unusual sightings at Holme Marsh should be reported to gary.aitch@norfolkwildlifetrust.org.uk (+ sightings books in each hide)**

Contacts

NWT Holme Dunes
The Firs,
Broadwater Road,
Holme-Next-The-Sea,
Norfolk PE36 6LQ
01485 525240

Norfolk Wildlife Trust
01603 625540

Key points

- **SSSI owned by the Norfolk Ornithologists' Association.**
- **Permit required (NOA members free, non-members £3).**
- **If you are visiting both NOA and NWT reserves, you need two permits.**
- **Dawn to dusk access for NOA members (track access gate is unlocked at all times). Non-members 9am - 5pm (best to phone prior to visit to check someone will be on site)**
- **Reserve closed Mondays.**
- **Friendly warden to tell you what is around.**
- **Not wheelchair accessible.**

Contacts

Norfolk Ornithologists' Association
01485 525406

SMALL BUT SUPERB – that's the best way to sum up a seven acre reserve that is particularly good for common, scarce and rare migrants in spring and autumn. A comfortable hide provides a perfect place from which to seawatch throughout the year. This is a good place to find your own migrants as the reserve is small and easy to cover.

Target birds

All year – **Barn Owl (85%), Marsh Harrier (60%).** *Summer* – **Black-tailed Godwit (90%), Avocet (80%).** *Spring/autumn* – **Passage migrants.** *Winter* – **Raptors (25%).**

Other possible bird species

All year
Little Grebe
Great Crested Grebe
Fulmar
Cormorant
Sparrowhawk
Kestrel
Red-legged Partridge
Grey Partridge
Oystercatcher
Lapwing
Tawny Owl
Great Spotted Woodpecker
Goldcrest
Treecreeper
Reed Bunting

Summer
Terns
Cuckoo
Hirundines
Sedge Warbler
Reed Warbler
Whitethroat
Blackcap
Other warblers
Spotted Flycatcher

Spring/autumn
Shearwaters
Gannet
Skuas
Kittiwake
Terns
Auks
Long-eared Owl
Wryneck
Yellow Wagtail
Redstart
Whinchat
Wheatear
Barred Warbler
Yellow-browed Warbler
Firecrest
Red-breasted Flycatcher
Pied Flycatcher
Red-backed Shrike

Winter
Divers
Grebes
Brent Goose
Wigeon
Teal
Goldeneye
Red-breasted Merganser
Hen Harrier
Golden Plover
Grey Plover
Winter thrushes
Siskin

Occasional
Hobby
Grasshopper
Warbler
Merlin
Peregrine
Short-eared Owl

Background information and birding tips

THIS SMALL reserve, the site of Norfolk's only accredited observatory, attracts migrants by the mist net full in spring and autumn. Ringing takes place all year round and you may be lucky to witness birds being ringed at the observatory when you visit.

You should be observant all the way along the access track to the grass car park, as the fields to your right are one of the best places in Norfolk to see Barn Owl at all times of year.

Park in the roped-off grass car park to the right of the track and not by the white house on the left. Follow the Shrike signs to the entrance of the NOA reserve, to the right of the white house. Before doing any more birding, obtain your permit from the Observatory office situated along the only path on the reserve (narrow and uneven).

ALL YEAR **OS MAP 132** **TF 714448**

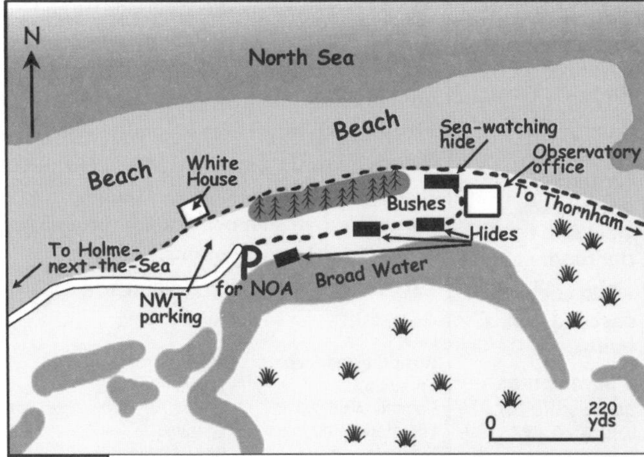

In spring and autumn, a spell in the seawatching hide could prove a profitable starting point, provided you are able to negotiate the steep flight of steps. Obtain a key for this hide from the Observatory office. The best time for seawatching is at high tide when the birds will be much closer. Some of the small pine trees partially block the view in places. At peak seawatching times, the hide can become quite full, so don't fall out (literally!) over the best viewing spot. And don't ignore this hide in winter, as this stretch of coast is excellent for divers and seaduck.

There are also two hides along the footpath to the Observatory office, both overlooking a sheltered 'valley' populated by thick bushes. In spring and autumn, sit quietly in one of these hides and you will be amazed at what pops out of the thick cover. The sun seems to catch this spot in the afternoons and due to the shelter of the surrounding pines, the area is highly attractive to tired migrants. Spend as long here as you can.

The only other hide on the NOA reserve overlooks Broadwater and the marsh beyond. This is a good place to watch breeding waders in spring and summer. Avocet and Black-tailed Godwits are virtually guaranteed at this time of year. In winter, watch out for raptors and wildfowl.

Access details

(Approx. two miles NE of Hunstanton).

From Hunstanton head E on A149 to left turn (sign-posted NOA Watchpoint/NNT Reserve). Continue on this road for about half a mile, then turn right onto a rough track just before you reach the toilet block (note there are no facilities on site). Drive slowly as track is very bumpy.

Pass through the entrance gate to the NWT and NOA reserve, telling the person in the hut you are only visiting the NOA part of Holme. If you intend visiting the NWT part of the reserve, you MUST purchase a separate permit.

Follow the gravel track down to the end and park on the right in the roped-off grass car park. Do not park by the white house unless you have purchased a permit for the NWT reserve.

Broadwater itself holds common wildfowl species and Reed and Sedge Warblers can be seen in the surrounding vegetation in summer. Marsh Harriers quarter the marsh at most times of year.

Other nearby sites

Blakeney Point, NWT Cley Marshes, Holkham NNR, Kelling Quags, Kelling Heath, Salthouse Beach, Salthouse Heath, Swanton Novers, NOA Walsey Hills, Wells Woods.

HORSEY AREA

Key points

- **Owned by the National Trust.**
- **Large pay and display car parks, with other areas viewable from the road.**
- **Mill car park costs £3 per hour.**
- **Some areas accessible for wheelchair users.**
- **Terrain is level but mostly along muddy paths, especially in winter.**
- **Small shop at Horsey Mill for snacks and drinks. Opening hours: Early March-Easter & Oct-Xmas, weekends only; Easter-July, five days a week; July-Oct, seven days a week.**

NOT ONLY is this area one of the best places in Norfolk for raptors, it is also one of the only places in Britain where you might see Cranes during the year. This is a large area to cover, incorporating Horsey Mill, Horsey Mere and Horsey Gap but there is usually much to see.

Target birds

All year – **Marsh Harrier (90%), Crane (60%), Bearded Tit (30%).** *Winter* – **Hen Harrier (50%), Merlin (25%).** *Summer* – **Grasshopper Warbler (hear 60%; see 15%).** *Spring/autumn* – **Passage migrants.**

Other possible bird species

All year
Little Grebe
Great Crested Grebe
Cormorant
Common wildfowl
Common waterbirds
Sparrowhawk
Kestrel
Lapwing
Common waders
Common gull species
Barn Owl
Green Woodpecker
Sky Lark
Meadow Pipit
Pied Wagtail
Stonechat
Jay
Common finches
Reed Bunting

Winter
Divers
Grebes
Seaduck
Bewick's Swan
Whooper Swan
Pink-footed Goose
Winter thrushes

Summer
Hobby
Sandwich Tern
Common Tern
Little Tern
Hirundines
Sedge Warbler
Reed Warbler
Other warblers

Spring/autumn
Shearwaters
Gannet
Skuas
Wryneck
Yellow Wagtail
Ring Ouzel
Redstart
Whinchat
Wheatear
Firecrest
Pied Flycatcher
Red-backed Shrike

Occasional
Short-eared Owl

Background information and birding tips

THOUGH a large area to cover, Horsey can be well worth the effort at any time of year but, as winter is the most exciting from a birdwatching point of view, that's where I will start.

The main targets in winter are raptors and Cranes. The small, resident Crane population roams widely during the day but the birds have several favourite areas. These include the fields around Brograve Farm (TG 444242), Walnut Farm (TG 452246) and Horsey Mill itself.

I have found the best place for Cranes (and raptors) is the pull-in on the right 0.6 miles to the south of Horsey Mill on the B1159. If you wait in your car for a while (the longer the better) you should see Crane, Hen Harrier, Barn Owl and Marsh Harrier and possibly Short-eared Owl and Merlin.

Scan the surrounding fields regularly, as raptors and Cranes appear as if out of thin air and usually vanish just as quickly! If you miss any of the above species during the day, visit Stubb Mill in the evening for almost guaranteed views of them.

Also along this road from Horsey Mill to West Somerton, you may find small numbers of Bewick's or Whooper Swans but I haven't seen any during numerous visits in recent winters. The wintering Pink-footed Goose flock seems to be becoming more elusive too but again, scan the fields thoroughly along the B1159. They are usually seen in flight, either side of the road in the morning and at dusk.

If you fancy stretching your legs, you have a couple of choices. Park in Horsey Mill car park, then cross the main road along the permissive footpath directly to the dunes (a permissive footpath is one that is permitted for use by the owner).

Scan the fields on the way for Cranes and raptors plus winter thrushes, Meadow Pipits, Sky Larks, waders, etc. Once you have reached the dunes, you can walk left or right along the footpath, or down to the sea. Left is to Horsey Gap, right is to Winterton Dunes.

Horsey Gap is good for seaduck such as Long-tailed Ducks, Red-breasted Mergansers, Common and Velvet Scoters, or scarcer grebes such as Slavonian and Red-necked. You should also get reasonable views here of Red-throated Divers.

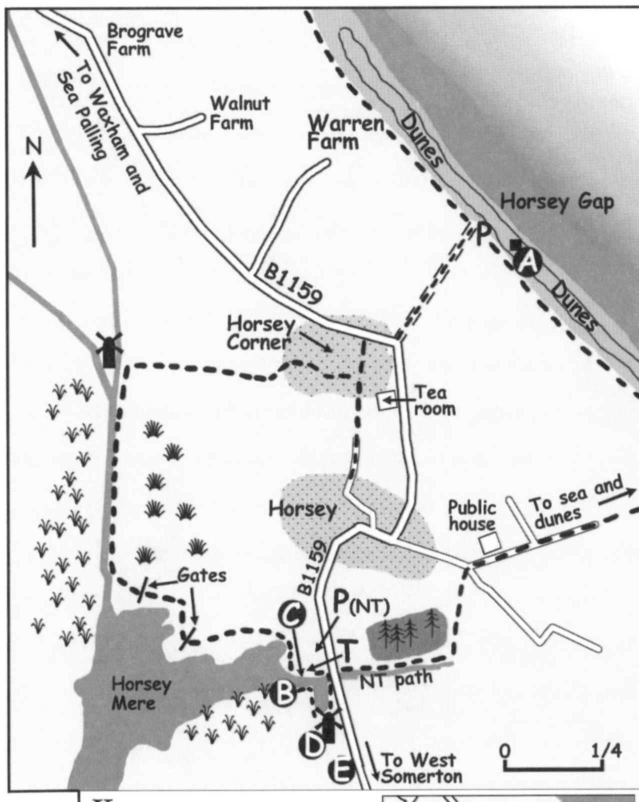

Key

A - Pill box good for Stonechat
B - Viewpoint for wheelchair users
C - Mooring
D - Horsey Mill
E - Lay-by for raptor watching

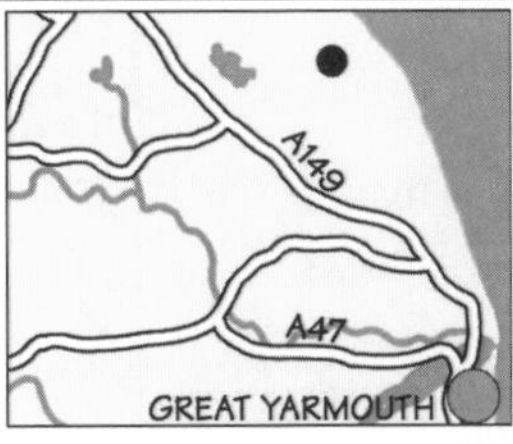

Access details

(Approx. ten miles N of Great Yarmouth).

***HORSEY MILL:* The car park is between Stalham and Martham on B1159, a loop road to the coast off A149 between Great Yarmouth and North Walsham/ Stalham. The main Horsey Mill car park is well sign-posted on brown tourist signs about two miles N of West Somerton.**

***HORSEY GAP:* Exactly one mile N of Horsey Mill car park. Heading N on B1159, there is a sharp left bend with a rough track to the right. This track leads to a large beach car park with access to coast and dunes.**

Key points

- **Mooring for boats small enough to get under Potter Heigham bridge.**
- **Boats for hire in summer from shop at mill.**
- **Telescope recommended.**
- **Footpath map available in shop.**

Contacts

Warden
01493 394961

The National Trust, East Anglia Regional Office
01263 733471

General Broads Authority
01603 610734

Rowing boat hire
01493 393511 (around £10 for half a day).

Along the dune footpath, you will almost certainly encounter one or two handsome Stonechats: the derelict pill box seems to be a favoured perch. A few Snow Buntings may be present on the beach during some winters. Of course, you can also gain access to the coast by parking in the Horsey Gap car park (see Access section) and this may be a wise alternative in bitterly cold weather!

Alternatively, from the mill car park, you can walk past the mill to a viewpoint over the mere and reeds. This is an excellent place for wheelchair users to sit to scan for raptors, Cranes, wildfowl and Bearded Tits. The viewpoint is part of the new 'Easy Access' network of trails. The longer you sit here, the more you will see, with Marsh Harrier being virtually guaranteed.

Across the dyke from the viewpoint is a narrow, muddy footpath running along the northern edge of Horsey Mere, accessed from the mill car park. Along this path, you cross a rough field, before going up a couple of steps to a raised bank. This does not give views over the mere but is a suitable place to wait for raptors and Cranes coming in to roost, though not as good as Stubb Mill.

This footpath continues to Horsey Corner, from where you can get back to the car park by taking either the road, or the dune footpath via Horsey Gap. The choice is yours.

The centre of attention at times of spring and autumn passage will be the dunes (as far south as Winterton and as far north as Sea Palling). I suggest you park in the Horsey Gap car park and explore the dunes and bushes as far as your energy levels allow.

Wheatears are seen regularly, as early as mid to late March, with Ring Ouzels not far behind. Bushes should be scanned for Redstarts, Wrynecks, Pied Flycatchers, Goldcrests, warblers, Whinchats, Tree Pipits, Red-backed Shrikes, etc. Anything is possible, so keep your eyes peeled.

Whimbrels may be passing overhead or stopping off in the fields around the dunes. Marsh Harriers will almost certainly be seen but Hen Harrier sightings drop off during these periods. Barn Owl is another resident species that can still be seen in the fields and dunes at these times.

At sea, the wintering ducks will be departing, being replaced by Little, Sandwich and Common Terns. In autumn, the ducks return and the terns may well be harassed by passing skuas. All four species are recorded annually, though Arctic Skua is the most common. Other possible passage birds at sea include Razorbill, Guillemot,

Other nearby sites

Breydon Water, Burgh Castle, Buxton Heath, NWT Cockshoot Broad, Great Yarmouth Beach, Great Yarmouth Cemetery, NWT Hickling Broad, Haddiscoe Marshes, Halvergate Marshes, NWT Stubb Mill (winter), NWT Ranworth Broad, Winterton Dunes.

Manx and Balearic Shearwaters, Kittiwake and Little Gull.

Summer is probably the quietest time to pay a visit. Marsh Harriers usually show well in the fields across the road from Horsey Mill but the Cranes will be very elusive.

On the mere, Common Terns are very active and noisy and close views can be obtained from a boat (either your Broadland hire boat or from a hired rowing boat – see phone number in contacts section). You may also be lucky enough to see Bearded Tits in the reeds from the viewpoint accessed along the short footpath from Horsey Mill.

Reed and Sedge Warblers are common around the Mere and hirundines sweep across the car park, dodging the visitors as they go. Swallows even nest in the thatched toilet block in the car park. At this time of year they are sometimes pursued by a Hobby or two.

In the dunes, Stonechats are raising their families. Grasshopper Warblers can be heard reeling from nearby bushes but are hard to locate. Whitethroats and Reed Buntings are busily feeding their young and usually show well in the bushes along the dune footpath and around the Horsey Gap car park. At sea, terns are constantly coming and going, while Ringed Plovers trot along the beach. Also look out for grey seals offshore.

The dunes in summer attract a wide range of scarce species of wildlife including grass snake, natterjack toad, emperor dragonfly, Essex skipper and dark green fritillary and also many different varieties of plants. The all-round naturalist could spend the whole day in the dunes area of Horsey alone!

The sheer variety of species to be seen is worth the effort of covering this extensive area. In winter, I tend to drive around, scanning for birds, or pull off and wait for an hour or two at a good vantage point. In times of passage, it can be an exciting place to explore to find your own birds – concentrate on hedgerows and bushes and you may strike lucky.

Cranes should brighten any birding trip to the Horsey area.

Key points

- **Part of Bure Marshes National Nature Reserve.**
- **Can only be reached by boat.**
- **Open April to mid-September, (Sunday to Thursday, 10am - 5pm).**
- **Free admission.**
- **Free temporary mooring for reserve visitors, free 24-hour mooring opposite at Salhouse.**
- **Boat occasionally runs from Salhouse Broad Quay to reserve entrance (£3 adults, £1.50 children in 2005), more details and bookings on 01603 721144.**
- **Fully boardwalked, two hides, both up sets of stairs.**
- **No dogs.**
- **Free binoculars in hides.**
- **Insect repellent advisable.**

Contacts

English Nature, Norfolk Office. 01603 620558.

HOVETON is a small scenic reserve which can only be reached by boat. A variety of common bird species can be seen on a stop-off during your Broadland boating holiday and there are many other attractions to make this a place to recommend for the all-round naturalist.

Target birds

Summer – **Common Tern (May to the end of July, 95%).** *All year* – **Marsh Tit (60%), Marsh Harrier (20%), Lesser Spotted Woodpecker (very secretive here, 1%).**

Other possible bird species

All year
Great Crested Grebe
Cormorant
Common waterfowl
Gadwall
Teal
Other common wildfowl
Kingfisher
Green Woodpecker
Great Spotted Woodpecker
Pied Wagtail
Goldcrest
Long-tailed Tit
Other common woodland birds
Treecreeper
Jay

Summer
Cuckoo
Hirundines
Sedge Warbler
Reed Warbler
Blackcap
Chiffchaff
Willow Warbler

Occasional
Hobby

Background information and birding tips

HOVETON GREAT BROAD is a Site of Special Scientific Interest within the Bure Marshes National Nature Reserve complex. It is managed by English Nature and is a very scenic place to visit when on a Broads boating holiday. While I would not pay £30-plus to hire a boat for the morning to visit this site specifically, as part of a holiday itinerary it is well worth spending an hour here.

Before your visit you can download an excellent reserve pamphlet from the English Nature website (http://www.english-nature.org.uk/about/teams/team_photo/HovetonNatTrail.pdf) detailing the history and ecology of Hoveton.

When you arrive you will find that the numbers on the pamphlet correspond to the markers on the nature trail. This pamphlet is also available at the reserve gate. It is advisable to check opening times before you visit as I have turned up to find the gate locked even though the reserve was supposed to be open!

From the temporary mooring, you enter the reserve through a wooden gate (on the left as you stand with your back to the river). There is usually a warden present to hand out information leaflets and collect your entrance fee. It is then simply a matter of following the boardwalk around the reserve. This passes through a wet wood (alder carr), past a reed-fringed broad and back to the river mooring.

One of the two hides overlooks the broad. Common Terns nest on wooden platforms on the lake and Reed and Sedge Warblers should be seen in the reeds and bushes around the edges of the broad. Common waterfowl and ducks such as Great Crested Grebes, Tufted Ducks and Grey Herons should also be present and it is worth scanning the marsh opposite the hide for Marsh Harriers. Cormorants are likely to be on show and loafing gull species will include Black-headed and Lesser Black-backed Gulls.

The other hide is a good place to see common woodland birds and wildfowl such as Teal and Gadwall.

Numerous common bird species can be found in the woods as well as slightly more scarce species such as Great Spotted Woodpecker, Marsh Tit and Treecreeper. Lesser Spotted Woodpeckers are present at Hoveton but during the period the reserve is open to the public, they are very secretive indeed.

All along the trail are information boards telling you about the creation and management of Hoveton Broad and, better still, there are lots of marked plants for ignoramuses like me.

The reserve is packed with many scarce plants and dragonflies and makes for a very pleasant stroll for an hour or so. If nothing else, it makes a great place to practise your first mooring after collecting your boat from Wroxham and to stretch your legs in beautiful surroundings.

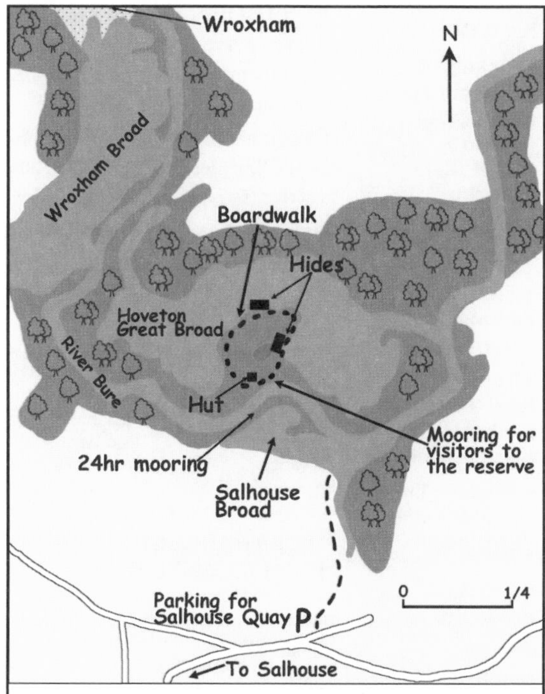

Access details

(Approx 6.5 miles NE of Norwich)

This site can only be reached by boat!

Follow the River Bure E from Wroxham for about 40 minutes. You will pass two entrances to Wroxham Broad on your right and then an obvious mooring site for Salhouse Broad will come into view, also on the right. Immediately opposite the Salhouse mooring is temporary mooring for visitors to Hoveton reserve on the left.

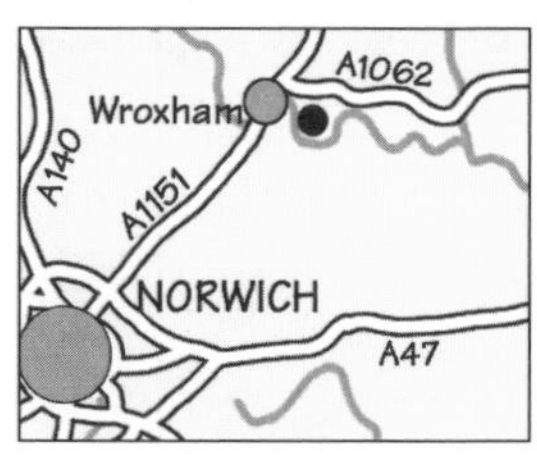

Other nearby sites

Breydon Water, NWT Cockshoot Broad, Great Yarmouth Beach, Hardley Flood, NWT Hickling Broad, Horsey, How Hill NNR, NWT Martham Broad, NWT Ranworth Broad, RSPB Surlingham Church Marshes, Ted Ellis Reserve.

HOW HILL NNR

Key points

- Tickets for trail from Toad Hole Cottage, (80p in 2005), trail leaflet available.
- Free entry to Toad Hole.
- Free car parking & boat mooring
- Terrain is level along muddy paths, some gravelled.
- Walking boots recommended.
- No dogs.
- Toilets available.
- Insect repellent advisable.

Contacts

How Hill, How Hill, Ludham, Great Yarmouth NR29 5PG
Tel. 01692 6788555
www.how-hill.org.uk

General Broads Authority
01603 610734

HIDDEN away in the Norfolk Broads, this superb reserve is easy to visit by boat or car for a very pleasant stroll through mixed habitats. Another Broadland site for the all-round naturalist.

Target birds

Spring/summer/autumn – **Avocet (75%), Cetti's Warbler (hear 55%, see 20%), Bearded Tit (45%), Marsh Harrier (60%), Little Ringed Plover (25%).**

Other possible bird species

Summer

Great Crested Grebe
Shelduck
Other common wildfowl
Common waterbirds
Sparrowhawk
Kestrel
Hobby
Oystercatcher
Lapwing
Snipe
Redshank
Common Tern
Turtle Dove
Cuckoo
Kingfisher
Green Woodpecker
Great Spotted Woodpecker
Sky Lark
Meadow Pipit
Pied Wagtail
Hirundines
Common scrub birds
Sedge Warbler
Reed Warbler
Grasshopper Warbler
Other warblers
Marsh Tit
Long-tailed Tit
Jay
Siskin
Redpoll
Reed Bunting

Occasional

Lesser Spotted Woodpecker

Background information and birding tips

THIS EXCELLENT but often ignored, reserve is run by the How Hill Trust but owned by the Broads Authority. The well-marked circular trail (about one and a half miles long) takes the visitor through many different habitats, each with its own particular bird species.

The car park affords a good overview of Reedham Marshes and it is worth pausing awhile for a glimpse of Marsh Harrier. The large grassy area here is an excellent place for a picnic and for active childrens' games.

Once you have purchased a ticket to enter the reserve from Toad Hole Cottage, the path cuts through a meadow, which is one of the best places in Norfolk to see swallowtail butterflies. Sedge and Reed Warblers sing from the bushes and reeds in this area.

A hide overlooks the Wolfson scrape where Little Ringed Plovers and Avocets sometimes breed and Common Terns occasionally visit. Shelducks breed here, along with common waterfowl such as Mute Swan, Moorhen, Coot etc.

Reed and Sedge Warblers sing from the vegetation on the edges of this scrape from May to August. The bushes are home to the resident, skulking Cetti's Warbler.

Opening times

Trail - open Easter, April, May and October daily 10.30am-5pm. June-Sept daily 9.30am-6pm (tickets from Toad Hole Cottage, 80p in 2005).
Toad Hole Cottage - open Easter, April, May & Oct Mon-Fri 10.30am-1pm & 1.30-5pm. Sat & Sun 10.30am-5pm. June-Sept daily 9.30am-6pm. Free entry.
Wildlife Water Trail - every hour on the hour. April, May & Oct at weekends, Bank Holidays, Easter week & local half term 11.00am-3pm. June-Sept daily 10-5pm (tickets from Toad Hole Cottage, £4 for adults in 2005, £8 for families).

Watch out for Bearded Tits in any stretch of reeds around the reserve.

After the first hide, the trail takes you along a straight, open path. Scan Clayrack Marshes to your left for Marsh Harriers and listen for Grasshopper Warblers reeling. You then reach Crome's Broad, a tranquil lake overlooked by a hide. This is the best place to look for Kingfishers and Common Terns and you will also get close views of common waterbirds. Ospreys and Black Terns may visit this broad on passage.

The trail also passes through a wet woodland (Gale Wood) where you should see Marsh Tits, Willow Warblers, Blackcaps, Chiffchaffs and many species of common birds. Further on, you will pass through an area of larger trees – a good place to see Great Spotted Woodpeckers and Jays.

A recent addition to How Hill's attractions is a 50 minute wildlife boat tour on an electric boat. The tour passes along reed-fringed dykes and is led by an experienced wildlife guide.

The paths can get muddy but there are some boardwalks and more substantial gravel paths for wheelchair users. Some paths are muddy no matter what time of the year you visit, so wheelchair users are strongly advised to contact the Trust before visiting to ensure access is possible.

The Broads Authority has purchased 36ha of land (Buttle Marsh) adjacent to the southern end of the reserve and is managing the area for Bitterns. This can be reached by a footpath from How Hill Staithe (walk downstream).

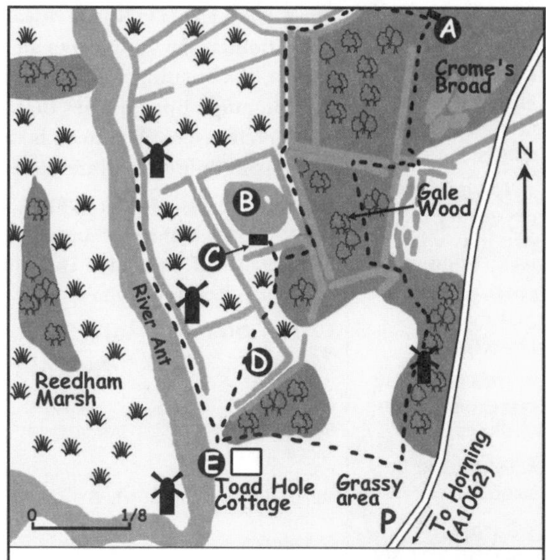

Key

A - Hide
B - Wolfson Scrape
C - Hide
D - Meadow for swallowtail butterflies
E - Mooring

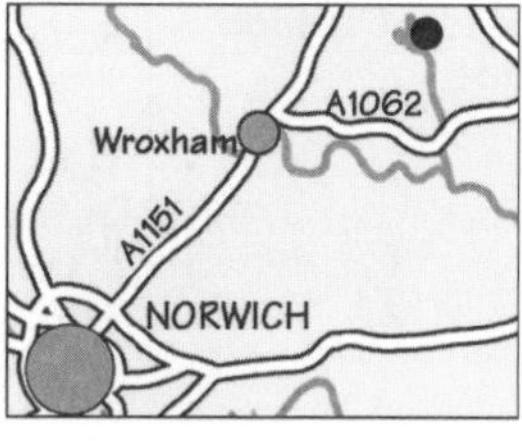

Access details

(Approx. 11 miles NE of Norwich)

***BY CAR:* From Wroxham, take A1062 (sign-posted to Potter Heigham) through Horning towards Ludham. After crossing Ludham bridge (if you reach Ludham village you have gone too far) take left turn (sign-posted Turf Fen).**

Effectively, this involves going straight on down a narrow lane where the A1062 turns sharply right.

Take second turn left, (just after red phone box), sign-posted How Hill. Follow lane to a sign for How Hill Nature Reserve and park in the car park for Toad Hole Cottage.

Walk across the grassed area towards the blue sign (similar to the one at the edge of the grass), then to the cottage to purchase an entry ticket.

***BY BOAT:* Head E from Wroxham on River Bure, then N up River Ant.**

The reserve's mooring is sign-posted on right, just after third windmill (not counting the one at the junction of the Bure and Ant). It is a short walk to Toad Hole Cottage.

HUNSTANTON

Key points

- **Food, toilets and other facilities in town centre.**
- **No walking necessary but you may wish to stroll along the prom or beach (sandy, flat terrain).**
- **Area regularly disturbed by dog walkers.**
- **Telescope useful.**
- **Purple Sandpipers only present at high tide.**

Contacts

Hunstanton Tourist Information, Town Hall
The Green, Hunstanton
Norfolk PE36 6BQ
Tel: 01485 532610
Fax: 01485 533972
Email: hunstanton.tic
@west-norfolk.gov.uk

HUNSTANTON is an ideal place for a birdwatching holiday. In addition to all the facilities you would expect in a bustling resort town, it offers excellent seawatching opportunities that are also accessible to wheelchair users. The town is the best place in Norfolk to see Purple Sandpiper in winter and Fulmar all year round.

Target birds

All year – **Fulmar (95%), Mediterranean Gull (50%).** *Winter* – **Purple Sandpiper (45%), Eider (60%), Common Scoter (40%), Long-tailed Duck (30%), Velvet Scoter (20%).** *Autumn* – **Passage seabirds.**

Other possible bird species

All Year
Cormorant
Oystercatcher
Ringed Plover
Sanderling
Dunlin
Turnstone
Kittiwake
Gull species

Spring/autumn
Shearwaters
Gannet
Skuas
Guillemot
Razorbill

Summer
Tern species

Winter
Divers
Grebes
Brent Goose
Goldeneye
Red-breasted Merganser
Grey Plover
Bar-tailed Godwit

Occasional
Scaup
Snow Bunting

Background information and birding tips

AS A BUSTLING seaside town Hunstanton can be busy at all times of year. Though Fulmars are virtually resident, it is probably only worth viewing them in winter when it is relatively quiet – though even at this time of year dog walkers can disturb the waders on the beach.

My favourite birdwatching position is on the prom at the bottom of the cliff. From this vantage point, except for a short period from mid September to late October, it is possible to sit in your car and scope the sea while Fulmars fly overhead. From the sea wall here you also get a good overview of the beach and rocks.

In winter if you wish, you can walk north along the beach for the chance of Snow Buntings (irregular visitors), or south where the groynes are renowned for roosting Purple Sandpipers around the jet-ski ramp at high tide. Also check the beach around the ramp for loafing Mediterranean Gulls. When the tide is out, Brent Geese feed among the rocks on the beach under the cliffs.

Alternatively, you may view the sea from the top of the cliffs by parking on the road near the lighthouse. This has the advantage of giving the viewer height to see birds at longer range and the shelters can afford less hardy seawatchers a degree of, well, shelter.

The number and variety of sea-duck varies from year to year but there is usually something out there. Red-breasted Mergansers,

Goldeneyes, Great Crested Grebes and Eider are the commonest species and up to 3,000 Common Scoters can range from here to Titchwell. Look out for the white wing-flashes of the scarce Velvet Scoters in among their cousins. Long-tailed Duck used to be very regular here but I haven't been as successful in recent years. The grass area by the shelters can be good for close views of Oystercatchers and Turnstones. Snow Buntings sometimes frequent the large grass car park by the lighthouse.

In spring and autumn, check the bushes around the golf course for migrants but **do not trespass on the course itself**.

Hunstanton is always worth visiting on the way to other more illustrious sites to see if there is anything around. In autumn, especially in strong onshore winds, you may be rewarded with sightings of one or more species of skua (Great and Arctic being the most common) or Manx, Balearic and Sooty Shearwaters. If nothing else, you will usually get fantastic views of Fulmars.

Hunstanton provides a good base for a birding trip. Members of the Hawaiian tourist board were so impressed during a visit to the town that they now recommend all Hawaiians pay a visit to "this beautiful place"! And who am I to argue?

Other nearby sites

Brancaster Marsh, Dersingham Bog, Gypsy Lane, NWT Holme Dunes, NOA Holme Observatory, Ken Hill Wood, King's Lynn Docks, NOA Redwell Marsh, Sandringham, RSPB Snettisham, RSPB Titchwell Marsh, Wolferton Triangle, Snettisham Coastal Park.

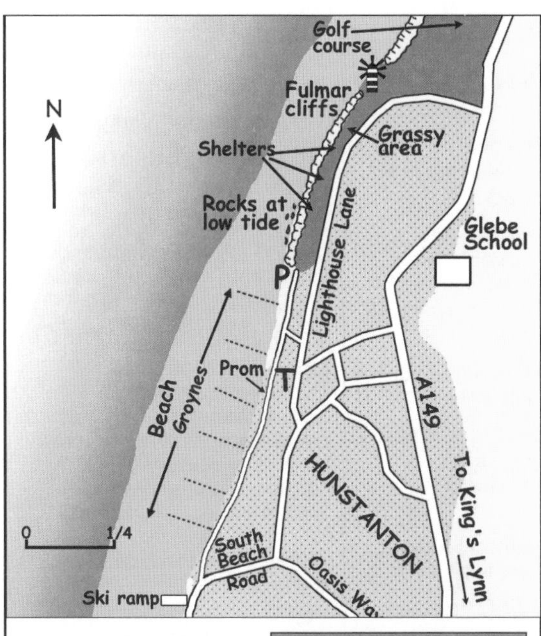

Access details

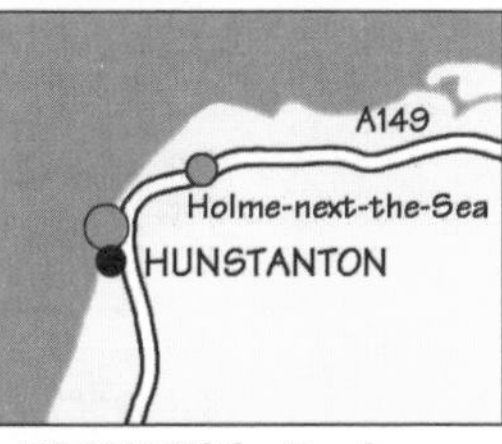

To the best birdwatching area, follow signs from A149 to 'Cliff Car Park' down Lighthouse Lane (B1161). Park along this road by the large grassed area, near one of the shelters and look out to sea from the cliff-top.

You may also continue towards the town centre, turning right down a small private road after the grassy area (signed 'private road, chalets only') – if you reach the main road you have gone too far. Parking here does not present a problem at off-peak times. Turn right at the bottom and park at the end for close views of the cliffs, beach and sea. This is excellent when the weather is foul or for wheelchair users. Walk N or S along the beach if you wish to stretch your legs.

The jet-ski ramp (approx. TF 668398) for Purple Sandpipers can be reached along the beach by walking about a mile S (towards Heacham), or by car by following signs for 'South Beach and Car Parks' from roundabout on A149. Go down this road (Oasis Way), then straight over the roundabout onto South Beach Road. At the bottom of the short hill, turn left and park about 50 yards along next to a café. Walk up onto the seawall – this is the jet-ski ramp where the Purple Sandpipers roost at high tide.

KELLING HEATH

Key points

- **Many small car parks.**
- **Level terrain on narrow peat tracks.**
- **Several possible Nightjar areas can be viewed from the car.**
- **Torch advisable.**
- **Insect repellent advisable.**
- **Many paths to explore – don't get lost!**

Contacts

None

FOR A PERFECT site to end a summer's day on the North Norfolk coast, head for this area of heath which is an excellent place to see Nightjars.

Target birds **Nightjar (90%), Wood Lark (40%).**

Other possible bird species

Summer	Sky Lark	*Occasional*
Sparrowhawk	Meadow Pipit	Hobby
Kestrel	Hirundines	Long-eared Owl
Woodcock	Common scrub birds	Tree Pipit
Tawny Owl	Common finches	
Green Woodpecker	Yellowhammer	

Background information and birding tips

KELLING is a large area of heathland famous for its Nightjar population. In my experience, these birds don't show as well as at other sites (Roydon Common, Salthouse Heath, Dersingham Bog, Sandringham) but it is a pleasant area to stroll around and find your own 'churrers'.

This site certainly doesn't seem to attract many birdwatchers so you may find yourself enjoying the displays of these amazing birds on your own. The Nightjars start 'churring' just before dark but don't usually show until after dark.

The main car park is a good starting point to listen for Nightjars. If you cannot hear any here, follow the wide track at the north end of the car park to where it starts to go slightly uphill. There is also a small patch of trees on your right. This has been a good area to see Nightjars in recent years. Incidentally, this path leads to the A149 near Kelling where you can walk to the shingle beach (see Kelling Quags).

There are several smaller car parks leading off from the road, any of which give access to the heath and its avian bounty. Once you have found yourself a car park not occupied with a courting couple, you will find a choice of paths to explore. Any may be good for Nightjars, so listen for the first distinctive sounds and follow the nearest track but stay on the path at all times.

The heath is a traditional site for Tree Pipit, present from mid-May until late August. However, they have been absent in the last couple of years but this will hopefully be a temporary blip, so still check for them.

You should also see common birds such as Yellowhammers, Green Woodpeckers and Sky Larks. Summer's Swallows, Swifts and House Martins are sometimes hunted by a Hobby, with Kestrels and Sparrowhawks more commonly seen.

There is a slight chance of Long-eared Owl at Kelling and some of the habitat looks good for Nightingale though I have never heard one here. Woodcocks are regularly seen roding at dusk. Wood Larks have recently taken up residence on the heath. They can be anywhere on here, so listen for their mournful song (early morning is best).

At the southern end of the heath is a wide public footpath (signed on a wooden post). Wheelchair users can access the heath down this track in their car (with care). There is a small lay-by half way down where you can park and listen out for Nightjars. At the end of the track is a wide area in which to turn the car around.

You may get a bit of noise disturbance from the camp sites nearby. If you are camping yourself, you might just be able to hear Nightjars from your tent/caravan or even catch a glimpse of one as they hunt insects around the campsite lights.

Nearby, Kelling Triangle (TG 090410) used to turn up an occasional Wood Warbler in spring but they seem to have deserted the area. It may still be worth exploring in spring for migrants though.

Access details

(Approx. seven miles W of Sheringham).

Follow A149 to Weybourne (about two miles W of Sheringham). Turn off immediately opposite Weybourne church, sign-posted Kelling Heath and NN Railway (Church Street).

Follow this road as it bends to the right and becomes Holt Road. In 0.7 miles, the road passes through a small wood, then opens out to gorse-lined hedgerows.

When you see the hedgerows, look for small, hidden turn-offs onto the heath. The second turn on the left takes you to a grass car park overlooking the heath (good for wheelchair users to scan the heath).

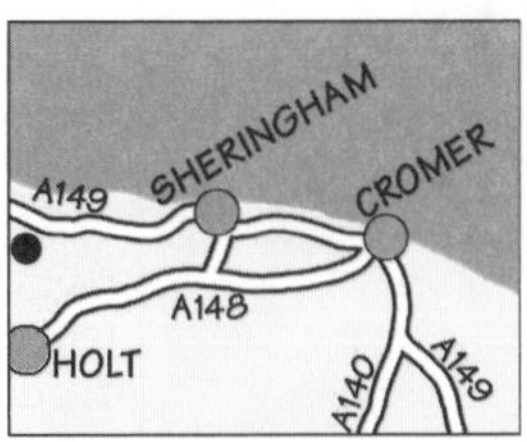

Also on the left, there is a track marked 'public footpath' that you can drive down to park in a small lay-by (approx. TG 101416). The track leads to the NN railway crossing where you can turn around.

The main car park is on the right approx. 0.25 miles past the public footpath sign on your left.

Other nearby sites

Blakeney Point, NWT Cley Marshes, Holkham NNR, Holkham Park, Kelling Quags, Swanton Novers.

Key points

- Public footpath, open at all times.
- Paths can be muddy even in summer.
- Level terrain along a rough track, then steep shingle sea wall.

Contacts

Norfolk Ornithologists Association, 01485 525406

KELLING QUAGS is an often overlooked reserve, partly managed by the Norfolk Ornithologists' Association and the Kelling Estate. This site attracts several species of common breeding birds and a few rarities. Because the pool is small, the visiting birdwatcher can obtain close views of many birds and, because it is under-watched, you might just find something special for yourself.

Target birds

All year – Barn Owl (50%). *Spring* – Sand Martin (95%), Garganey (20%). *Summer* – Little Gull (40%). *Autumn* – Passage seabirds, waders and migrants.

Other possible bird species

All year
Cormorant
Shelduck
Gadwall
Shoveler
Kestrel
Red-legged Partridge
Grey Partridge
Oystercatcher
Ringed Plover
Lapwing
Redshank
Common gull species
Sky Lark
Pied Wagtail
Meadow Pipit

Summer
Black-headed Gull
Sandwich Tern
Common Tern
Little Tern
Hirundines
Sedge Warbler
Reed Warbler
Whitethroat
Blackcap
Chiffchaff
Willow Warbler

Spring/autumn
Shearwaters
Gannet
Ruff
Whimbrel
Greenshank
Green Sandpiper
Wood Sandpiper
Common Sandpiper
Skuas
Little Gull
Black Tern
Yellow Wagtail
Hirundines
Whinchat
Wheatear

Winter
Divers
Grebes
Brent Goose
Wigeon
Sea ducks
Stonechat
Winter thrushes

Occasional
Hobby
Winter raptors
Short-eared Owl

Background information and birding tips

KELLING QUAGS, or Kelling Water Meadows as it is also known, is partly managed and owned by both the Norfolk Ornithologists' Association and the Kelling Estate. A hedge-lined track from the parking area leads down to a smallish pool. The hedges and surrounding fields are good in winter for common finches and thrushes and Whitethroat, Blackcap etc in spring and summer. The hedges should be checked for migrants in autumn and spring with Redstart and Pied Flycatcher possible.

In winter, the pool and surrounding meadow hold small numbers of Gadwall, Tufted Duck, Wigeon, Shoveler etc along with Shelduck and loafing gulls.

This area is a good place to watch out for early arriving migrants such as Black Tern, Martins, etc. Passage waders can include Greenshank, Whimbrel, plus Common, Green and Wood Sandpipers.

During summer, Black-headed Gulls raise their chicks on the island in the middle of the lake and Little Gulls can also be seen on the

reserve from May to September. Sand Martins, House Martins, Swallows and Swifts should all be skimming for insects.

After the pool, the footpath splits into two. The right hand side cuts across a 'causeway' through a small reedbed and continues on to a shingle beach. The path straight on wends its way through fields towards Salthouse and Cley.

When walking across the 'causeway', listen for Reed and Sedge Warblers in spring and summer. From the beach, you can spend time seawatching. In summer, Sandwich, Common and Little Terns will be busy fishing offshore.

From July to October watch out for Manx Shearwaters and all four skua species, especially in drizzly or foggy conditions with onshore winds. In winter, look out for divers, grebes and sea ducks including Red-breasted Mergansers, Common Scoters and Long-tailed Ducks.

Infrequent visitors can get the impression that there isn't much to see at Kelling but if you wait for a while something interesting usually turns up. The Quags have a good record of producing some good birds.

In 2001, a Dusky Warbler and a White-winged Black Tern were found. 2004 produced a Citrine Wagtail and a White-rumped Sandpiper visited in the autumn of 2005.

Be prepared for the unexpected! For instance, in the winter of 2005/6 a Bittern spent the whole time in a grass field completely out in the open and the Marbled Duck that dropped into the reserve during May 2000 is still being discussed to this day as to whether it was a wild bird or a 'fence hopper'.

This is a pleasant one mile walk from the car to the beach and back with plenty of common bird species to be seen along the way. You may even find something special.

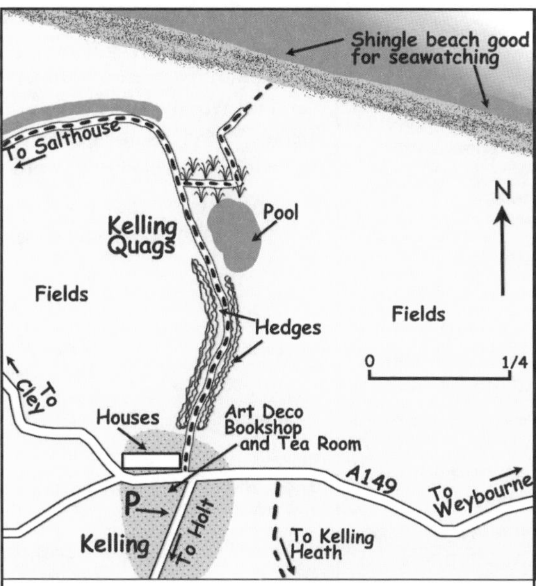

Access details

(Approx. 4 miles W of Sheringham).

Kelling village, turn left off the A149 on a road signposted to Holt (there is a bookshop and tearoom on this corner). Park sensibly on this narrow road and take care not to block residents' access. When leaving the site take extra care as this road joins the A149 on a very nasty double blind bend!

Wherever you park, take care not to block resident's access and be very careful when manoeuvring as the parking is on a blind, double bend.

Follow the track down to the meadows and onwards to the shingle beach.

SHERINGHAM
CROMER
A149
A148
HOLT
A140
A149

Other nearby sites

Blakeney Point, NWT Cley Marshes, Felbrigg Hall, Kelling Heath, Salthouse Beach, Salthouse Heath, Swanton Novers, NOA Walsey Hills, Weybourne.

KEN HILL WOOD

Key points

- **Extensive woodland, with occasional views to Snettisham Marsh and The Wash.**
- **Free access at all times.**
- **Free parking.**
- **Terrain is fairly level with some slight inclines.**
- **A 1.25 mile circular route, or explore as you fancy.**
- **Allow at least two hours to explore.**
- **Obey all 'Private' signs along the route.**
- **Paths can be muddy in winter, or after rain.**
- **Dogs on leads.**

Contacts

None

MIXED WOODLAND is a scarce habitat in Norfolk's coastal area, so this large patch situated between RSPB Snettisham reserve and Hunstanton, is well worth a visit. Ken Hill Wood is excellent for many common woodland bird species as well as one or two scarce ones. An added bonus is that you will meet very few other humans during your visit.

Target birds

All year – **Lesser Spotted Woodpecker (March, 50%, rest, 20%), Crossbill (20%).** *Spring/summer* – **Wood Lark (50%).**

Other possible bird species

All year
Sparrowhawk
Kestrel
Woodcock
Stock Dove
Barn Owl
Little Owl
Tawny Owl
Green Woodpecker
Great Spotted Woodpecker
Sky Lark
Goldcrest
Marsh Tit
Nuthatch
Treecreeper
Common woodland birds
Jay
Siskin

Summer
Marsh Harrier
Cuckoo
Hirundines
Warblers

Winter
Pink-footed Goose
Winter thrushes

Spring/autumn
Redstart
Wood Warbler
Firecrest
Pied Flycatcher

Background information and birding tips

CONSIDERING how many birders visit Snettisham, it is surprising how few are tempted to explore this wood. A walk at any time of year will produce encounters with common woodland birds but you'll also get a nice view over to The Wash in some places and there may be a few migrants to be found during times of passage.

Ken Hill Wood is a good place to see Crossbills but as with any site, they can be extremely elusive. In some years hardly any are seen, in others they seem to be in every pine tree. Wood Larks have recently colonised one or two clearings and all three species of woodpeckers are present. Lesser Spotted Woodpeckers are best seen in March and April when they perform their fluttering display-flight.

The route described below gives the visiting birdwatcher the best chance of connecting with the target species, though feel free to explore further as long as you observe the numerous 'Private Land' signs dotted throughout the wood.

From the car park, take the wide track at the back of the house, which soon narrows and bends into the wood. Not far along this path, there is a sign nailed to a tree stating 'Ken Hill Estates, dogs on leads'. Go through the gate here and you will see a field to your left. Stand at the edge of the field for an overview of The Wash. In winter, this is a good place to watch Pink-footed Geese leaving their roost at Snettisham. From late February you should see a Wood Lark displaying over this field and

in summer, watch the area for Marsh Harriers.

Once through the gate, follow the path keeping the field to your left and the wood on your right. After about 500 yards you reach a gate and an obvious barn in the field. Scan for Barn Owls, raptors, etc.

Bear right here into the wood (left takes you down to the coast). The path is fenced on both sides so you cannot go wrong. This area is probably the best for migrants in spring and autumn. Pied Flycatchers and Redstarts are regular visitors though neither are numerous. Yellow-browed Warbler, Firecrest, Red-breasted Flycatcher and Pallas's Warbler must all be distinct possibilities in September and October.

The path bears right, then eventually goes down a steepish hill. There are numerous side paths to explore in this area off to the right (paths to the left are all marked private). As you continue down the hill, pine trees become more numerous, so listen for the loud '*chip, chip*' calls of Crossbills.

At the bottom of the hill is a narrow concrete bridge over a small creek. Do not go over this bridge or you will reach the A149, instead turn right. After about 150 yards, the path reaches a T-junction with a wider track at a clearing. This is a good area for Treecreepers, Siskins, Coal Tits, Nuthatches and Great Spotted Woodpeckers. Turn right to skirt the clearing, then into more pine trees. Not long after this is another clearing, which is a good place to see a Green Woodpecker and maybe a Wood Lark.

Turn left at this clearing, then immediately right to bring you back to the gate with the Ken Hill Estates sign. Turn left back to the car park.

Adding the birds seen out towards The Wash and Snettisham, plus all the common woodland birds, you may well have seen 40 species on your walk, depending on the time of year.

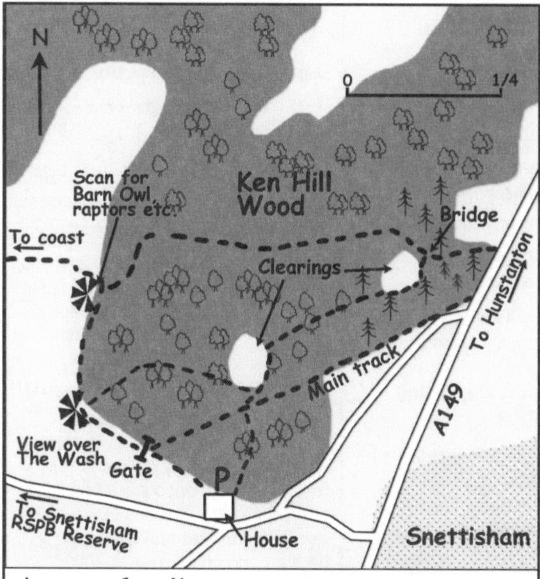

Access details

(Approx. five miles S of Hunstanton).

Turn off A149 between King's Lynn and Hunstanton at brown tourist signs for Snettisham Beach/ Snettisham RSPB. After 0.2 miles, on a left bend, is a house. The car park is behind this house, accessed through a red and white height barrier pole.

Take the wide track behind the house, which then narrows and enters the wood. Follow the paths as described in the text.

A149
A148
KING'S LYNN
A47

Other nearby sites

RSPB Snettisham, Snettisham Coastal Park, Dersingham Bog, Sandringham, Wolferton Triangle.

KING'S LYNN DOCKS

Key points

- **Free access at all times.**
- **All dock areas viewable from the road.**
- **Do not enter any fenced areas.**
- **Terrain is flat. Hedgerows viewed along a wide, rough track.**
- **Park sensibly! Do not block access for lorries.**
- **Low tide is best for gulls at the shellfish outfall.**

Contacts

Associated British Ports: King's Lynn.
01553 691555

WHILE this is not the most scenic site in Norfolk, it is the place that attracts gull aficionados, as it has a reputation for attracting rarer species at any time of year.

Target birds

All year – **Glaucous Gull (15%).** *Summer* – **Yellow-legged Gull (50%).**

Other possible bird species

All year		***Summer***
Cormorant	Turnstone	Common Tern
Common wildfowl	Common gull species	Whitethroat
Oystercatcher	Sky Lark	Blackcap
Ringed Plover	Meadow Pipit	
Curlew	Pied Wagtail	***Winter***
Redshank	Common scrub birds	Redwing
	Common finches	Fieldfare

Background information and birding tips

KING'S LYNN docks may lack glamour but it is the area most often frequented by gulls and gull freaks! It has a good track record of producing a Glaucous Gull or two in winter and one lingered here on and off all year in 2001.

Gulls sometimes loaf on the water in the dock near the weighbridge (20 yards into the site on the right). If not, they may be around the Fisher Fleet shellfish factory outfall, about 200 yards down the dock road.

The outfall, situated at the end of the dock road, is on the opposite bank to where you park, immediately before you reach the River Great Ouse. Look for a mud bank with a few large rocks scattered around. Low tide is best, when the gulls pick tasty morsels off the rocks.

In winter, it is worth checking the River Ouse for common wildfowl such as Tufted Ducks and Goldeneyes, or maybe Smew or Goosander in harsh weather. In summer, Common Terns fish the river, competing with the less dainty Cormorants.

The common gull species can still be found here in the summer months but winter is the time of year when gull enthusiasts eye the flocks to pick out

Glaucous Gull is a much sought-after species for lovers of Larids.

a Yellow-legged Gull from its Herring Gull cousins.

If you enjoy impressing your friends by being able to tell an immature Herring Gull from an immature Lesser Black-backed Gull then this is the place for you (or the place to practise ageing gulls if you aspire to this feat). At low tide scan the river banks for waders such as Redshank, Curlew, Turnstone and Oystercatcher.

Though the Fisher Fleet area is relatively quiet, remember that this is a working dock and you should expect heavy lorries to be passing regularly.

After checking the docks, you may wish to scan the extensive hedgerows for common scrub birds (Dunnock, Wren, Robin, etc). Drive to the river, then bear right along a pitted, rough track. This runs for more than 1.5 miles alongside the river, bordered by hedges all the way. This area is especially worth checking in spring and autumn for migrants.

In November 2001, a Barred Warbler and a Serin were both present, showing the potential of the site (and demonstrating my potential for peering into dense foliage for hours on end without seeing these special birds)!

The track eventually leads to Lynn Point, which is a good area to find Brent Geese and wintering raptors but you are very exposed to the elements!

In summary, King's Lynn docks are worth a detour from the A149 at any time of year to see what is around.

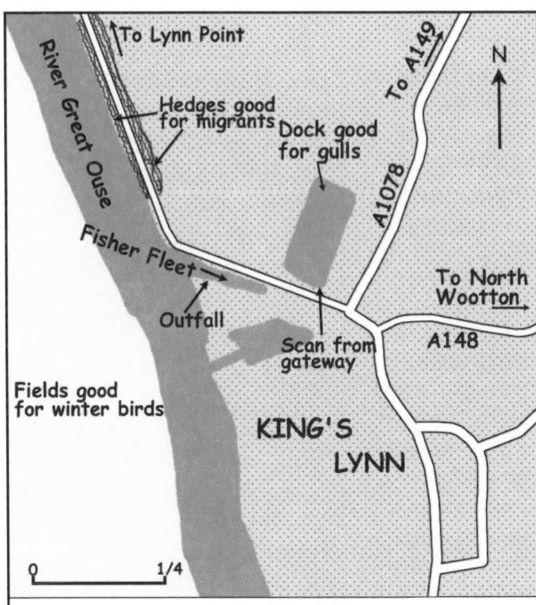

Access details

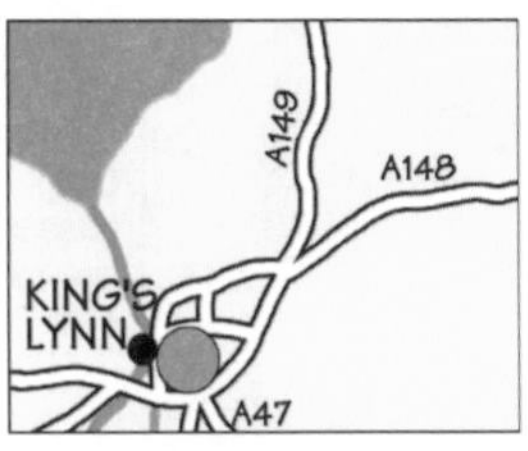

Follow signs for 'docks' leaving the King's Lynn bypass (A149) at northernmost roundabout onto A148 (sign-posted King's Lynn/South Wootton). At South Wootton, go straight through traffic lights, then the road becomes the A1078 (still signed to the docks). Follow this road for 3.8 miles then turn right into the docks, immediately before the sharpish left bend.

The dock on the right after 20 yards is good for loafing gulls. The Fisher Fleet is straight on from here, with trawlers docked on the left, (if you reach the river, you have gone too far).

At the River Ouse end of the fleet, there is a small shellfish factory outfall, which is the best place for gulls. PLEASE DO NOT BLOCK THE ROADS. HEAVY LORRIES USE THIS ROAD FREQUENTLY.

Other nearby sites

Brancaster Marsh, Dersingham Bog, NWT Holme Dunes, NOA Holme Observatory, Hunstanton, Ken Hill Wood, NOA Redwell Marsh, Roydon Common, Sandringham, RSPB Snettisham, RSPB Titchwell Marsh, Tottenhill gravel pits, Wolferton triangle.

RSPB LAKENHEATH FEN

Key points

- **Free access at all times.**
- **Managed by the RSPB.**
- **The Flash is on private land and can only be viewed from the footpath.**
- **Terrain is level along rutted grass paths and sandy tracks.**
- **Unsuitable for wheelchairs.**
- **The RSPB aims to make this the largest wetland area in the country.**

Contacts

Warden: 01842 828662 (9.00am - 5.00pm)

RSPB East Anglia Office 01603 661662

This site is renowned as the best place in Britain to see Golden Orioles. The RSPB is currently expanding Lakenheath to 5,000ha of reedbed and pools, creating the country's largest wetland area to attract breeding Bitterns and Bearded Tits.

Target birds

Spring/summer – **Golden Oriole (hear 80%, see 50%), Marsh Harrier (85%), Hobby (80%), Black Tern (May, 15%).**

Other possible bird species

Spring/summer

Great Crested Grebe
Common wildfowl
Shelduck
Gargeney
Common waterbirds
Sparrowhawk
Kestrel
Water Rail
Lapwing
Redshank
Common Sandpiper
Common Tern
Turtle Dove
Cuckoo
Great Spotted Woodpecker
Sky Lark
Hirundines
Kingfisher
Pied Wagtail
Common scrub birds
Grasshopper Warbler
Sedge Warbler
Reed Warbler
Whitethroat
Other warblers
Common woodland birds

Occasional

Bittern
Wood Sandpiper
Bearded Tit
Lesser Spotted Woodpecker

Background information and birding tips

THE RSPB HAS big plans for Lakenheath Fen. They have already planted more than 200,000 reeds with a resultant increase in breeding numbers of Reed and Sedge Warblers. In future years this reserve will become a prime site to see Bitterns and Bearded Tits. In the meantime, this remains the place to encounter Golden Orioles.

From mid-May, if you visit at the right time of day, you will almost certainly hear the flutey calls of the males drifting from the poplars but seeing one takes much patience. Their stunning colours blend in perfectly with their surroundings and you may have to wait quietly for an hour or two for good views of one. The most likely sighting will be a fleeting glimpse as an individual flies between poplar plantations.

I suggest a very early morning visit from mid-May onwards for best results. As the day wears on, the Golden Orioles become quieter, though one can occasionally be seen. It is best to position yourself where you can view the edge of a plantation where you may see the orioles flying from one block of trees to another.

Once the orioles are feeding young, controlled viewing facilities at the nest site may be possible. This varies from year to year: good views of the nest were possible in 2004 but not in 2005.

Do not enter the woods under any circumstances. The orioles are very sensitive to disturbance, so please stay on the paths at all times. If you see anyone behaving suspiciously, report them to RSPB staff.

There are two marked trails from the car park. The Washland Trail takes you onto the raised bank

alongside the Little Ouse River. The White Trail leads along the back of the first poplar plantation, through a reedbed, up to the second plantation before looping back to the car park below the Washland Trail. Please note that there is no access from the White Trail to the Washland Trail, unless you return to the car park.

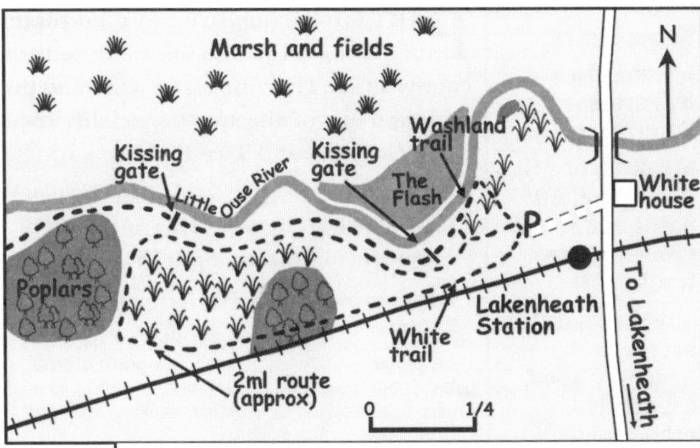

Walking along the marked paths, you will pass areas of reeds where Reed Warblers will entertain you. Many Sedge Warblers and one or two Grasshopper Warblers will be singing from the bushes and Whitethroats and Blackcaps are numerous.

The area known as The Flash holds breeding Great Crested Grebes among other common waterbirds and Common Terns are regular visitors. In May, one might be lucky enough to see Black Terns and Garganeys on The Flash, while at passage times the banks should be closely scanned for waders such as Wood, Common and Green Sandpipers.

Hobbies are a common sight in spring and summer as they hunt the numerous dragonflies and hirundines over the reedbeds (as many as 20 have been recorded at one time!). I have found the area looking towards the back of the second plantation to be the best for this elegant raptor.

A pair of Marsh Harriers regularly hunt over the first reedbed, between the first two plantations, sometimes giving very close views from the designated paths. Unfortunately, I have yet to see Bearded Tits here, though this will undoubtedly change in the near future.

I have seen Lesser Spotted Woodpecker in the poplars, though not very often. Much more likely are Turtle Doves and Cuckoos: the latter show particularly well at Lakenheath. You may even see a Kingfisher as it zooms down the Little Ouse.

For those interested in county boundaries, you will have to keep an eye on which birds you tick off for Suffolk and which you count for Norfolk. The Little Ouse is the county border, so the poplars are technically in Suffolk while The Flash is in Norfolk. For those people less 'sad' than me this does not matter one single jot!

Access details

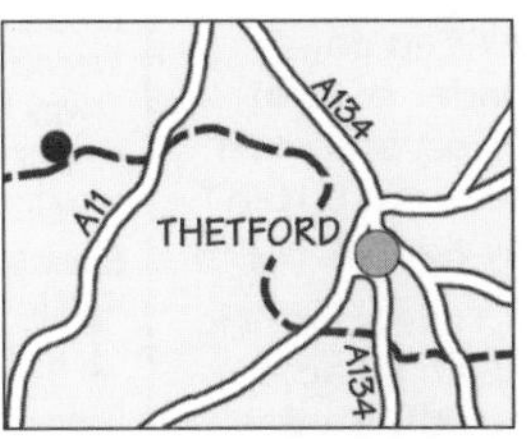

(Approx. 13 miles SE of Downham Market and 9.5 miles W of Thetford).

Situated off B1112 (Feltwell to Lakenheath road). From Feltwell, head S through Hockwold cum Wilton. Cross over a channel, then just after the next bridge (over the Little Ouse River) turn right onto a track to the car park (RSPB sign). This car park is not very obvious but is situated opposite a white house. If you reach Lakenheath station you have gone too far.

Walk back towards the Ouse along a very short footpath. Follow this rough track for approx. 150 yards to the car park. The Washland Trail is signed to the right (up to the raised bank alongside the Little Ouse River), the White Trail goes off to the left (up to the railway line and through a reedbed).

Key points

- **Managed by Forest Enterprise.**
- **Terrain is flat, with hard paths and rough gravel/ grass trails.**
- **Wheelchair access is generally good, especially in arboretum.**
- **Keep dogs under control as several each year are bitten by adders.**
- **Toilets, with disabled access, are situated nearby at Lynford Stag (TL 814919).**
- **Excellent FE footpath map available (see Contacts section).**

Contacts

Forest Enterprise
01842 810271

High Lodge Forest Centre
01842 815434

PART OF the huge Thetford Forest in The Brecklands of Norfolk, Lynford has become the best place in the county to see Hawfinches in winter, with a good chance of finding many of the area's speciality species (Nightjar, Wood Lark, Crossbill and Tree Pipit) in spring and summer.

Target birds

All year – **Lesser Spotted Woodpecker (30%), Crossbill (40%).** *Winter* – **Hawfinch (70%).** *Spring/summer* – **Nightjar (90%), Tree Pipit (85%), Wood Lark (85%).**

Other possible bird species

All year
Little Grebe
Great Crested Grebe
Common wildfowl
Sparrowhawk
Kestrel
Woodcock
Tawny Owl
Kingfisher
Woodpeckers
Marsh Tit
Common woodland birds
Nuthatch
Treecreeper
Jay
Siskin
Redpoll

Spring/summer
Cuckoo
Hirundines
Garden Warbler
Spotted Flycatcher

Occasional
Goshawk
Long-eared Owl
Grey Wagtail

Background information and birding tips

THE ARBORETUM, set within the huge Thetford Forest area of Norfolk, is run by Forest Enterprise which maintains several tracks through the woods. Some of these are suitable for wheelchair users, others not but most of the key species can be seen by those with mobility difficulties. Similar birds can be found nearby at the Lynford Stag picnic site, which also has toilet facilities, including ones for wheelchair users.

Between December and March Lynford has become the place to see Hawfinch in the county. They are usually to be found quietly feeding on the floor under the large hornbeam trees in The Paddock. There is a bench along the track from the southern car park, my favourite place to sit and scan for these elusive but beautiful birds. Crossbills sometimes sit in the tops of these trees. Early mornings are best.

At the back of the arboretum is Lynford Lake, which is good for common wildfowl and waterfowl. The alders around this lake attract Lesser Redpoll and Siskin. Many common species also frequent the arboretum, so you should obtain good views of Green and Great Spotted Woodpeckers, Marsh Tits, Treecreepers and Nuthatches.

In spring and summer, I prefer to park in the car park to the south of the arboretum. This car park gives you access to the blue (1.5 miles) and the green (1 mile) trails, which both lead you to the scenic west end of Lynford Lake, which is excellent for summer visitors, including Garden Warbler.

The longer trail leads you up Sequoia Avenue, which is where I have had most success with Crossbills at Lynford. Watch out for them flying overhead, almost always alerting you to their presence by their loud contact calls. Both trails lead to a bridge over the narrow part of the lake

where you may be lucky enough to see a Kingfisher.

This southern car park is a highly recommended spot for Nightjars, Wood Larks and Tree Pipits. From the car park, turn right along the top of a paddock (good for butterflies) until you reach a wooden barrier. Go past the barrier (it is to keep out cars, not people) and scan the clearing on your right for Nightjars in the evening and Wood Larks in the morning. Tree Pipits are most easily seen when they display during May and early June.

Long-eared Owls breed in Thetford Forest but you will be extremely lucky to see one. The best chance is in May when the hungry young squeak to attract the attention of the adults. Goshawk is the other scarce species of the area.

The whole area is ever changing, as some parts of the forest are felled and previously cleared areas regenerate. Any clearing should hold its own Nightjars or Wood Larks; they are there for you to discover your own special place! One such clearing is accessed opposite the minor road to West Toffs at TL 838879, an excellent spot for both Nightjars and Wood Larks.

Lynford Gravel Pits to the north can be accessed from the main car park (itself a good place to see Crossbills). Walk to the bottom left of the car park and take a narrow muddy track through the trees. After a few yards, cross the road looking out for quarry lorries. Follow the stony path running alongside the fenced off road (**do not walk along the road**) for 100 yards when it brings you to a small hide overlooking a deep lake.

Great Crested Grebes are resident here and are joined in winter by Tufted Ducks, Pochard and other common wildfowl. It is always worth checking here when visiting the arboretum as Ferruginous Duck and Great Northern Diver have been found on the pits.

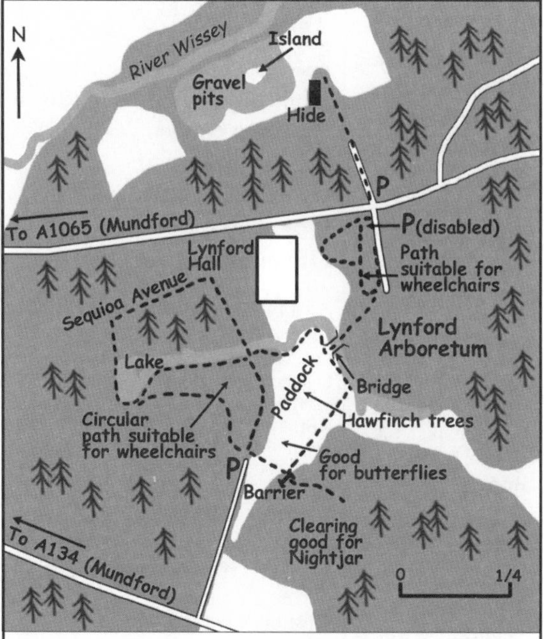

Access details

(Approx. 7 miles NW of Thetford).

Lynford is served by two car parks: On A134 (Downham Market to Thetford road) at the Mundford roundabout take the exit N to Swaffham. Then take first right turn, signed to Lynford Hall. Follow road past the hall to the car park sign-posted on the left (disabled drivers may park in the arboretum itself, signed on the right).

Alternatively, at the roundabout at Mundford head S towards Thetford but immediately take the minor road on left sign-posted to Lynford Lakes. Follow the road to the left turn, sign-posted to the lakes. Park in the designated car park at the end of this rough track.

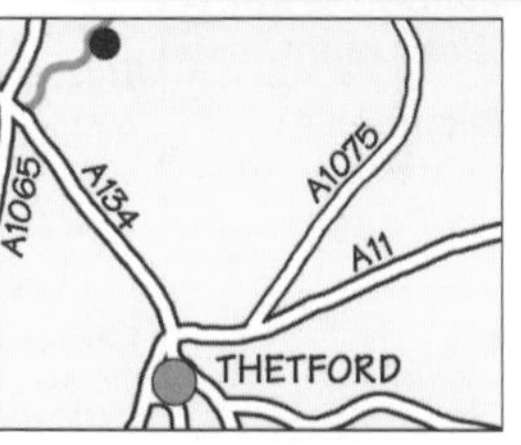

47 NWT MARTHAM BROAD NNR

Key points

- **Free access at all times.**
- **Managed by Norfolk Wildlife Trust.**
- **Site is a designated SSSI.**
- **Information board along Martham footpath.**
- **Terrain is level along grass and mud paths. Can be wet at all times of year.**
- **Not wheelchair friendly.**
- **Mooring available at West Somerton (£2 per night).**
- **Facilities in public house in West Somerton.**

Contacts

Norfolk Wildlife Trust
01603 625540

General Broads Authority
01603 610734

MARTHAM is a lesser-known Broadland site, close to Hickling and Horsey, which attracts many of the species associated with its larger neighbours. The two public footpaths that border Martham are excellent places to see wintering raptors, Bearded Tits and common wildfowl.

Target birds

All year – **Bittern (10%), Crane (30%), Marsh Harrier (80%), Bearded Tit (55%), Cetti's Warbler (hear 50%, see 15%).** *Winter* – **Common wildfowl (100%), Hen Harrier (40%).**

Other possible bird species

All year
Great Crested Grebe
Cormorant
Common wildfowl
Common waterbirds
Sparrowhawk
Kestrel
Common gull species
Barn Owl
Kingfisher
Great Spotted Woodpecker
Sky Lark
Meadow Pipit
Common woodland birds
Corvids
Common finches
Reed Bunting

Summer
Common Tern
Sedge Warbler
Reed Warbler
Other warblers

Winter
Pink-footed Goose (in flight)
Winter thrushes

Occasional
Bewick's Swan
Whooper Swan
Smew
Merlin
Peregrine
Hobby

Background information and birding tips

I FEEL it is a great shame that Martham Broad is often overlooked, as it is a Norfolk Wildlife Trust site that offers some close encounters with many sought-after species.

A walk along the eastern footpath towards Horsey Mill should reward the visiting birdwatcher with good views of Marsh Harrier at any time of year and the chance of Hen Harrier, Merlin and Peregrine overhead in winter. Cranes regularly fly over at all times of year. If you catch the light right – early morning – you will get stunning views of some or all of the above species!

If you wish to see Martham Broad itself, take the footpath from West Somerton village. This footpath affords views over the water for close encounters with many species of common wildfowl at all times of year. You should expect Tufted Duck, Pochard, Mallard, Gadwall, Teal, Shoveler and Shelduck, though numbers decrease during the summer months.

Bearded Tits show best at the southern end of the Broad, though usually only in flight. If you want closer views, go to Hickling Broad nearby. In the wood itself, you should hear a Cetti's Warbler or two if the sun is shining. They are more vocal in spring but I once heard one here in November.

Spend a little time on the footpath at the edge of the broad and scan the reeds. A Bittern is often seen flying from one area of reeds to another, or if you are really lucky feeding at the edge of the reedbed.

Scarcer visitors such as Smew, Scaup and grebes sometimes

supplement the common birds at Martham in winter and Black Terns occasionally drop in on passage.

In summer, a tern nesting platform can be studied from the footpath. Common Terns nest here and provide an hour's entertainment watching their comings and goings. When the sea is rough, Sandwich and Little Terns may visit the broad. Reed and Sedge Warblers take up residence and Marsh Harriers are seen daily. Having said that, summer is probably the quietest time to visit Martham.

A little further along, a few muddy islands can be seen from the footpath. Terns use these islands for roosting, as do Oystercatchers and maybe a few passing waders at migration time (Common and Green Sandpipers for instance). The footpath continues all the way to Acle alongside the River Thurne.

The path along the northern end of the broad runs north from the pull-in by West Somerton channel to the road, halfway between the village and Horsey Mill. Turn right (as the path reaches the road) to complete a circular route back to West Somerton, though watch out for traffic. It is very easy to forget about cars when a Hen Harrier is hovering next to you or a flock of Cranes is flying overhead!

Other nearby sites

NWT Alderfen Broad, NWT Barton Broad, Great Yarmouth Beach, Great Yarmouth Cemetery, Hardley Flood, NWT Hickling Broad, Horsey, How Hill NNR, NWT Stubb Mill, NWT Upton Fen, Winterton Dunes.

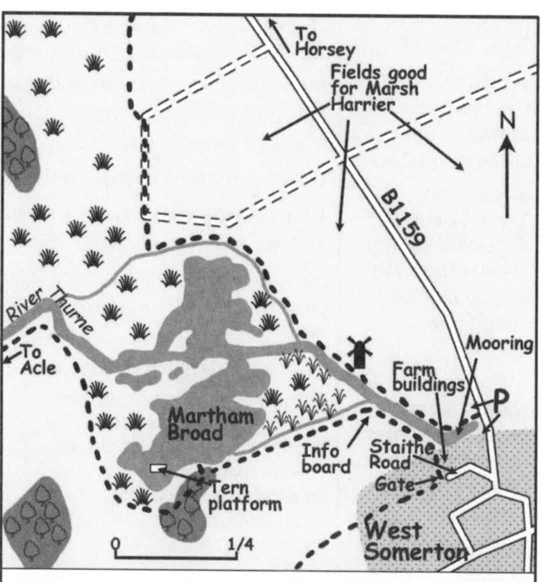

Access details

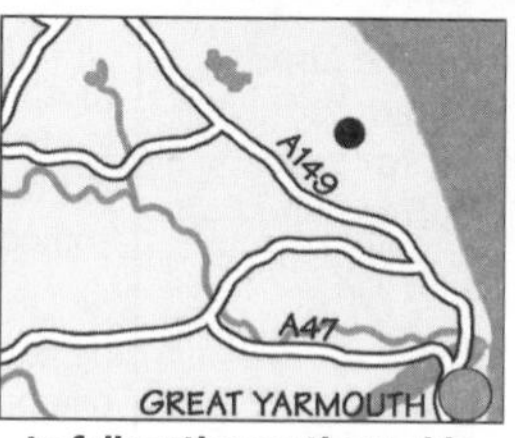

(Approx. nine miles N of Great Yarmouth).

BY CAR: **From A149 (Cromer to Great Yarmouth road) take B1152 NE to Martham (two miles S of Potter Heigham). Continue through Martham to West Somerton, then head N on B1159 towards Horsey. Park in one of the two large pull-ins by the channel, 200 yards after the tricky junction with the B1159 to Winterton.**

Take the waterside footpath to view the fields along the eastern side of Martham Broad (good for raptors), or walk back into West Somerton for about 75 yards and turn right into Staithe Road (best views of the Broad and reeds). After 100 yards, bear left past the farm to where the Tarmac joins a rough path. Where the grass path starts, turn right through a kissing gate to follow the southern side of the channel. This path reaches a wood in a quarter of a mile. Pass through another kissing gate and, after a further 100 yards, a narrow path runs through the trees to the water's edge.

BY BOAT: **For small craft only, as you will have to negotiate Potter Heigham bridge. West Somerton moorings are situated N of Potter Heigham bridge. You have to sail across Martham Broad to get to the moorings. Approximately a 40 minute trip from Potter Heigham.**

Key points

- **Difficult to view the marsh from a wheelchair.**
- **National Trust Tower is accessed up steep stairs but marsh can be seen from car park.**
- **Tower and toilets usually locked in winter (always locked when I have visited).**
- **Pay-and-display car park.**
- **Arrive about an hour before dark for best results.**

Contacts

The National Trust
01263 733471

FAMED as the place from which to catch boats to Blakeney Point, Morston is not so well known as a fantastic place to stand and watch raptors and Brent Geese flying in to roost in winter. Until now, that is!

Target birds *Winter* – Brent Goose (90%), Hen Harrier (75%), Barn Owl (60%), Merlin (20%).

Other possible bird species

Winter

Pink-footed Goose	Marsh Harrier	Rock Pipit
Little Egret	Grey Plover	Meadow Pipit
Common waterfowl	Other common waders	Pied Wagtail
Kestrel	Common gull species	Corvids
	Sky Lark	Common finches

Background information and birding tips

THOUGH rarely visited by birders in winter, Morston can pay dividends for the patient viewer. The observation tower provides an excellent vantage point to view raptors on the marsh as they pass through to roost at Warham Greens.

Hen Harriers tend to come into roost quite late in the day and Merlin is by no means guaranteed but there should be plenty to keep you occupied until they do appear.

A Little Egret or two can usually be found in the channels and on one particularly memorable visit I was entertained by two Barn Owls hunting along the sea wall, one of which flew right over the car and landed on a post in the car park.

Shortly after, several skeins of Brent Geese flew across the magnificent orange sky (or Norfolk Sunset as it is known to those privileged to witness it) to roost on the main channel. Sometimes birdwatching can be hard work but experiences like that make the effort well worthwhile.

If you arrive early, it may be worth strolling onto the marsh, using the obvious muddy footpath alongside the wide boat channel to get a better view of the main Blakeney Channel. As well as geese and waders, you may be rewarded with a diver or one of the rarer grebes (a Great Northern Diver overwintered in 2000 & 2001).

The muddy channels close to the observation tower provide good views of Redshank, Curlew, Ringed Plover, Grey Plover, Dunlin and Lapwing when the tide is out. I had a pleasant surprise in January 2001 when I found a Greenshank feeding in one such creek. Was it an early arrival or hardy wintering individual?

If you do walk along the paths, watch out for feeding flocks of finches and larks. There is a chance that you may encounter Twite or Rock Pipits mixed in with the Sky Larks and finch flocks.

You can walk out onto the marsh, east towards Blakeney harbour or west towards Stiffkey. If you take the latter route, after about a mile, you reach what is called Stiffkey Fen.

This is a privately owned area of flooded fields, which attract passage waders, such as, Wood,

Common, Curlew and Green Sandpipers, Little Stints, Whimbrels and Greenshank in spring and autumn. It is also a favoured haunt of Garganey in spring.

In summer, the area becomes crowded with holidaymakers and boaters and is probably best avoided unless you wish to catch a boat out to Blakeney Point for the seal and tern colonies (highly recommended).

In summary, this is an excellent place for a quiet hour's birding on a fine winter's evening and it should produce one or two goodies. It would be even better if the National Trust opened the observation tower more often to allow birdwatchers to get out of the biting wind.

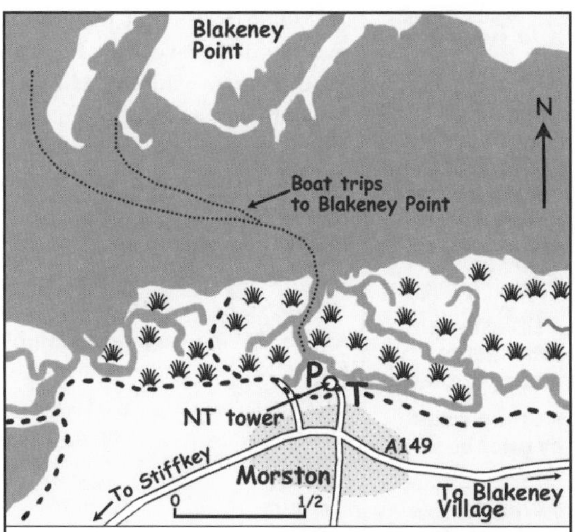

Access details

(Approx. 9.6 miles W of Sheringham).

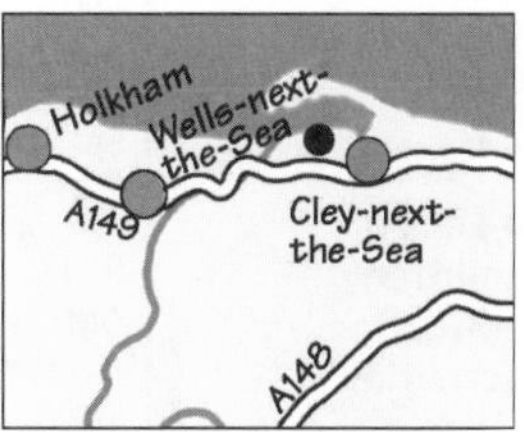

About two miles W of Blakeney village on A149, Morston Quay is sign-posted on a brown tourist sign. Follow rough track to pay-and-display car park, watching out for some vicious speed humps.

The National Trust watch tower overlooks the marsh and creeks but unfortunately this is locked in winter, as are the toilets. However, a balcony on the tower provides a good vantage point to watch raptors and geese coming in to roost.

For those wishing to stretch their legs, footpaths run east to Blakeney and west to Stiffkey from the car park along the raised sea wall (slightly raised grass bank would be a better description).

Other nearby sites

NWT Cley Marshes, Felbrigg Hall, Holkham NNR, Holkham Park, Salthouse Beach, Stiffkey Fen, NOA Walsey Hills.

PENSTHORPE

Key points

- **Free parking.**

Open 10am - 5pm April – Dec (£7 in 2006) and 10am - 4pm Jan – March (£6 in 2006).

- **No dogs.**
- **Level terrain; some paths muddy at times.**
- **Group visits by prior booking please.**
- **Wheelchairs available (first come, first served).**
- **Restaurant.**
- **Lots of children's education activities.**

Contacts

Visitor Centre
01328 851465
E-mail:
info@pensthorpe.com
www.pensthorpe.com

CONSISTING of more than 500 acres of formerly flooded gravel pits, Pensthorpe is famous as a place to see captive wildfowl. However, a large part of the site is a nature reserve, a haven for wild birds and animals. There are several SSSIs on site including a flood meadow and old pasture. Around 100 species of wild birds breed at Pensthorpe.

Target birds

All Year – **Common wildfowl, Lesser Spotted Woodpecker (<5%), Grey Wagtail (40%), Willow Tit (60%).** *Spring/summer* -– **Honey Buzzard (40%), Marsh Harrier (60%), Avocet (75%), Grasshopper Warbler (hear, 60%, see, 5%), Spotted Flycatcher (70%).** *Autumn* – **Passage waders.**

Other possible bird species

All year
Great Crested Grebe
Little Grebe
Cormorant
Grey Heron
Egyptian Goose
Shelduck
Common waterbirds
Sparrowhawk
Buzzard
Kestrel
Red-legged Partridge
Grey Partridge
Pheasant
Water Rail
Oystercatcher
Little Ringed Plover
Lapwing
Woodcock
Snipe
Common gull species
Stock Dove
Barn Owl
Little Owl
Kingfisher
Green Woodpecker
Great Spotted Woodpecker
Sky Lark
Pied Wagtail
Starling
Common scrub birds
Goldcrest
Marsh Tit
Nuthatch
Treecreeper
Bullfinch
Lesser Redpoll
Other common finches
Jay
Other corvids
Reed Bunting

Winter
Bewick's Swan
Meadow Pipit
Winter thrushes
Siskin

Spring/summer
Hobby
Common Tern
Turtle Dove
Cuckoo
Sand Martin
Other hirundines
Sedge Warbler
Reed Warbler
Lesser Whitethroat
Whitethroat
Garden Warbler
Blackcap
Chiffchaff
Willow Warbler

Spring/autumn
Ringed Plover
Dunlin
Redshank
Greenshank
Green Sandpiper
Wood Sandpiper
Common Sandpiper
Curlew
Black-tailed Godwit
Ruff
Yellow Wagtail

Occasional
Little Egret
Bittern (winter)
Winter raptors
Osprey (passage)
Long-eared Owl (winter)
Nightingale (summer)
Bearded Tit
Tree Sparrow
Cetti's Warbler

Background information and birding tips

YOU MAY BE wondering why I have included a wildfowl collection in a wild bird site guide and I must admit to thinking long and hard about whether to incorporate Pensthorpe into this book. However, once you visit, you will realise that Pensthorpe is much

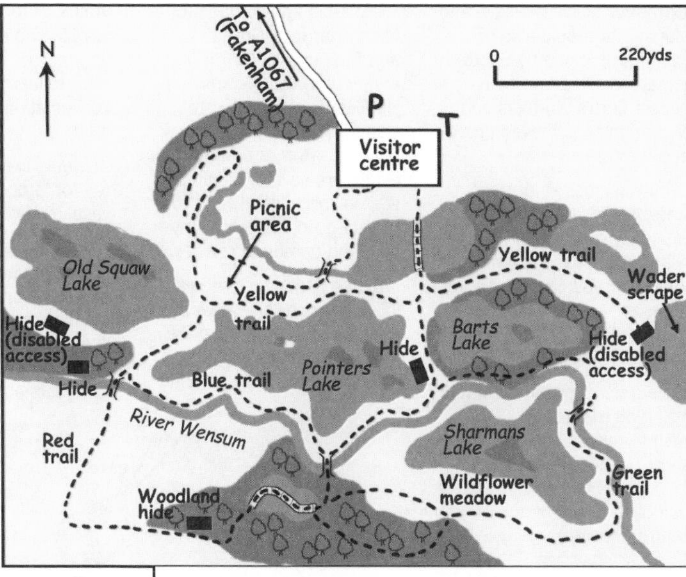

more than a 'bird zoo', being set in 500 acres of land including several SSSIs.

The estate is owned and managed with wildlife in mind by Bill Jordan, of Jordan's cereals fame and serves as a benchmark for farming practices in the UK. Some of the estate is run as a conservation grade farm bursting with wildlife of all forms. The Pensthorpe Conservation Trust is also instrumental in the Corn Crake release scheme in the Cambridgeshire Fens. With all this in mind, it is obvious that this site is worthy of coverage.

Access details

(1 mile east of Fakenham)

From the Fakenham bypass roundabout (adjacent to the football ground), take the A1067 signed to Norwich. Go straight on at the next roundabout, then left onto Pensthorpe Road at the next roundabout (still signed to Norwich). The park entrance is 1 mile along this road on your right (signed Waterfowl Park & Nature Reserve).

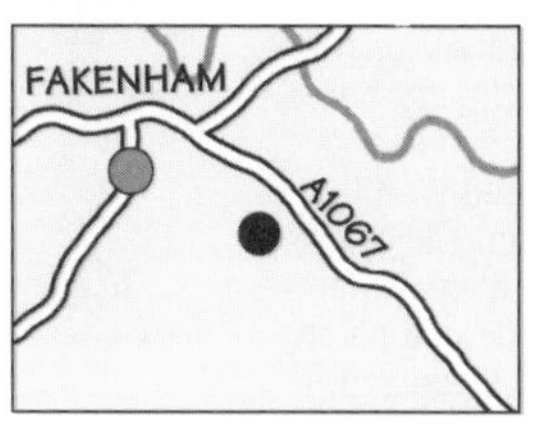

When you arrive, you will pass through the shop and visitor centre, then through the captive birds' pens. However, you are soon onto the reserve itself and have a number of trails from which to choose. I tend to ignore the captive wildfowl, which no doubt attract wild birds on site. The trouble is you cannot tell which is wild and which is captive so I suggest you cannot safely 'tick' any duck or goose here.

After leaving the pens, the trails are well marked on colour-marked posts. The yellow trail is of little interest until you reach the wader scrape. This is overlooked by a hide (wheelchair accessible). The scrape attracts passage waders in spring and autumn and the islands are safe nesting sites for Oystercatchers, Shelduck, Avocets and occasional Little Ringed Plovers.

Retrace your steps to follow the blue markers. The path circles Pointer's Lake (wildfowl in winter, Little and Great Crested Grebes all year) or you can branch off along the green trail. In summer, the bushes along either path will be bursting with warblers. Listen out especially for Grasshopper Warbler and Lesser Whitethroat.

The green trail takes you through a wet wood (carr), home to many common woodland birds. This is the most likely place to catch sight of a Lesser Spotted Woodpecker but they are extremely elusive. Willow and Marsh Tits should also be seen here, joined by Spotted Flycatchers in summer. I expect Cetti's Warblers and Nightingales to move in here in the future!

You will cross an ancient water meadow (the path is usually muddy), alive with butterflies in summer. Wherever you cross the River Wensum, keep an eye open for the resident Grey Wagtails and Kingfishers.

The green trail joins the red trail (you may wish to take a short cut here and follow the blue trail back to the centre/café etc). There are patches of reed and sedge along the red path, home to Sedge and Reed Warblers in summer. There is also a small hide in a patch of woodland. I like to sit here for quite a while as one is treated to very close views of many woodland species (including six species of tit!).

Whenever you reach a spot where you can scan your surroundings, look out for Honey Buzzards passing over in summer. Pensthorpe is very close to the Sennowe Estate, hence HBs are seen almost daily between mid May and early September.

Also keep an eye open for Marsh Harriers, Goshawks and Buzzards all year round and Peregrines, Merlins and Hen Harriers in winter, though sightings are few and far between. Dotted around the estate are several feeding stations allowing visitors to get close up views of many common passerine species.

An entry fee of £7 seems a lot to get onto a reserve but one has to bear in mind the other attractions available. This is a great place to bring your kids to learn about wildlife and conservation and you may even go on a 'safari tour' to learn more about conservation grade farming methods.

I would like to see a separate fee for 'proper' birders and casual visitors, though I realise this is impractical.

In the meantime, if a rare bird turns up, a reduced fee is usually negotiated for 'twitchers' (such as when a Squacco Heron turned up a few years ago).

Lapwing is one of many species to breed among the captive birds at Pensthorpe.

Other nearby sites

NWT Syderstone Common, Sculthorpe Moor, Flitcham Abbey Farm, Swanton Novers, Great Ryburgh, Pentney Gravel Pits, NWT Roydon Common, King's Lynn Docks.

PENTNEY GRAVEL PITS

Key points

- **Access at all times.**
- **Park sensibly – all roads heavily used by gravel lorries.**
- **Be careful of heavy trucks in the bridge area.**
- **Telescope very useful.**
- **Best to arrive early in summer, as the Leisure Park area is busy with holidaymakers.**
- **Viewing the Leisure Lake is from the road, so wheelchair access is good.**
- **Portaloo 200 yards off path at main pit.**

Contacts

None

VIEWS OF THIS working gravel pit – renowned for its breeding Little Ringed Plovers, Sand Martins and Nightingales – can be obtained from a public footpath alongside the River Nar. At other times of year, common waterfowl dominate the scene. The lakes at the Pentney caravan site hold common waterbirds, including Egyptian Geese, which can be scanned from the road.

Target birds *All year* – Common wildfowl (100%) Yellow-legged Gull (30%). *Summer* – Sand Martin (100%), Little Ringed Plover (75%), Nightingale (hear 30%, see 5%). *Spring/autumn* – Passage waders.

Other possible bird species

All year
Great Crested Grebe
Cormorant
Egyptian Goose
Water Rail
Common wildfowl
Common waterbirds
Sparrowhawk
Kestrel
Common gull species
Kingfisher
Green Woodpecker
Great Spotted Woodpecker
Sky Lark
Pied Wagtail
Jay
Other corvids
Bullfinch
Other common finches
Yellowhammer
Reed Bunting

Spring/autumn
Ringed Plover
Little Stint
Curlew Sandpiper
Ruff
Whimbrel
Greenshank
Green Sandpiper
Wood Sandpiper
Common Sandpiper
Black Tern
Yellow Wagtail

Summer
Common Tern
Hobby
Hirundines
Grasshopper Warbler
Sedge Warbler
Reed Warbler
Lesser Whitethroat
Other common warblers

Winter
Goldeneye
Winter thrushes

Background information and birding tips

A CASUAL glance might suggest Pentney Pits has little to offer birdwatchers but it is worth a diversion off the A47 at all times of year.

The main area of interest is the working pits, accessed from the track running east from High Bridge. Follow the rough, grass path (checking the ditch for Sedge Warblers in summer and Kingfishers all year round) until it joins a wide gravel track. There are many viewpoints along the way and several paths down to the pits.

The first pit holds many loafing gulls throughout the year, which may include Yellow-legged and Caspian, possibly joined by Iceland and Glaucous in winter. These birds visit from the Blackborough End Tip, visible in the background.

The second pit along has a couple of sandy islands and muddy edges. This is the best area for Little Ringed Plover in summer and any passage waders in spring and autumn. Check the reeds for Reed Warbler and Reed Bunting. Also scan the fields to your right for thrushes, gamebirds, Lapwings and grazing wildfowl.

Further along, you come to a large pit which attracts Common

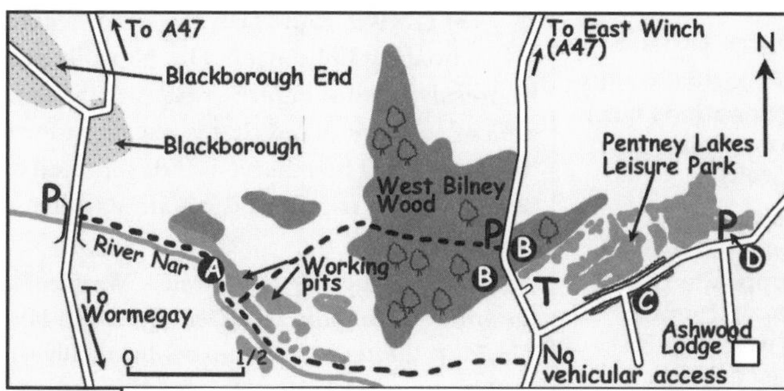

Terns in summer (and maybe Black and Arctic Terns on passage) and winter ducks. Eventually, you reach the main working pit with a poplar plantation to your right.

If you fancy a really long walk, continue along the footpath until it meets a road. Turn left and follow the road to the Leisure Park and West Bilney Woods. Go through the wood and turn left at the top of the track to return to the public footpath alongside the River Nar. Turn right to get back to High Bridge.

The pit by the Leisure Lakes can be viewed from the verge opposite the track to Ashwood Lodge.There is a lot of disturbance but it is worth a quick stop, as rare grebes (e.g. Black-necked) have been seen here in winter among the common wildfowl. Little Ringed Plovers sometimes frequent the muddy edges.

This area is best visited early in the morning before the holidaymakers have stirred from their caravans. Be warned that lorries use this road at all times of the day and travel at a fair rate of knots.

Nightingales are declining here but there were still nine singing males found during the last full survey taken in 1999. One was also reported to be singing in April 2002. The trick is to drive slowly along the road – from late April to late May – listening for their beautiful song.

Key

A Viewpoint for working pits
B Cover for Nightingales
C Hedgerows along roadside
D Viewpoint for Pentney Lakes (suitable for wheelchairs)

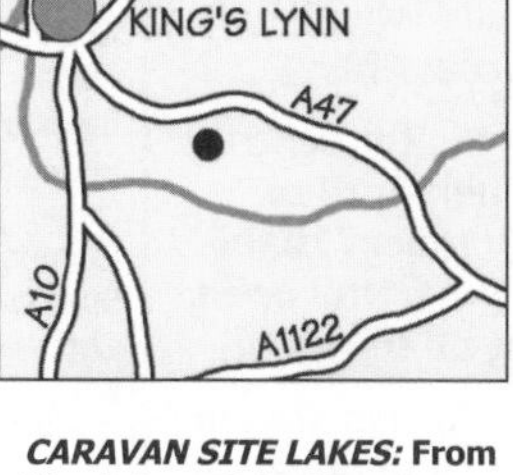

Access details

(Approx. 5.5 miles SE of King's Lynn).

***WORKING PITS:* From King's Lynn, take the A47 signed to Norwich (ignoring brown signs for "Pentney Lakes"). After approx. 3 miles take East Winch Road, signed to Waste Disposal Tip. After 1 mile, take first left (signposted "Waste Recycling Centre", immediately before 7.5 tonne restriction sign). Go past recycling centre, down hill, right at sharp bend to a T-junction. Turn left and drive 0.4 miles to bridge. Park carefully in small layby on right before you cross the bridge (room for two cars). The public footpath is signed both ways along the River Nar (take the left track as you face the bridge, crossing the ditch and then over a stile). DO NOT BLOCK ANY FARM GATES.**

***CARAVAN SITE LAKES:* From King's Lynn take the minor road off to the right following the brown tourist signs for 'Pentney Lakes'. Follow to the entrance of Pentney Lakes Leisure Park. The area of bushes just before this entrance used to be good for Nightingales, as did the area around the sandy pull-in for West Bilney Wood (TF 699133).**

To view the pits, go past the Leisure Park entrance and turn left at the sharp bend by the house (straight on is access for lorries only). After one mile, park on the left-hand verge opposite track to Ashwood Lodge (if you reach the ancient cross on the right you have gone too far).

There is a small car park at the entrance to West Bilney Wood (see Access section). Follow the wide track through the pine trees and you should see Goldcrest, Coal Tit, Great Spotted Woodpecker, Treecreeper and maybe even Tawny Owl and Crossbill.

NWT RANWORTH BROAD

Key points

- Free car park (donations box) near Ranworth Staithe.
- No toilets on site – use block opposite the Maltster pub (wheelchair accessible).
- Level terrain, fully wheelchair accessible.
- Visitor centre open April to October (10am-5pm), trail open at all times.
- Groups should book in advance.
- No cycling or dogs.
- Electric boat from Ranworth Staithe to the visitor centre and NWT Cockshoot Broad (80p in 2005).
- Boat trips tour Ranworth Broad (£3 in 2005 but phone to see when they are running)
- Play area, book sales, sightings board, snacks at centre.

VISIT NWT Ranworth Broad for a pleasant diversion on a boating holiday on The Norfolk Broads. There is an impressive visitor centre at Ranworth, accessed through an area of wet woodland that is excellent for many common bird species. The reserve is a designated SSSI. You may also wish to take a trip from the staithe to the visitor centre on the electric boat.

Target birds

All year – Cetti's Warbler (hear 60%, see 10%). *Summer* – Common Tern (100%), Marsh Harrier (15%), Bearded Tit (5%). *Winter* – Common wildfowl (100%).

Other possible bird species

All year
Great Crested Grebe
Cormorant (large roost)
Egyptian Goose
Shelduck
Common wildfowl
Common waterbirds
Sparrowhawk
Common gull species
Kingfisher
Great Spotted Woodpecker
Common scrub birds
Marsh Tit
Common woodland birds
Common finches
Reed Bunting

Summer
Cuckoo
Hirundines
Summer warblers

Winter
Wigeon
Gadwall
Teal
Shoveler
Pochard

Occasional
Lesser Spotted Woodpecker
Osprey

Background information and birding tips

PART of the Bure Marshes NNR, Ranworth Broad is a good site for wheelchair users to observe birds, insects and flora, as the 500 yard trail is a boardwalk throughout.

The Norfolk Wildlife Trust visitor centre, where Ranworth Broad can be viewed through the windows, is easily accessible to wheelchair users, though the upstairs viewing area can only be reached by steps.

There is a sightings board near the entrance so you can see what you missed on the way in. An ice cream goes down a treat here while you are watching the Common Terns rearing their young on the nesting platforms near the centre. An Osprey regularly drops in on spring passage. In 2002 this could be seen from the visitor centre but in 2005 it could only be seen from the boat trips on Ranworth Broad itself.

Once you have found the reserve (sign-posting from the car park could be improved), it provides a very pleasant stroll through wet woodland (known as carr) where you may encounter many common species, plus Cetti's Warblers singing from the thick cover.

In winter, NWT Ranworth Broad attracts a large number of wildfowl but the centre itself is closed. This sometimes means viewing

Contacts

Norfolk Wildlife Trust
01603 625540

Broadland Conservation Centre, Ranworth, 01603 270479

General Broads Authority
01603 610734

Access details

(Approx. 8 miles NE of Norwich).

BY CAR: **From B1140 (Acle to Wroxham road), follow signs into South Walsham village. In village centre take the road N to Ranworth. Follow road for 1.1 miles to a junction of roads at The Maltster public house (pub on left, Granary Stores straight ahead). Turn right here, following signs to the Conservation Centre car park about 30 yards down on the right, indicated by a brown tourist sign.**

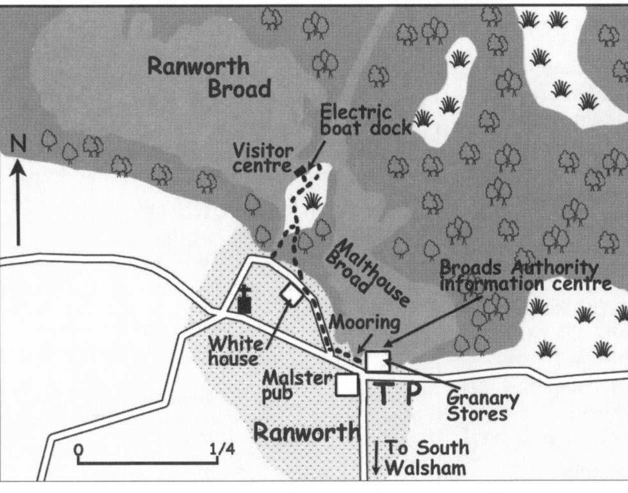

Walk back to the pub and Ranworth Staithe. Look for a Norfolk Wildlife Trust sign indicating the start of the walk to the Conservation Centre (the electric boat to the visitor centre also leaves from this area). Follow boardwalk (adjacent to the road, running west) towards church to its end. Turn immediately right (do not go straight on to the church) and follow for 0.2 miles to reserve entrance on the right (opposite a large white house). Follow the boardwalk through the alder carr to the visitor centre.

BY BOAT: **Head W from Wroxham along River Bure, through Horning and moor up at Ranworth Staithe. The reserve notice board is on the right near the shop. Follow the directions above to the visitor centre or catch the electric boat from the staithe (small fee payable).**

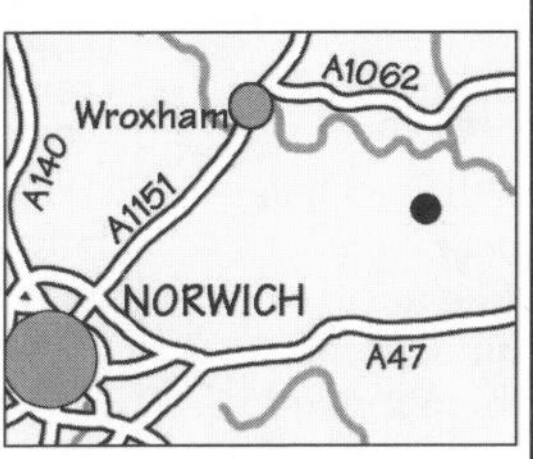

can be uncomfortable from the boardwalk due to the lack of shelter but as the Broad is usually swarming with Pochards, Shovelers, Teal, Tufted Ducks and Great Crested Grebes, it is worth the effort.

All in all, there is something here for everyone. The reserve is also good for butterflies and dragonflies in summer and a visit is usually an enjoyable one, though the trip might be made more endurable by using insect repellent.

Probably the most exciting sight for birdwatchers is the roost of more than 400 Cormorants throughout the year.

An added attraction for visitors is the boat trip around Ranworth Broad. This visits areas not viewable from the visitor centre and the informative guide will make this an interesting excursion. You must phone before your visit to check when this boat is running (it is a separate trip from the one from Ranworth Staithe to the visitor centre). This is the only way to see Bearded Tits at this site and up until at least July 2005, the regular Osprey.

Other nearby sites

Breydon Water, Buxton Heath, NWT Cockshoot Broad, Great Yarmouth Beach, NWT Hickling Broad, Hoveton Great Broad, How Hill NNR, RSPB Strumpshaw Fen, NWT Upton Fen, Winterton Dunes.

NOA REDWELL MARSH

Key points

- Access for NOA members dawn-dusk, non-members 9am - 5pm after obtaining key from NOA Holme Observatory (£5 deposit).
- The key fits all NOA reserve hides. If your membership has lapsed, please return your key!
- Fully boardwalked for wheelchair access.
- Wheelchair users gain free access to hide, non-NOA members must phone prior to their visit to ensure someone is available to unlock the hide.
- Telescope useful.
- Fieldguide in hide for reference.
- Sightings book in hide.

Contacts

Norfolk Ornithologists' Association
01485 525406

EVEN THOUGH you have to obtain a key to gain access to Redwell's hide, it is well worth the effort as it has become the place to see Green and Wood Sandpipers in north Norfolk in spring and autumn.

Target birds

All year – Barn Owl (90%). *Spring/autumn* – Green Sandpiper (60%), Wood Sandpiper (40%).

Other possible bird species

All year
Egyptian Goose
Common wildfowl
Common waterbirds
Marsh Harrier
Kestrel
Lapwing
Redshank
Snipe
Common gull species
Sky Lark
Meadow Pipit
Pied Wagtail
Common scrub birds
Corvids
Common finches

Winter
Brent Goose
Wigeon
Teal
Other common wildfowl
Winter thrushes

Summer
Black-tailed Godwit
Avocet
Hobby
Turtle Dove
Hirundines
Sedge Warbler
Lesser Whitethroat
Whitethroat
Blackcap

Spring/autumn
Little Ringed Plover
Little Stint
Ruff
Greenshank
Common Sandpiper
Yellow Wagtail

Occasional
Little Egret
Hen Harrier (winter)

Background information and birding tips

REDWELL MARSH comprises 35 acres of marshland with an excellent wader scrape that attracts many bird species all year round.

The hide is accessed along a boardwalk from the Holme access track and is fully wheelchair accessible. To gain access to the hide you must first obtain a key from the NOA Holme Observatory (directions on page 119).

The scrape attracts numerous Green and Wood Sandpipers in spring and autumn, as well as Common and Curlew Sandpipers, Ruff, Little Stints, Whimbrels and Greenshanks.

A few Yellow Wagtails regularly visit in spring and are usually to be found around the hooves of the resident cows. A Little Egret may drop in at any time of year.

In summer, small numbers of Avocets and Black-tailed Godwits may visit the marsh and, overhead, you may be lucky to see a Marsh Harrier or Hobby.

Winter brings an array of common wildfowl to Redwell. Expect to see Wigeon, Tufted Ducks, Gadwall, Teal and Mallards. If these species become agitated, scan the marsh for a Hen Harrier, Merlin or Peregrine.

At any time of the year, Redwell Marsh is an excellent place to see a Barn Owl. A vigil in the hide for any reasonable length of time should result in superb views of this special bird.

Finally, don't neglect to scan the hedgerow alongside the boardwalk leading to the hide. This can hold several bird species, such as Goldfinch, Greenfinch, Bullfinch,

Linnet, Dunnock and Blackbird which may all be encountered at any time of year. They will be joined by Sedge Warbler, Blackcap and Whitethroat in summer.

The telegraph pole at the entrance seems to attract the local Great Spotted Woodpecker, especially when displaying in spring.

Redwell Marsh makes for an excellent diversion when combined with a visit to the NOA and NWT reserves. A full day's birding in the Holme area can be very rewarding whatever time of year you visit.

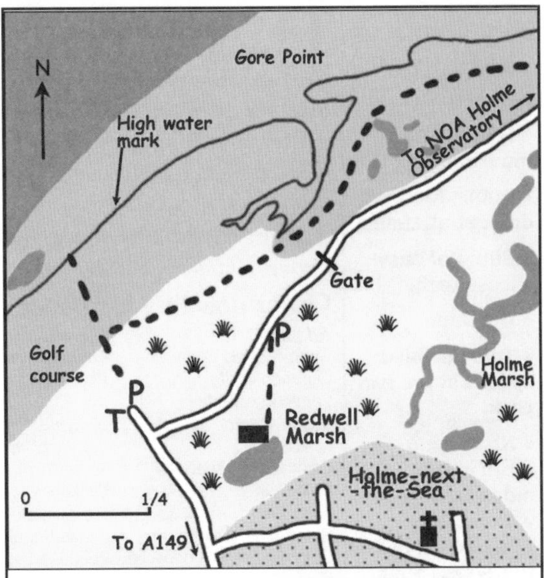

Access details

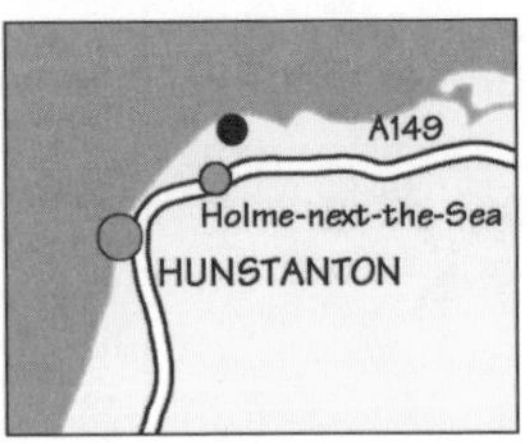

(Approx. 2 miles North East of Hunstanton).

From Hunstanton head E on A149 to left turn (sign-posted NOA Watchpoint/NNT Reserve). Continue on this road for about half a mile, then turn right onto a rough track just before you reach the toilet block (note there are no facilities on site). Drive slowly as track is very bumpy. Go to the NOA Holme Observatory (see page 107 for instructions) to obtain a key and follow their directions for parking.

Be careful not block the gate to the marsh as it will obstruct wheelchair users. Follow the short boardwalk to the hide.

Other nearby sites

Brancaster Marsh, Gypsy Lane, NWT Holme Dunes, NOA Holme Observatory, Hunstanton, Ken Hill Wood, Sandringham, RSPB Snettisham, RSPB Titchwell Marsh.

ROCKLAND BROAD

Key points

- Free car parking.
- Free 24-hour mooring.
- Public footpath open at all times.
- 800m of easy-access path.
- One hide.
- Two disabled spaces in the car park.
- No turning room in the hide for large wheelchairs. You may have to reverse 50m along the path to turn around.
- Facilities in the pub when open.

Contacts

General Broads Authority
01603 610734

RSPB Strumpshaw Fen
01603 715191

HEAD FOR this pleasant reserve in Broadland if you are keen to see or hear Cetti's Warbler. This is one of Norfolk's premier sites for the skulking species. Rockland is ideal for those on a boating holiday though it is not teeming with rarities. The Broad itself supports many common water birds and the marshes usually attract a Marsh Harrier in summer.

Target birds

All year – **Cetti's Warbler (hear, 80%, see, 25%).** *Spring/summer* – **Marsh Harrier (55%).**

Other possible bird species

All year
Great Crested Grebe
Common wildfowl
Common waterfowl
Sparrowhawk
Kestrel
Common gull species
Barn Owl
Kingfisher
Green Woodpecker
Great Spotted Woodpecker
Sky Lark
Meadow Pipit
Pied Wagtail
Common scrub birds
Corvids
Common finches
Reed Bunting

Summer
Common Tern
Turtle Dove
Cuckoo
Hirundines
Sedge Warbler
Reed Warbler
Lesser Whitethroat
Whitethroat
Blackcap
Chiffchaff
Willow Warbler

Winter
Winter wildfowl
Winter thrushes

Spring/autumn
Arctic Tern
Black Tern
Yellow Wagtail

Occasional
Hobby

Background information and birding tips

ROCKLAND is a small and mostly overlooked Broad but has many delights to offer the visiting birdwatcher. It is probably my most successful place to see Cetti's Warbler in the county. And yes, I did write **see** Cetti's!

The birding starts in the car park where common species such as Chaffinch, Goldfinch, House Sparrow, Robin, etc can be encountered. In summer, Sedge and Reed Warblers sing from the vegetation around the staithe car park.

If the area is peaceful, listen out for a Kingfisher along the mooring channel. First thing in the morning is best. Walk slowly along the path. You might hear a Cetti's Warbler in any of the bushes along the way. There is a bench about 150 yards from the gate where I like to sit and wait to see what pops out of these bushes. Patience is needed to catch a glimpse of a Cetti's.

After the stile, the path runs atop a raised bank. There are one or two gaps in the bushes along the path, allowing you to view Rockland Broad. Watch out for terns in the summer and ducks in the winter. Common Tern is most numerous here but Black and Arctic Terns pass through occasionally in spring.

The bushes and reeds along the path should also produce Sedge and Reed Warblers and Whitethroat. The marsh on your right is a good place to see Marsh Harriers if you are lucky.

Green and Great Spotted Woodpeckers inhabit the trees at the back of the marsh to your right and they can sometimes be seen flying along the edges of the wood. Yellow Wagtails may be seen in the fields, especially in spring.

You eventually reach a hide, managed by the RSPB. This is the best place to view water birds such as Great Crested Grebe, Coot, Moorhen, Grey Heron, Mute Swan, Tufted Duck, Pochard, Gadwall etc.

The windows at either end of the hide look into thick bushes and are excellent places to get a fleeting glimpse of Cetti's Warblers.

The easy-access path ends here but a muddy path continues through bushes and continues alongside the marsh up to the River Yare. You may get closer views of Marsh Harrier here.

You can now retrace your steps to the car park or continue along the footpath, which rejoins the minor road at Claxton. You will then have to turn right along the road back to Rockland Staithe (approx 3.5 miles round walk).

You can also walk to the Ted Ellis reserve from Rockland's car park. Walk onto the road and turn right. After 150 yards, turn right along a farm track (signed "playground") and follow through to Surlingham Wood and the Ted Ellis Trust car park (approx. 1 mile).

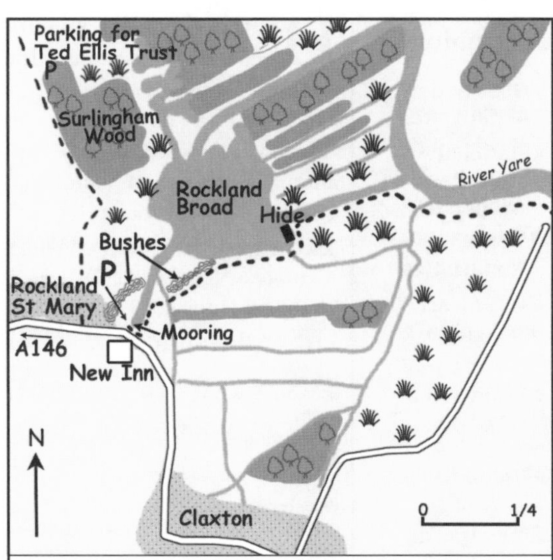

Access details

(Approx. 6.5 miles E of Norwich).

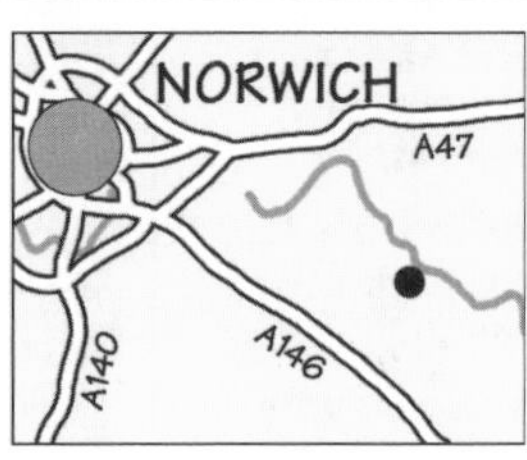

BY CAR: **From A47 Norwich bypass, turn onto A146 (sign-posted Lowestoft and Norwich). Head SE on this road (i.e. away from Norwich) for about 100 yards until first set of traffic lights. Turn left to Bramerton. Stay on this minor road to Rockland then follow signs for Claxton (basically you are staying on this minor road throughout). Beyond the houses in Rockland, follow the small sign on left directing you to 'Rockland Staithe Car Park'. If you reach the New Inn, you have gone too far (the car park is almost opposite the pub). Do not park in the pub car park.**

From the designated car park follow the path over a small bridge towards the pub. The footpath to the reserve starts after you have crossed the mooring channel and continues to the River Yare.

BY BOAT: **The reserve is situated along the River Yare about half an hour's journey SE from the Brundall boat yards. Moor in the channel at Rockland Staithe.**

Other nearby sites

Breydon Water, RSPB Buckenham Marshes, Cantley, Great Yarmouth Beach, Hardley Flood, NWT Hickling Broad, Horsey Mere, RSPB Strumpshaw Fen, RSPB Surlingham Church Marshes, Ted Ellis Reserve.

NWT ROYDON COMMON

Key points

- **SSSI and RAMSAR site.**
- **National Nature Reserve, managed by NWT.**
- **No facilities.**
- **Use insect repellent in summer.**
- **Open at all times, free access and parking.**
- **Access along sandy tracks, which can be wet after rain. Mostly level terrain.**
- **Car track to car park very rough.**
- **Access very difficult for wheelchair users.**
- **A torch may be useful on Nightjar trips.**
- **Telescope essential for watching raptors.**

Contacts

Norfolk Wildlife Trust
Tel 01603 625540

HERE'S A Norfolk Wildlife Trust reserve that is equally good in summer and winter. Hen Harriers coming into the raptor roost can be seen from November to March, joined occasionally by a Merlin. In summer, Nightjars show well at Roydon. The whole reserve is packed with rare and scarce animals, insects and plants, making it a fantastic place for the all-round naturalist to visit.

Target birds

Winter – Hen Harrier (90%), Merlin (25%). *Summer* – Nightjar (90%), Tree Pipit (60%), Wood Lark (70%), Nightingale (hear, 60%, see 20%).

Other possible bird species

All year
Sparrowhawk
Kestrel
Grey Partridge
Lapwing
Snipe
Woodcock
Curlew
Stock Dove
Tawny Owl
Barn Owl
Common scrub birds
Marsh Tit
Green Woodpecker
Great Spotted Woodpecker
Sky Lark
Meadow Pipit
Pied Wagtail
Jay
Common finches
Yellowhammer
Reed Bunting

Winter
Jack Snipe
Winter thrushes

Spring/summer
Hobby
Hirundines
Grasshopper Warbler
Lesser Whitethroat
Other warblers

Occasional
Long-eared Owl
Short-eared Owl

Background information and birding tips

ROYDON COMMON is a famous raptor roost site. A visit here in winter will almost certainly result in sightings of a couple of Hen Harriers along with Kestrel, Sparrowhawk and, occasionally, Merlin.

The standard procedure is to turn up an hour before dusk between late October and early March (though I have found December through to February to be the optimum period) and scan the Common. The harriers can appear as if out of nowhere, so be alert.

Keep a close eye on Carrion Crows as any raptor in the area will be welcomed by a mass of mobbing corvids! I was alerted to the presence of a female Hen Harrier in 05/06 by such a kerfuffle. The graceful raptor was soon joined on the heath by another female and a male, as well as two Barn Owls. Hen Harriers normally head towards the back of the Common and fly around before landing on the ground to roost.

Good numbers of Jack Snipe are present in winter but seeing them involves a trek in freezing cold water up to your knees!

In summer, NWT Roydon Common is a good place to see Nightjars. Up to 20 churring males can be heard on the reserve. To see one, take the main track from the car park until you reach a junction with another sandy track (approx 200 yards on your left). The Nightjars can be anywhere along this second track, as well as Wood Lark and Tree Pipit. Nightjars can usually be seen as close as the

Access details

(Approx. four miles E of King's Lynn).

FOR RAPTORS: **From the King's Lynn bypass, take A148 towards Cromer. After approx. 300 yards turn right (sign-posted to Grimston and Congham Hall Herb Garden). After 0.6 miles, take the sandy track on the right (with the wooden public footpath sign). Park in gravel car park after 250 yards. From car park, walk through the new gate then along the sandy track for about 100 yards. Take the first track on your left (blocked by a huge log) which opens out onto a flat, grassy area that overlooks the Common.**

FOR NIGHTJARS: **(Also general access to the heath and bog) follow directions as above but after the new gate, take second track on your left (by the NWT Roydon Common noticeboard). Nightjars can be seen anywhere from this track. This track passes through the reserve then on to Grimston Warren, a newly acquired NWT reserve that is being restored to bog (currently no access but can be viewed from the fence).**

FOR NIGHTINGALES: **(TF 697228) Follow instructions as for raptors (above) but instead of using car park, travel further along the Grimston road to just before the road junction. There is a small car park on the right that is not easy to see (if you reach the road junction sign-posted to Roydon, you have gone too far). The bushes around the car park and the nature trail that starts from this car park are very good for Nightingales.**

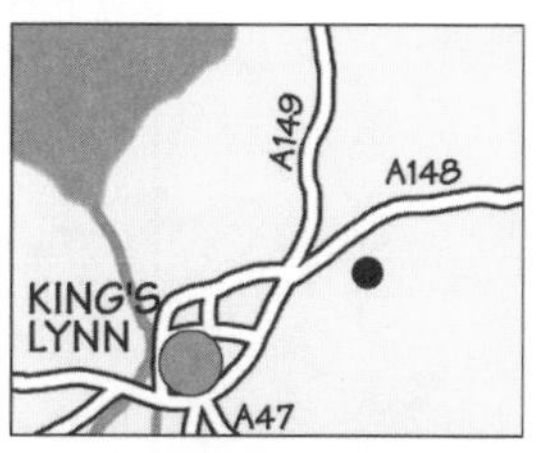

junction of the two main tracks, approximately 300 yards from the car park.

Wheelchair users and people with mobility difficulties may park on the access track before reaching the NWT car park and scan the heath for raptors from their car. Unfortunately, it is unlikely that you will see Wood Lark or Nightjar from here in summer.

Nightingales are present at Roydon in respectable numbers. Park in the eastern car park, taking care on this busy road. Nightingales are usually audible from this car park, from mid April (approx 18th). Cross over a stile and follow the way-marked NWT trail through the wet wood.

The wood and pools along this trail are excellent for insects as well as birds. The wide, grass track accessed from the east of the car park (left as you turn in to the car park) is also excellent for butterflies and eventually leads to a sandy track. Turn right along the sandy track (this is, unbelievably, a 60mph road!) and you reach the gates to Roydon Common (on your right, follow the track to the raptor roost car park) and Grimston Warren (on your left, no formal trails yet).

This is one of the top 500 nature reserves in the country and a lot of work goes into maintaining the habitat for all kinds of flora and fauna. The result is that Roydon Common, as well as being an excellent site for raptors and breeding birds, is also host to an amazing number of rare plants, dragonflies and moths.

SALTHOUSE HEATH

Key points

- **Access at all times.**
- **Park sensibly.**
- **The only walking necessary is along level Tarmac roads.**

Contacts

None.

BETWEEN MAY and August, head for the heath at dawn or dusk as this site probably holds the best watched Nightjars and Nightingales in the county. It is especially good for wheelchair-bound birdwatchers as all target birds may be seen from the road.

Target birds

Summer – **Nightjar (85%), Tree Pipit (May display flight 80%), Nightingale (hear 80%, see 40%).**

Other possible bird species

Summer

Hobby	Tawny Owl	Common woodland birds
Woodcock	Great Spotted Woodpecker	Warblers
Cuckoo	Hirundines	Yellowhammer
	Common scrub birds	

Background information and birding tips

THE NAMES of the two most noteworthy species to be seen at Salthouse Heath give a clue to their habits. 'Night' suggests that both species, Nightingale and Nightjar, are only to be found during darkness. This is not strictly true of course but it is necessary to be on site at dawn or dusk for the best chance of locating either of these evocative species.

Nightingales arrive from about April 17 but I suggest you visit the Heath from a week later to be sure of connecting with one. I prefer to arrive around dawn on a mild day and listen for their beautiful, far-carrying song. It doesn't usually take long to locate a singing Nightingale but seeing it is another matter!

The most promising place to look is in bushes lining the triangle of roads west of the crossroads where you park (see map). I have listened for an hour to a bird singing continually from thick cover three yards in front of me without catching a glimpse of the little devil.

Even more annoying was the fact that it kept moving from bush to bush and I still didn't see it! Eventually, I obtained good views, demonstrating the benefits of patience.

There are stories of more than one Nightingale singing in full view on trees that haven't yet developed their leaves (in April) but I have never experienced this myself. Yet. The junction of the triangle of roads at TG 071422 is supposed to be a good place for this.

Nightingales do sing through the day, especially on warm spring ones and in the evenings. This means you can turn up an hour before dark, listen to the Nightingales, then head back along the road for the chorus of Nightjars.

The Nightjars on Salthouse Heath are probably the most watched (listened to) in Britain. On most nights there are several people standing around waiting for the first '*churrs*' of these birds. They arrive in mid to late May and entertain visiting birdwatchers until August.

Once parked, you need go no further. Male Nightjars should start 'churring' on the Heath north and south of the road just as it is getting dark. If you are really lucky, you may see one perched in a bare tree while it does its vocal impression of a distant moped. This is probably more likely on the north side of the road, the bird being silhouetted against the sunset. What better way to end a day in Norfolk?

As the light dims, flying Nightjars can usually be seen over the road and a close encounter with a one is certainly a life-enhancing experience!

Please remember that both Nightingales and Nightjars are sensitive to disturbance, so please do not chase after them or tape-lure them. If you see bad behaviour at this site, please remonstrate with the perpetrator.

The heath is a traditional site for Tree Pipit, present from mid-May until late August. However, they have been absent in the last couple of years but this will hopefully be a temporary blip, so still check for them.

Wood Larks seem to be colonising Salhouse but I have never been lucky enough to see them at this site. They should be singing from late February through to May, if you fancy searching for one but you must remain on the paths at all times.

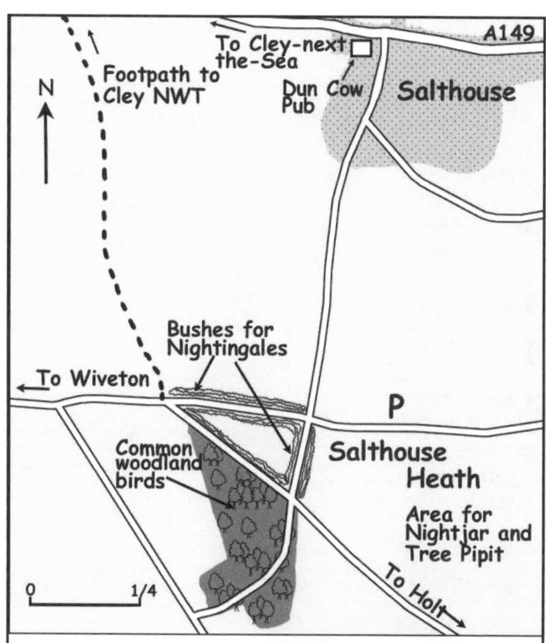

Access details

(Approx. 6 miles W of Sheringham).

From A149 turn inland on a minor road (S) at the Dun Cow pub. After one mile, you reach a crossroads. Turn left and park on the verge wherever you can find a space. This is the area to hear and see Nightjars.

For Nightingales, walk back to the crossroads and listen for their loud song. For either species, it should not be necessary to enter the heath.

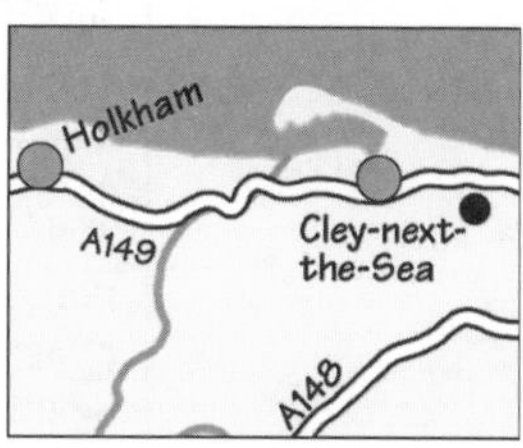

You may also walk from Cley NWT/Walsey Hills to Salthouse Heath (or vice versa) along the public footpath

Other nearby sites

Blakeney Point, NWT Cley Marshes, Felbrigg Hall, Kelling Quags, Salthouse Beach, Swanton Novers, NOA Walsey Hills, Weybourne

NWT SALTHOUSE MARSHES

Key points

- Free access at all times.
- Marsh can be viewed from the road so suitable for wheelchair users.
- Terrain is level along shingle bank.
- Areas either side of beach car park owned by the National Trust.

Contacts

None.

IN RECENT winters, Salthouse has established itself as one of the most reliable places to see Snow Buntings in Norfolk, occasionally joined by a Shore Lark or two. The flood pools along the access road give the visiting birdwatcher the chance to obtain close views of common wader species, while the shingle seawall is a handy place from which to seawatch.

Target birds

Winter – Barn Owl (65%), Seabirds (40%), Snow Bunting (25%), winter raptors (20%), Shore Lark (10%). *Spring/autumn* – Passage waders, passage seabirds, Lapland Bunting (5%). *Summer* – Marsh Harrier (80%), Little Tern (80%).

Other possible bird species

All year
Cormorant
Kestrel
Common waders
Common gull species
Sky Lark
Meadow Pipit
Pied Wagtail
Reed Bunting

Winter
Divers
Grebes
Brent Goose
Wigeon
Long-tailed Duck
Common Scoter
Goldeneye
Red-breasted Merganser
Hen Harrier
Merlin
Peregrine
Guillemot
Razorbill
Winter thrushes

Spring/autumn
Shearwaters
Gannet
Garganey
Little Ringed Plover
Little Stint
Temminck's Stint
Curlew Sandpiper
Ruff
Whimbrel
Greenshank
Green Sandpiper
Wood Sandpiper
Common Sandpiper
Skuas
Arctic Tern
Yellow Wagtail
Wheatear

Summer
Sandwich Tern
Common Tern

Background information and birding tips

SALTHOUSE MARSHES, to all intents and purposes, is an extension of NWT Cley Marsh reserve, thus the range of species to be seen is similar to its larger, more illustrious neighbour.

In winter, if you walk west towards Cley, you pass the area favoured by Snow Buntings and Shore Larks, known as the Little Eye (the small hump visible from the car park). Both species are possible though not recorded annually.

If you are lucky, a Lapland Bunting may also be present in this area, though they are more usually seen on autumn passage. The pools to your left should be scanned for common wader species, which may be joined by one or two Avocets in spring and summer.

Further west, look out for Barn Owl and Marsh Harrier. Up on the shingle sea wall, seawatching can be productive at all times of year. The terns, divers, grebes, ducks, shearwaters and skuas listed for Cley can all be seen at sea from Salthouse, at the right time of year.

To the east, you may follow

the Norfolk Coastal Path along the shore to Sheringham, via Gramborough Hill and Weybourne, birdwatching all the way.

The road to the beach is an excellent area to watch birds at close range but it is important to stay in your car to avoid disturbance. Waders can be very close to the road here, particularly, in autumn.

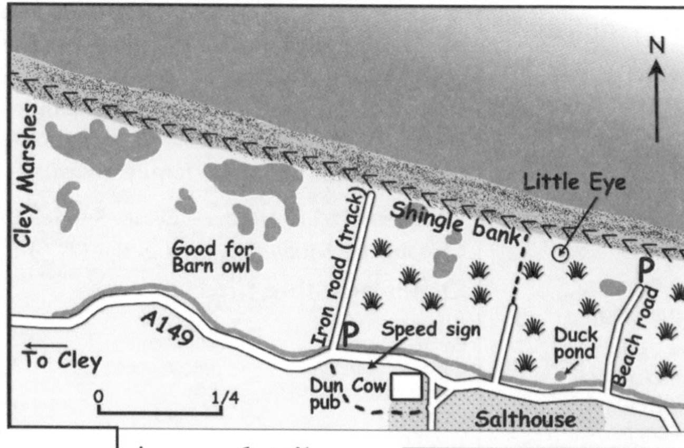

Little Stints are a speciality in September, while Green, Wood and Curlew Sandpipers can all give superb views. Redshanks are present all year round, possibly joined at migration times by a Greenshank or two. Whimbrels are regular visitors in spring.

Winter produces Brent Geese and Wigeon in the fields along the approach road. Yellow Wagtails can be seen here in spring and autumn and don't forget to watch out for one of the rarer races (Blue-headed, Syke's etc) among them.

Some birders prefer to park in the Iron Road car park and walk down to the Little Eye and seawall. This is generally a quieter route (less people, not less birds!) than from the beach car park but is essentially the same walk.

In between the Iron Road and Beach Road car parks, along the A149, is a small duck pond. This usually holds a few loafing gulls, predominantly Black-headed and common ducks which love to be fed by children of all ages! Occasionally, a Mediterranean Gull joins the throng.

This is also a good place to stop as you can feed yourself in the pub or shop and no, you can't count all the feral geese on your list!

Access details

(General area: approx. five miles W of Sheringham).

BEACH ROAD: **On A149, heading to Sheringham, you will pass the Dun Cow pub (on right) then the duck pond (on left) after leaving Salthouse village. Take the next road left, (0.4 miles past the pub) sign-posted 'Beach Road' and follow this down to the shingle car park, scanning fields from your car to avoid disturbing the birds. If available, use a small lay-by just after you have turned off the A149 for scanning.**

IRON ROAD: **Park in very small car park off A149, 1.2 miles E of Cley NWT visitor centre (approaching from Cley, if you reach the 40mph signs as you enter Salthouse, you have gone too far). Walk down the track to the shingle seawall.**

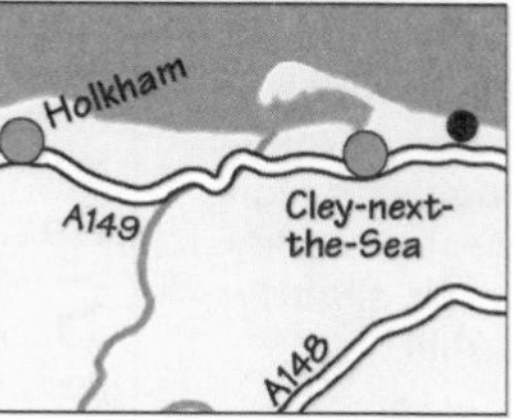

Other nearby sites

Blakeney Point, NWT Cley Marshes, Felbrigg Hall, Kelling Heath, Kelling Quags, Salthouse Heath, Sheringham, Swanton Novers, NOA Walsey Hills, Weybourne.

SANDRINGHAM ESTATE

Key points

- **House and some trails closed in winter.**
- **Country Park and Visitor Centre open all year.**
- **Free car parking.**
- **Toilets, including wheelchair access.**
- **Level terrain along rough paths or roads. Nightjars along a rough sandy track, slightly uphill.**
- **Shop, restaurant and tea-room.**
- **Plants for sale.**
- **Children's play area.**
- **Picnic site.**
- **Bird hide (not accessible to wheelchair users).**

Contacts

Public Enterprises, The Estate Office, 01553 772675 www.sandringhamestate.co.uk E-mail: enquiries@sandringhamestate.co.uk

FAMOUS as the winter home of the Royal Family, Sandringham is also the summer home to Nightjar and permanent home to many common woodland species of birds. The expanse of ancient woodland with easy access, coupled with several non-birding attractions, make this an ideal place for the whole family to visit.

Target birds

All year – **Lesser Spotted Woodpecker (25%), Crossbill (15%).** *Summer* – **Nightjar (90%).**

Other possible bird species

All year
Common wildfowl
Common waterbirds
Sparrowhawk
Kestrel
Woodcock
Tawny Owl
Green Woodpecker
Great Spotted Woodpecker
Sky Lark
Goldcrest
Nuthatch
Treecreeper
Coal Tit
Marsh Tit
Jay
Siskin
Redpoll
Other finches

Summer
Cuckoo
Hirundines
Warblers
Spotted Flycatcher

Spring/autumn
Redstart
Passage migrants

Background information and birding tips

SANDRINGHAM'S magnificent mixed woodland is home to many birds. A maze of footpaths through the woods connects the many parking places along the minor road to the main car park.

The pines around the main car park are excellent for Crossbills. Be prepared to stand for a while (or sit in your car), listening out for their loud '*chip chip*' calls. Early mornings are best, when they may come down to drink from the puddles in the car park. I find the Jays are tamer here than anywhere else I know.

Along the approach road, look out for feeders hanging from the trees: these are great places to see woodland birds at close range, especially in winter.

The colour-marked trails, (blue is one mile long, yellow two miles long), start from the children's play area to the left of the Sandringham shop. They weave in and out of the woods and are excellent walks to see common woodland species. All three woodpecker species are present but Lesser Spotted Woodpeckers are scarcest, especially when the trees are in full leaf. The best time to find them is in late March/early April when they are displaying.

The yellow trail splits from the blue one and leads to a hide overlooking a small pool. A few minutes here should produce good views of many common species and possibly a Crossbill flock coming down to drink.

The trails can be tricky to follow as the yellow and blue paint marks on tree trunks are sometimes hard to see. The arrows are sometimes ambiguous, too. If you go more than 100 yards without seeing a coloured spot on a tree, I suggest you retrace your steps.

The trails may prove difficult for wheelchairs to negotiate but no matter, as there is a scenic drive (sign-posted from the main access road) that follows the general route of the trails and all species can be seen in this manner.

There are also several flat 'rides' that pass between the trees while a tractor carries tourists around the estate for a small fee.

From the end of May to the end of August, Sandringham is one of the best places in Norfolk to see Nightjars. My favourite area is accessed from a small, muddy lay-by at approximately TF 679273. Park here and walk into the young plantation.

Nightjars can be seen close to the lay-by on wires, or for better views walk along the sandy track (heading left as you enter the plantation) for about 300 yards. You reach another set of wires crossing the track. Turn right along a wide track, following the wires.

I like to stand very quietly by a telegraph pole and Nightjars usually come and sit on the pole or wires immediately above my head, deafening me with their churring call. You should not try attracting Nightjars by flapping a white handerchief. Not only does this disturb the birds, it isn't necessary!

If you cannot find my little pull-in, don't worry, most of the clearings in the area hold this evocative species. The area around the Camping & Caravan Club site is another good place to see and hear them. Follow the brown tourist signs to the entrance of the camp site and park in any of the pull-ins in the area.

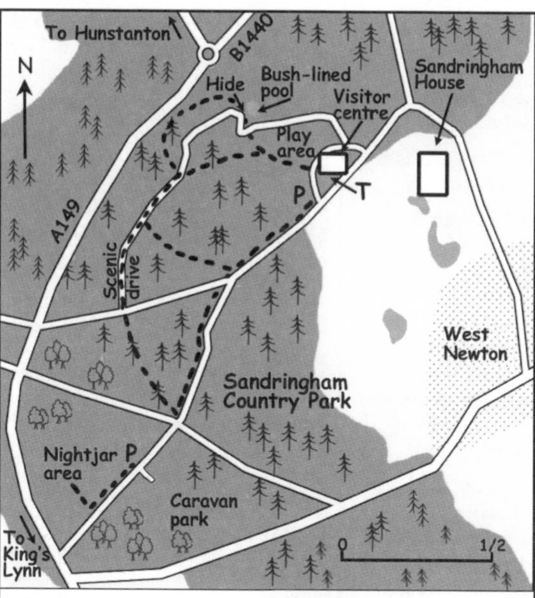

Access details

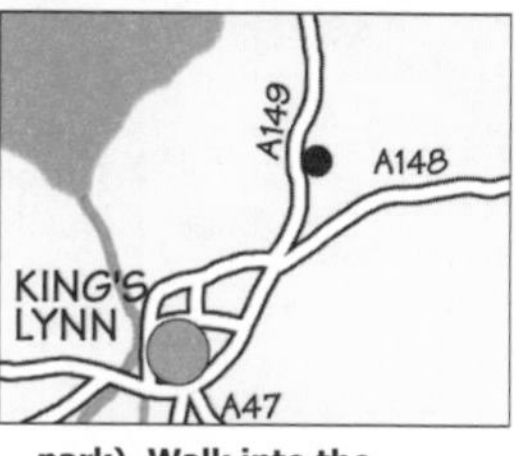

(approx. 6 miles N of King's Lynn).

The Sandringham Estate is well sign-posted from A149 (about six miles N of King's Lynn town centre).

Follow minor road down to the main car park (1 mile) or pull off wherever takes your fancy to walk into the woods. The 'Scenic Drive' is sign-posted off on the left of the access road.

FOR NIGHTJARS:
From King's Lynn take the 2nd right turn after the one to West Newton. The pull-ins on the right give access to prime Nightjar areas. You can also carry on down the road and turn right (sign-posted to the caravan site).

After half a mile, pull in to the verge on the right (virtually opposite the entrance to the caravan park). Walk into the plantation, turn left and follow the sandy track up to where it meets some telephone wires. The track on the right here is excellent for Nightjars.

From Hunstanton, turn off A149 left at the Sandringham brown camping site signs. The pull-ins along this minor road give access to prime Nightjar areas.

Alternatively, continue on road and turn right sign-posted to the caravan site, then follow instructions above.

Key points

- **Many paths accessible by wheelchair.**
- **Many trails to explore.**
- **Trail leaflet available (£3.50, covering the whole of Thetford Forest) from Forest Enterprise offices in village (open 9am - 4.30pm).**
- **Early mornings best for most species, except Nightjar which can be seen at dusk.**
- **Insect repellent advisable in summer.**

Contacts

Forest Enterprise, East Anglia Division
01842 810271

High Lodge Forest Centre
01842 815434

MANY A HAPPY hour can be spent exploring the woods and clearings of this beautiful area in the heart of Breckland. It is a large area to cover but several sought-after species such as Nightjar, Wood Lark, Golden Pheasant and Hawfinch can be found in the vicinity.

Target birds

All year – **Hawfinch (25%), Lesser Spotted Woodpecker (40%), Golden Pheasant (5%), Crossbill (25%), Goshawk (20%), Long-eared Owl (1%).** *Summer* – **Nightjar (90%), Tree Pipit (75%), Wood Lark (75%), Redstart (40%).** *Winter* – **Brambling (50%).**

Other possible bird species

All year
Sparrowhawk
Kestrel
Woodcock
Stock Dove
Tawny Owl
Kingfisher
Green Woodpecker
Great Spotted Woodpecker
Sky Lark
Meadow Pipit
Goldcrest
Marsh Tit
Coal Tit
Nuthatch
Treecreeper
Jay
Siskin
Redpoll
Yellowhammer

Summer
Hobby
Turtle Dove
Cuckoo
Hirundines
Whitethroat
Garden Warbler
Blackcap
Other warblers
Spotted Flycatcher

Occasional
Firecrest (breeds occasionally)

Background information and birding tips

MANY OF THE scarcer species on offer here, for example Crossbill, Goshawk and Hawfinch, can be very elusive, due to the size of the area. However, Nightjars and Wood Larks can be very easy to locate.

I have given directions to the St. Helen's picnic site near Santon Downham but many species can be seen from any suitable pull-in along the roads and tracks in the forest. St. Helen's picnic site, however, gives easy access to many of the birds and has a few facilities, with more in nearby Santon Downham village.

The orange-marked trail from St. Helen's car park is a circular route, about a quarter of which is in Suffolk. Walk to the back of the car park and you will see a pinky/orange, solid path. In winter, scan under the trees at the back of the car park for Bramblings. Head right along the path to a tunnel under the railway line. From here, you may walk right (to the Holy Well and Oratory) or straight ahead. I usually walk ahead to a clearing and then bear left to more excellent clearings for Woodlark, Nightjar, Woodcock and Goshawk.

Any stand of pines may produce Crossbills, any dense cover could hide Golden Pheasants and look out for Redstarts in summer in mature woodland. Also in summer, any clearing along the orange trail (or in the whole of the Thetford Forest!) should be scanned for Wood Lark, Goshawk (late Feb – April best) and Tree Pipit during the day and Nightjar and Woodcock at dusk.

ALL YEAR | **OS MAP 144** | **TL 827874**

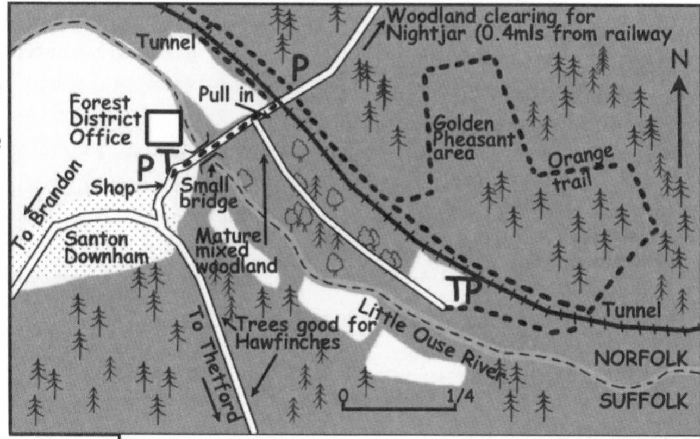

Access details

(Approx. 3.5 miles NW of Thetford).

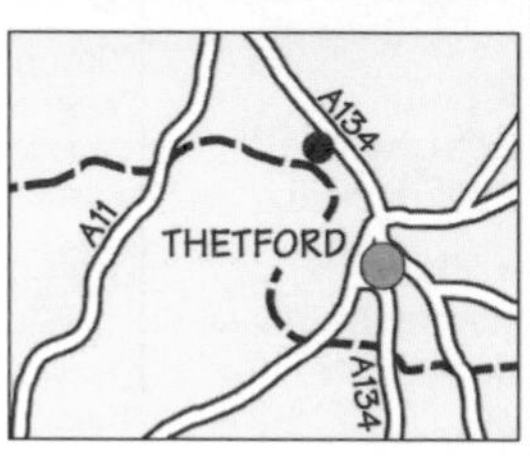

From Thetford, take the B1107, sign-posted Brandon. Take the first right turn (after approx. 3 miles) signed to Forest District Offices. As you drive down this road, keep an eye open for Hawfinch in the lime trees on either side. Follow this road to the Forest Office car park or continue to St. Helen's picnic site car park. For St. Helen's, go past the offices and continue along the narrow road, cross the small bridge, then turn right immediately after this bridge (if you cross over the railway line you have gone too far). The car park is 0.75 miles down this road.

The orange trail eventually leads to a road by a railway crossing, near a bridge over the Little Ouse River. The wood by the bridge is an excellent place to stand and wait for the resident Lesser Spotted Woodpecker to put in an appearance. The estate office car park is another good vantage point for this species (plus there is a shop there for your provisions). The river should be scanned for Kingfisher and any bridge over the Little Ouse is an excellent vantage point to watch bats at dusk

From the road, railway, river junction you now have a choice: straight ahead (following the orange trail markers) to more clearings, right along the road for Wood Larks and Nightjars, or left through the Forestry Office car park to the Suffolk side of the walk.

If you choose to go straight ahead, pass through the sandy car park, then through the barrier marked 'Protect Wildlife. Dogs On Lead'. This track continues for several miles alongside the railway line and gives access to many clearings, which are good for both Wood Larks and Nightjars. Don't forget to regularly scan the sky for raptors passing overhead.

If you don't want to walk far along this track, the orange trail bears left through a tunnel, about 400 yards from the barrier. Scan the meadow for Snipe and Lapwing and the creek for the rare Des Moulin's whorl snail. The orange trail then rejoins the road at the river bridge, continuing through Suffolk back to St. Helen's car park.

On the walk up the road (right) from the railway line, after half a mile or so you will come across a large clearing either side of the road. This is the best area in Santon Downham for Wood Larks and Nightjars. Early mornings from February to May are best for the former species and dusk from mid-May to the end of August for the latter. While you are waiting for the Nightjars to show, listen out for the begging calls of young Long-eared Owls, or the squeaks and honks of a roding Woodcock.

If you choose the Suffolk option, (the final third of the orange trail), you may wish to divert along the road leading to Thetford to scan the trees for Hawfinch, particularly in winter (see map).

SCULTHORPE MOOR

Key points

- **Leased & managed by the Hawk and Owl Trust.**
- **Free parking.**
- **Open daily except Mondays 8 am - 6pm, April – Sept and 8am - 4pm, Oct – March (open at other times by prior arrangement.**
- **Fully boardwalked nature trail.**
- **Hide wheelchair accessible.**
- **SSSI.**
- **Sightings book in hide.**
- **More trails planned.**
- **Portaloo.**

Contacts

Warden: Nigel Middleton, (Mobile 07867 572 794)
E-mail: nigel@sculthorpemoor.fsnet.co.uk
www.sculthorpemoor.co.uk

The Hawk & Owl Trust, PO Box 100, Taunton, TA4 2WX
(0870 9903889)
www.hawkandowl.org

A DESIGNATED SSSI, Sculthorpe Moor is 17 hectares of reedbed, valley fen, alder carr and woodland. It is being lovingly restored by the Hawk and Owl Trust for wildlife and the local community.

Target birds

All Year – **Willow Tit (70%), Barn Owl (50%), Marsh Harrier (50%), Lesser Spotted Woodpecker (15%).** *Summer* – **Spotted Flycatcher (70%), Grasshopper Warbler (hear, 75%, see, 10%), Nightingale (hear, 60%, see, 10%).** *Winter* – **Brambling (55%), Hen Harrier (25%).**

Other possible bird species

All Year
Little Grebe
Red-legged Partridge
Grey Partridge
Pheasant
Sparrowhawk
Kestrel
Woodcock
Common gull species
Stock Dove
Collared Dove
Tawny Owl
Kingfisher
Green Woodpecker
Great Spotted Woodpecker
Sky Lark
Goldcrest
Marsh Tit
Treecreeper
Nuthatch
Jay
Other corvids
Bullfinch
Other common finches
Reed Bunting
Yellowhammer

Spring/summer
Hobby
Turtle Dove
Cuckoo
Hirundines
Sedge Warbler
Reed Warbler
Blackcap
Willow Warbler
Chiffchaff

Spring/autumn
Passage waders

Winter
Winter wildfowl
Lapwing
Winter thrushes
Siskin
Lesser Redpoll

Occasional
Winter raptors
Bittern
Little Egret
Honey Buzzard
Common Buzzard

Background information and birding tips

SCULTHORPE MOOR Community Nature Reserve comprises 42 acres of reedbed, valley fen, alder carr and coppiced woodland leased from the parish council by the Hawk and Owl Trust. The Trust is working to restore these habitats for the good of birds and wildlife.

Currently, there is a hide and 700 metres of boardwalk around the coppiced wood but there are plans to open up a wader scrape, a tower hide, a further 700 metres of boardwalk and an education centre. It is a nice reserve at the moment but when complete in 2007 it will be a fantastic little wildlife refuge.

After parking your car in the rough area along the access track, walk to the temporary visitor 'hut', a further 400 yards down the track. The boardwalk begins by the hut (disabled visitors may park here). There is a Barn Owl box right by the hut and it is worth scanning the surrounding fields to see if the occupant is out and about.

The boardwalk splits but you can walk either way as it is a circular route. Whichever way you choose to go, walk slowly and quietly. In winter, Brambling, Siskin and Redpoll may be seen. In summer, listen for warblers such as Chiffchaff and Willow Warbler. You

may be lucky and spot one of the resident Lesser Spotted Woodpeckers but Great Spotted is much more likely.

Along the way, you will cross the Main Drain. Either bridge over the drain may produce a sighting of a Kingfisher. There are also several benches along the boardwalk, ideal places to sit quietly to see what emerges from the trees to visit the feeders. This is the best place to see Willow Tit (a scarce species in Norfolk) but Marsh Tits also occur here so be prepared to compare these two very similar species!.

The Frank Jarvis hide overlooks a feeding station and a meadow. I love to sit in here, mainly to watch the mice and voles take seed from the floor beneath the feeders. This is a great place to see Bramblings in winter, affording superb views of this elusive finch. Many species of common woodland and scrub birds come to the feeders to delight visitors to the hide.

While in the hide, don't forget to scan the meadow at the back of the wood. The Barn Owl is seen from here virtually daily and a Marsh Harrier occasionally floats over the field. There are fieldguides in the hide to aid identification and a sightings book to let you know what has been seen.

A further boardwalk is planned to take birdwatchers to the River Wensum and a tower hide. This will allow visitors a splendid overview of the extensive reedbed, home to Bearded Tit, Marsh Harrier and Water Rail. In summer, you will see Reed Warblers here and it is hoped Bitterns will be attracted to breed.

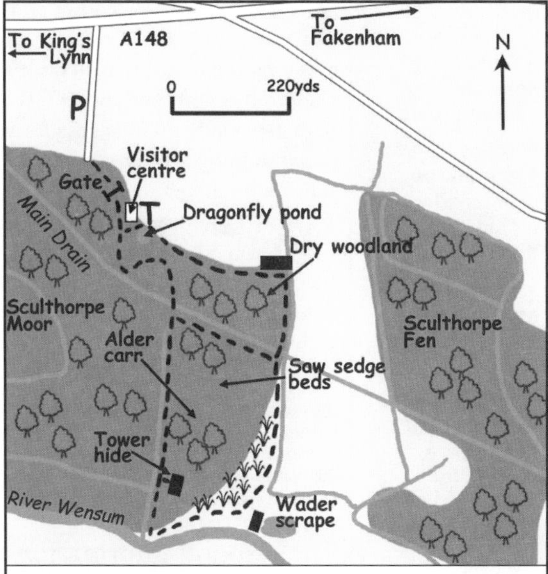

Access details

(1 mile west of Fakenham)

From King's Lynn, take the A148 road to Fakenham. Go through East Rudham and past the turn-offs for Dunton. Look out for a turning on your right to Sculthorpe Mill and you know you are close. There is a road to Sculthorpe on your left but you need the next turning on your right (The Drift), almost directly opposite the second turning left to Sculthorpe (there is a hand-made board for 'Sculthorpe Moor Community Nature Reserve'). The car park is down this track to your right, signed on a Hawk & Owl Trust board. Park your car and walk down the access track to the reserve entrance.

Fakenham
A148
A1065

There will also be a wader scrape to attract passage waders such as Green, Wood and Common Sandpipers and maybe breeding Little Ringed Plover, Avocet, etc, though the path to the scrape will be closed during April – mid Aug to protect breeding birds.

Sculthorpe Moor is well worth a visit as I write this but when fully open - by the end of 2007 - it will become one of those hidden 'must-visit' little Norfolk gems.

SHERINGHAM

Key points

- A sheltered seawatching vantage point.
- Toilet block on the promenade, including disabled toilets.
- Early mornings or evenings seem best.
- Access via footpaths to flat terrace, perfect for wheelchairs.
- Free parking.
- Some shelter available on the prom for wheelchair users down a steep ramp.

Contacts

None

IN THE RIGHT weather conditions – strong onshore winds with a bit of mist or rain – seawatchers intent on enjoying the offshore bird bounty can take advantage of sheltered accommodation on the seafront at Sheringham, with especially good access for wheelchair users. The target percentages below are for when the conditions are ideal for seawatching.

Target birds

Spring/autumn – **Arctic Skua (60%), Great Skua (40%), Manx Shearwater (35%), Little Auk in November (10%), Balearic Shearwater (10%), Sooty Shearwater (5%), Grey Phalarope (5%), Pomarine Skua (5%), Long-tailed Skua (3%), Leach's Petrel (2%), Sabine's Gull (1%), Storm Petrel (1%).**

Other possible bird species

All year	Summer	Winter
Fulmar	Gannet	Red-throated Diver
Cormorant	Kittiwake	Wigeon
Common wildfowl	Tern species	Common Scoter
Common waders	Hirundines	Red-breasted Merganser
Common gull species		Auks

Background information and birding tips

SHERINGHAM'S Leas area is arguably the best seawatching spot in the county. In the right weather conditions (and sometimes even in seemingly unfavourable conditions), close views can be had of many of the passage seabird specialities.

From late July, Manx Shearwaters should be seen in small numbers with the chance of one or two Balearic Shearwaters passing, too. However, it is in autumn when this spot can really produce the goods. Unfortunately, the best conditions for seawatching are strong onshore winds with rain or mist, which can make birding very uncomfortable. At Sheringham there is help at hand in the form of a large shelter on the prom with seats: luxury!

From this vantage point and in the conditions described above, the hardy birdwatcher can settle down to enjoy some excellent seawatching. Birds you can anticipate include all four skua species, Sooty Shearwater and Sabine's Gull, all of which are seen with some regularity, especially in September.

If you are even luckier you may pick out a Leach's or European Storm-petrel, or something even more special such as a Fea's Petrel!

Tardy Common, Sandwich and Little Terns can be seen at this time, as well as Gannets, Fulmars, Kittiwakes and common gull species. Common wader species are seen daily and ducks on passage are usually noted too.

In truth, the majority of birders here are waiting for a biggie to come along (Fea's Petrel, Tropicbird, etc) but you will have to put in many hours to stand a chance of that happening – unless you are extremely lucky.

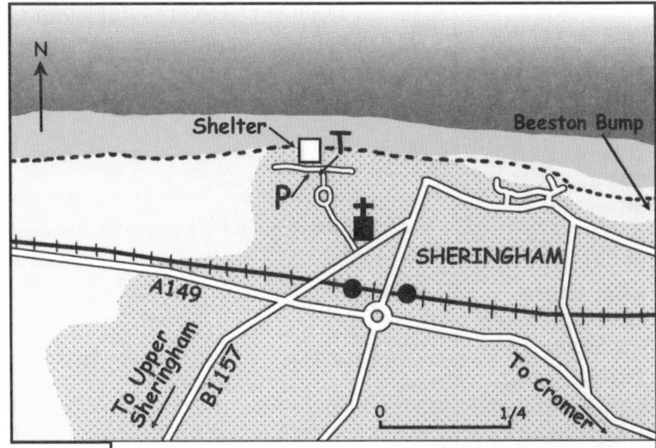

Late October into early November sees Little Auks passing in variable numbers. Strongest passage comes after prolonged spells of northerly or north-westerly winds.

When seabirds are passing in large numbers, the atmosphere in the shelter can be electric as every few seconds someone picks out something new to test your ID skills.

A quick glance at the TV weather charts the previous night should help you decide if an early morning trip to the prom is going to be worthwhile. However, if things do look promising, arrive early as the shelter can get packed full of fellow nutters, erm, I mean seawatching fanatics.

In addition to seawatching, the area to the east of the town, as far as Cromer, has become renowned as a raptor migration hotspot. In spring and autumn species can include Buzzard, Marsh Harrier, Sparrowhawk and an occasional Goshawk.

Nearby, Baston Bump (TG 168433) has a track record of attracting migrants in spring and autumn and is a good place to view visible migration of species such as Tree and Meadow Pipits and winter thrushes.

Wheelchair users can park on the flat platform at the top of the prom or move down the steepish ramp to shelter under the bridge. The latter option restricts your field of view but it has kept me dry on many an occasion!

Access details

(General area: Sheringham town centre).

From A149, turn into the town down Church Street, opposite B1157 to Upper Sheringham. Cross railway bridge and follow road to the church (about half a mile). Turn left into The Boulevard where you will find a small roundabout with a cenotaph on it. Take the second exit from the roundabout (dead end) and park by the concrete bridge straight ahead of you. This is the area known as The Leas.

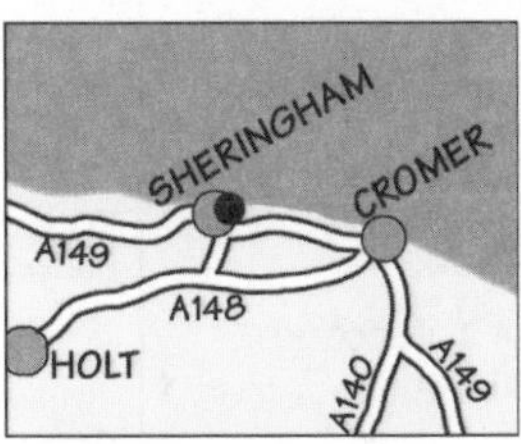

Walk through the arch onto a terrace, which gives a superb view of the sea. If the weather is poor, go down the steps into a shelter with seats.

Other nearby sites

Blakeney Point, NWT Cley Marshes, Holkham NNR, Salthouse Beach, NOA Walsey Hills, Warham Greens, Wells Woods, Weybourne.

SNETTISHAM COASTAL PARK

Key points

- **Free access at all times.**
- **Car park: summer £2.50 all day, £1.50 after 3pm, free in winter (in 2005).**
- **Car park locked 10.30pm – 8.30am.**
- **Mostly level terrain but some steep banks.**
- **Some paths muddy after rain.**
- **Seawatching hide.**
- **Telescope useful.**

Contacts

Warden: M. Vowser, Village Farm, Hill Rd, Ingoldisthorpe, King's Lynn, Norfolk PE31 6NZ (014854 41239)

King's Lynn Borough Council, Kings Court, Chapel St, King's Lynn, Norfolk PE30 1EX (015537 961241)

SNETTISHAM COASTAL (or Country) Park comprises 143 acres of marsh, scrub, reedbed and open water. It includes Heacham Harbour and is bordered by The Wash so a respectable number of species is possible whenever you visit.

Target species

All Year – **Waders.** *Summer* - **Grasshopper Warbler (hear 90%, see 50%).** *Winter* – **Pink-footed Goose (90%).** *Spring/autumn* – **Passage seabirds and migrants, Mandarin Duck (30%).**

Other possible bird species

All Year
Little Grebe
Great Crested Grebe
Fulmar
Common wildfowl
Common water birds
Marsh Harrier
Sparrowhawk
Kestrel
Red-legged Partridge
Grey Partridge
Water Rail
Common waders
Common gull species
Barn Owl
Kingfisher
Green Woodpecker
Great Spotted Woodpecker
Sky Lark
Common scrub birds
Corvids
Bullfinch
Other common finches
Yellowhammer
Reed Bunting

Summer
Avocet
Black-tailed Godwit
Hobby
Turtle Dove
Cuckoo
Sand Martin
Other hirundines
Sedge Warbler
Reed Warbler
Lesser Whitethroat
Whitethroat
Blackcap
Chiffchaff
Willow Warbler

Winter
Divers
Grebes
Sea ducks
Merlin
Peregrine
Purple Sandpiper
Short-eared Owl
Grey Wagtail
Stonechat
Winter thrushes

Spring/autumn
Shearwaters
Gannet
Whimbrel
Other passage waders
Kittiwake
Skuas
Ring Ouzel
Whinchat
Wheatear
Garden Warbler
Spotted Flycatcher
Pied Flycatcher
Other passage migrants

Occasional
Montagu's Harrier
Shore Lark
Nightingale
Barred Warbler
Bearded Tit
Snow Bunting

Background information and birding tips

SNETTISHAM COASTAL Park was established in 1984. It makes for a pleasant stroll after visiting the nearby RSPB reserve at any time of year. More than 120 species have been recorded in the park or on the adjacent beach and mudflat (The Wash).

When you enter the beach car park (free in winter), park immediately on the right. The entrance to the park is across a little wooden bridge. At migration times, it may be worth scanning the conifers bordering the car park to see if any birds have arrived. A good indicator species is Goldcrest: if they are in the pines, other species may have arrived too. There is an information board just inside the park.

If you fancy starting from a different way, walk onto the seawall from the car park. Turn

right to get to Heacham, left if you want to visit the toilet block. (Note that you should not try to access the RSPB reserve this way, do so only from the RSPB car park). You can walk all the way along this new seawall to Heacham south beach (approx. 2 miles), viewing The Wash on your left and the Coastal Park on your right. About a mile along the seawall, you reach a wooden hide, ideal for viewing The Wash in inclement weather.

The mud should hold several species of waders such as Grey Plover, Oystercatcher, Knot, Turnstone, Dunlin, Golden Plover, Curlew, etc, etc joined by Whimbrel, Curlew Sandpiper, etc in spring and autumn.

Wader-watching is best in winter but birds began to flock to the mudflat from July onwards. June is the quietest month but whatever time of year you visit, choose to view this area when the sea is reasonably close if you wish to see more than dots on the mud.

Also in winter, be in position on the seawall at dawn and dusk and you should be treated to thousands of Pink-footed Geese flying overhead. Views are probably better on the RSPB reserve but the Coastal Park is an acceptable alternative if you don't fancy the extra walking.

When the tide is fully in, look out for grebes and divers in winter and skuas and shearwaters passing in autumn. Seaducks such as Common Scoter and Eider could be present at any time of year, Long-tailed Duck and Red-breasted Merganser joining them in winter.

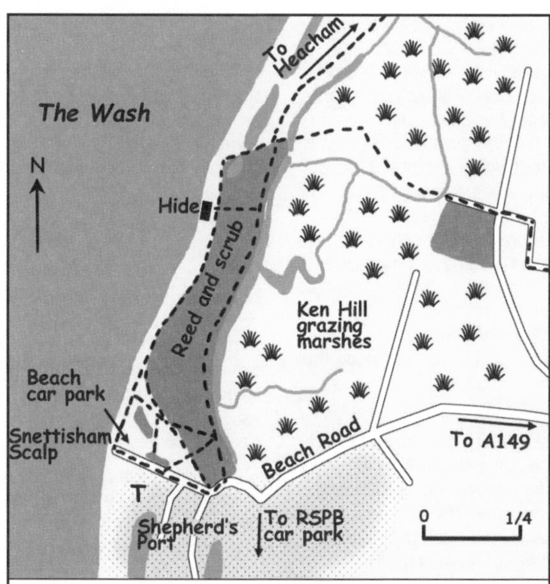

Access details

(Approx. 5 miles south of Hunstanton)

Follow the brown tourist signs to 'Snettisham Beach and RSPB reserve' from the A149 Dersingham bypass. Follow this narrow road for 1.9 miles to where it ends at the beach car park. Walk along the main seawall or go into the park via the wooden walkway on the right near the car park entrance.

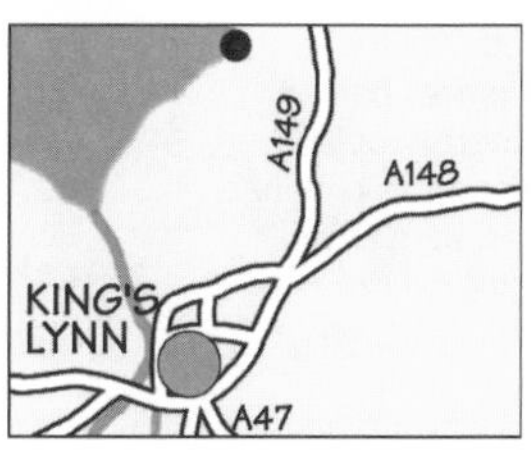

In spring and autumn, the Coastal Park is well worth exploring fully. Wheatear, Ring Ouzel and Whinchat are annual visitors and anything may turn up in favourable conditions.

The bushes attract passage warblers, which join the breeders such as Lesser Whitethroat, Whitethroat and Blackcap. Nightingales can also be heard occasionally but are not present every year.

During the spring and summer, Snettisham is probably the best place in Norfolk to see Grasshopper Warblers. Seven or more

birds can be heard reeling from isolated bushes and usually show well with a bit of patience. Walk into the park from the beach car park and head left along a wide stony path. After about 400 yards, there is a narrow, muddy path on your right leading into the heart of the park, which takes you past some bushes in the reeds. In my experience, this is the best place for 'Groppers', though they can be heard anywhere along the main track too.

This narrow path leads to the secondary seawall, accessed up some steps. Turn left along the uneven, grass track and head towards Heacham (right takes you back to the beach car park access road). There is a channel on your right with a marsh behind. Kingfishers fly along this channel and Barn Owls hunt over the marsh. In winter, scan the marsh for grazing geese, wildfowl and Short-eared Owl.

This track affords excellent views over the park on your left. There is an extensive reedbed, home to Reed and Sedge Warblers in summer and Reed Buntings year round. It can only be a matter of time before Bearded Tits take up residency and it also looks good for a wintering Bittern or two (though I have never seen one here).

There are several creeks and pools to your right, all should be checked for wildfowl on the water and waders on the muddy edges. Mandarin Ducks sometimes stop in spring, though cannot be guaranteed and can be elusive.

After about a mile (opposite the hide on the main seawall) you have a choice. You can go down the steep seawall bank into the heart of the park, or you may wish to carry on along the track towards Heacham. Another footpath leads off to your right, heading for Ken Hill Wood.

If you choose the Heacham route, the track bends inland. Once you reach the town you can return to the beach car park via the main seawall, making this a pleasant circular walk (approx 5 miles). The open areas of water on your left are excellent for hirundines in summer, usually pursued by a Hobby or two (I was entertained by a couple here for over an hour in July 2005).

The varied habitats of the Coastal Park ensure an enjoyable and usually productive, hour or two's bird watching at any time of year. It is situated between Hunstanton to the north, Ken Hill Wood to the east, The Wash to the west and Snettisham RSPB to the south, making this stretch of Norfolk a perfect base for a birdwatching weekend.

Panicking birds may be a sign that a lethal Peregrine is in the area. By Alan Harris

Other nearby sites

Dersingham Bog, Gypsy Lane, NWT Holme Dunes, NOA Holme Observatory, Hunstanton, Ken Hill Wood, King's Lynn Docks, NOA Redwell Marsh, NWT Roydon Common, Sandringham, RSPB Titchwell Marsh, Tottenhill Gravel Pits, Wolferton Triangle, RSPB Snettisham.

RSPB SNETTISHAM

VISIT SNETTISHAM at high tide and you will be treated to one of the great avian spectacles of Britain, if not the world. Thousands of waders swarm over The Wash in an ever-changing maelstrom of feathers (my eloquence is not enough to truly describe the scene to you: you will just have to go to see for yourself). Many thousands of Pink-footed Geese also roost on The Wash here and it is a real treat to watch them depart to their feeding grounds at dawn.

Target birds

All year – Wader roost (100%), Barn Owl (60%), Short-eared Owl (10%). *Winter* – Pink-footed Goose (dawn & dusk, 90%), Peregrine (40%), Snow Bunting (30%), Scaup (20%). *Summer* – Avocet (90%), Marsh Harrier (60%). *Spring/autumn* – Passage waders (100%).

Other possible bird species

All year
Cormorant
Common wildfowl
Kestrel
Common waders
Common gull species
Sky Lark
Meadow Pipit
Pied Wagtail
Common finches
Reed Bunting

Winter
Brent Goose
Goldeneye
Red-breasted Merganser
Hen Harrier
Merlin
Golden Plover
Grey Plover
Knot
Sanderling
Black-tailed Godwit
Bar-tailed Godwit
Winter thrushes

Summer
Common Tern
Hirundines
Sedge Warbler
Reed Warbler
Grasshopper Warbler
Whitethroat
Other warblers

Spring/autumn
Little Stint
Curlew Sandpiper
Spotted Redshank
Greenshank
Green Sandpiper
Common Sandpiper
Yellow Wagtail
Whinchat
Wheatear

Occasional
Bittern
Smew
Montagu's Harrier
Hobby

Background information and birding tips

ENSURE YOU get the best out of Snettisham by checking the time of high tide before visiting. If you catch the place at low tide you could be in for a very miserable visit!

The best time for watching the thousands of waders is at high tide three to four days either side of a full moon. This is because the Wash is a vast area of mud and the sea only pushes the waders within viewable distances when the tide is at its highest. You should be in position at least 90 minutes before the high tide to get the best experience.

The downside of a full moon is that for three to four days either side, geese movements become unpredictable, as the extra light allows them to remain on their feeding grounds throughout the night. **Please view the geese from the Rotary hide as they can be disturbed by people standing on the bank.**

Key points

- **Open at all times.**
- **Obey all 'Anglers Only' signs.**
- **Paths can be very muddy in winter.**
- **Three sets of steps to negotiate – otherwise flat terrain.**
- **Disabled drivers can park close to first hide by prior arrangement (at least 5 working days in advance).**
- **Wader roost best 3-4 days either side of a full moon. Arrive at hide up to 90 minutes before high tide.**
- **To view geese at dawn or dusk avoid 3-4 days either side of a full moon when geese movements become unpredictable.**

ALL YEAR **OS MAP 132** **TF 652329**

Catch Snettisham at the right time and the spectacle of thousands of waders swirling through the air will leave you breathless. A number of species roost throughout the year, except in June, with numbers highest in winter. It cannot be overstated just what a stunning sight they make. I urge you to witness this magnificent avian spectacular and marvel at the sheer number of birds present.

To reach the roost you have to walk nearly two miles through the reserve, though wheelchair users and people with mobility difficulties can take their car up to the first hide – Rotary Hide. This must be arranged with the warden at least five working days before your visit.

You will pass several pits on the way to The Wash, which are good for Tufted Duck, Pochard, Goldeneye, Gadwall, Mallard, etc and several fields good for Barn Owl, thrushes and finches. The bushes and hedgerows hold common garden birds throughout the year, joined by Whitethroat and sometimes Grasshopper Warbler in summer.

Once on the seawall, follow the wide track to the hides or the seats overlooking The Wash. Look out for Snow Bunting on the shingle in winter. There is also a circular route that cuts across two pits and through a field of rough grass (good for Sky Larks, Meadow Pipits and owls).

Access details

(Approx. five miles S of Hunstanton).

Snettisham reserve is well sign-posted from A149's Dersingham bypass, 6.5 miles N of King's Lynn. Follow brown tourist signs for 'Snettisham Beach and RSPB reserve' down Beach Road. Continue for 1.5 miles to the signed car park on the left. If you arrive before 7.30am or after 9pm, you may have to park near the gate and walk through onto the access road. Follow the new footpath from the car park for 1.5 miles to the hides.

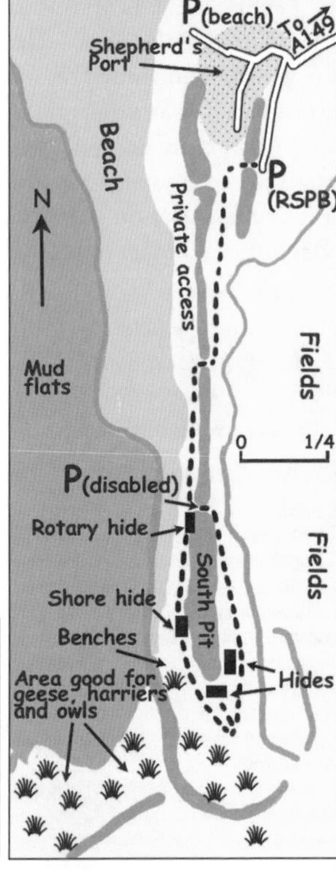

The most numerous wader is Knot. In winter they look plain grey, dumpy birds but if you visit in July/August many will show remnants of their red breeding plumage, whereas others will be grey. This gives the impression of someone having paved the mud with pretty bricks but a glance through your binoculars/telescope will reveal thousands of Knot constantly shifting position as the tide comes in.

Also in the mayhem, you should be able to pick out species such as Bar-tailed Godwit, Dunlin, Sanderling, Turnstone, Grey Plover, Curlew, Ringed Plover and Redshank. And the fun really starts when a bird of prey comes in to teduce the throng by one. The waders take to the air in huge, swirling flocks to unsettle the raptor.

On very high tide days, many of the waders come in to roost on the southernmost pit, affording excellent views from the hides surrounding the lake. This also give photographers ample opportunity to obtain close-up wader shots.

This pit is good for passage waders too and in summer, Black-headed Gulls, Common Terns and one or two pairs of Avocets nest on the islands here. In winter, this pit is the favoured place for Smew and Scaup.

A winter walk at Snettisham can be a very cold experience so wrap up warmly. On the sea wall there is no respite from the bitter wind but the old saying 'no pain, no gain' is usually proven to be well-founded. And don't be lulled into thinking summer will be much warmer either: always be prepared for anything at Snettisham!

A final word about the beach car park area. This is reached by continuing past the RSPB car park turn off, following signs to the 'Beach'. There is no access to the RSPB reserve from here but the Snettisham Coastal Park is adjacent to the car park (see page 172). The park is probably the best place in Norfolk to see Grasshopper Warbler, along with common finches and scrub birds. There is also a good chance of migrants in spring and autumn.

In winter, if you walk north from here, you can usually get views of Wigeon and other wildfowl on the marshy grasslands behind the second sea wall. You may also be treated to a good view of Pink-footed Geese flying over.

If you plan your trip carefully, Snettisham is **the** place in Norfolk, if not Britain, to witness one of the great marvels of the bird world; a mass wader roost. And that's not taking into account the 40,000 Pink-footed Geese flying overhead at dusk or dawn!

Thousands of Golden Plovers flock to Snettisham in winter.

Other nearby sites

Dersingham Bog, Gypsy Lane, NWT Holme Dunes, NOA Holme Observatory, Hunstanton, Ken Hill Wood, King's Lynn Docks, NOA Redwell Marsh, NWT Roydon Common, Sandringham, RSPB Titchwell Marsh, Tottenhill Gravel Pits, Wolferton Triangle, Snettisham Coastal Park.

Key points

- **Essential to check tide times before visiting.**
- **Wader ID charts in some hides, plus sightings sheet.**
- **Free access for members and non-members alike.**
- **Toilets open all year in beach car park (don't turn in to reserve car park but carry on to the end of road).**
- **Café open in summer adjacent to car park entrance gate.**
- **Dogs on leads.**

Contacts

The Warden,
The Business Centre,
43a Lynn Road
Snettisham,
King's Lynn,
Norfolk PE31 7LR.
Tel: 01485 542689
E-mail: snettisham@rspb.org.uk
http://www.rspb.org.uk/reserves/guide/s/snettisham/index.asp

NWT SPARHAM POOLS

Key points

- Level terrain along narrow grass and mud paths.
- Not suitable for wheelchairs (though Grey Wagtail habitat is viewable from the road).
- Paths can be muddy after rain.
- Free access at all times.
- No facilities other than a car park.

Contacts

Norfolk Wildlife Trust
Tel 01603 625540

HEAD for these reclaimed gravel pits along the River Wensum if you want to add Grey Wagtail to your Norfolk list, though there are many commoner bird species as well. Local attractions for non-birding family members are Dinosaur World and the Norfolk Wildlife Park.

Target birds

All year – Grey Wagtail (65%). *Summer* – Common Tern (95%), Spotted Flycatcher (70%). *Winter* – Goosander (70%).

Other possible bird species

All year
Little Grebe
Great Crested Grebe
Cormorant
Common wildfowl
Common waterbirds
Sparrowhawk
Kestrel
Common gull species
Kingfisher
Green Woodpecker
Great Spotted Woodpecker
Sky Lark
Meadow Pipit
Pied Wagtail
Common scrub birds
Marsh Tit
Bullfinch
Other common finches
Common woodland birds
Reed Bunting

Summer
Oystercatcher
Cuckoo
Turtle Dove
Sand Martin
Other hirundines
Sedge Warbler
Lesser Whitethroat
Whitethroat
Blackcap
Chiffchaff
Willow Warbler

Winter
Goldeneye
Winter thrushes
Siskin
Redpoll

Spring/autumn
Passage waders
Yellow Wagtail

Occasional
Garganey
Egyptian Goose

Background information and birding tips

SPARHAM POOLS is a Norfolk Wildlife Trust reserve, reclaimed from former gravel workings. Lying north-west of Norwich, the pits and surrounding habitats are home to many common species all year round and offer a peaceful alternative to the nearby tourist traps of Dinosaur World and the Norfolk Wildlife Park.

Once you have found the NWT car park, (and it will take you a little while), there is a circular path round the pits. You can't get lost as the path does not veer off but leads you back to the car park whichever way you choose.

The track takes you through bushes and trees with occasional views over the pools themselves. Scan the islands in the pools for Egyptian Geese, Oystercatchers and Common Terns, which all nest in summer. You should see plenty of common wildfowl whatever time of year you visit, though numbers increase in winter. Shovelers, Gadwalls, Mallards, Pochards and Tufted Ducks are joined by Goldeneyes and Teal in winter. Sparham has become a reliable site for Goosanders in recent winters, a welcome addition to any cold day's birding.

In the south-eastern corner of the pools, there is a private gravel pit which may be worth checking for waders such as Common, Green, Curlew and Wood Sandpipers, Greenshank, Ruff, Little Ringed Plover, etc during migration periods. These new pits seem to be a favourite site for any gulls that may be around, though a telescope may be needed to see them well.

The field adjacent to the road, near the car park, should be scanned for pipits, wagtails and larks especially when wet. The bushes and trees on the reserve should produce many species such as Bullfinch, Marsh Tit, Long-tailed Tit, Siskin, Redpoll, Great Spotted and Green Woodpeckers, etc.

Fifty yards from the entrance to the reserve is the best place to see Grey Wagtail in Norfolk. They are resident around the bridge over the River Wensum, though can go missing for long periods. To view the area, walk to the bridge from the NWT car park, as there is no other parking nearby. In summer, the wagtails are joined by Spotted Flycatchers around the bridge.

This is a decent site to spend an hour or two wandering around. The mile circular route should reveal many common species of birds, though the more often you can visit, the more you will see. It is the sort of place which turns up a really rare bird once every 20 years and it is the dedicated 'patch-watcher' who will be rewarded.

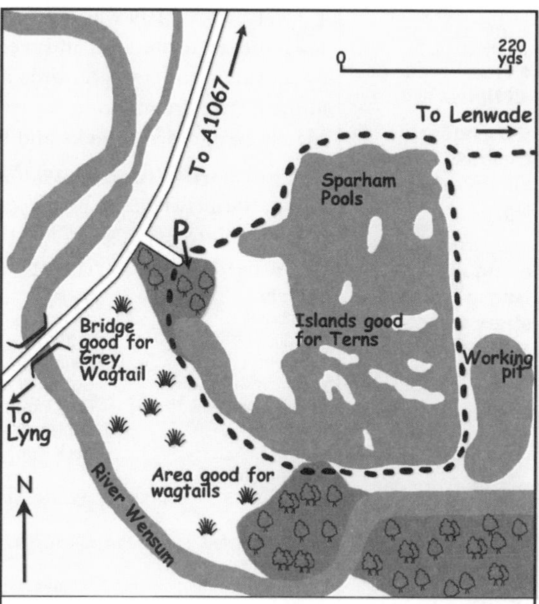

Access details

(Approx: 11.5 miles NW of Norwich).

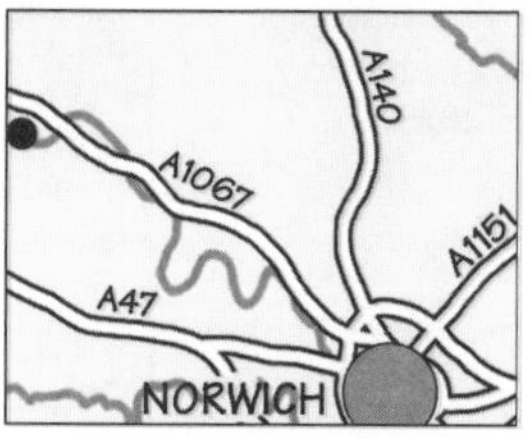

From the Norwich outer ring road, take A1067 NW for approximately 11 miles (sign-posted Bawdeswell).

A mile beyond Lenwade, turn left down Lyng Road (sign-posted Lyng) and continue for 0.8 miles (if you reach the river bridge you have gone too far).

Turn down a narrow track on left to the car park (50 yards from the bridge).

This is well hidden as the NWT sign is pointing towards Lyng village, so you will probably have to turn around at the bridge and return to find the car park (look out for the wooden public footpath sign, also well hidden!).

Once in the car park, you can take the path signed with yellow arrows (slightly uphill at 11 o'clock as you drive down the entrance track) or bear right from the access track along a narrow muddy path.

Ignore the path with the NWT sign as it doesn't lead anywhere.

Other nearby sites

NWT Buxton Heath, Swanton Novers, Great Ryburgh, Pensthorpe Wildlife Park, NWT Syderstone Common, NWT Wayland Wood, Blickling Hall.

STIFFKEY FEN

Key points

- **Free access at all times.**
- **Do not trespass. Obey all 'Private' signs.**
- **Terrain is level along muddy tracks (some stiles and steps may need to be negotiated).**
- **Not suitable for wheelchair users: view marsh from car parks at Morston or Stiffkey.**
- **Telescope very useful.**
- **Facilities available in village.**

Contacts

The National Trust, East Anglia Regional Office
01263 733471

STIFFKEY FEN was farmed for 200 years but was returned to wetland and reedbed in 1996. A large area of open water attracts waterbirds all year round. The islands at the centre are magnets for waders and the surrounding marsh, hedgerows, creeks and fields can be alive with birds.

Target birds

Winter – **Wildfowl (100%), winter raptors (75%), Barn Owl (75%).** *Spring/autumn* – **Passage waders, passage migrants.**

Other possible bird species

All year
Cormorant
Shelduck
Little Egret
Common wildfowl
Common waterbirds
Marsh Harrier
Kestrel
Common waders
Great Spotted Woodpecker
Sky Lark
Meadow Pipit
Pied Wagtail
Common scrub birds
Corvids
Common finches
Reed Bunting

Winter
Brent Goose
Pink-footed Goose
Scaup
Wigeon
Merlin
Peregrine
Golden Plover
Grey Plover
Winter thrushes
Rock Pipit

Spring/autumn
Scaup
Little Stint
Ruff
Whimbrel
Greenshank
Green Sandpiper
Wood Sandpiper
Common Sandpiper
Yellow Wagtail
Redstart
Whinchat
Wheatear
Winter thrushes
Barred Warbler
Goldcrest
Spotted Flycatcher
Pied Flycatcher

Summer
Breeding waders
Breeding gulls
Terns
Hobby
Hirundines
Sedge Warbler
Reed Warbler
Other warblers

Background information and birding tips

STIFFKEY FEN can be approached from three directions: by walking along the North Norfolk Coastal Path from Morston or Stiffkey or by the public footpath from the A149. Any of these walks will produce many species of birds at any time of year.

From the lay-by on the A149, carefully cross the road, go through a gap in the hawthorn hedge and turn left. Follow the grass path (checking the hedge for scrub birds and migrants and the fields for gamebirds, buntings, finches, etc) for approx. 300 yards. Cross the A149 again and head slightly right for a few yards before crossing a stile onto a muddy footpath (if you cross the stream on the A149 you have gone too far). You reach another stile, an excellent vantage point to scan the Fen!

Follow the footpath for 500 yards onto the seawall (up a few steps), with The Fen on your right. You can now turn left to Stiffkey (1.5 miles) or right to Morston (1.25 miles) along the Norfolk Coastal Path. This junction is a good place to scan for raptors in winter. They roost at Warham Greens, about 2.5 miles to the west but can be

seen flying over the marsh in front of you up to two hours before dark.

With a telescope, you can also scan Blakeney Channel from here for terns in summer and wildfowl in winter. The muddy channels are excellent for waders at all times of year (a Lesser Yellowlegs overwintered here in 04/05).

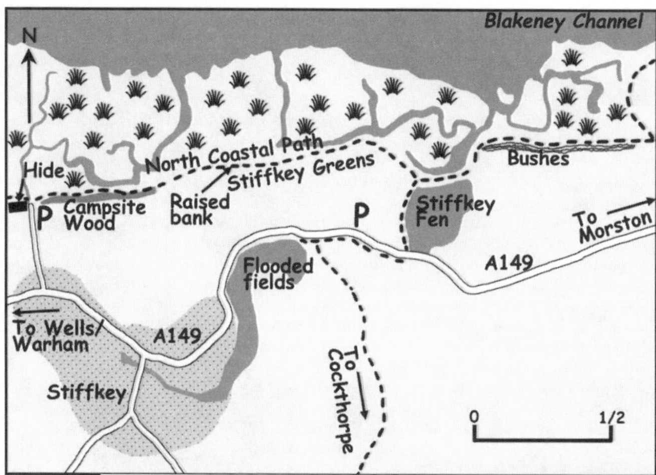

Whether you choose to walk east or west, check the bushes along the path in spring and autumn as anything may turn up. Barred Warblers are regular vagrants in autumn and you should see commoner species such as Goldcrest, Garden Warbler, Whinchat, Redstart, etc, etc.

Stiffkey Fen itself can be viewed from either the footpath from the A149 or the Coastal Path in winter but in summer, vegetation makes it difficult to view the Fen from the A149 footpath so vertically-challenged individuals may have to climb the seawall to view the site.

The open water of the Fen is home to common wildfowl such as Tufted Duck, Pochard, Shelduck, Egyptian Goose, Gadwall, etc, joined by Goldeneye in winter. Scaup regularly drop in on passage (unfortunately, they don't seem to stay for the winter) and Brent Geese frequently come in to bathe in winter.

Access details

(Approx 4 miles east of Wells-Next-The-Sea)

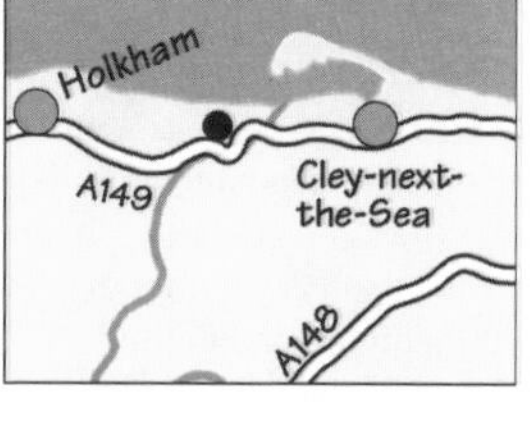

From Wells, go through Stiffkey village (20mph), passing the Red Lion pub on your left.

After 1.2 miles (and several nasty bends!), park in the muddy lay-by on your left (room for about 5 cars). Cross the road, go through a gap in the hedge and turn left for The Fen or right to the flooded field.

***STIFFKEY NT CAR PARK:* (TF 965439)**

From A149, turn down Greenway (unadopted road) at the western end of Stiffkey village (first left in Stiffkey if approaching from Wells). The car park is 500 yards down this track. Walk W to Warham Greens and Wells-Next-The-Sea, or E to Stiffkey Fen and Morston Quay.

The muddy islands attract waders at all times of year. Avocets breed and you can also see Little Ringed Plovers and Black-tailed Godwits in summer. Passage periods bring Green, Wood and Common Sandpipers, Ruff, Whimbrel, Curlew Sandpiper, Little Stint, etc. In winter, the water level usually covers the islands so wader-lovers should turn their attention to the channels along the Coastal Path.

From the A149 lay-by, you also have access to a wonderful flooded field, alive with Wigeon and Lapwing in winter and common waders and wildfowl all year round. Park in the lay-by (never on

STIFFKEY FEN

Common Sandpiper might be expected at Stiffkey during passage times.

the A149) and cross the road. Go through the gap in the hedge and turn right. Follow the grass path for 0.2 miles when it meets the public footpath to Cockthorpe. View the flood/scrape from this junction but be careful not to flush the birds.

Stiffkey Fen can also be reached from a car park in Stiffkey village. Turn down Greenway and park in the National Trust car park at the end. The Norfolk Coastal Path runs east or west from here or you can walk onto the marsh to try to find winter flocks of Twite, Rock Pipits, Snow Buntings, etc (but keep to footpaths!).

Walk right from the car park to reach Stiffkey Fen. In autumn, the narrow strip of wood (Campsite Wood) running east (right) from the rear of the car park should be explored thoroughly. The stunted trees here have an 'enchanted forest' feel and attract species such as Redstart, Pied Flycatcher, Spotted Flycatcher in spring and Yellow-browed Warbler, Firecrest, etc, etc in spring and autumn.

In winter, this car park is an ideal place for wheelchair users to sit and watch for raptors passing over the marsh, with Brent and Pink-footed Geese also likely. If people fancy a bit of shelter, there is a small viewing hut ('hide' is too strong-a word for it!) just to the left of the car park, accessed up a couple of steps.

Visiting birdwatchers could easily spend the whole day in the area. The Fen, flood pools, marsh, hedgerows and channels provide differing habitats for you to explore and you may also wish to combine your visit with a boat trip to Blakeney Point from Morston.

Other nearby sites

Blakeney Point, NWT Cley Marsh, Felbrigg Hall, Holkham NNR , Holkham Park, Morston Quay, Salthouse Beach, NOA Walsey Hills, Warham Greens.

RSPB STRUMPSHAW FEN

PATIENCE is a virtue at this popular RSPB reserve which features many different habitats and is excellent all year round for a half or full day's birdwatching. Basically, the longer you stay on the reserve, the more you will see, though some of the sought-after species can be very elusive!

Target birds

All year **– Marsh Harrier (95%), Bearded Tit (70%), Willow Tit (75%), Lesser Spotted Woodpecker (65%), Cetti's Warbler (hear 60%, see 15%), Bittern (20%).** ***Winter*** **– Hen Harrier (80%).** ***Summer*** **– Grasshopper Warbler (hear 40%, see 10%), Hobby (25%), Garganey (25%).**

Other possible bird species

All year
Great Crested Grebe
Cormorant
Common wildfowl
Water Rail
Common waterbirds
Sparrowhawk
Kestrel
Woodcock
Common gull species
Kingfisher
Green Woodpecker
Great Spotted Woodpecker
Sky Lark
Meadow Pipit
Pied Wagtail
Jay
Common scrub birds
Common woodland birds
Marsh Tit
Willow Tit

Winter
Common wildfowl
Redpoll

Spring/autumn
Osprey
Greenshank
Green Sandpiper
Common Sandpiper

Summer
Hobby
Common Tern
Yellow Wagtail
Hirundines
Sedge Warbler
Reed Warbler
Garden Warbler
Grasshopper Warbler
Other warblers
Spotted Flycatcher

Occasional
Goosander
Spotted Crake
Savi's Warbler (rare)

Key points

- **Managed by the RSPB.**
- **Entry is free to RSPB members, non-members £2.50 family ticket (in 2006).**
- **Open from sunrise to dusk every day except Christmas Day.**
- **Only one hide accessible to wheelchairs.**
- **Manned reception hide with updated sightings board.**
- **Toilet block on site.**

Background information and birding tips

VISITORS to Strumpshaw Fen should be prepared to walk quite a distance if they wish to see everything on offer as it is a large reserve. It is a popular birding venue at all times of year with sought-after species being relatively easy to see – with patience.

Your walk starts at the visitor centre just inside the reserve. It is worth lingering around the car park as Lesser Spotted Woodpeckers regularly visit the mature trees here, one of the most reliable sites in Norfolk to see them.

Next stop is the reception centre. On view should be common water birds and wildfowl, plus the chance of a Marsh Harrier. The dead branch protruding across the water to your right is a favoured perch of the resident Kingfisher. This is also the place to be at dusk in winter when a few Hen and Marsh Harriers gather to roost, sometimes joined by a large flock of Starlings.

My preferred route then proceeds through a small wood, home to several resident species of common woodland birds. It is also home to one of the last remaining Norfolk colonies of Willow Tits, so wait around to try to pick them out from the more numerous Marsh Tits.

Access details

(Approx. seven miles E of Norwich)

Leave A47 Norwich to Great Yarmouth road at the roundabout sign-posted to Brundall. Continue along this minor road for 0.4 miles. Bear left at the sharp bend onto The Street (sign-posted Brundall Station). Negotiate mini-roundabouts and the traffic-calmed area until, after 1.1 miles, you go under a railway bridge. Look for the sign for RSPB Strumpshaw Fen, turning right (Stone Road), then immediately right again (Low Road). Continue to RSPB car park (muddy verge!) by the railway line. Walk across the railway line at the crossing to the reception centre.

OR: From A47, turn S at signs to Cantley/Beighton (just where the road becomes a dual carriageway) into Lingwood village. In Lingwood, take the left turn (sign-posted to Station/ Strumpshaw/Cantley & Freethorpe) along Station road.

Continue past the station to a T-junction. Turn right to Strumpshaw/Norwich, along Norwich Road. Go into Strumpshaw village and turn left (at signs for Strumpshaw Fen and Household Waste Disposal Site) then immediately right down Low Road at the small brown RSPB sign (easily missed). Follow this road down to the RSPB car park.

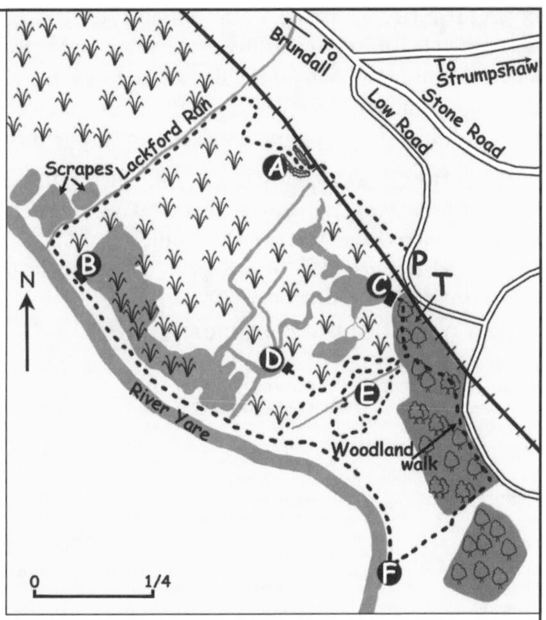

Key

A Best bushes for Cetti's
B Tower hide
C Visitor Centre
D Fen hide
E Summer meadow
F Pumphouse

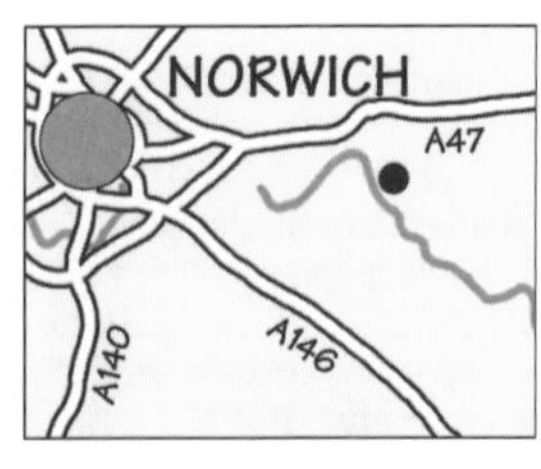

From the wood, walk along the wide, sandy track to Fen Hide. Listen for Grasshopper Warblers reeling from the isolated bushes in the reeds here. The hide gives a view over the large reedbed so watch out for Bittern, Marsh Harrier and Bearded Tit at all times of year.

If the fancy takes you, you can walk through the wood along the Woodland Trail. This takes you to the River Yare footpath, where you can turn right to join up with the Fen Hide footpath.

The walk alongside the Yare should produce Great Crested Grebes and Sedge Warblers in the bushes on the water's edge (summer only). Listen out too for Cetti's Warbler here, though further along the trail is better.

Half a mile from Fen Hide is the Tower Hide, accessed up a steep flight of steps. The climb is worth the effort though as Tower Hide affords superb views over the whole reserve. Sit here for as long as you can to increase your chance of seeing the more desirable species.

A long wait in Tower Hide may produce a flight view of one of the breeding Bitterns, or scan along the channels for one feeding at the edge of the reeds. This species bred at Strumpshaw in 2001, rewarding the RSPB's hard efforts to attract them. In winter, the lagoons hold a good selection of common wildfowl, joined in spring by a Garganey or two.

Once you have had your fill from Tower Hide, continue along the footpath by the River Yare. Very soon, this path bears right to run alongside a small stream called the Lackford Run.

The hide that used to overlook a fine wader scrape has disappeared but you can still see the scrape from the path. Be careful not to flush the birds.

The bushes along the Lackford path hold common finches and scrub birds (Dunnock, Wren, etc) and also Cetti's and Grasshopper Warblers. In the summer of 2001 and 2002, this was the best place to sit and listen at dusk to the strange call of a Spotted Crake or two.

Further along this path, you enter an area of what can only be described as a swamp, accessed along a boardwalk. This area, stretching a couple of hundred yards to the railway crossing, is the best place to see the Cetti's Warblers. They are easy to hear but do like to hide in the thick cover. Be patient! Look out, too, for Willow Tits here.

Once you have crossed the railway line, take the wide track to the right back to the car park (past a cottage). This completes a long, circular route, which produces many common and scarce species no matter what time of year you visit. You should encounter at least a couple of the target species but you may be unlucky and see nothing. The longer you stay, the more chance you have of seeing the birds.

Strumpshaw Fen is also an excellent place for other wildlife. In summer, many species of dragonfly and butterfly can be seen along with many scarce plants.

Key points

- **Hearing Loop installed at reception centre for hard of hearing visitors.**
- **Terrain is level along muddy paths.**
- **Well-marked trails (with distances).**
- **Steep steps to Tower Hide.**
- **Picnic tables by reception.**
- **Cycle rails by reception.**

Other nearby sites

Breydon Water, RSPB Buckenham Marshes, Buxton Heath, Cantley Beet Factory, Great Yarmouth Beach, Great Yarmouth Cemetery, Hardley Flood, Rockland Broad, RSPB Surlingham Church Marshes, Ted Ellis Reserve.

NWT STUBB MILL

Key points

- **£3 fee for non NWT members.**
- **Do not park at the watchpoint itself. Park in NWT Hickling Broad car park and walk back to the mill.**
- **Access road can be very muddy or flooded.**
- **Getting a wheelchair onto the viewing bank is impossible but birds may be viewable from the end of the access road.**
- **Wellingtons essential.**
- **NWT visitor centre closed in winter, though toilets usually open.**

Contacts

The Warden, Hickling Broad National Nature Reserve 01692 598276

Norfolk Wildlife Trust 01603 625540

THE BEST PLACE in the country to see Cranes in winter and Norfolk's leading site to see Merlin, Hen and Marsh Harriers is simply a slightly raised mud bank where you can stand to get panoramic views of the favourite roosting site of these four sought-after bird species.

Target birds

Winter – **Marsh Harrier (99%), Crane (85%), Hen Harrier (85%), Merlin (60%), Barn Owl (70%).**

Other possible bird species

Winter

Pink-footed Goose (in flight)
Wigeon (in flight)
Sparrowhawk
Kestrel
Lapwing
Woodcock
Common gull species
Sky Lark
Meadow Pipit
Pied Wagtail
Common scrub birds
Winter thrushes
Jay
Common finches

Background information and birding tips

HARDY birdwatchers are virtually guaranteed to see Cranes in winter at this famous site, the only area in Britain where this is possible. It is also an excellent place to see Merlin and Hen and Marsh Harriers as they come in to roost.

It is best to arrive at the raptor watchpoint at least an hour and a half before dusk to stake your claim on a good viewing position. Regularly scan the fields, as raptors seemingly appear from nowhere. In recent winters, up to 22 Cranes, more than 30 Marsh Harriers, up to four Hen Harriers and a couple of Merlins have visited the roost on a regular basis. Barn Owls are also frequently seen.

If it is raining it is probably worth postponing your visit. The birds still fly in to roost but I have found that they tend to hunker down quickly in wet weather. Apart from that, there is no shelter here so you'll get wet too! If it is foggy there is absolutely no point in visiting the site.

If the weather is fine, the raptors quarter the fields in search of a last meal before roosting. I have noted that Hen Harriers tend to come in later than the other birds, so do not despair if it is getting late and you still haven't seen one. The Merlins will quite often be seen mobbing the harriers and, if you are lucky, you may see one land on a fence post in reasonable light.

Once on the ground, the Cranes can be surprisingly difficult to see. This sounds impossible for a four foot tall, three foot long shaggy mop but it is remarkable how they melt away into the tall grass when feeding.

This is a fantastic way to end a day's birding in this corner of Norfolk. What could be better than listening to the evocative '*cronk, cronk*' of the Cranes as they fly over two species of harrier being mobbed by a lightning-fast Merlin?

Other species seen from the watchpoint include a thousand or so Pink-footed Geese flying over to roost, Woodcock, Jay, Fieldfare, Redwing, Kestrel and Sparrowhawk.

One cautionary note: it is highly

WINTER | OS Map 134 | TG 428222 

likely that the road to the mill watchpoint will be flooded, or at best very muddy, so wear Wellingtons.

Birdwatchers tend to spend the day in the Horsey/ Martham area, searching for the Cranes and raptors, or on the NWT's Hickling Broad reserve, then end up at the Stubb Mill roost in the late afternoon – a perfect winter day out.

In recent winters the watchpoint has become very busy with birders. The earlier you arrive the more likely you are to get a place on the bank

Also look out for the Chinese water deer, a small introduced species.

N
To Hickling Green (A149)
Private track
Raised mud bank
Viewing point for raptor roost
P
Visitor Centre
Stubb Mill
NWT Hickling Broad
Bittern hide
0
1/4

Access details

(approx. 14 miles NE of Norwich)

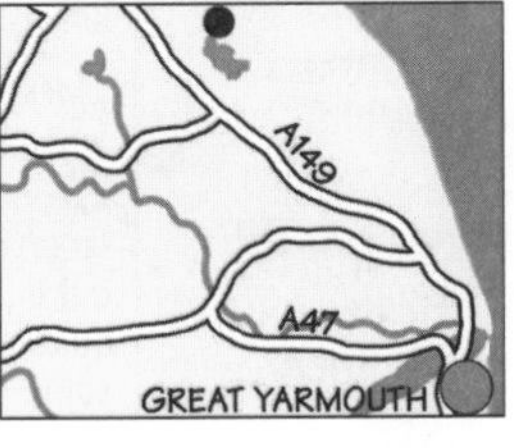

From A149, about one mile south of Potter Heigham, turn NE at the sign-post to Hickling. Follow all the way to Hickling Green, then turn right at The Greyhound public house.

Follow the brown duck signs to the Norfolk Wildlife Trust's car park. DO NOT DRIVE DOWN TO THE MILL. Disabled drivers should phone the warden for permission to drive closer to the viewing area.

From the car park, retrace your steps down the road. After about 100 yards you will reach an obvious cross roads (straight on is a private farm track).

Turn right down the muddy road and walk for about half a mile down to the disused Stubb Mill. Do not enter the mill and cottage grounds but watch the fields from between the red posts on the obvious raised mud bank where the track ends (TG 437222).

There is free entry to NWT members but non-members should pay a fee. This is difficult as the visitor centre is closed in winter and I have never seen a warden on site to issue permits. The raised bank can get crowded at times so get there early to reserve your place.

Other nearby sites

Breydon Water, RSPB Buckenham Marshes, Burgh Castle, Great Yarmouth Beach, Haddiscoe Marshes, NWT Hickling Broad, Horsey, NWT Martham Broad, RSPB Strumpshaw Fen.

67 RSPB SURLINGHAM CHURCH MARSHES

Key points

- **Open at all times.**
- **Circular route along rough paths. Some shallow steps en route.**
- **Limited free parking by church. Be considerate to church users on Sundays.**
- **One hide.**
- **Not suitable for wheelchair users.**
- **Boots or Wellingtons advisable.**
- **Keep dogs under control.**
- **Stick to paths at all times.**
- **RSPB notice board at Surlingham church.**
- **Sightings record board and ID posters in hide.**

Contact

RSPB Mid-Yare Reserves
01603 715191
E-mail: strumpshaw@rspb.org.uk

RSPB East Anglia Office
01603 661662

SOMETIMES REWARDING, sometimes quiet for birds, the Surlingham site is a small RSPB reserve in Broadland that deserves more attention from birdwatchers. It is always worth calling in to see what is around at any time of year.

Target birds

All year – **Bearded Tit (40%), Cetti's Warbler (hear 60%, see 20%).** *Winter* – **Jack Snipe (25%), Hen Harrier (50%).** *Spring/autumn* – **Passage waders.** *Summer* – **Marsh Harrier (30%), Grasshopper Warbler (hear 50%, see 10%).**

Other possible bird species

All year
Great Crested Grebe
Cormorant
Gadwall
Shoveler
Other common wildfowl
Common waterfowl
Sparrowhawk
Kestrel
Water Rail
Snipe
Barn Owl
Kingfisher
Green Woodpecker
Great Spotted Woodpecker
Sky Lark
Meadow Pipit
Pied Wagtail
Long-tailed Tit
Corvids
Common finches
Reed Bunting

Winter
Winter wildfowl
Jack Snipe
Winter thrushes

Summer
Hobby
Cuckoo
Hirundines
Yellow Wagtail
Sedge Warbler
Reed Warbler
Grasshopper Warbler
Whitethroat
Blackcap

Background information and birding tips

SURLINGHAM Church Marshes is one of the lesser known RSPB reserves. It is quite difficult to find but is worth the effort. Though quite a small area (68ha), it holds some desirable species for the visiting birdwatcher.

My suggested route starts from Surlingham Church. Follow the reserve sign-post straight down the grassy track past the cottage. This runs downhill along a bush-lined path to a dyke. The hedgerow is good for common scrub birds (Robin, Blackbird, Dunnock, etc) and common finches. The path soon reaches the River Yare and runs adjacent to it all the way to the hide.

While on the grass path by the river, listen out for Cetti's and Grasshopper Warblers in the thick bushes in spring and summer, neither species is easy to see. Common species on the river itself include Coot, Moorhen, Grey Heron and Great Crested Grebe, with a good chance of Kingfisher.

The hide is reached by a short grass path to your right (on your left if approaching from the Ferry House pub). The hide overlooks a large pool, that holds breeding Gadwall and Shovelers. In front of the hide you should see Reed and Sedge Warblers in summer and Bearded Tits all year.

Cetti's Warblers may also show in the bushes around the hide all year round. If the water level in the pool is low, watch the muddy edges for the resident Water Rails and passage waders such as Green and Common Sandpipers.

In summer, Marsh Harriers may patrol the reserve and in winter, Hen Harriers are seen regularly from the hide at dusk. In winter, the pools become flooded and attract decent numbers of common wildfowl such as Tufted Duck, Pochard and Shelduck.

The marshy edges of the pool should be scrutinised for Jack Snipes in winter. This is probably the best place to see them in Norfolk.

After the hide, you can either retrace your steps to the car or boat, or complete the circuit of the reserve. As the river bends to the left, the footpath bears right and skirts a marshy field that is good for Snipe, Lapwing and Pied Wagtail, with Yellow Wagtails regularly recorded in spring.

You will then reach a T-junction of public footpaths. You should turn right along a narrow, boardwalk towards the gun club. The marshes are regularly shot over but only on Sundays and Thursdays after 10am.

After the gun club, the path becomes a rough farm track. Follow this for another quarter of a mile back to the car park, scanning the bushes and small wood for common woodland birds and finches.

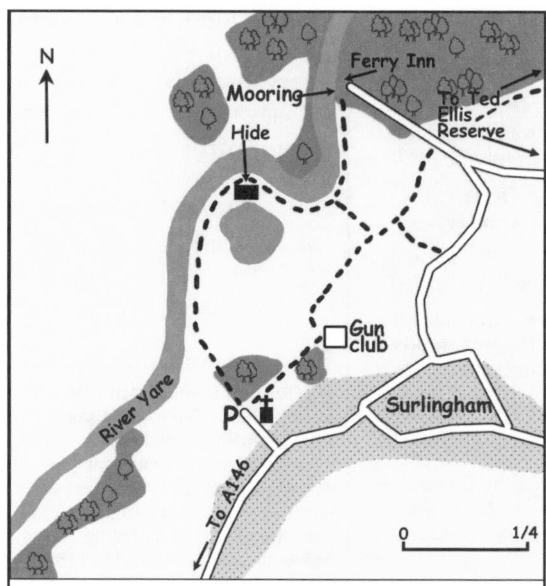

Access details

(Approx. five miles E of Norwich)

BY CAR: **From A47 Norwich bypass, turn onto A146 (sign-posted to Lowestoft & Norwich). After 100 yards, turn left to Bramerton and Kirby Bedon at first set of traffic lights.**

After 2.5 miles you will reach a green with the Bramerton village name-post on it. Turn left here (no destination signposted) and continue all the way into Surlingham.

Take a left turn in Surlingham village down Church Lane (a dead end), sign-posted to the Church and park there. The reserve is sign-posted either straight on or to the right by the cottage (circular route).

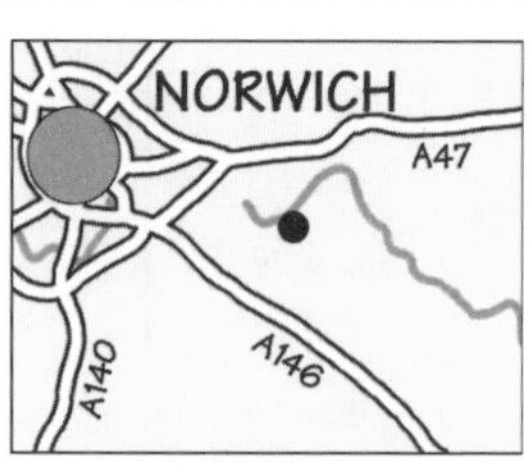

BY BOAT: **Moor up at the Ferry House pub, which is about half way between Norwich and Rockland Broad on the River Yare.**

There is a permissive footpath running south to the RSPB reserve. Follow this until you reach a small wooden bridge. The reserve starts immediately after the bridge, marked by the RSPB sign. The hide is on the left just after the bridge.

Other nearby sites

Breydon Water, RSPB Buckenham Marshes, Cantley Beet Factory, Great Yarmouth Beach, Hardley Flood, How Hill NNR, Rockland Broad, RSPB Strumpshaw Fen, Ted Ellis Reserve, NWT Upton Fen.

SWANTON NOVERS NNR

Key points

- No access to woods.
- No walking involved.
- Donation requested.
- Telescope recommended.
- Information leaflets in box by entrance gate.
- No facilities.
- Dogs on leads.

Contacts

English Nature
01603 620558

Site Manager
01485 543044

THIS RESERVE provides a viewpoint over Swanton Great Wood, the summer home of both Buzzards and Honey Buzzards. There is no access to the wood, so you will just have to wait in the car park for the raptors to appear.

Target birds

Buzzard (95%), Honey Buzzard (40%), Hobby (80%).

Other possible bird species

Spring/summer

Sparrowhawk
Kestrel
Marsh Harrier
Lapwing
Turtle Dove
Sky Lark
Hirundines
Common scrub birds
Whitethroat
Blackcap
Corvids
Common finches
Yellowhammer

Background information and birding tips

HONEY BUZZARDS have nested in Swanton Great Wood since 1989 and have raised at least ten youngsters in this ancient woodland. The pair were joined by Buzzards a couple of years later. More than 50 species of birds nest in the woods but access is by permit only: and no, you won't get one, so don't bother asking!

This site is owned by the Astley Estate but is managed by English Nature. The owners ask for donations from visitors, which they put towards the renovation of the church in Swanton Novers. The donation box is situated at the entrance gate. There is usually an English Nature warden on hand for advice and a friendly chat.

Honey Buzzards arrive around mid-May and by June should be incubating eggs. This means they become more elusive until July/August if nesting has been successful.

Even on a good day the Honey Buzzards can be out and about for long periods, so patience is a requirement you'll need in abundance. If it is raining, don't waste your time visiting as all raptors will be sheltering.

Scan the whole area at regular intervals as the HBs (as they are commonly known) can appear as if out of thin air. Due to the popularity of the raptor watchpoint at nearby Great Ryburgh, visitors to Swanton Novers should now find themselves alone to admire the HBs.

While waiting, you will be entertained by a Hobby or two and several Common Buzzards. Study each buzzard very carefully. If you are familiar with the flight outline of a Common, picking out a Honey will be much easier when they finally appear.

When the two buzzard species are in the air together, be sure to note the raised wings of the Common and the flat wings of the Honey. Honey Buzzard also has a more protruding head with longer wings and tail than Common. If you are really lucky, you may see an HB perform its wing-clapping display.

Yellowhammers can be seen coming and going to nests nearby and they have been known to nest in the car park itself (I nearly had the embarrassment of running over a nest a few years ago).

Also, keep an eye on the bird

END May-MID Sept **OS MAP 133** **Approx. TG 011302** 

table in the bottom right hand corner of the car park field as this is kept topped up with seed for the Greenfinches, Goldfinches, etc to feed on (and the occasional Tree Sparrow in winter).

Though most birders head for Great Ryburgh these days, due to the fact that Honey Buzzards show better and more frequently than at Swanton Novers, it is still worth spending a couple of hours here.

Firstly, Great Ryburgh is difficult for wheelchair users to get good views. In contrast, Swanton offers an all round view of the woods so access for disabled birders isn't an issue. Secondly, now most people have moved elsewhere, Swanton can be a very peaceful place to study the area's raptors.

Other nearby sites

Blakeney Point, Cley NWT, Great Ryburgh, Holkham Park, Kelling Heath, Kelling Quags, Pensthorpe, Salthouse Heath, Sculthorpe Moor, NWT Syderstone Common, Walsey Hills NOA.

Access details

(Approx. 5 miles E of Fakenham).

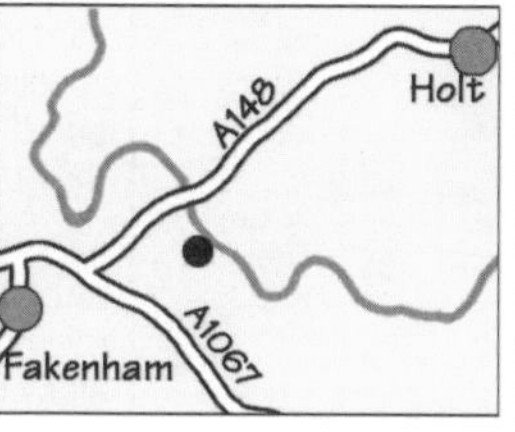

At the roundabout in Holt, on the A148 King's Lynn to Cromer road, turn off onto B1110 to East Dereham. After about five miles, cross the B1354 (you need to turn right then immediately left, sign-posted Guist). After a further two miles, turn right at the crossroads to Fulmodeston.

The raptorwatch car park is 0.4 miles on the right: turn into the field at the wooden signposts. Park in the field and view the surrounding woods.

If approaching from Fakenham on the A148, take the turning off right after the Fakenham bypass, sign-posted "Fulmodeston 2 miles" (opposite the Kettlestone Road crossroads – if you reach The Green Man pub you have gone too far). Follow through to Fulmodeston where you go straight over at the crossroads down Hindolveston Road.

Follow the road down to the raptorwatch car park on the left after 3.3 miles (turn into the field at the brown sign – if you reach the B1110 crossroads you have gone too far).

Key points

- **Free access and parking at all times.**
- **Dogs on leads.**
- **No facilities.**
- **SSSI.**
- **Information board in car park.**
- **Stay on paths at all times.**

Contacts

Norfolk Wildlife Trust, 01603 625540
www.wildlifetrust.org.uk/norfolk

A HIDDEN GEM comprising 24 hectares of acidic heathland that holds several sought-after species, including one of the last remaining Willow Tit colonies in the county.

Target Species

Spring/summer – Nightjar (40%), Wood Lark (90%), Willow Tit (50%).

Other possible bird species

Spring/summer	Cuckoo	Garden Warbler
Pheasant	Barn Owl	Lesser Whitethroat
Red-legged Partridge	Tawny Owl	Grasshopper Warbler
Grey Partridge	Green Woodpecker	Other summer warblers
Sparrowhawk	Great Spotted Woodpecker	Corvids
Kestrel	Sky Lark	Bullfinch
Hobby	Hirundines	Other common finches
Stock Dove	Pied Wagtail	Yellowhammer.
Turtle Dove	Common scrub birds	

Background information and birding tips

THIS NORFOLK WILDLIFE Trust-owned reserve is one of the best places in Norfolk to see Wood Larks. Very few people visit Syderstone so you may be able to admire this heathland speciality in solitude. Nightjars sometimes breed on the common and, when they do, they show well.

The first important message has to be aimed at dog owners. Please keep them on a lead and do not allow them to splash about in the pools. These pools are home to natterjack toads and your dog's anti-flea powder will pollute the water and kill this rare amphibian.

Syderstone is criss-crossed by a maze of paths. From the car park, head directly away from the road down a narrow, muddy path. This path leads through bushes and trees with the farm and fields to your right. After 300 yards you reach a junction with a wide farm track. Turn left along this track then immediately right along a wide, grass path (you can also carry on at the junction through the woods, or turn left on the farm track and immediately left again). After a few yards the path opens into a clearing, one of several good sites for your target species.

If you carry along this path, you pass through some bushes, excellent for Willow Tit. This species is now virtually extinct in Norfolk so I have made this a target bird for Syderstone. The path then opens out to a newly-cleared area ideal for Wood Larks and Nightjars. Spring mornings are best for locating Wood Larks. Listen for their mournful song, which can be very ventriloquistic! For Nightjars, you need to arrive at dusk and wait for the churring to start

Basically, the whole of the Common continues in a similar vein. The paths pass through bushes and trees and into clearings. If you find someone waiting for birds to show in one clearing and you want to enjoy your birdwatching in peace, just walk a few hundred yards and you will find a clearing of your own.

While you are waiting for the

target species, you should see a range of commoner birds. Green Woodpeckers will be hard to miss as will common scrub birds such as Wren, Robin, Blackbird, etc, etc. A Barn Owl may be seen hunting over the Common at dawn and dusk and a Hobby may zip through chasing a Swallow or House Martin.

Linnets breed at Syderstone as do many common warblers including Willow, Garden and Grasshopper Warblers, Chiffchaff, Whitethroat, Blackcap and Lesser Whitethroat. Listen out for the gentle cooing of a Turtle Dove, the reeling of a Grasshopper Warbler, the scalding '*tip*' of a Great Spotted Woodpecker, the unobtrusive call of a Bullfinch or the cuckooing of a Cuckoo (obviously!).

From the car park, the NWT reserve continues across Mill Lane. Cross the road and follow the muddy path through a patch of pleasant, shady woodland. Common woodland birds, including a few warblers, are here but otherwise there is little of interest on this side of the road.

Syderstone Common can be viewed from a separate car park located immediately after the left fork (Mill Lane) as you approach from the B1454. This large car park is ideal for wheelchair users and people with mobility difficulties to get Nightjar and Wood Lark on their lists! Face away from the road and scan the Common; both species can be seen from the car park but you may have to wait a while.

A path leads onto the Common from this lower car park (go down a narrow path and turn right along a wider track, which eventually leads to the track to the 'higher' car park). This path joins several other tracks criss-crossing the area, ideal for exploring the Common.

In summary, you can explore Syderstone Common along any one of the footpaths and you should see the target birds and many more besides. This is a sensitive site so you should keep to the footpaths at all times: remember, it is not just the birds that live here; there are many scarce plants and animals that you may harm if you do not behave sensibly!

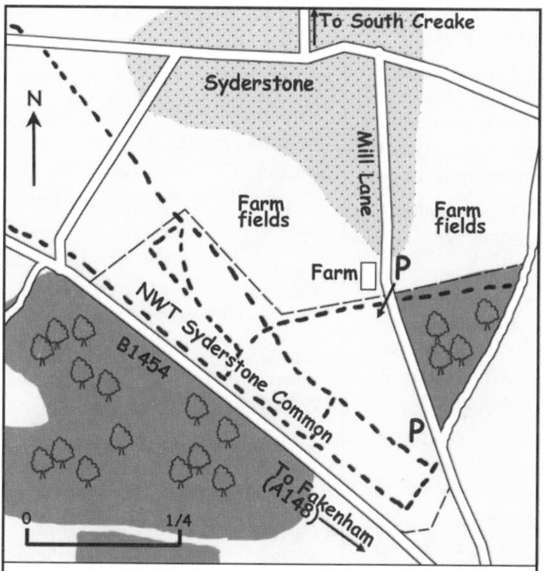

Access details

(Approx 4 miles west of Fakenham)

Take the A148 from King's Lynn to Fakenham. Approx. 4 miles before you reach the Fakenham by-pass, turn left on the B1454 (signed to Docking/Hunstanton). In 1.3 miles turn right at the sign for Wicken Green and Syderstone PO & store. After a further 0.3 miles you reach the Syderstone village sign where you take the left fork (Mill Lane). The small, unmarked car park is up the hill on your left after 0.2 miles, immediately before the metal gate to a large metal farm barn.

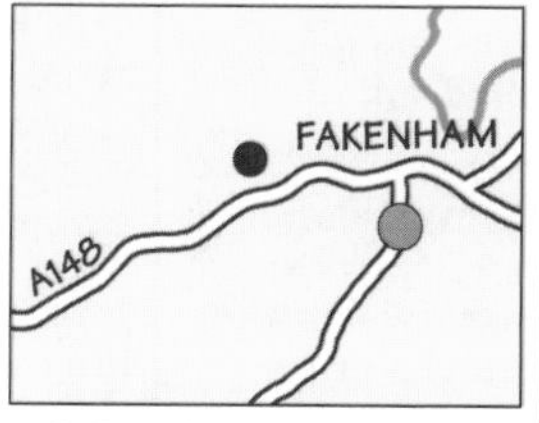

TED ELLIS TRUST NATURE RESERVE

Key points

- **Free parking and access every day but please give generously at donations box.**
- **Small visitor centre with toilets.**
- **Very limited wheelchair access (the hide/ visitor centre is accessible).**
- **Reserve leaflets and maps in dispenser in car park.**
- **Hide is full of info boards plus drawing paper for children.**
- **Level terrain, along muddy tracks, boardwalks and uneven grass paths.**
- **Keep to paths at all times.**
- **No cycles on reserve but bike rails behind warden's hut.**
- **Use insect repellent.**
- **No dogs.**

HERE is a beautiful reserve hidden in the southern part of the Norfolk Broads that offers a pleasant stroll at any time of year to see many common and scarce bird species, plus many other types of wildlife.

Target birds

All year **– Cetti's Warbler (hear 75%, see 20%), Bearded Tit (30%), Lesser Spotted Woodpecker (March/April 60%, rest 10%).** ***Summer*** **– Marsh Harrier (75%), Nightingale: hear 80%, see 10%).**

Other possible bird species

All year
Great Crested Grebe
Little Grebe
Common wildfowl
Common waterbirds
Sparrowhawk
Kestrel
Common gull species
Woodcock
Red-legged Partridge
Grey Partridge
Little Owl
Barn Owl
Kingfisher
Green Woodpecker
Great Spotted Woodpecker
Pied Wagtail
Common scrub birds
Marsh Tit
Common woodland birds
Jay
Reed Bunting

Winter
Hen Harrier
Winter thrushes

Summer
Hobby
Turtle Dove
Cuckoo
Sedge Warbler
Reed Warbler
Other warblers
Spotted Flycatcher
Hirundines

Occasional
Bittern
Osprey

Background information and birding tips

TED ELLIS was a well-known writer and broadcaster who died in 1986. This reserve, sometimes known as Wheatfen Broad, is owned by the Ted Ellis Trust and is a wonderful memorial to a respected naturalist.

The Trust's Patron, David Bellamy, once said of this reserve, "Wheatfen Broad is, in its way, as important as Mount Everest or North America's redwood forests. It is probably the best bit of fenland we have because we know so much about it. That is purely because one man gave his life trying to understand it - Ted Ellis".

It is a well hidden reserve near Surlingham but once you have found it I predict you will return again and again to stroll along the three miles of paths. Your first port of call should be the leaflet dispenser in the car park. This is an excellent publication that tells you what you can see on the reserve and where you can see it (don't forget to put a donation in the box).

The trails pass through many different habitats, all of which can hold several desirable species. Cetti's Warblers seem to show themselves frequently, particularly in the bushes by Wheatfen Broad. Lesser Spotted Woodpeckers inhabit the woods but as they

Contacts

Ted Ellis Trust at Wheatfen Nature Reserve, Surlingham, Norfolk.

Wheatfen Broad, The Covey, off The Green, Surlingham, Norwich, Norfolk NR14 7AL.

Warden: David Nobbs - 01508 538036. Email: wheatfen@aol.com

www.wheatfen.org.uk

can be secretive, try visiting on a fine day in March when they will be drumming and displaying. Also in spring, you should see the resident Bearded Tits in the extensive reedbed or catch a glimpse of a Nightingale in the thick bushes. In summer they are joined by good numbers of Reed Warblers at Wheatfen.

In summer, after strolling along the path through the reeds hoping for a glimpse of the Marsh Harriers, you can walk to the River Yare. From here you can see Great Crested Grebe, Coot, Moorhen and quite probably Kingfisher as you wave to the passing boats. However, be warned that this path may be closed, even in summer, as the reserve can be very wet underfoot.

This is a superb site for the all-round naturalist. There are some excellent birds to be seen (including an occasional Bittern) but the place is also alive with scarce and rare plants, butterflies (17 species) and dragonflies (14 species).

You are guaranteed a very friendly welcome from the staff who are only too pleased to tell you what can be seen and the current warden, David Nobbs, is one of the friendliest chaps you could wish to meet.

It is possible to walk from the reserve to Rockland Broad. Leave the car park and turn left along the access track (away from the way you drove in). This track passes alongside Surlingham Wood and eventually (approx 1 mile) comes out onto the main road at Rockland St Mary. Once on the road, turn left to the New Inn and the path to Rockland Broad (approx 150 yards).

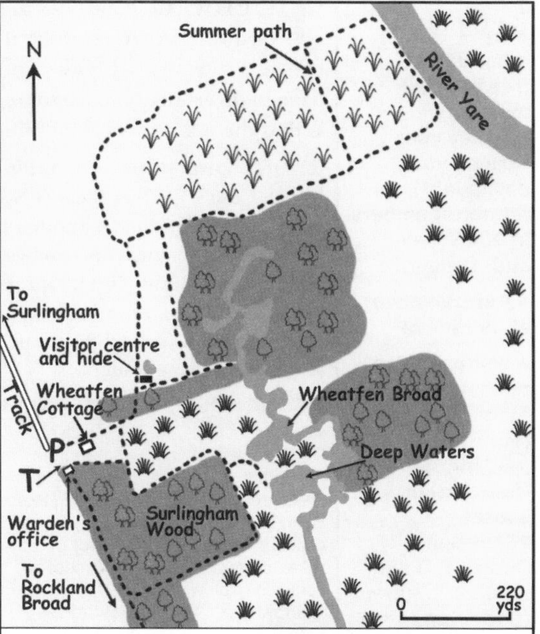

Access details

(Approx. six miles E of Norwich).

From A47 Norwich bypass, turn onto A146 (sign-posted Lowestoft). Head SE for about 100 yards until first set of traffic lights, where you turn left to Bramerton and Kirby Bedon.

After 2.5 miles you reach a junction with the Bramerton village name-post on a patch of grass. Turn left (not sign-posted anywhere!) and continue all the way into Surlingham.

In Surlingham, go through the village to a small pond. Take the next left turn (The Green). Follow for half a mile and turn right down The Covey (sign-posted to the

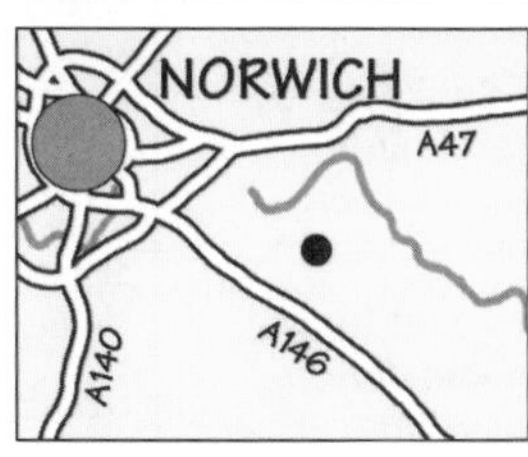

Ted Ellis reserve).

This road becomes a rough track and the reserve is well sign-posted at the end of this track.

The trail to the hide is straight on as you enter the car park, access to the wood is behind the small wooden warden office. Pick up a leaflet before you enter the reserve for more detailed trail directions.

RSPB TITCHWELL MARSH

Key points

- Car park free to RSPB members (display your card on your dashboard), £4 for non-members in 2006 (pay-and-display).
- Reserve open at all times.
- Visitor centre opening times: 10am-4pm (Mon-Fri) and 9.30am-5pm (Sat-Sun) in winter. 10am-5pm (Mon – Fri) and 9.30am-5.30pm (Sat – Sun) in summer.
- Café closes half an hour earlier than visitor centre.
- Toilet block in car park, including disabled access.
- Regular guided walks.
- Visitor centre sells books, clothes, binoculars etc.
- Binoculars for hire (£2).

TITCHWELL continues to shine as the premier site for birdwatchers in Norfolk, if not in Britain. I find it hard to visit the county without popping into Titchwell, even if I have to divert many miles to do so! The simple reason for this is that there is always something to see.

Target birds

All year – Little Egret (85%), Bearded Tit (75%), Cetti's Warbler (hear 80%, see 45%), Bittern (20%), Marsh Harrier (90%). *Winter* – Spotted Redshank (70%), Red-throated Diver (65%), seaduck and grebes (65%), Purple Sandpiper (60%), Black Brant (60%), raptors (40%). *Spring* – Avocet (99%), Little Gull (90%). *Summer* – Avocet (99%), Marsh Harrier (95%), Mediterranean Gull (25%), Little Gull (90%). *Autumn* – Passage seabirds, passage waders.

Other possible bird species

All year
Little Grebe
Cormorant
Shelduck
Eider
Common Scoter
Velvet Scoter
Common wildfowl
Sparrowhawk
Kestrel
Water Rail
Black-tailed Godwit
Common waders
Barn Owl
Great Spotted Woodpecker
Sky Lark
Meadow Pipit
Pied Wagtail
Long-tailed Tit
Corvids
Bullfinch
Linnet
Reed Bunting

Winter
Brent Goose
Pintail
Goldeneye
Red-breasted Merganser
Hen Harrier
Merlin
Peregrine
Water Rail
Golden Plover
Grey Plover
Knot
Woodcock
Guillemot
Razorbill
Stonechat
Common ('Mealy') Redpoll
Lesser Redpoll

Spring
Garganey
Little Ringed Plover
Black-tailed Godwit
Whimbrel
Greenshank
Little Gull
Sand Martin
Yellow Wagtail

Summer
Sandwich Tern
Common Tern
Little Tern
Turtle Dove
Hirundines
Sedge Warbler
Reed Warbler
Whitethroat
Blackcap
Chiffchaff
Lesser Whitethroat
Willow Warbler

Autumn
Shearwaters
Gannet
Garganey
Hobby
Avocet
Little Ringed Plover
Little Stint
Curlew Sandpiper
Ruff
Whimbrel
Greenshank
Green Sandpiper
Wood Sandpiper
Common Sandpiper
Grey Phalarope
Skuas

Occasional
Hobby (summer)
Short-eared Owl (winter)
Spotted Crake (autumn)

ALL YEAR **OS MAP 132** **TF 751438**

Background information and birding tips

THE BEAUTY of Titchwell is that there is always something to see, no matter what the weather conditions, no matter what time of year you visit. You are guaranteed half a day's birding at least and at certain times of the year a whole day can be spent tootling around. This really is a five star reserve that deservedly draws big crowds, so if you like your privacy see the Gypsy Lane site (page 96).

Birdwatching starts in the car park. The surrounding bushes are full of common birds eager to share your food and Chaffinches and Robins often come to take crumbs off your wing mirror.

Before leaving the car park you should have 'ticked off' Blackbird, Robin, Dunnock, Song Thrush, Long-tailed Tit, Blue Tit, Great Tit, Greenfinch, Goldfinch, House Sparrow, Woodpigeon, Collared Dove and if lucky a Bullfinch or two, a wintering Chiffchaff or Blackcap. In summer Turtle Dove, Willow Warbler and Blackcap join the throng.

Follow the marked path from the car park to the visitor centre. This takes you through some dense scrub and alder trees. In winter, a Woodcock can regularly be seen roosting just off the path, usually in full view. Check the alders for redpoll species and Siskins. In summer, the bushes are full of common scrub birds and warblers.

Feeders by the visitor centre are popular and Bramblings can join common species in winter.

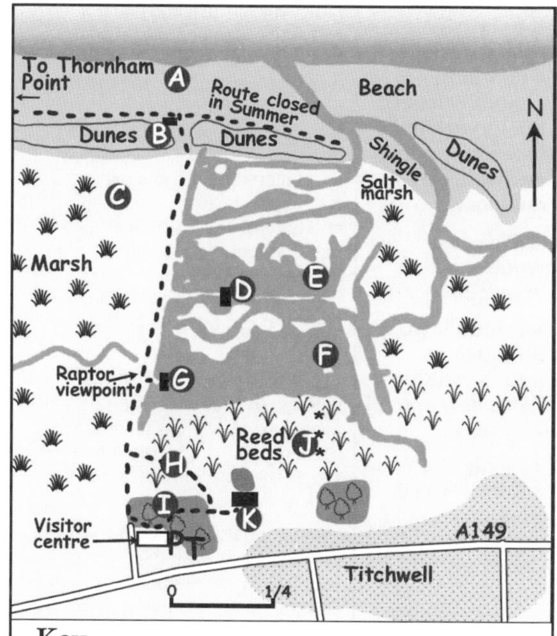

Key

A Pill box (good for Purple Sandpiper
B Viewing platform
C Bare ground (good for buntings/ finches
D Parrinder Hide
E Lagoon
F Lagoon
G Island Hide
H Meadow Trail
I Feeding tables
J Dead trees (good for Marsh Harriers
K New Fen Hide

Access details

(Approx : five miles E of Hunstanton).

The reserve is sign-posted off A149, between the villages of Thornham and Titchwell. There is a large car park on site. The reserve is accessed via a public footpath, which is open at all times.

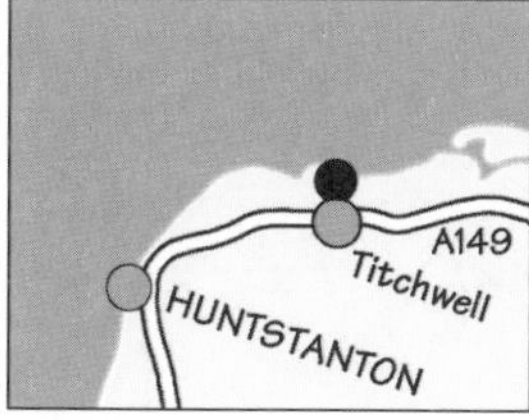

The main reserve lies either side of a 1km track down to the sea. The only deviations allowed are down the short paths to the hides, though unless it is raining heavily it is hardly necessary to enter them as birds seem unperturbed by our constant comings and goings on the main track.

The closest hide to the visitor centre is the Fen

Key points

- **Footpath generally level but wheelchair users may need assistance at one point.**
- **All hides wheelchair accessible.**
- **Dogs allowed on the main path but not in hides or along Fen Trail.**
- **Picnic site adjacent to car park.**

Contacts

RSPB Titchwell Marsh nature reserve, Titchwell, Norfolk PE31 8BB
Tel 01485 210779
E-mail: titchwell@rspb.org.uk

Hide, which is reached along a 250 metre long boardwalk from the visitor centre. This hide affords excellent views across the reeds for breeding Marsh Harriers in summer and roosting Hen Harriers in winter. Bearded Tits should be encountered here and a patient wait should result in a sighting of a Bittern. Thanks to heavy management of the reedbed, Bitterns now breed at Titchwell. Sightings are usually of a bird in flight and can be quite brief, so be alert!

You should also hear a Cetti's Warbler on your walk along the boardwalk. A pair has taken up residence but can be tricky to see as they skulk in the dense undergrowth and bushes.

Rejoin the main track via the boardwalk and scan the fields to your left. These are good for Barn Owl (mornings and evenings best) all year round and Golden Plover and Lapwing flocks in winter. Look to your right in the ditches for Water Rail (best in winter) or a flyover Woodcock at dusk.

Follow the track and check the reeds on your right for Bearded Tits (windless days are best). I have found autumn the best time to get close views, as the adults feed their noisy young right next to the path.

Marsh Harriers regularly quarter the reeds for prey in spring and summer, often chased by a Lapwing or two. In summer, the reedbed is alive with Reed Warblers and Reed Buntings, while Wrens and Sedge Warblers sing from the small bushes and trees.

Look over the bank to your left at regular intervals for raptors and geese in winter. Redshanks take flight at the slightest thing and are often your indicator that a raptor is in the vicinity. Also on the marsh in winter, you should see Snipe, Curlew and Wigeon feeding in the grass. Brent Geese are guaranteed in winter and spring (sometimes up until May) and for the last eight winters they have been joined by a Black Brant, their American cousin. This is also a good place to look for Little Egret at any time of the year. They occasionally fly over the path giving excellent views, especially at dusk.

Two paths lead off to your right, the first to Island Hide and the second to Parrinder Hide, both of which overlook lagoons. The former is good for spotting Bearded Tits and Water Rails and in recent autumns this area has regularly attracted a Spotted Crake.

A good selection of ducks can also be seen from Island Hide during the year, along with common wader species. If you are lucky, you may be able to pick out a Mediterranean Gull from the swirling throng of noisy Black-headeds. This hide also gives a good view over the reedbed for Marsh Harrier and possibly Bittern. In spring and summer, this hide is the best place to observe Little Gull, usually flying at the back of the lagoon. Up to 12 birds are seen regularly.

Parrinder Hide is good for viewing breeding Avocets and close views of autumn waders such as Little Stint and Curlew Sandpiper. In winter, Pintail can be seen from here, often at the back of the lagoon and Water Pipits are sometimes seen on the islands.

The lagoons attract longer-legged waders such as Spotted Redshank, Black-tailed and Bar-tailed Godwits.

Unfortunately, 'Sammy' The Black-winged Stilt has passed away after 14 long years in residence. The islands in the lagoons attract waders such as Ringed Plover, Dunlin and Ruff, joined by Little Ringed Plover in summer and Little Stint and Curlew Sandpiper in autumn.

Where the track ends at a boardwalk onto the beach, there is an area of bare ground to the left. In recent winters, this has been an excellent area for feeding flocks of Goldfinches and Linnets but Shore Larks and Twite have become scarce here.

If the birds are not here, try walking east (right) along the beach. The area of pebbles around here is another good place for all the above species and Snow Bunting, though none can be guaranteed as they tend to roam along the beach as far as Hunstanton and Holkham. Each winter is different, so check recent records to ensure you are not disappointed. To avoid disturbing birds, only take this route in winter and do not attempt to walk onto the salt marsh, which can be dangerous.

To view the sea/beach you can either sit on the wooden viewing platform (good for wheelchair users but too bouncy for easy telescope use) or settle down out of the wind on the beach. Winter should produce large numbers of waders on the beach and an unpredictable number of sea duck/grebes/divers out to sea. High tide is best as all birds are closer to the viewer at this time.

The old, now derelict, pill box is an excellent place to see regular Purple Sandpiper in winter as well as Turnstone. Sanderling, Dunlin, Ringed Plover, Bar-tailed Godwit and Oystercatcher are usually present all year. Grey Plover and Knot join the party in the autumn and remain into late spring.

Common Scoters can be present all year round, though they range as far as Hunstanton so cannot be guaranteed. Some years up to 3,000 can be seen and in other years hardly any. Also watch out for the white wing-flashes of Velvet Scoter among the Commons.

Winter sea enthusiasts can have their days enlivened by regular Red-throated Divers and, if lucky, the not so regular Black-throateds or Great Northern Divers. Long-tailed Ducks are unpredictable in their numbers as are Slavonian and Red-necked Grebes. One or two Guillemots and Razorbills are regularly seen in winter. The onset of spring is heralded in late March by the return of Sandwich Terns, joined by Little and Common Terns in May.

Autumn seawatching, preferably in a strong onshore wind, can be very good from the beach at Titchwell. Skuas are regularly seen, with Great and Arctic being the commonest but Pomarine and Long-tailed are occasionally spotted. Manx Shearwaters can virtually be guaranteed from August to October and look out for the rarer shearwaters (Sooty, Balearic, Great and Cory's). Little Auks pass by in November.

Titchwell has an excellent record for turning up rarities. A few years ago a Franklin's Gull and a Laughing Gull were seen together and I have seen two Penduline Tits here (not at the same time), the second only minutes after I had seen a Rough-legged Buzzard fly over the Black-winged Stilt!

In recent years, Arctic Redpoll, White-rumped Sandpiper, Stilt Sandpiper, Purple Heron, Gull-billed Tern and White-tailed Eagle are among a host of rarities recorded and scarcities such as Red-necked Phalarope, Temminck's Stint and Spotted Crake are almost expected.

Other nearby sites

Brancaster Marsh, Choseley Barns, Dersingham Bog, Gypsy Lane, NWT Holme Dunes, NOA Holme Observatory, Holkham Hall, Holkham NNR, Hunstanton, Ken Hill Wood, King's Lynn Docks, Sandringham, RSPB Snettisham, Swanton Novers, NOA Redwell Marsh, NWT Roydon Common, Wolferton Triangle.

TOTTENHILL GRAVEL PITS

Key points

- **The pits can be viewed at all times from the road.**
- **Do not enter the fenced-off areas.**
- **No walking necessary.**
- **Wheelchair users may find pits obscured by bushes.**

Contact

None

THIS FLOODED gravel pit, which is a traditional wintering site for Smew in varying numbers, can be viewed from the road. Rumours of Nightingales present in the thick bushes along the roadside are unsubstantiated by me. The pits are private and you must not enter the site.

Target birds *Winter* – Smew (65%).

Other possible bird species

Winter
Great Crested Grebe
Cormorant
Common waterfowl
Wigeon
Gadwall
Teal
Shoveler
Goldeneye
Egyptian Goose
Other common wildfowl
Sparrowhawk
Common gull species
Great Spotted Woodpecker
Kingfisher
Goldcrest
Nuthatch
Treecreeper
Pied Wagtail
Common scrub birds
Long-tailed Tit
Common woodland birds
Common finches
Reed Bunting

Early spring
Sand Martin
Swallow
House Martin

Background information and birding tips

TOTTENHILL continues to attract wintering Smew in varying numbers but Willow Tits, its other speciality, have disappeared from the site. Winter wildfowl are drawn here because the pool is sheltered by trees and so rarely freezes over. 700-plus Pintail, 300-plus Pochard and 200-plus Teal have been counted on the lake, along with Goldeneye, Tufted Duck, Gadwall, etc.

While scanning the lake for Smew, you should also see more common ducks such as Wigeon, Tufted Duck, Pochard and Goldeneye. Smew can remain on site until April, by which time you will be able to watch the comical head-tossing courtship displays of the drake Goldeneye as they try to impress the females who are usually more occupied with feeding.

Tottenhill is a traditional wintering site for Smew.

Great Crested Grebes should also be present and coming into their resplendent breeding plumage by February. Look out or their elaborate courtship rituals, including the famous 'weed dance' and synchronised head bobbing and shaking.

Several species of common woodland birds frequent the trees. By the end of March, you should also encounter the first Chiffchaffs, Blackcaps and Sand Martins of the year as they pour in from their African wintering grounds.

In the summer months the bushes along the road completely obscure the view of the pits. Besides, bird activity is confined to very common species which are readily seen elsewhere, so a visit is probably only advised while the Smew are in residence, unless you wish to investigate reports of Nightingales in the area.

The large pit on the left of the A10, just past the junction with the A134, attracts a large number of common wildfowl but do not be tempted to stop on either road as they are very busy at all times.

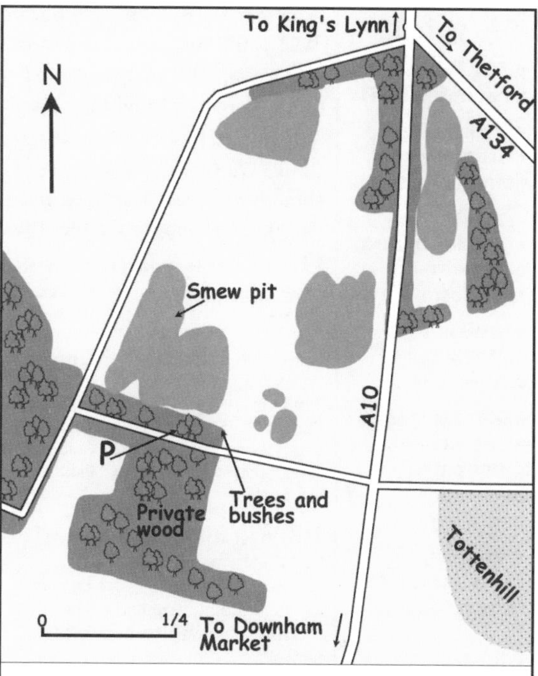

Access details

(Approx. 4 miles S of King's Lynn).

From King's Lynn, take A10 S towards Downham Market. Ignore the turn-off to Thetford (A134) after four miles but a mile after this junction there is a crossroads.

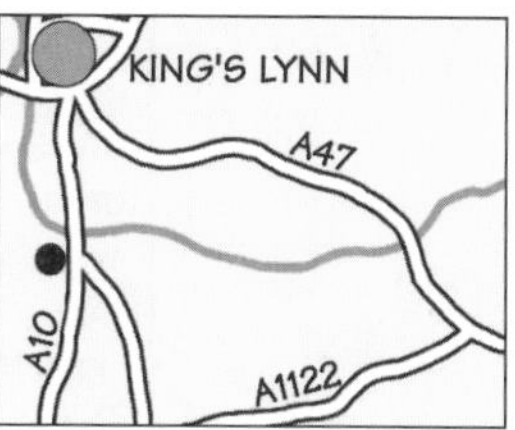

Take the minor road to the right, then park on the right after another half a mile in the very small pull-off. The gravel pits can be viewed from the road here.

Other nearby sites

Blackborough End Tip, Flitcham Abbey Farm, Hunstanton, Ken Hill Wood, NWT Roydon Common, Sandringham, RSPB Snettisham, WWT Welney, Wolferton Triangle.

73 NWT UPTON BROAD AND MARSHES

Key points

- **Site is a designated SSSI.**
- **Phone NWT warden before going on to the reserve.**
- **Small car park, otherwise no facilities.**
- **Trail not suitable for wheelchairs.**
- **Terrain is level along muddy, grass paths and a short boardwalk.**
- **Walking boots (at least) recommended.**

Contacts

Norfolk Wildlife Trust
01603 625540

General Broads Authority
01603 610734

UPTON FEN is very hard to find but once on site, you'll discover it is a fantastic place for the all-round naturalist, with plenty of bird species to please those visitors only interested in feathered wildlife!

Target birds

All year – **Nightingale (hear 60%, see 10%), Cetti's Warbler (hear 50%, see 5%), Lesser Spotted Woodpecker (March 40%, rest 5%).** *Summer* – **Marsh Harrier (80%), Hobby (60%), Grasshopper Warbler (hear 50%, see 5%).**

Other possible bird species

Spring/summer
Sparrowhawk
Kestrel
Water Rail
Woodcock
Turtle Dove
Cuckoo
Green Woodpecker
Great Spotted Woodpecker
Sky Lark
Meadow Pipit
Hirundines
Common scrub birds
Sedge Warbler
Reed Warbler
Lesser Whitethroat
Whitethroat
Garden Warbler
Blackcap
Chiffchaff
Willow Warbler
Goldcrest
Marsh Tit
Long-tailed Tit
Reed Bunting

Very occasional
Savi's Warbler

Background information and birding tips

THIS Norfolk Wildlife Trust reserve is perhaps best known for its dragonfly populations but it has much to offer the birdwatcher as well.

There is a blue, way-marked trail around the reserve, consisting of muddy grass paths and boardwalks (the long loop is 3km, the short trail is 1.6km).

You should see Sky Lark, Linnet, Yellowhammer, Goldfinch, etc along the hedges and in the fields as you approach the car park.

The walk starts at the Turf Ponds, small pools just inside the reserve entrance. This is an excellent area for dragonflies, while birds can include Garden Warbler, Blackcap, Chiffchaff, Kestrel, Sparrowhawk, Swallow, Swift and House Martin. Listen out for the explosive song of Cetti's Warbler.

Follow the marked trail straight ahead into a wet woodland. Migrants include Willow Warbler, Blackcap, Garden Warbler and Chiffchaff. Goldcrest and Marsh Tit are seen regularly. Common woodland birds are seen and heard here too.

The wet woodland, or carr, is the best place to try to see Nightingale. You should hear them from late April onwards but seeing one in the thick cover is another matter.

The wood opens out to a cleared area, which is an excellent place to see Whitethroats and Sedge Warblers. There is usually a Grasshopper Warbler reeling from cover at the back of the clearing.

Green and Great Spotted Woodpeckers are sometimes seen flying along the edge of the woodland. Look out for elusive Lesser Spotted Woodpeckers here too. The best times are March and early April when they are in display flight. This spot is also a good place to see swallowtail butterflies.

The trail then splits into two at

a blue marker. The right fork takes you along a dyke to the viewpoint. The left hand path is a short cut back to the car park. On the way to the viewpoint, you should see Reed Warblers and Reed Buntings.

The path opens out to a marsh, which is an excellent place to stand and wait for Hobbies pursuing hirundines and dragonflies, as well as enjoying views of Marsh Harriers as they scour the ditches for prey.

The path rejoins the main track after about a quarter of a mile. You should turn right towards the Turf Ponds and car park, listening and watching for warblers and scrub birds in the bushes along the way.

A combination of birdwatching, dragonfly and butterfly watching and plant finding will guarantee a successful visit to this first-rate little site. As well as the excellent birds - a Savi's Warbler took up residence in 2000 - this is a superb place for rare butterflies (swallowtail), dragonflies (Norfolk hawker) and plants (marsh fern).

Walking boots are recommended at all times and you really need that insect repellent; the mosquitos here are the most vicious I have found anywhere in the world!

I forgot my repellent on one visit and was fortunate to escape with all limbs intact. It was very satisfying to watch a Norfolk hawker devour one of these mozzies, back-end first, giving it a taste of its own medicine. Isn't nature wonderful!

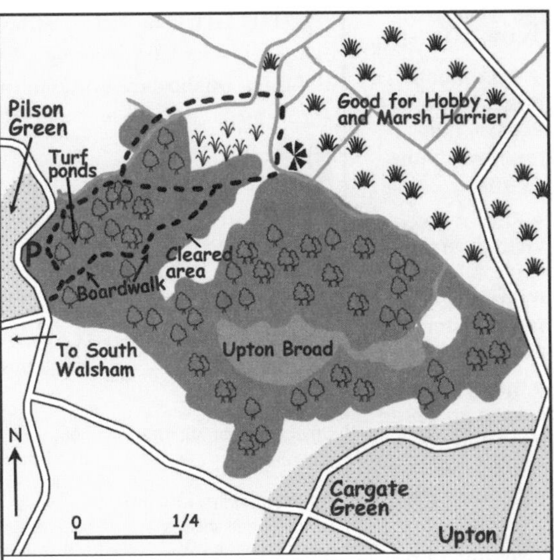

Access details

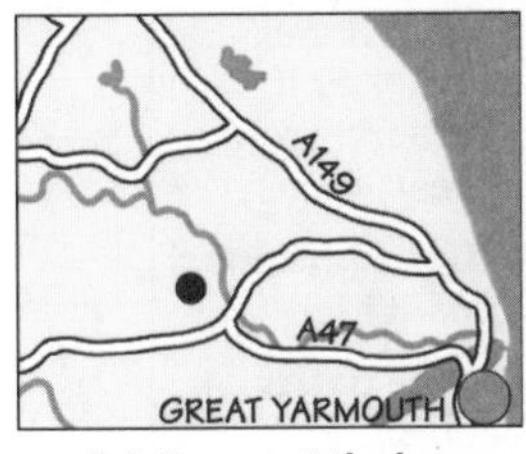

(Approx. ten miles NE of Norwich).

Upton Fen can be a devil to find! Basically, you need to head for Pilson Green, NE of South Walsham. From the B1140 (Wroxham to Acle road), follow signs for South Walsham/Ranworth.

In the village, keep heading E, past the church, then take the left turn sign-posted to Pilson Green/Fairhaven Water Gardens.

Take second left turn (ignoring the one signed to 'Broad') sign-posted 'Upton 1 mile'. Once past the houses, take the first left down Low Road, which is a dead end.

The small reserve car park is approx. 200 yards on the right, just before the house. If you have made it this far, you deserve to see everything on the reserve!

Other nearby sites

Breydon Water, Buxton Heath, NWT Cockshoot Broad, Great Yarmouth Beach, NWT Hickling Broad, Hoveton Great Broad, How Hill NNR, NWT Ranworth Broad, RSPB Strumpshaw Fen, Ted Ellis Reserve, Winterton Dunes.

Key points

- **NOA members dawn to dusk access, non-members 9am - 5pm.**
- **Report to visitor centre on arrival. Non-members need a permit (donation asked for).**
- **Small visitor centre accessed up steep steps (sells books and bird reports).**
- **£5 deposit for key which fits all NOA hides. Return key if membership lapses!**
- **ID & sightings book in hide**
- **Some paths level, some steep but all are narrow.**
- **Warden usually present.**
- **Telescope very useful.**

Contacts

Norfolk Ornithologists' Association
01485 525406

THE HIDE at Walsey affords an excellent panoramic view over Cley Marshes. Even though the reserve is tiny, the thick bushes are home to many breeding warblers and scrub birds. I feel it is a special place just to sit to see what comes into view.

Target birds

All year – **Barn Owl (60%), Bittern (5%).** *Spring/autumn* – **Passage migrants.** *Winter* – **Water Pipit (60%), raptors (15%).** *Summer* – **Marsh Harrier (99%), Lesser Whitethroat (65%), Grasshopper Warbler (hear 50%, see 5%), Cetti's Warbler (hear 60%, see <10%).**

Other possible bird species

All year
Little Grebe
Egyptian Goose
Other common wildfowl
Sparrowhawk
Kestrel
Common waders (distant)
Common gull species
Common scrub birds
Common finches
Reed Bunting

Winter
Brent Goose
Winter thrushes

Summer
Hobby
Turtle Dove
Cuckoo
Hirundines
Sedge Warbler
Reed Warbler
Other warblers

Spring/autumn
Passage migrants
Redstart
Whinchat
Wheatear
Winter thrushes
Barred Warbler
Yellow-browed Warbler
Firecrest
Pied Flycatcher
Red-backed Shrike

Background information and birding tips

THERE IS always something to see on or from this reserve. Though it is small (three acres, owned by the Norfolk Ornithologists' Association) it is covered by thick bushes and gorse, ideal for attracting migrants in spring and autumn.

These have included Yellow-browed Warbler, Hume's Leaf Warbler, Barred and Icterine Warblers, Red-backed, Woodchat and Great Grey Shrikes, Firecrest, Wryneck etc. A couple of Cetti's Warblers have recently colonised the reserve and can be heard singing throughout the year.

The extensive area of gorse at the top of the hill is usually closed but if a rarity is found, the warden opens up the footpath. There are two narrow paths cutting through the bushes. I recommend pausing at regular intervals to see what pops out of cover as the bushes really are quite thick.

Another feature of Walsey is the panoramic views of NWT Cley Marshes from the hide at the top of the hill (£5 deposit for key). From here you may obtain distant views of some of Cley's specialities or watch for visible migration. For instance, a Bittern is sometimes seen flying across the reeds. Water Pipits can be seen around the channel opposite the reserve car park in winter and 'scope views of Avocets, Brent Geese and various species of ducks can be obtained at appropriate times of the year.

Viewing over Cley Marshes

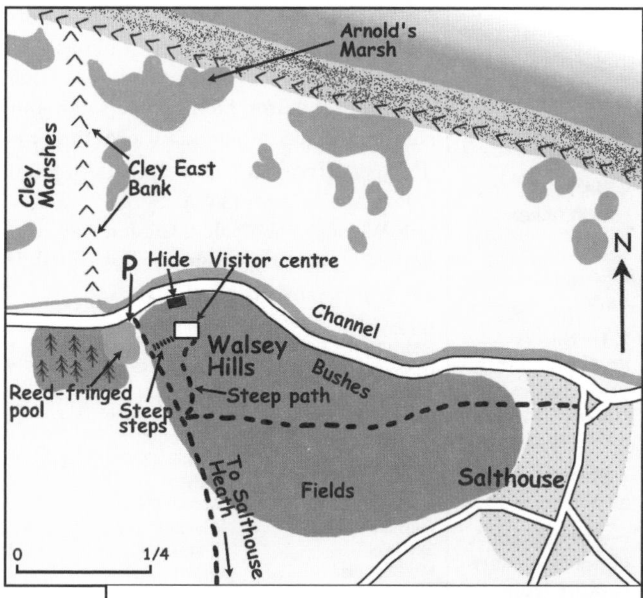

produces regular raptor sightings, including Hen, Marsh and (occasionally) Montagu's Harriers. Merlin, Peregrine, Kestrel and Sparrowhawk are also seen regularly. Barn Owls are noted on a daily basis.

In summer, an array of warblers breed on the reserve. These include the locally scarce Lesser Whitethroat, along with the more common Blackcap, Whitethroat, Willow Warbler, Chiffchaff and Garden Warbler. Grasshopper Warblers are often heard from the car park but seldom seen. Also on the reserve in summer, warm days can produce sightings of adder, slow worm and common lizard as well as a wide range of butterflies.

In summary, this is an excellent reserve and it is worth spending time here to wander the paths, looking for migrants or the commoner breeding birds. Alternatively, you could spend an hour or two basking in the sun while eating your sandwiches, looking out over Cley marshes. The bird feeder below the visitor centre is worth keeping an eye on as well. Don't mind the regular swarm of flies in summer, they don't bite!

The reserve is open from dawn to dusk every day. The reserve is also the best place to see adders in summer when up to three of these beauties bask on the grass by the visitor centre.

You may also wish to walk from Walsey to Salthouse Heath along a public footpath (just over one mile) or vice versa if you wish.

Access details

(General area: six miles W of Sheringham.

Head E from Cley on A149 towards Sheringham. About half a mile after passing the NWT Cley Marsh visitor car park on right, turn onto the rough lay-by on the right signed 'NOA Watchpoint' (virtually opposite Cley East Bank).

All visitors should enter the reserve via the path leading from the car park and report to the small visitor centre up the steep steps on the left.

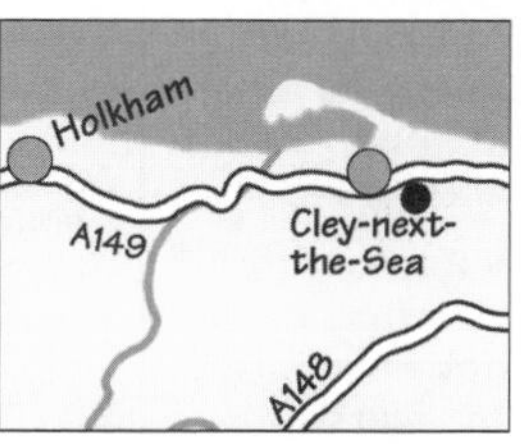

Other nearby sites

Blakeney Point, NWT Cley Marsh, Felbrigg Hall, Kelling Heath, Kelling Quags, Morston Quay, Salthouse Beach, Salthouse Heath, Sheringham, Stiffkey, Swanton Novers, Weybourne.

WARHAM GREENS

Key points

- **Part of the Holkham National Nature Reserve.**
- **Narrow, rough access roads.**
- **Small car parks.**
- **Terrain is level along grass paths. Narrow, muddy paths to marsh.**
- **Stay on paths at all times.**
- **Wheelchair users may view raptors from car parks but the paths are definitely not accessible.**
- **Raptor roost watchers must not walk onto the marsh.**

Contacts

English Nature
01603 620558

THIS expanse of saltmarsh holds populations of some scarce Norfolk breeders and has gained a reputation in recent years as a passage migrant hotspot, especially in autumn. In winter, Hen Harriers come in to roost at dusk, sometimes accompanied by a Merlin or two.

Target birds

Winter – **Hen Harrier roost (75%), Rock Pipit (70%), Merlin roost (30%).** *Spring/autumn* – **Passage migrants (e.g. Wheatear, Whinchat, Garden Warbler, Barred Warbler, etc).** *Summer* – **Breeding waders (60%), Marsh Harrier (70%).**

Other possible bird species

All year
Shelduck
Lapwing
Snipe
Curlew
Redshank
Kestrel
Grey Partridge
Black-headed Gull
Barn Owl
Sky Lark
Meadow Pipit
Pied Wagtail
Starling
Reed Bunting

Spring/autumn
Dunlin
Whimbrel
Greenshank
Green Sandpiper
Common Sandpiper
Wryneck
Yellow Wagtail
Bluethroat
Black Redstart
Redstart
Whinchat
Wheatear
Ring Ouzel
Winter thrushes
Barred Warbler
Lesser Whitethroat
Blackcap
Goldcrest
Firecrest
Pied Flycatcher

Summer
Hobby
Terns
Hirundines
Sedge Warbler
Whitethroat
Blackcap
Chiffchaff
Willow Warbler

Winter
Brent Goose
Wigeon
Seaduck
Short-eared Owl
Stonechat
Twite
Snow Bunting

Background information and birding tips

WARHAM GREENS is part of Holkham National Nature Reserve. It first came to my notice when I heard of a strange harrier in the fields here, rumoured to be a Pallid Harrier. After spending an hour trying to find the place, the bird turned out to be a Montagu's but was still thrilling to see. Since then, Warham has produced several Barred Warblers and a Blyth's Reed Warbler to mention but a few goodies.

Summer is the quietest period, though Shelduck, Redshanks and Black-headed Gulls all nest on the marsh. The hedgerows around the car parks hold Whitethroats, Blackcaps and Chiffchaffs and common scrub species and the bushes along the edge of the marsh attract breeding Sedge Warblers.

Marsh Harriers occasionally hunt over the marsh but are more easily seen elsewhere. One July, I drove down the deserted track and was treated to a delightful family party of two adult and six young Grey Partridges dust-bathing in the car park.

The main attraction in winter is the raptor roost. Hen Harriers are seen daily between December and

February, appearing from about an hour before dark. Merlins are also regularly seen here but are never guaranteed.

Sharing the marsh in winter are varying numbers of Brent Geese and Wigeon. A Short-eared Owl is occasionally seen but Barn Owls are noted more regularly. A few Twite may be among the flocks of Goldfinches, Linnets, Greenfinches etc and if you are really lucky maybe even a Snow Bunting or two. Rock Pipits also winter in good numbers but can be hard to locate.

Warham's reputation as a migrant trap, particularly in autumn, is well founded. The bushes running east and west from the car parks can hold species such as Redstart, Chiffchaff, Willow Warbler, Blackcap, Pied Flycatcher, Garden Warbler, etc. Be alert too for something a little special, such as Firecrest or Barred Warbler.

If you walk west from the main car park, check the small, bush-lined hollow on the left after about 400 yards, rather grandly called 'the quarry'. This is a nice sheltered, sun-trap, ideal for attracting migrants.

The marsh and bushes around the edges of the marsh should be checked for migrant Wheatears and Whinchats etc but don't ignore the sky for a passing Honey Buzzard or, more likely, migrating thrushes, hirundines, etc.

The pools and creeks on the marsh may attract passage waders such as Greenshank, Whimbrel, Little Stint, etc along with Yellow Wagtails in spring.

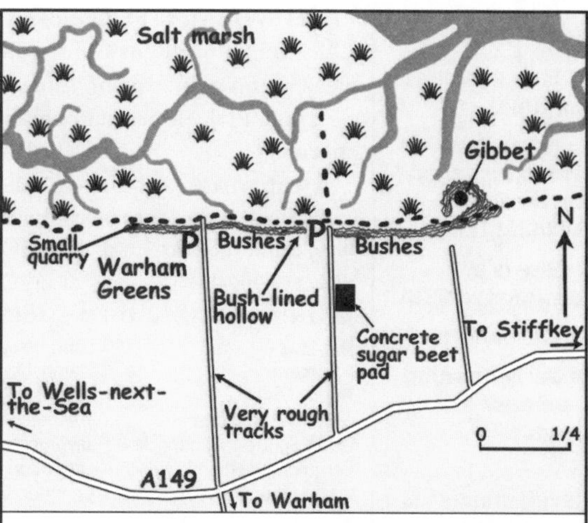

Access details

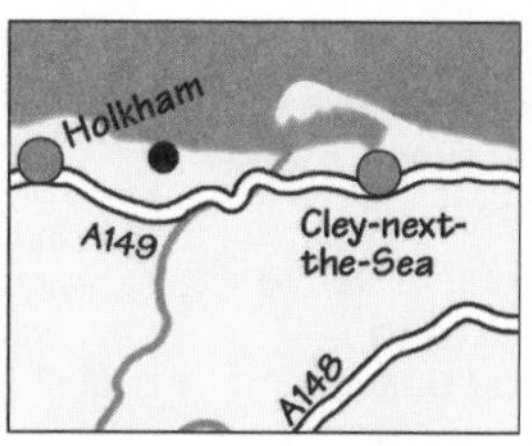

(Approx. 1.5 miles E of Wells-Next-The-Sea).

Head E from Wells along A149 towards Sheringham. To find the most convenient Warham car park turn N onto a very rough track opposite the turn-off to Warham (look for a small, partly hidden sign-post). The track is signed 'not suitable for vehicles'. If you worry about the suspension on your car, park here and walk the rest of the way. If not, drive slowly to a small car park at the end (about half a mile).

From here walk straight ahead onto the marsh, or to the left or right to view the bushes during passage periods. Raptors can be seen from the car park but particularly recommended is the area surrounding The Gibbet, a strange metal structure on a concrete base, 500 yards to the right.

A smaller car park is at the end of an even rougher track about a quarter of a mile W of this one. Do not park on concrete sugar beet pad used by farmers and large farm vehicles. Do not block access for any farm vehicles.

Other nearby sites

Blakeney Point, NWT Cley Marsh, Felbrigg Hall, Holkham Park, Holkham NNR, Salthouse Beach, Sheringham, Stiffkey, NOA Walsey Hills, Wells Woods, Weybourne.

NWT WAYLAND WOOD

Key points

- **Free access at all times**
- **An ancient wood managed by Norfolk Wildlife Trust.**
- **Site is a designated SSSI.**
- **Car parking.**
- **Early morning and dusk are best.**
- **Terrain is level, mainly along uneven grass paths.**
- **Can be wet at all times. Muddy in winter.**
- **Never leave paths to see Golden Pheasants.**
- **Too boggy for wheelchairs but birds can occasionally be seen from car park.**

Contacts

Norfolk Wildlife Trust
01603 625540

Wayland Tourism Association,
c/o Wayland Hall,
Middle Street, Watton,
Norfolk IP25 6AG
(01953 884224)
www.wayland-tourism.org.uk

THIS BEAUTIFUL ancient coppiced woodland remains a reliable site for Golden Pheasant. It is especially pleasant on a fine spring morning when the sun-dappled clearings make a perfect backdrop to a stunning dawn chorus.

Target birds

All year – **Golden Pheasant (40% - early morning and dusk are best), Lesser Spotted Woodpecker (March 40%, other months 15%).** *Spring/summer* – **Nightingale (hear 50%, see 10%).).**

Other possible bird species

All year		***Summer***
Sparrowhawk	Long-tailed Tit	Cuckoo
Tawny Owl	Marsh Tit	Hirundines
Green Woodpecker	Nuthatch	Warblers
Great Spotted Woodpecker	Treecreeper	Spotted Flycatcher
Common woodland birds	Jay	
Common scrub birds	Other corvids	
	Common finches	

Background information and birding tips

SOME SAY small is beautiful and NWT Wayland Wood is relatively small (35ha) and definitely beautiful (despite it being the inspiration for the Babes In The Woods fairy tale). If you pick the right day and time, as you get out of your car in the car park, the sun will be slicing through the trees to light the grass 'rides' perfectly. To complete the picture you should hear the raucous 'strangled chicken' call of Golden Pheasants!

To see the birds here walk through the metal gate from the car park, then follow the muddy, grass path for approximately 50 yards. You'll then reach a clearing in front of you, with a grass path (or 'ride') to your right.

The best place for the Golden Pheasants is in the thick bushes alongside the right-hand grass path. You can either stand very quietly at the junction of the car park path and grassy ride, or walk quietly along the ride to peer into gaps between bushes. Display some patience and you should be successful. Fortunately, the Golden Pheasants here are very vocal. At other sites they cease calling in June but at Wayland they seem to like the sound of their own voices and I have heard even them calling in late August at midday.

Norfolk Wildlife Trust is coppicing some of the thick cover here to improve the habitat for numerous species of birds. This intensive management has enabled the return of Nightingales to the reserve and their song can be heard from the end of April deep within the thick scrub.

Unfortunately, this work seems to have disturbed the Goldies and sightings in early 2006 were few and far between.

Stand quietly in the clearing opposite the area recommended for Golden Pheasants and you will be surrounded by Marsh Tits, Nuthatches, Great Spotted Woodpeckers and Jays, as well as Great, Blue and Long-tailed Tits and other common species.

Lesser Spotted Woodpeckers have been seen in these woods but are always elusive. A summer visit to Wayland should produce numerous warbler species including Blackcap, Goldcrest, Willow Warbler, Chiffchaff and Garden Warbler.

You may wish to follow the NWT way-marked route along a grass 'ride' all the way around the wood but I have found the first patch of wood up to the cleared area is the best for all the birds.

The way-marked footpath is a circular route that eventually leads back to the clearing near the car park. It is only about a mile in length, if that and Golden Pheasants can be seen on any of the paths if you remain quiet. To be honest, though, the rest of the walk can be quite unproductive compared to the car park area.

Just one word of caution: some birders have been known to leave the paths to search for pheasants. If you see this happening tell them bluntly that you will not stand for such behaviour. Not only are they disturbing the birds; it is very poor fieldcraft. They may see the rear end of a petrified Goldie hurtling away from them but a pheasant won't be seen again for a few hours after that. Simply standing still should produce views of one scratching contentedly in the leaf litter, dazzling you with their plumage.

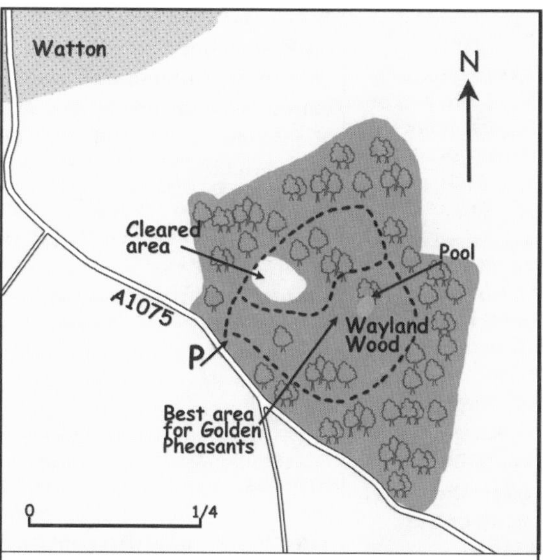

Access details

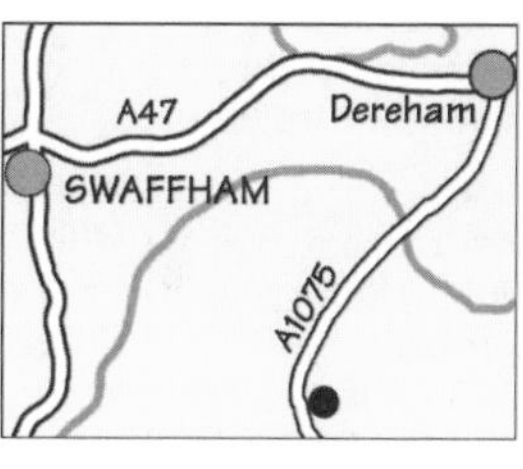

(Approx. 10.5 miles NE of Thetford).

Turn S off A47 (King's Lynn to Norwich road) at Dereham onto A1075. After approximately seven miles you will pass through Watton village followed by a right turn signposted 'Thompson 3 miles/Merton 1.5 miles'.

Ignore the turn-off and keep going on A1075 until you see SLOW signs painted on the road, followed by a public footpath signpost to a track on your left.

Immediately after this track there is a narrow entrance to the reserve car park on the left, indicated by a brown tourist sign. This entrance is 0.4 miles past the national speed limit signs in Watton.

Other nearby sites

Barnhamcross Common, NWT East Wretham Heath, Fordham, NWT Foulden Common, RSPB Lakenheath, Lynford Arboretum, Santon Downham, NWT Sparham Pools, NWT Weeting Heath.

NWT WEETING HEATH

Key points

- **Open from April 1 to end of August (check with contacts below for changes).**
- **Reserve open 7am to dusk, visitor centre open 9am- 5pm (can close if no voluntary wardens).**
- **Site is a designated SSSI.**
- **Terrain is level along gravel paths.**
- **Access to hides is up short, wooden ramps.**
- **Hides and visitor centre are fully wheelchair accessible, though paths are rough with tree roots protruding slightly.**
- **£2.50 entrance fee to non-NWT members in 2006.**

Contacts

Norfolk Wildlife Trust
01603 625540
www.wildlifetrust.org.uk/norfolk
admin@norfolkwildlifetrust.org.uk

WEETING is a superb Breckland reserve famous for its breeding Stone-curlews. The hides are accessed along short paths through a pleasant conifer wood, packed with common woodland species. As well as the Stone-curlews, you should obtain excellent views of Wood Larks from the hides. A superb little place!

Target birds

Spring/summer – **Stone-curlew (90%), Wood Lark (90%), Marsh Harrier (60%), Buzzard (60%), Hobby (60%), Little Owl (60%).**

Other possible bird species

Spring/summer
Sparrowhawk
Kestrel
Lapwing
Common gull species
Green Woodpecker
Great Spotted Woodpecker
Hirundines
Sky Lark
Meadow Pipit
Common scrub birds
Wheatear
Mistle Thrush
Summer warblers
Goldcrest
Spotted Flycatcher
Common woodland birds
Marsh Tit
Corvids
Siskin
Linnet
Other common finches

Occasional
Tree Pipit
Crossbill

Background information and birding tips

WANT TO SEE Stone-curlew and Wood Lark? Then head for NWT Weeting Heath. There are other sites, of course but please avoid these to prevent them being targeted by egg collectors.

The return of heathland species to Weeting each spring depends entirely on the rabbit population busy nibbling away, keeping the plants low enough for Stone-curlews and Wood Larks to nest. You may see both species from either the east or west hides. Wood Larks usually nest close to the hides, especially the west one.

The Stone-curlews nest further away, sometimes out of sight over the ridge. Patience may be required to see these ground-nesting birds but they usually show in the end. These large migrant birds are nocturnal, so an early morning or evening visit is best, though they can be seen at all times of day. Be aware, however, that there can be a wicked heat haze during the day, which can severely hamper viewing.

If you are lucky, you may even hear the eerie call of the Stone-curlew, a loud, haunting '*tudlooweeet tudlooweet*' (when you hear it, you will know what I mean).

Recently Marsh Harriers and Buzzards have started nesting in the area and both species visit Weeting Heath on a regular basis. Scan the trees at the back of the heath for a chance of seeing them. From the west hides, a good scan of the trees and fence posts on your right should reveal a Little Owl.

While waiting for the target species to show, you will be entertained by Green Woodpeckers, Mistle Thrushes and Lapwings on the heath. Rabbits are abundant, sometimes chased by stoats

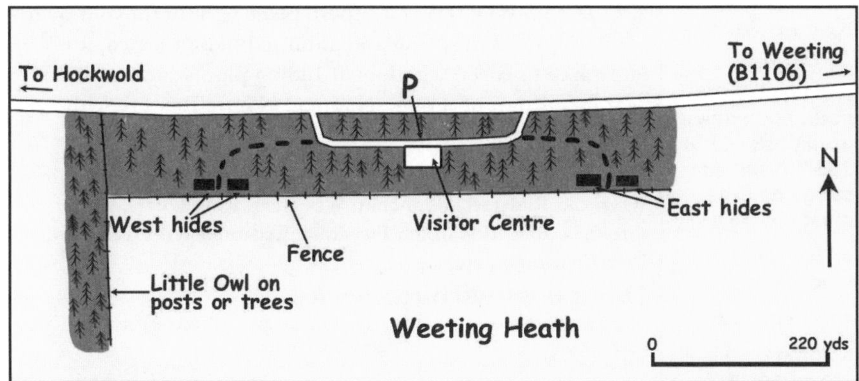

(beware mistaking the former for Stone-curlews in extreme heat haze conditions!). Wheatears may be seen on passage.

In the pine trees surrounding the hide, you should see Spotted Flycatcher, Marsh Tit, Long-tailed Tit, Blackcap, Goldcrest, etc. Crossbills and Tree Pipits are seen occasionally.

The new visitor centre stocks a good selection of books for sale. One may also purchase chocolate bars and hot drinks. There is a display explaining the history and biology of Weeting, a sightings board, an extensive supply of tourist information leaflets and a wheelchair friendly toilet.

Please note that the visitor centre may close at any time of day if the warden needs to be out and about on the reserve itself.

All in all, this is a first-class little reserve and you are guaranteed a friendly welcome from the wardens, who are only too happy to spend time with you to show you what is on the reserve.

Visiting birdwatchers who spend a leisurely hour or two here will see many sought-after Breckland species, though be sure to remain quiet throughout your visit to avoid disturbing these sensitive, vulnerable species.

Access details

(Approx. 7.5 miles NW of Thetford).

Head N on A1065 from Brandon towards Swaffham. Immediately after crossing the railway turn left onto B1106, signposted to Weeting.

After about 1.5 miles turn left at the green to Hockwold. After a further 1.5 miles the reserve is sign-posted off to the left. Park in the car park and obtain your permit from the new visitor centre (NWT members free). The centre is open from April to August.

Other nearby sites

Barnhamcross Common, NWT East Wretham Heath, Fordham, NWT Foulden Common, RSPB Lakenheath, Lynford Arboretum, Santon Downham, NWT Sparham Pools, NWT Weeting Heath.

Key points

- **Large pay and display car park, open dawn until dusk (£3 in 2006, disabled badge holders must pay also).**
- **Two toilet blocks on site.**
- **Café on site.**
- **Some tracks are wheelchair accessible (after negotiating a tight kissing gate).**
- **Terrain is level along a wide track but several narrower paths are steep.**
- **Managed by English Nature as part of its Holkham NNR.**
- **Dogs on leads allowed.**

Contacts

English Nature
01603 620558

WELLS WOODS is a superb place to hunt for your own migrants in spring and autumn but be warned, it is a large area to cover, with lots of hiding places for the birds, as it forms part of a huge National Nature Reserve with Holkham Pines.

Target birds

Spring/autumn – **Passage migrants including: Wryneck, Redstart, Whinchat, Wheatear, Ring Ouzel, winter thrushes, Barred Warbler, Firecrest, Red-breasted Flycatcher, Pied Flycatcher, etc.**

Other possible bird species

Spring/autumn
Woodcock
Common gull species
Green Woodpecker
Great Spotted Woodpecker
Sky Lark
Meadow Pipit
Hirundines
Common scrub birds
Lesser Whitethroat
Garden Warbler
Blackcap
Chiffchaff
Willow Warbler
Goldcrest
Common woodland birds
Treecreeper
Jay
Other corvids
Crossbill
Other common finches
Siskin
Redpoll

Background information and birding tips

THOUGH several species of bird such as Spotted Flycatcher breed in Wells Woods and common woodland birds, plus Crossbill and Jay, can be found all year round, the most productive periods to visit are during spring and autumn migration times, with autumn being the best.

Wells Woods is part of Holkham National Nature Reserve but I have split this site from Holkham Gap/Pines for ease of coverage. The whole area can provide a superb day searching for grounded migrants, though be warned that it is a huge area to cover thoroughly.

From the beach car park, take the path at the right hand edge of the boating lake. After a few yards the path splits left or straight on; the choice of route is yours and either is good for migrants.

The path straight ahead leads to a toilet block. The berry bushes opposite are excellent for warblers and it is well worth pausing here for quite some time to see what flits out of the thick cover. If it starts raining there is the added attraction of good shelter offered by the block's roof.

This path continues up a boardwalk into Wells Dell. This is a patch of wood criss-crossed by undulating paths and is a favoured area for migrants. This area should also be searched thoroughly. Another narrow path skirts the wood on its seaward side and runs the length of the forest to Holkham Gap.

Alternatively, take one of several paths behind the toilet block. These all lead to the wide path which you would have reached if you had taken the left fork just past the boating lake.

It sounds complicated but you cannot get lost as you either hit the beach on the northern side of the woods or the wide track to Holkham on the southern side. All areas can be good for migrants.

Another area renowned for rare and scarce migrants is the Drinking Pool. This is difficult to find but is best reached by the following route: take the left-hand path after leaving the car park. Follow to a T-junction then turn right along a wide track.

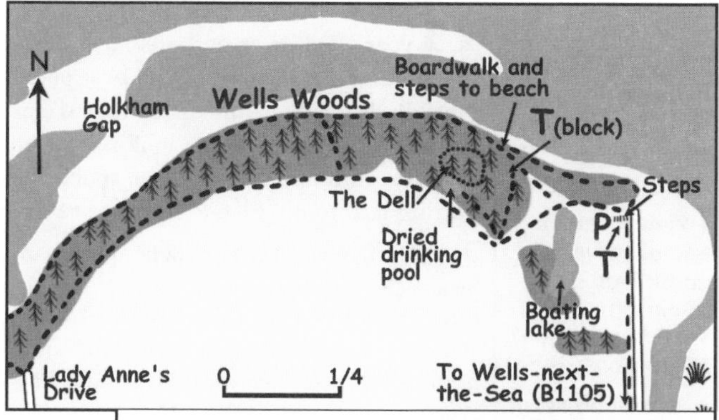

Continue on this track when it bends to the left (ignore the wide track into the wood) and carry on for about 150 yards until you see a single pine tree and a single bramble bush on the right of the path, with what looks like a grass lay-by behind them. The drinking pool is reached by continuing beyond the single pine tree and taking the next path on the right for about 100 yards.

Once you have found the pool (it took me 75 minutes the first time I tried) wait quietly around the edge and see what pops out of the surrounding bushes. Though it has virtually dried out, the pool area still attracts rare, scarce and common migrants.

It is hard to say which species you will see in Wells Woods but bear in mind the following advice to help you find something interesting. I always try to find a sheltered area of berry bushes, ideally with a bit of sun on them. This usually produces Garden Warbler, Blackcap, Dunnock, Wren and Blackbird and hopefully a Barred Warbler in autumn.

Another tip is to find a feeding flock of tits (or rather wait for it to find you). Scarce migrants such as Firecrests and Yellow-browed Warblers tend to join these flocks, so scrutinise them carefully.

Wells harbour can be very good for wintering wildfowl and grebes, especially in harsh weather. The harbour wall can be reached from the beach car park via some steps adjacent to the car park exit or from Wells town centre.

Also scan the fields to the west of the harbour wall for geese and winter thrushes.

Wells Woods can be a frustrating place. I have wandered around in the rain with just a Redstart and two Garden Warblers to show for three hours' birding but as soon as the sun came out so did the hidden migrants!

Access details

(Approx. 15 miles E of Hunstanton).

About half way between Sheringham and Hunstanton, turn off A149 at the sign-posts for Wells Quay/Wells Beach. In the town, follow signs for Beach Car Park and Pinewoods Caravan Site. This road runs adjacent to Wells harbour and ends in a large pay and display car park. The path into the wood starts at the western end of the car park, behind of boating lake.

Alternatively, park in Lady Anne's Drive, opposite the main entrance to Holkham Park and walk east (right) at the bottom. This takes you through Wells Woods and to the car park/toilets after about a mile and a half.

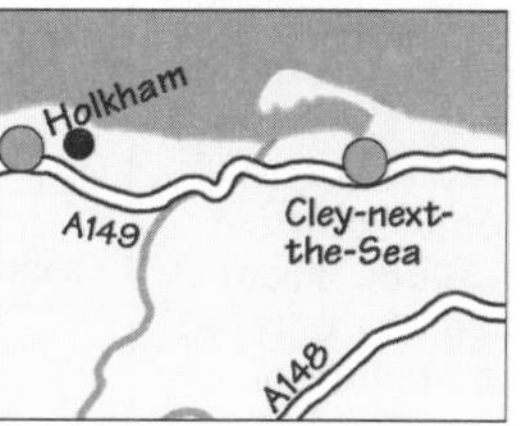

WWT WELNEY

Key points

- **Obtain permit (£3.90 in 2006 for non-members) at visitor centre.**
- **Visitor centre and observatory open: Mon-Tue 10am-5pm, Wed-Sun 10am-8pm.**
- **Afternoon swan feeds: Noon & 3.30pm, late Oct - mid March daily feed with live commentary at 3.30pm. From Dec 26 - end Feb an additional swan feed at 12 noon.**
- **Floodlit swan feeds: 6.30pm early Nov-end Feb, every night except Mondays and Tuesdays. N.B. Be in Observatory for 6.30pm when live commentary starts. Feed starts at 6.45pm.**
- **The tea room is open: Mon/Tue 10am-4.30pm Wed/Thu/Fri 10am-5.30pm Sat/Sun 10am-6pm.**

HIGHLY RECOMMENDED to visit at all times of year, Welney is perhaps most famous for its wildfowl spectaculars and is indeed the best place to see wild swans in Norfolk. My wife would argue that Welney should be more famous for its heated hide looking out onto the wildfowl lakes! In summer, many scarce species breed on the reserve, putting it onto my Five-Star-Rated reserve list.

Target birds

All year – **Whooper Swan (100%), Bewick's Swans (100%: a few injured birds of both species remain throughout the year), Corn Bunting (60%), Tree Sparrow (20%).** *Winter* – **Pintail (99%), Peregrine (65%), Brambling (10%).** *Spring/summer* – **Avocet (95%), Little Ringed Plover (80%), Black-tailed Godwit (80%), Marsh Harrier (65%), Garganey (40%).** *Autumn* – **Passage waders (40%).**

Other possible bird species

All year
Great Crested Grebe
Cormorant
Common wildfowl
Sparrowhawk
Kestrel
Red-legged Partridge
Grey Partridge
Lapwing
Snipe
Redshank
Common gull species
Barn Owl
Little Owl
Kingfisher
Green Woodpecker
Great Spotted Woodpecker
Sky Lark
Meadow Pipit
Pied Wagtail
Corvids
Common finches
Yellowhammer
Reed Bunting

Winter
Common wildfowl
Winter thrushes

Summer
Common Tern
Oystercatcher
Turtle Dove
Hirundines
Yellow Wagtail
Sedge Warbler
Reed Warbler
Whitethroat
Blackcap

Passage
Little Gull
Arctic Tern
Black Tern
Ringed Plover
Little Stint
Temminck's Stint
Curlew Sandpiper
Dunlin
Ruff
Whimbrel
Greenshank
Green Sandpiper
Wood Sandpiper
Common Sandpiper
Grey Wagtail
Winter thrushes

Occasional
Willow Tit
(Tundra) Bean Goose
Pink-footed Goose
Smew
Hen Harrier
Merlin
Short-eared Owl
Hobby

Background information and birding tips

WELNEY is owned by the Wildfowl and Wetlands Trust and is worth a visit at any time of year. It is particularly famous for its winter birds when the feeding of swans and ducks is a feature of many a family visit. Every afternoon and most evenings, a staff member scatters a wheelbarrow load of grain for the wildfowl.

From spring 2006, visitors to Welney have been able to enjoy a brand new, eco-friendly visitor centre. Access to the observatory is via a new bridge so birders will no longer have to cross the road to reach the sanctity of the heated hide! The Welney website has details of all the energy-saving features of the new centre: well worth a read.

From the comfort of the heated observatory, you will see thousands of wildfowl in winter. Recent counts include 1,150 Mallard, 1,720 Pintails, 7,700 Wigeon, 1,800 Teal, 4,750 Pochards, 3,700 Bewick's Swans and 1,000 Whooper Swans! And one thing is for sure; the Mallards you see here are truly wild birds.

During the day, the wild swans feed on potatoes left out by sympathetic farmers in the surrounding fields and can be hard to locate. Avoid disturbing the swans as any break in feeding could be disastrous for the birds. The heated hide on the reserve gives a much better view of all the species and can be very welcome on a wild, freezing cold day!

The feeders around the visitor centre are alive with finches, sometimes including scarce Bramblings. An added bonus is the fact that you can watch birds filling their stomachs while you fill yours in the café! Corn Buntings are usually seen sitting on the 'phone wires along the main road and Tree Sparrows are sometimes seen around the farm near the visitor centre.

Recent winters have seen the regular occurrence of a small number of Tundra Bean Geese (the smaller race of Bean Goose) and a Smew or two. Peregrine Falcons regularly hunt the

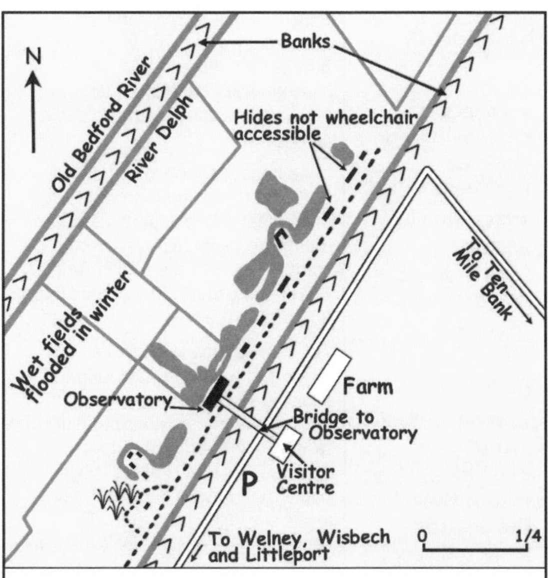

Access details

(Approx. seven miles S of Downham Market).

From the north: The reserve is off A10, seven miles S of Downham Market ('Ten Mile Bank/Welney' on a brown tourist sign). Follow road for 0.8 miles to a bridge. Turn left, then immediately right down Station Road (there is a brown tourist sign but it is difficult to see). Follow Station Road for about 4.5 miles to the reserve car park on the left. Be warned: this road is straight but keep your speed down as there are severe undulations and potholes along the route.

From the south: From Ely, head N on A10 to Littleport. Turn left onto A1101 towards Wisbech. After about four miles the road turns sharply right to run alongside a high bank. At the next sharp left bend, take the minor road straight on. The reserve centre is approximately 1.3.miles further on.

ducks and their presence is generally indicated by mass panic among the wildfowl. If everything goes up in the air, quickly scan for a Peregrine or other raptor, such as Hen Harrier, Merlin, Short-eared Owl or Sparrowhawk.

Spring sees the arrival of Garganey, Avocet, Little Ringed Plover and Black-tailed Godwit. Garganey

Key points

- **Toilets on-site, including disabled facilities.**
- **Free hire of wheelchairs (one motorised, two self-wheeled).**
- **Binocular hire (£1).**
- **Hearing loop installed in main hide. This means that the hearing-impaired can enjoy the sounds of birds on the marsh, which is a superb idea.**
- **There is a well stocked shop for books, bird food, etc.**
- **Picnic site.**
- **Pond dipping facilities.**

Contacts

The Wildfowl & Wetlands Trust, Hundred Foot Bank, Welney, Wisbech PE14 9TN
TEL: 01353 860711
E-Mail: info.welney@wwt.org.uk
www.wwt.org.uk/visit/welney/

appear in late March/early April and usually show well to visitors but become more elusive as the season wears on. Marsh Harriers have also recently started breeding at Welney.

The Little Ringed Plovers usually breed on the island in front of the main hide, giving superb views as they raise their chicks. A useful comparison with the similar Ringed Plover can usually be made as they argue over the best feeding areas.

In summer, the WWT opens up a two and a quarter mile long trail allowing visitors the chance to explore the marsh, home to Black-tailed Godwits and other breeding waders. This trail is along rough paths that may be flooded if water levels are high in the area. The short reedbed boardwalk is also worth a look-see.

Avocet chicks can be seen from mid-June, along with odd-looking Shelduck youngsters. Several injured Bewick's and Whooper Swans also summer at the reserve. Turtle Doves often sit on the phone wires along the access road in summer.

The main hide is the most popular viewpoint but there are several more hides that overlook the marshes. Most are wheelchair accessible but paths may become muddy after prolonged rain, making access difficult.

For those who like to count their Mallard flocks in peace, there are one or two glass-fibre mini-shelters along the track which hold one person; they look like Portaloos but some hardy birders prefer them to the luxurious heated hide.

This is a very good reserve at all times of year. There is usually a warden in the main hide to show the visitor what is around. Most birdwatchers turn up in winter when the wildfowl are in attendance but this reserve should not be overlooked in spring and autumn – one or two species of wader usually drop in on passage – or summer.

Corn Buntings are a familiar sight on wires around Welney.

WEYBOURNE

THOUGH at first glance this seems a poor place for birds, as it is merely a grassy cliff-top, Weybourne is an excellent, easy-to-cover area to find migrant birds in spring and autumn. The cliff here is a superb seawatching vantage point at all times of year.

Target birds

Winter – Seabirds. *Spring/autumn* – Passage migrant passerines, passage seabirds. *Summer* – Sandwich Tern, Roseate Tern (occasional), Common Tern, Arctic Tern, Little Tern.

Other possible bird species

All year
Cormorant
Common waders
Common gull species
Sky Lark
Meadow Pipit
Pied Wagtail
Common finches
Reed Bunting

Winter
Red-throated Diver
Great Crested Grebe
Red-necked Grebe
Slavonian Grebe
Pink-footed Goose
Brent Goose
Eider
Common Scoter
Velvet Scoter
Goldeneye
Red-breasted Merganser
Hen Harrier
Merlin
Peregrine

Spring
Hirundines
Yellow Wagtail
Black Redstart
Whinchat
Wheatear
Ring Ouzel

Summer
Hirundines
Sedge Warbler
Reed Warbler
Whitethroat
Blackcap

Autumn
Sooty Shearwater
Manx Shearwater
Balearic Shearwater
Gannet
Skuas
Kittiwake
Little Auk
Black Redstart
Winter thrushes

Background information and birding tips

WEYBOURNE is a site with an excellent track record of attracting migrants in spring and autumn. It is also a good seawatching site at all times of year, though Sheringham offers a bit more shelter in bad weather conditions.

Your birding starts in the car park, where to your left, a small area of reeds holds Reed Buntings all year round plus Reed and Sedge Warblers in summer. The small pond sometimes attracts common wildfowl and waterbirds, mainly Mallard and Coot. The bushes behind you are on private land but you can see into them from the car park to check for migrants.

From the car park, there is a choice: If you choose to walk right (east), go up the slight incline onto the cliff top and follow the grass track. After about half a mile there is a hedgerow near a cottage, which is worth searching for migrants in spring and autumn.

The extensive grassy area attracts Sky Larks and Meadow Pipits all year and migrants such as Yellow Wagtails and Ring Ouzels in spring and autumn. Rarer species such as Short-toed Lark are a distinct possibility. In winter, raptors sometimes hunt over this area.

The cliff is a superb place from which to seawatch. In winter, look out for Great Crested, Red-

Key points

- **Pay and display car park.**
- **Steepish incline onto the cliff, then flat track.**
- **Free access at all times.**
- **A public house and shop close by.**

Contacts

None

necked and Slavonian Grebes, all three diver species, Red-breasted Mergansers, Goldeneye, Long-tailed Ducks and Velvet and Common Scoters.

In spring, you may be able to see incoming migrants make landfall, or winter visitors such as Fieldfares and Redwings departing for warmer climes. In autumn, the reverse happens.

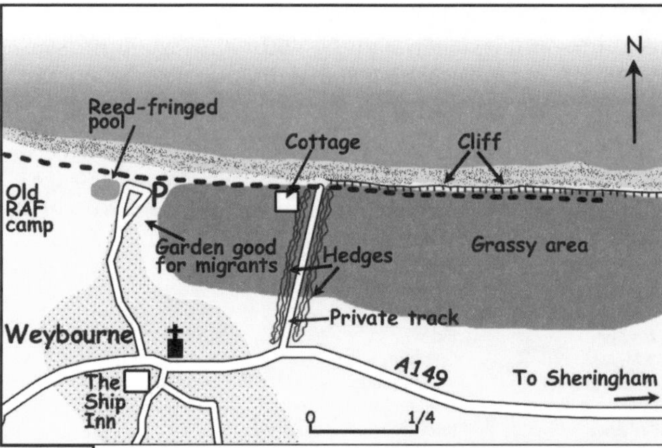

Nothing is guaranteed, of course but watch the weather forecasts to assist you in deciding whether to visit Weybourne at migration times. In spring, if there is a low pressure system over East Anglia coupled with high pressure over the rest of Europe, then sit and watch the birds stream in! In autumn, high pressure over Scandinavia with a low pressure system over Britain and onshore winds is likely to produce the best results.

In summer, terns will be fishing offshore and, from late July onwards, watch out for species such as Manx Shearwater, all four species of skua, Sabine's Gull etc.

If you walk west (left) from the car park, the going is slightly rougher but there are some good fields and bushes that attract migrants, especially around the disused RAF camp. Ring Ouzel and Black Redstart are specialities around this area. It is possible to walk all the way to Kelling Quags and beyond, to Cley and Blakeney Point if you so desire. On foggy or drizzly spring and autumn mornings the whole area can be dripping with newly arrived migrants.

My personal Weybourne triumph came on July 21, 2001 when I decided to do some seawatching before heading up to Kelling Heath for Nightjar. The first bird I saw out to sea, as I stood on the shingle by the car park, was a Caspian Tern!

Access details

(Approx: three miles W of Sheringham).

Turn off A149 in Weybourne village opposite The Ship Inn (from Hunstanton this is just before the church, from Sheringham just after the church). Follow this rough road down to a pay-and-display car park at the end. Walk E (right) onto the cliff or W (left) to the disused RAF camp.

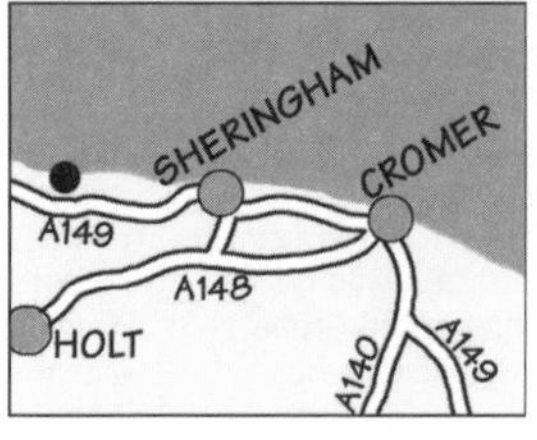

Other nearby sites

All year – Blakeney Point, NWT Cley Marsh, Felbrigg Hall, NOA Kelling Quags, Salthouse Beach, NOA Walsey Hills.

Summer – Kelling Heath, Salthouse Heath, Swanton Novers.

A SITE with much birding potential within two miles of Norwich city centre, Whitlingham Country Park consists of open water, woodland, ancient quarries and a marsh. It can get busy during school holidays and at weekends but there are always some tranquil parts in which to see a range of common bird species.

Target species *All year* – Common water and woodland birds (100%).

Other possible bird species

All year
Little Grebe
Great Crested Grebe
Cormorant
Grey Heron
Common waterfowl
Egyptian Goose
Sparrowhawk
Kestrel
Common gull species
Stock Dove
Tawny Owl
Kingfisher
Great Spotted Woodpecker
Green Woodpecker
Sky Lark
Pied Wagtail
Common scrub birds
Blackcap
Goldcrest
Jay
Other corvids
Tree Sparrow
Common finches
Reed Bunting

Winter
Common wildfowl
Lapwing
Grey Wagtail
Meadow Pipit
Winter thrushes

Spring/ summer/ autumn
Common Tern
Cuckoo
Sand Martin
Other hirundines
Reed Warbler
Sedge Warbler
Summer warblers

Occasional
Rarer grebes (winter)
Marsh Harrier
Hobby
Oystercatcher
Little Ringed Plover
Mediterranean Gull
Little Gull
Arctic & Black Tern (passage)
Passage waders (spring/ autumn)
Wheatear (passage)
Brambling (winter)

Background information and birding tips

WHITLINGHAM Country Park has been developed from former gravel workings and is managed by the Whitlingham Charitable Trust with assistance from The Broads Authority. It lies just two miles from Norwich city centre and comprises several developing habitats that attract many common species of birds. It was opened in 2004, so these habitats have still to mature but the potential is there for this to be a very good birdwatching site.

You can start your walk from a number of points in the park. The beauty of Whitlingham is that you can cover the whole site in one go or visit one of the distinctly different areas as the mood takes you. These include the two broads, a mature wood and a small marsh. Each bit has its own car park so lazy birders, such as me, or people with just a few minutes to spare at lunchtime can drive between/to areas to maximise birding time!

The downside of this easy access and proximity to a large city is that the park can become very busy, especially at weekends and holiday times. There are usually some areas that remain quiet and there are always birds to see.

The main car park is situated adjacent to Whitlingham Great

Key points

- **New visitor centre opened Easter 2006.**
- **Pay-and-display car park (£1 up to 2hrs, £3 longer, orange badge holders free).**
- **No dogs in Little Broad area, July 1 – August 31.**
- **River bus from Norwich in summer.**
- **Boating activities possible for non-birders.**
- **Leaflet detailing colour-marked routes.**
- **Broadland boat mooring on site (24 hour).**

Contacts

Whitlingham Country Park Ranger 01603 610734 www.nccoutdooreducation.co.uk (01493 368129)

Whitlingham Charitable Trust, C/o Broads Authority, 18 Colgate, Norwich NR3 1BQ (01603 610734)

Beccles Broads Information Centre on 01502 713196.

River bus: 01603 701701

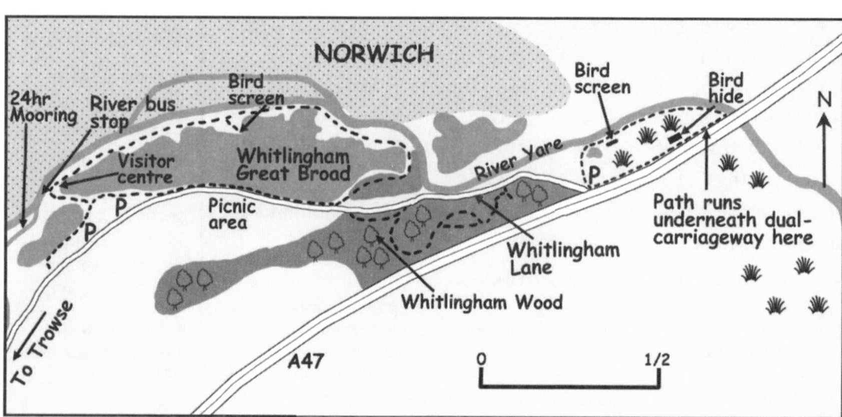

Broad, probably the principal feature for visiting birdwatchers. A level path runs around the whole broad, although the 'quiet' end can be viewed from a pull-in along the access road.

From the main car park, walk into the reserve (not forgetting to pay-and-display). The path splits the two broads. Little Broad has Reed and Sedge Warblers in summer though this broad acts as the main boating lake so it can be a very disturbed area!

Once you are away from the hustle and bustle of the new visitor centre (opening Easter 2006) and the education centre, follow the path that runs alongside the broad (on your right) and the River Yare (on your left).

The path is lined with trees and bushes where you should see resident common finches and scrub birds joined by warblers in summer (Blackcap, Willow Warbler, Chiffchaff, Whitethroat, etc). You may wish to walk up the bank on your left at regular intervals to see what is on the river (Great Crested Grebe and other common waterbirds should be expected and Kingfisher is a possibility). There are one or two narrow, grass paths off to your right that lead to the broad's edge, though these are principally for fishermen to use.

After approximately a quarter of a mile, you reach a gravel path signed to the 'Bird Screen'. Follow this track for about 75 yards to the screen, which overlooks the Great Broad (there is also an information board here). The posts in the water will be occupied by gulls or Cormorants but check for Kingfishers. The broad itself holds common ducks all year round (Tufted Duck, Gadwall, Mallard, etc) joined by Goldeneye, Pochard, Teal, etc in winter. Check the Little and Great Crested Grebes carefully as a Slavonian joined them in the winter of 05/06 and a Black-necked is possible in

Access details

Leave the A47 Norwich bypass on the A146 (dual carriageway) signed to Norwich, Lowestoft, Trowse & football traffic. After 0.6 miles, turn right on the ring road (A1054 to City Centre & Trowse). After 0.3 miles, turn right at the roundabout to Trowse. Go over a bridge and turn left onto Whitlingham Lane, (0.3 miles after the roundabout). Follow this road to your desired car park (Little Broad, Great Broad, Picnic Meadow, Woodland or Whitlingham Marsh – up to two miles from the start of Whitlingham Lane).

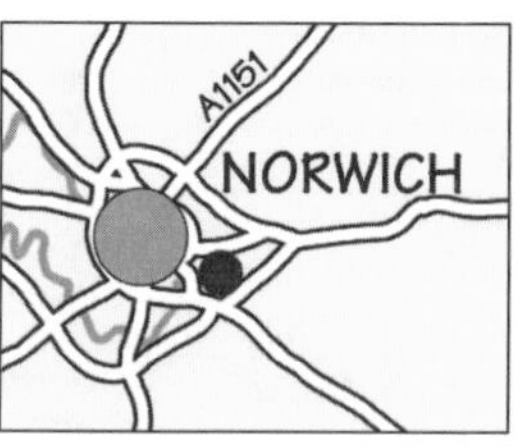

spring. The broad is home to Canada, Greylag and Egyptian Geese throughout the year. Check the islands from here for any waders and wildfowl (Little Ringed Plovers may breed on these islands).

The path continues to the far end of the broad. Check the rocky edges here first thing in the morning (before disturbance by dog-walkers, etc) for waders such as Common Sandpiper during spring and autumn passage times and Grey Wagtail in winter. You may also see birds coming down to this shallow edge to drink.

Follow the path to the opposite bank of the broad. You may choose to then divert left along the access road to the wood or marsh, or continue along the side of Great Broad to the car park and visitor centre (for refreshments?).

There is a picnic meadow along the access road, a pleasant place for an outdoor gathering. The woodland walk has its own car park, approximately one mile from the park entrance gate, on your right. This is surrounded by trees and you may see Great Spotted Woodpecker, Long-tailed Tit, Goldcrest, etc, etc from your car.

The woodland walk starts by walking along the access road (away from the park entrance), then across the grass/lawn to the grotty-looking toilet block (there are some cycle rails here also). Follow blue signs through the trees (the start of the path is not obvious behind the 'toilets'). Some of the way is quite steep.

There are one or two viewpoints into some shaded dells, ideal for feeding warblers and common scrub birds in inclement weather. The path loops around the wood, onto the access road and back to the car park.

Whitlingham Marsh (owned by Norwich County Council) car park is a further 0.3 miles from the woodland car park, just before you go under the A47. There is a weather-beaten information board in the car park. Follow the hard path that starts by the access gate and this leads you to the River Yare.

Turn right along a rough grass track and after 20 yards there is a bird screen overlooking the marsh. To be honest, better views can be obtained from the footpath! The marsh may hold Snipe, with Reed and Sedge Warblers in summer. There is also a large reedbed here but I haven't seen much in there.

The path continues through a patch of scrubby wood, which looks good for Cetti's Warbler, though I haven't heard of any in this area. You then have to walk under the A47 (very eerie as lorries thunder overhead) where the path continues to the right of the bridge stanchion.

After 100 yards, go through a wooden gate on your right. The muddy path leads to a boardwalk and hide. This overlooks a tiny pond, optimistically called a scrape. I believe the council are working towards making this a better area for wildlife, so the marsh will improve for birdwatchers too.

Retrace your steps back to the footpath and turn right to the car park (this is the old Norwich to Yarmouth road!) 400 yards along.

If you are feeling energetic, you can walk the whole country park from the main car park, following the course of the River Yare.

Non-birding members of your family may wish to try canoeing or other water-based activities available from the centre, or they can play on one of the two beach areas.

Whitlingham Country Park would make a superb local patch for a Norwich birder as it is the sort of place where some good birds will turn up if watched regularly.

Other nearby sites

NWT Sparham Pools, RSPB Surlingham Church Marshes, Ted Ellis Trust Reserve, Rockland Broad, NWT Foxley Wood, Blickling Hall.

Key points

- **National Nature Reserve and SSSI, managed by English Nature.**
- **Access on foot only.**
- **Avoid Little Tern colony. This is a Schedule 1 species and disturbing them is a criminal offence.**
- **Keep dogs under control.**
- **Keep to paths at all times as there are many rare plants and animals.**
- **Beach car park closes at 8pm in summer, 4pm in winter (£1 in 2006). Double yellow lines strictly enforced at all times of year but parking OK after 8pm, May – Sept. Alternatively, park at village Hall at Kings Corner (near the payphone) and walk to dunes.**
- **Toilet block in car park.**

MANY SCARCE plants, insects, dragonflies and animals can be found on the reserve and it is a superb place to find common, scarce and rare migrant birds in spring and autumn. In summer, Little Terns nest on the beach and Nightjars usually show well at dusk by the dunes. In winter, raptors regularly hunt over the dune system.

Target birds

All year – **Marsh Harrier (50%).** *Summer* – **Little Tern (95%), Nightjar (85%), Grasshopper Warbler (hear 55%, see 10%).** *Spring/autumn* – **Passage migrants.** *Winter* – **winter raptors (25%), Short-eared Owl (10%).**

Other possible bird species

All year
Sparrowhawk
Kestrel
Ringed Plover
Common gull species
Barn Owl
Tawny Owl
Green Woodpecker
Sky Lark
Meadow Pipit
Pied Wagtail
Common scrub birds
Stonechat
Corvids
Yellowhammer
Reed Bunting
Winter seaduck
Winter thrushes

Summer
Sandwich Tern
Common Tern
Cuckoo
Hirundines
Warblers

Spring/autumn
Shearwaters
Gannet
Skuas
Long-eared Owl
Wryneck
Richard's Pipit
Tawny Pipit
Yellow Wagtail
Bluethroat
Redstart
Whinchat
Wheatear
Ring Ouzel
Winter thrushes
Barred Warbler
Pallas's Warbler
Yellow-browed Warbler
Firecrest
Pied Flycatcher
Red-backed Shrike
Ortolan Bunting

Occasional overhead
Crane
Pink-footed Goose

Background information and birding tips

THE RESERVE is part of an extensive nine-mile-long dune system. In recent years, it has become one of the 'in-places' for birdwatchers to find rare and scarce migrants in Norfolk.

In truth, Winterton is much more than a migrant hotspot, with Nightjars and Little Terns on offer in summer, several raptor species to savour in winter and the possibility of some excellent seawatching in autumn.

After parking in the beach car park (or in the small pull-ins along the beach road) you have a choice of walking north or south through the dune system, though the southerly dunes are really only of interest in spring and autumn. At these times the bushes at the bottom of the hill can hold many common (Redstart, Pied Flycatcher, Goldcrest, etc), scarce (Firecrest, Barred and Icterine Warblers, etc) or rare (Pallas's Warbler, Dusky Warbler, etc) migrants.

In spring and autumn, all the dunes should be searched thoroughly for anything that moves! Wheatears, Whinchats, Ring Ouzels, pipits, wagtails, etc, should all be encountered and Wryneck and Red-backed Shrike are regularly reported from here. When I say search the dunes thoroughly, I mean stay on the paths criss-crossing the site, scanning regularly with your binoculars. This method usually pays dividends, with the added bonus of not disturbing other rare animals and plants in the process.

If you choose to head north, you may wander for many miles, passing Horsey Gap, Waxham and Sea Palling. All hold the promise of migrants popping up at any time. On the way, about 500 yards from the car park, you will find an object protruding from the sand. This is fancifully called 'The Totem Pole' and is often referred to in bird reports/ bird newslines, etc.

In addition to the migrants, you should encounter many resident species such as Kestrel, Yellowhammer, Meadow Pipit, Reed Bunting, Sky Lark, Green Woodpecker and the delightful Stonechat. Marsh Harriers and Barn Owls regularly hunt over fields to the west of Winterton Dunes (look towards Horsey Mill), with sightings almost guaranteed all year round for the former species.

In winter, this can seem a barren place. However, hardy walkers may be rewarded with sightings of Hen Harrier, Merlin, Peregrine and Short-eared Owl, though none are guaranteed. Skeins of Pink-footed Geese regularly fly overhead, especially in the early mornings and evenings.

Crane is another species to watch out for around the Winterton area, though they are usually seen more frequently around Horsey and at Stubb Mill. However, I had two adults and two juveniles fly overhead at Winterton in November 2001 (accompanied by a Sacred Ibis!), so keep your eyes peeled at all times.

The sea should not be

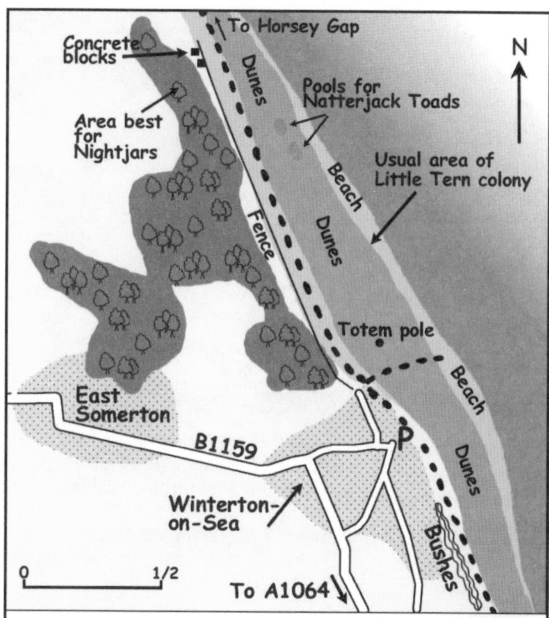

Access details

(Approx. eight miles N of Great Yarmouth).

FROM YARMOUTH: Follow signs for Caister-on-Sea along A1064. After a stretch of dual carriageway near Caister, you reach a roundabout. Take B1159 to Winterton (second exit) and continue for approximately 4.5 miles. As you enter Winterton village, take Hermanus Road on right, sign-posted 'Beach'. Turn right at T-junction (down The Craft), then park in the small lay-bys by the dunes, or in the car park at the end of the road. Walk left (N) or right (S) into the dunes, or straight ahead to the beach.

FROM THE NORTH AND WEST: Enter Winterton village along B1159 and follow signs to The Beach (along The Craft). Park in the small lay-bys alongside the dunes, or in the car park at the end of the road.

A149
A47
GREAT YARMOUTH

Key points

- **Café in beach car park.**
- **Terrain generally level along wide, rough, sandy tracks. Difficult wheelchair access.**
- **No horses.**
- **No motorbikes.**
- **If you see any disturbance at the Little Tern colony phone 07899 901566 immediately.**
- **Do not touch any strange objects on the beach – unexploded missiles turn up occasionally!**

Contacts

English Nature, Norfolk Office
01603 620558

The diminutive Little Tern forms a bustling breeding colony at Winterton.

ignored at Winterton either, as winter can produce reasonable numbers of Red-throated Divers, Red-breasted Mergansers, Common Scoters, Long-tailed Ducks and other scarce grebes and divers.

In summer, the main attractions are Nightjars and Little Terns. The tern colony (the largest in the UK) is usually north of the beach car park. Head for but do not approach too closely, the fenced-off area to watch the comings and goings of this fantastic species.

Also, usually hanging around this area are Oystercatchers, Turnstones and Ringed Plovers. Out to sea, you should see Common and Sandwich Terns busily fishing for food to raise their young at colonies nearby.

For Nightjars, take the main track north following the fence on your left, with trees at the back. Nightjars can be anywhere in this fenced-off area, though I have found the best spot to be about half a mile from the beach road, by the concrete blocks at the northern entrance to the reserve. Green Woodpeckers continually 'laugh' at waiting birders, while a Tawny Owl occasionally shows itself. If you wait quietly, Nightjars will come and perch on fence posts at the edge of the main track.

Winterton Dunes is home to one or two pairs of Grasshopper Warblers in summer, though they are extremely difficult to see. You will more likely hear them 'reeling' from the bushes dotted around the dunes. They may also join natterjack toad, Nightjar, Green Woodpecker, Woodcock and Tawny Owl in the dusk chorus for an uplifting end to the birdwatching day!

Other nearby sites

NWT Alderfen Broad, NWT Barton Broad, Breydon Water, Burgh Marshes, Great Yarmouth Beach, Great Yarmouth Cemetery, NWT Hickling Broad, How Hill NNR, NWT Martham Broad, NWT Ranworth Broad, Ted Ellis Trust Reserve.

THOUGH generally devoid of other interesting species, Wolferton is England's prime site to see the beautiful Golden Pheasant. As suggested by its name, the site is a triangle of roads, bordered by thick bushes. The pheasants occasionally emerge from these bushes to feed along the grass verges.

Target birds *All year* – Golden Pheasant (60%).

Other possible bird species

All year	Long-tailed Tit	***Winter***
Pheasant	Goldcrest	Pink-footed Goose
Tawny Owl	Common finches	(overhead)
Woodcock		
Great Spotted Woodpecker	***Summer***	***Occasional***
Common scrub birds	Warblers	Lesser Spotted Woodpecker
Common woodland birds		

Background information and birding tips

WOLFERTON TRIANGLE is a site of limited interest as regards species numbers but is the best site in the country for Golden Pheasants. Patient birdwatchers should be rewarded with good views of these gaudy introductions as long as certain rules are followed.

Though the target birds are present all year round, I have found early mornings and late afternoons in winter and spring provide the best chances of seeing a Goldie. The most important thing to remember is to never get out of your car or the pheasants will scuttle into the undergrowth.

Simply cruise very slowly around the triangle of roads keeping an eye on the grass verges for the birds. In my experience, the most productive stop-off is the small, muddy lay-by on the south-eastern edge of the triangle at TF 673277.

From here, it is possible to see into the wood where Goldies may be seen scratching for food in the leaf litter. If you see anyone in this wood, please ask them to leave!

While waiting for the Golden

Wolferton remains the best place in the country to see an elusive Golden Pheasant. By Alan Harris.

Key points

- **Woods are private – do not enter.**
- **No need to even get out of your car.**
- **Access at all times.**
- **Do not impede the progress of local traffic – keep checking the rear view mirror as you crawl along.**
- **Do not run over any pheasants!**

Pheasants to show, you can amuse yourself by watching some commoner bird species (Robin, Wren, Blackbird) or grey squirrels which sometimes approach the car.

Great Spotted Woodpeckers, Goldcrests and Coal Tits are regular visitors to the wood, Woodcocks may be roding overhead in spring and summer and if you are lucky, you may see on on the grass verges at dawn or dusk. Lesser Spotted Woodpeckers have been recorded in recent years.

The chance of connecting with Golden Pheasants is quite good, though there are horror stories of people visiting more than 100 times without success. I never used to struggle but in the last couple of years they seem to have become more elusive. I hope it isn't due to birders trespassing in the wood! Friends still regularly see the Goldies here though; one even phoned me to say he had seen them on the grass verge on the main A149! I have seen one or two males on each of my three visits in 2006 so I still rate your chances of seeing this species as relatively high

I suggest you call in at The Triangle early in the morning and if you don't see any Golden Pheasants within an hour, move on and return at dusk. One final tip: read up on how to distinguish between female Golden and Common Pheasants before you go to avoid embarrassment.

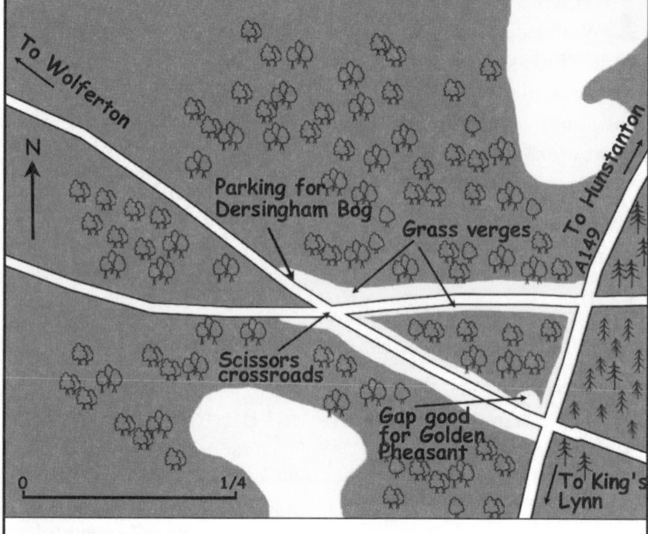

Access details

(Approx. five miles N of King's Lynn).
Between Hunstanton and King's Lynn off A149. Wolferton is sign-posted opposite the turn-off for Sandringham. Once off the A road, drive round the triangle of minor roads (about one mile in 'circumference') skirting the dense bushes.

Other nearby sites

Dersingham Bog, Flitcham Abbey Farm, Gypsy Lane, NWT Holme Dunes, NOA Holme Observatory, Hunstanton, NOA Redwell Marsh, Ken Hill Wood, NWT Roydon Common, Sandringham, RSPB Snettisham, RSPB Titchwell Marsh.

ACCESS TO SITES

THIS IS a quick-reference chapter to show the various ways you can reach your chosen destination. For instance, if you are relying on public transport, turn to the relevant page to see which reserves are easily accessible to you. You can then turn to the Site Guide page for more details sites listed in alphabetical order. Simple!

Take it as read that all reserves are accessible by car, with the exceptions of Berney Arms Marsh (see Halvergate Marshes), which can only be reached by train and Hoveton Great Broad, which can only be reached by boat.

SITES FULLY ACCESSIBLE TO WHEELCHAIR USERS

The sites listed on this page are ones I consider to be accessible by wheelchair users, and several have been field-tested by a disabled friend. However, I strongly advise that you check with the contact number listed on the Site Guide page for specific guidance before you visit. I apologise profusely now if you turn up at a site and it is not accessible to you. Please let me know if this happens and I will amend the details for future editions.

BARTON BROAD

COCKSHOOT BROAD

FLITCHAM ABBEY FARM

FORDHAM

HADDISCOE MARSH

HERBERT BARNES RIVERSIDE PARK

HICKLING BROAD Most of the reserve is accessible.

HUNSTANTON

KING'S LYNN DOCKS

RANWORTH BROAD

REDWELL MARSH Need key to hide from NOA.

ROCKLAND BROAD

SALTHOUSE HEATH

SCULTHORPE MOOR As of 2006, fully accessible. Some new parts – opening in 2007 – will not be accessible.

SHERINGHAM

STUBB MILL Restricted view of raptor roost.

SWANTON NOVERS

TITCHWELL MARSH Rough track. May struggle on last third of path.

TOTTENHILL GRAVEL PITS View from car.

WEETING HEATH Hides fully accessible, may need assistance on bumpy tracks to hides. Phone before your visit.

WELNEY Most of the reserve is accessible.

WOLFERTON TRIANGLE

ACCESS TO SITES

SITES PARTLY ACCESSIBLE FOR WHEELCHAIR USERS

Listed on this page are sites where I consider some sections can be reached by wheelchair users, together with a short description of the accessible area. Please check with the contact number listed on the Site Guide page before you visit.

BARNHAM CROSS COMMON Some species may be seen from car parks.

BLICKLING HALL Some estate roads and paths.

BRANCASTER MARSH Marsh viewable from the road and beach car park.

BUCKENHAM MARSH View along very wet, very rough access track.

BURGH CASTLE Marsh and Breydon Water viewable from the Angles Way footpath.

CHOSELEY BARNS Barns viewable from road, bunting fields not accessible

CLEY MARSHES Western end of the reserve from the visitor centre.

NWT EAST WRETHAM HEATH Wide track alongside reserve.

FARMLAND BIRD CENTRE Park by hide. Some farm tracks my be accessible.

FELBRIGG HALL Some of the woodland trail.

FOULDEN COMMON Should at least hear Nightingale from the car park.

GREAT RYBURGH Some of estate may be visible from car park. Better at Swanton Novers.

GREAT YARMOUTH BEACH Med Gulls from piers, Black Redstart from road.

GREAT YARMOUTH CEMETERY Some paths in churchyard.

HICKLING BROAD most of the reserve.

HOLKHAM HALL Trees viewable from estate roads. Tawny Owl track probably too muddy.

HOLKHAM NNR Washington Hide, Lady Anne's Drive, viewing platform behind Washington Hide, some of woods along sandy track.

NWT HOLME DUNES One large hide overlooking wader scrape, access track from car

HORSEY Mere viewable from 'Easy Access' track. Fields visible from the road.

HOW HILL NNR A few paths may be accessible. Check before you go.

KELLING HEATH Limited views over heath from small car parks.

KELLING QUAGS Access down a very rough track. Ask the NOA's opinion.

LYNFORD ARBORETUM Many paths wheelchair accessible. No access to the gravel pits.

MORSTON QUAY Limited view of saltmarsh from the car park.

PENSTHORPE Blue and yellow trails only.

PENTNEY GRAVEL PITS Leisure Lake viewable from the road, but of limited interest.

ROYDON COMMON Access down rough tracks, which can be wet. Ask the NWT first.

SALTHOUSE BEACH Fields visible from the road, including Snow Bunting area.

SANDRINGHAM Several tracks and roads, plus part of the trails.

SANTON DOWNHAM Several wide sandy tracks and tarmac roads.

SNETTISHAM Rotary hide. Phone at least five working days before you visit.

STIFFKEY Saltmarsh viewable from the NT car park.

STRUMPSHAW FEN Main hide, plus track to railway crossing, good for Cetti's Warbler.

NWT SYDERSTONE COMMON Some species may be seen from lower car park

WALSEY HILLS Lower path only. Narrow and muddy, but level.

WARHAM GREENS Very limited view of saltmarsh from car park.

WAYLAND WOOD May catch a glimpse of Golden Pheasant from car park.

WELLS WOODS Some wide, slightly rough tracks.

ACCESS TO SITES

ACCESS BY PUBLIC TRANSPORT

It is important to check for up-to-date information on all trains and buses BEFORE you travel.

- The Norfolk County Council Bus Information Line can be reached on 0870 608 2608.
- For train information, phone 08457 484950 www.nationalrail.co.uk.
- National Express Coaches phone 08705 808080 www.nationalexpress.com.
  see Contacts section on page 249 for websites and further contact details.

I have found by far the best website for planning a journey in Norfolk is:
http://www.travelineeastanglia.org.uk/scripts/webtriplanner.dll/journeys
where you can type in your set off point and destination, choose your mode of transport and time of travel and the website does the rest!
The Broads Authority produce a series of leaflets titled *Birds by Boat*, *Birds by Train* and *Birds by Bus* see contacts section, page 249.

The NWT offers a 50% discount off the reserve entry fee for anyone who can produce a valid ticket from public transport.

NWT ALDERFEN BROAD Nearest bus stop seems to be in Neatishead bus 36 from Norwich.

BARNHAM CROSS COMMON Train to Thetford; walk south for 1 mile.

NWT BARTON BROAD Bus 36 from Norwich to Neatishead; 10 min walk to the reserve.

BERNEY ARMS MARSHES Train to Berney Arms Station.

BLACKBOROUGH END TIP Train or coach to King's Lynn; bus X1 to Middleton; walk 1.5 miles to tip.

BLAKENEY POINT Train to Sheringham; Coasthopper bus 36 to Blakeney; boat to Point.

BLICKLING HALL Train or coach to Norwich then bus 44 or X5 to Aylsham.

BRANCASTER MARSH Train or coach to King's Lynn; Coasthopper bus 36 to Brancaster; walk onto marsh.

BREYDON WATER NORTH SHORE Train or coach to Yarmouth; walk along Weaver's Way footpath.

RSPB BUCKENHAM MARSHES Train to Buckenham Station adjacent to reserve.

BURGH CASTLE Train or coach to Great Yarmouth, then bus 7 to Burgh Castle.

NWT BUXTON HEATH Bus 45 runs along the B1149 from Holt.

CHOSELEY BARNS Train or coach to King's Lynn; Coasthopper bus 36 to Titchwell; walk 1 mile up hill to barn.

NWT CLEY MARSHES* Train to King's Lynn or Sheringham; Coasthopper bus 36 to reserve entrance.

NWT COCKSHOOT BROAD Train to Hoveton & Wroxham; bus 711 to Ranworth Broad; electric boat to Cockshoot. OR Train to Norwich; bus X1 to Acle; bus 711 to Ranworth; electric boat to Cockshoot Broad.

DENVER SLUICE Train or coach to King's Lynn: bus 37 to Denver; walk.

DERSINGHAM BOG Train or coach to King's Lynn; bus 40 or 41 to the main rd; walk through the Wolferton Triangle to reserve entrance.

NWT EAST WRETHAM HEATH Train to Thetford; bus 11A goes past reserve entrance.

FARMLAND BIRD CENTRE Train to Sheringham; Coasthopper bus 36 to Holt; bus 46 or 46A to Glandford; walk to reserve.

FELBRIGG HALL Bus 60 from Cromer runs on schooldays only. Best to get train to Sheringham; taxi to Felbrigg Hall.

FLITCHAM ABBEY FARM Train or coach to King's Lynn; bus X8 to Hillington; walk 2 miles to the farm.

FORDHAM Train to Downham Market; bus 37 to

ACCESS TO SITES
BY PUBLIC TRANSPORT

main road near Fordham; 15 min walk to canal bridge.

NWT FOXLEY WOOD Train or coach to Norwich; bus X56 to Fakenham; stop at Foxley War Memorial on the A1067; 30 min walk to reserve.

GREAT YARMOUTH BEACH Train or coach to Yarmouth; walk to beach.

GREAT YARMOUTH CEMETERY Train or coach to Yarmouth; walk to cemetery.

GYPSY LANE Train or coach to King's Lynn; Coasthopper bus 36 to Titchwell.

HADDISCOE MARSHES Train or coach to Yarmouth; buses 581 & 580 run over the viewing bridge.

HARDLEY FLOOD Train or coach to Norwich; bus X2 to Chedgrave; walk to Flood.

HERBERT BARNES RIVERSIDE PARK Train to Yarmouth; walk along the Angle's Way footpath to reserve.

NWT HICKLING BROAD* Train or coach to Norwich; bus 54 to Stalham; bus 737 or 12X to Hickling; 20 min walk to reserve .

HOLKHAM HALL Train or coach to King's Lynn or Sheringham; Coasthopper bus 36 to entrance gates.

HOLKHAM PINES Train or coach to King's Lynn or Sheringham; Coasthopper bus 36 to top of Lady Anne's Drive.

NWT HOLME DUNES Train or coach to King's Lynn; Coasthopper bus 36 to Holme; walk to reserve.

NOA HOLME BIRD OBSERVATORY Train or coach to King's Lynn; Coasthopper bus 36 to Holme; walk to reserve.

HORSEY Train or coach to Yarmouth; bus 1 or 1A to West Somerton; walk 2 miles to mill.

HOVETON GREAT BROAD Train to Wroxham; bus 711, 54 or 738 to Salhouse; boat from Salhouse Quay to Hoveton Broad mooring.

HOW HILL NNR Train or coach to Yarmouth; bus 736 or 837 to Ludham; walk 2 miles to reserve.

HUNSTANTON Train to King's Lynn; bus 40 or 41 to Hunstanton.

KELLING HEATH Train or coach to King's Lynn or Sheringham; Coasthopper bus 36 runs along A149; walk to reserve.

KELLING QUAGS Train or coach to King's Lynn or Sheringham; Coasthopper bus 36 runs along A149; walk to reserve.

KEN HILL WOOD Train to King's Lynn; bus 40 or 41 to the Snettisham turn off.

KING'S LYNN DOCKS Train or coach to King's Lynn.

RSPB LAKENHEATH FEN Train to Lakenheath Station adjacent to reserve.

LYNFORD ARBORETUM Train to Thetford; bus 136 to Mundford; 15 min walk.

NWT MARTHAM BROAD Train or coach to Yarmouth; bus 1 or 1A to West Somerton; 10 min walk .

MORSTON QUAY Train or coach to Sheringham or King's Lynn; Coasthopper bus 36 to Morston.

PENTNEY GRAVEL PITS Train or coach to King's Lynn; bus 32 to Pentney .

PENSTHORPE Bus X53 runs to the gates from Fakenham.

NWT RANWORTH BROAD Train to Hoveton & Wroxham; bus 711 to Ranworth Broad.

NOA REDWELL MARSH Train or coach to King's Lynn; Coasthopper bus 36 to Holme; walk to reserve.

ROCKLAND BROAD Train or coach to Norwich; bus 001 to Rockland St Mary.

NWT ROYDON COMMON Train or coach to King's Lynn; bus 48 runs past entrances to reserve.

NWT SALTHOUSE MARSHES Train or coach to King's Lynn or Sheringham; Coasthopper bus 36 runs along A149; walk down beach road.

SALTHOUSE HEATH Train or coach to King's Lynn or Sheringham; Coasthopper bus 36 to Dunn Cow pub; walk 1 mile up hill to heath.

SANDRINGHAM Train or National Express coach

ACCESS TO SITES
BY PUBLIC TRANSPORT

to King's Lynn, then bus 411 or Coastliner service from King's Lynn Bus Station.

SANTON DOWNHAM Train to Thetford; bus 200 or 358 to Brandon goes past access road.

SHERINGHAM Train or coach to Sheringham.

SCULTHORPE MOOR Train or coach to King's Lynn then bus X98 to top of access track The Drift.

SNETTISHAM COASTAL PARK Train or coach to King's Lynn; bus 40 or 41 to Snettisham turn off; walk 2 miles to beach car park.

RSPB SNETTISHAM Train or coach to King's Lynn; bus 40 or 41 to Snettisham turn off; walk 2 miles to reserve car park.

NWT SPARHAM POOLS Train or coach to Norwich; bus 29to Lyng goes past entrance.

STIFFKEY FEN Train or coach to King's Lynn or Sheringham; Coasthopper bus 36 goes past entrance.

RSPB STRUMPSHAW FEN Train to Brundall; walk 1.5 miles OR Train or coach to Norwich; bus 17A to strumpshaw; walk 0.5 miles to reserve.

NWT STUBB MILL Train or coach to Norwich; bus 54 to Stalham; bus 737 or 12X to Hickling; 20 min walk to watchpoint.

SWANTON NOVERS Train or coach to King's Lynn; bus X8 or 48 to Fakenham; bus 304 to Swanton Novers; 10 min walk to watchpoint.

SURLINGHAM CHURCH MARSH Train or coach to Norwich, then bus 001 to Loddon passes through Surlingham village.

NWT SYDERSTONE COMMON Train or coach to King's Lynn; bus X8 to West Rudham; bus 48 to Syderstone; 15 min walk to reserve.

TED ELLIS NATURE RESERVE Train or coach to Norwich; bus 001 to Rockland St Mary; 1 mile walk to reserve OR the same bus to Surlingham; walk 1.25 miles to reserve.

RSPB TITCHWELL Train or coach to King's Lynn; Coasthopper bus 36 to reserve entrance.

TOTTENHILL GRAVEL PITS Train or coach to King's Lynn; bus 37 to Tottenhill; walk to pit.

NWT UPTON FEN Train or coach to Norwich; bus X1 to Acle; bus 731 to Upton; walk 1.5 miles to reserve. OR bus 17 from Norwich to Upton.

NOA WALSEY HILLS Train or coach to King's Lynn or Sheringham; Coasthopper bus 36 to reserve entrance.

WARHAM GREENS Train or coach to King's Lynn or Sheringham; Coasthopper bus 36 to top of access track.

NWT WAYLAND WOOD Train or coach to Norwich; bus 31 to Watton stops near reserve.

NWT WEETING HEATH* Train to Brandon; bus 28, 143 or 145 to Weeting; walk 1 mile to reserve.

WELLS WOODS Train or coach to King's Lynn or Sheringham; Coasthopper bus 36 to Wells; walk to woods.

WWT WELNEY Train to Littleport or Ely; taxi to reserve 4 miles from Littleport.

WEYBOURNE Train or coach to King's Lynn or Sheringham; Coasthopper bus 36 to beach road.

WINTERTON DUNES Train or coach to Yarmouth; bus 1 to Winterton.

WHITLINGHAM COUNTRY PARK Number 58 and 58A bus route from Norwich. Also a river bus from Station Quay, Norwich, Norfolk 01502 713196.

WOLFERTON TRIANGLE Train or coach to King's Lynn; bus 40 or 41 to the triangle.

Authors note:

One other thing to bear in mind is that some of the more rural bus routes operate on 'Norfolk Time' i.e. half an hour either way of advertised time. I once stood in Halvergate for a bus that was 40 minutes late! **GOOD LUCK!**

ACCESS TO SITES

BROADLAND BOAT MOORINGS

These sites have mooring facilities at or close to the reserve, and these make for ideal stop-offs during your Norfolk Broads holiday. A river map is an essential aid to planning your holiday, and I can recommend the one produced by GEOprojects UK Ltd, 9-10 Southern Court, South Street, Reading RG1 4QS 0118 939 3567 as being the best.

BARTON BROAD Moor at Gay's Staithe and walk to reserve, about half a mile.

BREYDON WATER Moor on River Bure and walk past train station to view Breydon Water.

BERNEY ARMS MARSHES Free mooring at Berney Arms along the Berney Arms Reach of the River Yare at the west end of Breydon Water. A short walk to the reserve

BUCKENHAM MARSHES Free mooring at Cantley along the River Yare; walk back along the river footpath to Buckenham RSPB about 2 miles.

BURGH CASTLE Moor at Burgh Castle Marina and walk north for half a mile.

COCKSHOOT BROAD Moor in channel at reserve entrance.

GREAT YARMOUTH BEACH Moor on River Bure. 15 minute walk to beach.

GREAT YARMOUTH CEMETERY Moor on River Bure. 15 minute walk.

HALVERGATE MARSHES Moor in Yarmouth, then train to Berney Arms, then walk.

HARDLEY FLOOD Moor on River Chet near the Flood.

HERBERT BARNES RIVERSIDE PARK Moor at Yarmouth and walk to park

HICKLING BROAD Nearest mooring is at Hickling Sailing Club, over a mile away.

HORSEY Moor at Horsey Mill.

HOVETON GREAT BROAD Moor on River Bure at reserve entrance.

HOW HILL NNR Moor on River Ant at reserve entrance.

MARTHAM BROAD Moor at West Somerton on the River Thurne.

RANWORTH BROAD Moor at Ranworth village and walk 500 yards.

ROCKLAND BROAD Moor at Rockland staithe on the River Yare.

SURLINGHAM CHURCH MARSHES Moor at Ferry House and walk half a mile.

TED ELLIS TRUST RESERVE. Moor at Rockland Staithe on the River Yare and walk about a mile along a public footpath to the reserve see pages 157 and 195 for route OR moor at Ferry House, Surlingham, on the River Yare and walk along the river path or through village approx 3 miles.

NWT UPTON FEN Moor at Upton Dyke on the River Bure and walk 2 miles to the reserve.

WHITLINGHAM COUNTRY PARK 24 hour mooring on the River Yare adjacent to the Country Park.

THE NORFOLK BIRD LIST

Breeding numbers of Black-tailed Godwits are governed by water levels in suitable habitat. However, birds may grace any Norfolk marsh in summer.

NORFOLK BIRD LIST

THIS IS a run down of all species of birds which have been seen in Norfolk, detailing when and where to see them. This is mainly aimed at beginners who may not be aware of when and how often some species are present in the county. The list can be used as a checklist as there are boxes to record your Norfolk life list and an individual year.

I have to stress that these notes are from my personal experiences of the birds in Norfolk and many folk will disagree with my verdicts! For instance, I made 25 trips to Norfolk in 2001 and saw Marsh Harrier every single time, hence my assessment that they are common. Obviously, they aren't common in the true sense but you can't argue with a 100% strike rate! Also included are several races of species which are sometimes mentioned in bird magazines, and which may be given full species status in future (indicated by italics).

I have assigned all species to one of the following categories.

COMMON
Very abundant, or very easy to see even if there aren't many of them around.

SCARCE
Not very common, or hard to see in the field even if fairly abundant in numbers. Not likely to be seen by a casual visitor unless they are specifically looking for a particular species (eg. Hawfinch). See specific site pages for more detail of when to visit and how likely you are to see the target species.

MODERATELY RARE
Hardly any seen during the year, and certainly almost never by the casual visitor.

RARE
Probably only a handful of records, or several records many years ago.You will not see this species unless alerted to a new sighting by a pager or birdline service.

EXTREMELY RARE
Probably only one record in the history of record-keeping! Probably more chance of winning the National Lottery than seeing one of the species in this category on a casual visit. Only intrepid birders looking for rare birds will find one of these in a lifetime, or twitchers travelling to see these rarities are likely to see them.

NORFOLK BIRD LIST

.... **Red-throated Diver**	*Gavia stellata*	Relatively common at sea in winter. Rare inland.
.... **Black-throated Diver**	*G. arctica*	Fairly rare at sea in winter. Rare inland.
.... **Great Northern Diver**	*G. immer*	Fairly rare at sea in winter. Rare inland.
.... **White-billed Diver**	*G. adamsii*	Extremely rare.
.... **Pied-billed Grebe**	*Podilymbus podiceps*	Extremely rare.
.... **Little Grebe**	*Tachyaptus ruficollis*	Fairly common on inland waters.
.... **Great Crested Grebe**	*Podiceps cristatus*	Common at sea in winter. Breeds on inland waters, stronghold in The Broads.
.... **Red-necked Grebe**	*P. grisegena*	Scarce at sea in winter.
.... **Slavonian Grebe**	*P. auritus*	Scarce at sea in winter.
.... **Black-necked Grebe**	*P. nigricollis*	Mainly seen on passage on inland waters.
.... **Black-browed Albatross**	*Thalassarche melanophins*	Extremely rare.
.... **Fulmar**	*Fulmarus glacialis*	Relatively common resident. Hunstanton is the best place, or any seawatching site.
.... **Zino's/Fea's Petrel**	*Pterodroma madeira/fea*	Extremely rare.
.... **Black-capped Petrel**	*P. hasitata*	Extremely rare.
.... **Cory's Shearwater**	*Calonectris diomedia*	Rare passage sea bird. Late summer to October.
.... **Great Shearwater**	*Puffinus gravis*	Extremely rare passage seabird. Late summer to October.
.... **Sooty Shearwater**	*P. griseus*	Moderately rare passage seabird. Early autumn off seawatching sites.
.... **Manx Shearwater**	*P. Puffinus*	Scarce (but most common shearwater) passage seabird. Late summer to October at seawatching sites.
.... **Balearic Shearwater**	*P. mauretanicus*	Moderately rare passage seabird. Late summer at seawatching sites.
.... **Little Shearwater**	*P. assimilis*	Extremely rare.
.... **Storm Petrel**	*Hydrobates pelagicus*	Moderately rare seabird, from late July – late September.
.... **Leach's Petrel**	*Oceanodroma leucorhoa*	Moderately rare seabird. autumn.
.... **Gannet**	*Morus Bassanus*	Relatively common passage seabird. Autumn best.
.... **Cormorant**	*Phalacrocorax carbo*	Common resident at coastal sites plus inland waters.
.... **Shag**	*P. aristotelis*	Moderately rare passage seabird at seawatching points.
.... **Bittern**	*Botaurus stellaris*	Extremely secretive, scarce resident. Look over reedbeds at Hickling, Cley, etc. Best seen in icy weather when they may feed in open areas, but more often seen briefly flying over reedbeds.
.... **Little Bittern**	*Ixobrychus minutus*	Extremely rare.
.... **Night Heron**	*Nycticorax nycticorax*	Rare.
.... **Squacco Heron**	*Ardeola ralloides*	Extremely rare.
.... **Little Egret**	*Egretta garzetta*	Scarce but increasing records. Marshes all year, Titchwell a favoured site.
.... **Great White Egret**	*E. alba*	Rare.
.... **Grey Heron**	*Ardea cinerea*	Common resident at all wetlands.
.... **Purple Heron**	*A. purpurea*	Rare.
.... **Black Stork**	*Ciconia nigra*	Extremely rare.
.... **White Stork**	*C. ciconia*	Rare.
.... **Glossy Ibis**	*Plegadis falcinellus*	Extremely rare.
.... **Spoonbill**	*Platalea leucorodia*	One or two regularly seen each year: Titchwell, Holkham NNR and Breydon Water.
.... **Mute Swan**	*Cygnus olor*	Common resident on all wetlands.
.... **Bewick's Swan**	*C. columbianus*	Localised winter resident. Best at Welney.
.... **Whooper Swan**	*C. cygnus*	Localised wnter resident. Best at Welney.
.... ***(Tundra) Bean Goose***	*Anser fabalis rossicus*	Moderately rare winter visitor, mainly at Welney.
.... **(Taiga) Bean Goose**	*A.f. fabalis*	Up to 300 winter at Buckenham Marshes, Nov – Feb
.... **Pink-footed Goose**	*A. brachyrhynchus*	Thousands winter in Norfolk. Snettisham, Horsey and Holkham favoured sites. Seen in flight or on fields almost anywhere on north coast.
.... **White-fronted Goose**	*A. albifrons*	winter resident, best at Holkham and Buckenham.
.... **Lesser White-fronted Goose**	*A. erythropus*	Extremely rare winter visitor.
.... **Greylag Goose**	*A. Anser*	Common resident, feral population on all wetlands.

NORFOLK BIRD LIST

....	**Snow Goose**	*A. caerulescens*	Rare winter visitor. Probably all escapes!
....	**Canada Goose**	*Branta canadensis*	Common resident on all waters.
....	**Barnacle Goose**	*B. leucopsis*	Moderately rare winter visitor. Try Holkham.
....	**(Pale-bellied) Brent Goose**	*B. bernicula*	Moderately rare winter visitor amongst dark-bellied flocks.
....	***(Dark-bellied) Brent Goose***	*B.b. hrota*	Very common winter resident on all north coast marshes.
....	***Black Brant***	*B.b. nigricans*	Moderately rare winter visitor amongst dark-bellied Brent flocks. Titchwell and Cley are best bets.
....	**Red-breasted Goose**	*B. ruficollis*	Rare winter visitor. Scan Brent goose flocks.
....	**Egyptian Goose**	*Alopochen aegyptiacus*	Increasingly common feral resident on many Broadland rivers and coastal marshes.
....	**Ruddy Shelduck**	*Tadorna ferruginea*	Extremely rare, Recent records due to escapes?
....	**Shelduck**	*T. tadorna*	Common resident mostly on coastal marshes.
....	**Mandarin**	*Aix galericulata*	Rare.
....	**Eurasian Wigeon**	*Anas penelope*	Common winter resident, all marshes. One or two stay for winter.
....	**American Wigeon**	*A. americana*	Rare.
....	**Gadwall**	*A. strepera*	Common resident all waters.
....	**Teal**	*A. crecca*	Common winter resident. A few over-summer.
....	**Green-winged Teal**	*A. carolinensis*	Rare.
....	**Mallard**	*A. platyrhynchos*	Very common resident.
....	**Pintail**	*A. acuta*	Fairly common winter resident. Try Welney, with smaller numbers at Titchwell.
....	**Garganey**	*A. querquedula*	Scarce on passage, plus a few pairs breed: Cley, Hickling or Welney.
....	**Blue-winged Teal**	*A. discors*	Extremely rare.
....	**Shoveler**	*A. clypeata*	Common resident.
....	**Red-crested Pochard**	*Netta rufina*	Extremely rare.
....	**Pochard**	*Aythya ferina*	Common winter resident all waters, some breed.
....	**Canvasback**	*A. valisineria*	Extremely rare.
....	**Ring-necked Duck**	*A. collaris*	Rare.
....	**Ferruginous Duck**	*A. nyroca*	Rare.
....	**Tufted Duck**	*A. fuligula*	Common winter resident all waters, some breed.
....	**Scaup**	*A. marila*	Scarce winter visitor. Try Snettisham RSPB pits.
....	**Common Eider**	*Somateria mollisima*	Scarce sea duck. Try Titchwell all year round.
....	**King Eider**	*S. spectabilis*	Extremely rare.
....	**Steller's Eider**	*Polysticta stelleri*	Extremely rare.
....	**Long-tailed Duck**	*Clangula hyemalis*	Scarce winter sea duck. Coast between Hunstanton and Horsey.
....	**Common Scoter**	*Melanitta nigra*	Up to 3000 off the north coast. Hunstanton, Holme and Titchwell.
....	**Surf Scoter**	*M. perspicillata*	Extremely rare.
....	**Velvet Scoter**	*M. fusca*	Scarce sea duck in with Common Scoters – scan flock for white wing patches (see above).
....	**Bufflehead**	*Bucephala albeola*	Extremely rare.
....	**Goldeneye**	*B. clangula*	Fairly common winter visitor. At sea or on inland pits.
....	**Smew**	*Mergellus albellus*	Scarce winter visitor. Best at Tottenhill Pits, also Hickling and Snettisham.
....	**Red-breasted Merganser**	*M. serrator*	Fairly common at sea in winter. North coast sites.
....	**Goosander**	*M. merganser*	Scarce in winter. Try Denver Sluice, Sparham Pools.
....	**Ruddy Duck**	*Oxyura jamaicensis*	Scarce, but increasing, resident. Try East Wretham.
....	**Honey Buzzard**	*Pernis apivorus*	Rare breeder (possibly 2 pairs). Swanton Novers and Great Ryburgh mid May to mid September.
....	**Black Kite**	*Milvus migrans*	Extremely rare.
....	**Red Kite**	*M. milvus*	Rare. Flitcham Abbey Farm has recent records.
....	**White-tailed Eagle**	*Haliaeetus albicilla*	Rare winter visitor.
....	**Marsh Harrier**	*Circus aeruginosus*	Common in summer on all marshes. Scarce in winter, Horsey area best.
....	**Hen Harrier**	*C. cyaneus*	Scarce winter visitor. Roosts at Stubb Mill and Roydon Common are best. Arrive about an hour before dark.

NORFOLK BIRD LIST

.... **Pallid Harrier**	*C. macrourus*	Extremely rare.
.... **Montagu's Harrier**	*C. pygargus*	Rare breeder. Details not given at request of RSPB. Try any watchpoint or marsh. Sometimes seen on migration at Snettisham or Cley.
.... **Goshawk**	*Accipiter gentilis*	Scarce breeder. Try any vantage point in Thetford Forest from late Feb to early May for displaying birds.
.... **Sparrowhawk**	*A. nisus*	Common resident in virtually all woodland.
.... **Buzzard**	*Buteo buteo*	Moderately rare resident. Try Swanton Novers and Great Ryburgh.
.... **Rough-legged Buzzard**	*B. lagopus*	Usually one in the county in winter. Listen to telephone newslines for current site.
.... **Golden Eagle**	*Aquila chrysaetos*	Extremely rare.
.... **Osprey**	*Pandion haliaetus*	Scarce on passage. May and September best months.
.... **Kestrel**	*Falco tinnunculus*	Common resident everywhere.
.... **Red-footed Falcon**	*F. vespertinus*	Moderately rare spring vagrant.
.... **Merlin**	*F. columbarius*	Scarce winter visitor. Most marshes but best at Stubb Mill roost.
.... **Hobby**	*F. subbuteo*	Scarce but increasing summer visitor. Hickling and Weeting Heath best.
.... **Eleonora's Falcon**	*F. eleonorae*	Extremely rare.
.... **Gyrfalcon**	*F. rusticolus*	Extremely rare.
.... **Peregrine Falcon**	*F. peregrinus*	Scarce winter visitor, most marshes. Holkham NNR and Buckenham Marshes seem favoured spots.
.... **Red-legged Partridge**	*Alectoris rufa*	Common resident. Scan any field.
.... **Grey Partridge**	*Perdix perdix*	Declining resident in fields. Roydon Common best.
.... **Quail**	*Coturnix coturnix*	Present most summers in wheat fields. Bird newslines will tell you best place but they are rarely seen.
.... **Pheasant**	*Phasianus colchicus*	Common resident everywhere.
.... **Golden Pheasant**	*Chrysolophus pictus*	Scarce resident. Wolferton Triangle and Wayland Woods.
.... **Water Rail**	*Rallus aquaticus*	Secretive resident. More commonly seen in winter. Try Cley and Titchwell.
.... **Spotted Crake**	*Porzana porzana*	Moderately rare autumn visitor. Titchwell is a favoured haunt.
.... **Little Crake**	*P. parva*	Extremely rare.
.... **Baillon's Crake**	*P. pusilla*	Extremely rare.
.... **Corncrake**	*Crex crex*	Moderately rare passage migrant. Usually seen when flushed from Blakeney Point.
.... **Moorhen**	*Gallinula chloropus*	Common resident, all waters.
.... **Allen's Gallinule**	*Porphyrula alleni*	Extremely rare.
.... **Coot**	*Fulica atra*	Common resident, all waters.
.... **Common Crane**	*Grus grus*	Small population resident in Horsey/Hickling area.
.... **Little Bustard**	*Tetrax tetrax*	Extremely rare.
.... **Great Bustard**	*Otis tarda*	Extremely rare.
.... **Oystercatcher**	*Haematopus ostralegus*	Common coastal resident.
.... **Black-winged Stilt**	*Himantopus himantopus*	A single bird has taken up residence at Titchwell for last nine years.
.... **Avocet**	*Recurvirostra avosetta*	Fairly common breeder. Cley, Titchwell, Welney. Winter flock on Breydon Water as well as other seasons.
.... **Stone Curlew**	*Burhinus oedicnemus*	Moderately rare but increasing breeder. Weeting Heath, April to September.
.... **Cream-coloured Courser**	*Cursorius cursor*	Extremely rare.
.... **Collared Pratincole**	*Glareola pratincola*	Rare.
.... **Oriental Pratincole**	*G. maldivarum*	Extremely rare.
.... **Black-winged Pratincole**	*G. nordmanni*	Extremely rare.
.... **Little Ringed Plover**	*Charadrius dubius*	Moderately rare breeder. Welney best place, April to late August.
.... **Ringed Plover**	*Charadrius hiaticula*	Common coastal resident, plus inland scrapes.
.... **Killdeer**	*C. vociferus*	Extremely rare.
.... **Kentish Plover**	*C. alexandrinus*	Moderately rare spring vagrant. Favours Breydon Water.

NORFOLK BIRD LIST

....	**Greater Sandplover**	*C. leschenaultii*	Extremely rare.
....	**Caspian Plover**	*C. asiaticus*	Extremely rare.
....	**Dotterel**	*C. morinellus*	Moderately rare passage migrant.
....	**American Golden Plover**	*Pluvialis dominica*	Extremely rare.
....	**Pacific Golden Plover**	*P. fulva*	Extremely rare.
....	**Golden Plover**	*P. apricaria*	Common winter visitor. Snettisham or Titchwell best.
....	**Grey Plover**	*P. squatarola*	Fairly common winter visitor. Any coastal wader site.
....	**Sociable Plover**	*Vanellus gregarius*	Extremely rare.
....	**Lapwing**	*V. vanellus*	Common resident all marshes.
....	**Knot**	*Calidris canutus*	Common winter visitor. Snettisham at high tide.
....	**Sanderling**	*C. alba*	Common on beaches in winter.
....	**Semipalmated Sandpiper**	*C. pusilla*	Rare.
....	**Red-necked Stint**	*C. ruficollis*	Extremely rare.
....	**Little Stint**	*C. minuta*	Scarce passage wader. Autumn at Titchwell and Cley.
....	**Temminck's Stint**	*C. temminckii*	Passage wader. Cley in May is best.
....	**White-rumped Sandpiper**	*C. fuscicollis*	Rare.
....	**Baird's Sandpiper**	*C. bairdii*	Rare.
....	**Pectoral Sandpiper**	*C. melanotos*	Moderately rare vagrant, usually September.
....	**Sharp-tailed Sandpiper**	*C. acuminata*	Extremely rare.
....	**Curlew Sandpiper**	*C. ferruginea*	Passage wader, Titchwell in September is best.
....	**Purple Sandpiper**	*C. maritima*	Scarce winter visitor. One on the beach by the old pill box at Titchwell, a few by the ski-ramp at Hunstanton all at high tide.
....	**Dunlin**	*C. alpina*	Common resident wader. All pits and coast.
....	**Broad-billed Sandpiper**	*Limicola falcinellus*	Rare. Favours Breydon Water.
....	**Stilt Sandpiper**	*Micropalama himantopus*	Extremely rare.
....	**Buff-breasted Sandpiper**	*Tryngites subruficollis*	Rare. Usually in September.
....	**Ruff**	*Philomachus pugnax*	Fairly common resident, scarcer in winter. Cley, Holme, Titchwell, Snettisham, etc.
....	**Jack Snipe**	*Lymnocryptes minimus*	Moderately rare winter visitor. Very secretive. Surlingham, Holme, Cley, Roydon Common.
....	**Snipe**	*Gallinago gallinago*	Common resident on all marshes and pits.
....	**Great Snipe**	*G. media*	Extremely rare.
....	**Long-billed Dowitcher**	*Limnodromus scolopaceus*	Rare.
....	**Woodcock**	*Scalopax rusticola*	Common but secretive resident. Dusk at Buxton Heath and Holkham Park, winter from the Fen Hide boardwalk at Titchwell.
....	**Black-tailed Godwit**	*Limosa limosa*	Relatively scarce at all times of year. Try Breydon Water and Cley in winter, Welney and Cley in summer.
....	**Bar-tailed Godwit**	*L. lapponica*	Relatively common all year. Any wader hotspot in winter (Titchwell, Snettisham) and Titchwell in summer.
....	**Little Whimbrel**	*Numenius minutus*	Extremely rare.
....	**Whimbrel**	*N. phaeopus*	Scarce on passage. Try Blakeney Point, Cley, Breydon Water and Salthouse Beach.
....	**Curlew**	*N. arquata*	Common in winter, all marshes, scarcer in summer. Breeds at Roydon Common, Warham Greens.
....	**Spotted Redshank**	*Tringa erythropus*	A few winter at Titchwell. Passage best at Snettisham.
....	**Redshank**	*T. totanus*	Common on all pits and marshes all year.
....	**Marsh Sandpiper**	*T. stagnatilis*	Extremely rare.
....	**Greenshank**	*T. nebularia*	Scarce on passage. Cley, Breydon Water, Snettisham, Holme, etc.
....	**Greater Yellowlegs**	*T. melanoleuca*	Extremely rare.
....	**Lesser Yellowlegs**	*T. flavipes*	Rare.
....	**Solitary Sandpiper**	*T. solitaria*	Extremely rare.
....	**Green Sandpiper**	*T. ochropus*	Common passage wader. Holme is good but all scrapes should have some.
....	**Wood Sandpiper**	*T. glareola*	Scarce passage wader. Cley, Holme, Salthouse Beach are all favoured areas.
....	**Terek Sandpiper**	*Xenus cinereus*	Rare.
....	**Common Sandpiper**	*Actitis hypoleucos*	Relatively common on passage. See Green and Wood Sandpipers for favoured sites

NORFOLK BIRD LIST

.... **Spotted Sandpiper**	*A. macularia*	Rare.
.... **Turnstone**	*Arenaria interpres*	Common resident on coast.
.... **Wilson's Phalarope**	*Phalaropus tricolor*	Extremely rare.
.... **Red-necked Phalarope**	*P. lobatus*	Cley in May is a traditional stop-over. Moderately rare.
.... **Grey Phalarope**	*P. fulicarius*	Moderately rare from seawatching points in autumn.
.... **Pomarine Skua**	*Stercorarius pomarinus*	Moderately rare seabird. Autumn best but sometimes seen in winter.
.... **Arctic Skua**	*S. parasiticus*	Scarce on Autumn passage. From late July harassing terns at sea.
.... **Long-tailed Skua**	*S. longicaudus*	Moderately rare seabird. Autumn best.
.... **Great Skua**	*S. skua*	Scarce seabird. Best from August to October harassing birds at sea.
.... **Mediterranean Gull**	*Larus melanocephalus*	Moderately rare breeder. Best seen on Great Yarmouth beach.
.... **Laughing Gull**	*L. atricilla*	Rare.
.... **Franklin's Gull**	*L. pipixcan*	Rare.
.... **Little Gull**	*L. minutus*	Scarce on passage at Titchwell, Breydon Water, Kelling Quags etc. May is best.
.... **Sabine's Gull**	*L. sabini*	Moderately rare autumn seabird at seawatching points.
.... **Bonaparte's Gull**	*L. philadelphia*	Extremely rare.
.... **Black-headed Gull**	*L. ridibundus*	Very common breeder and resident. All waters and marshes.
.... **Slender-billed Gull**	*L. genei*	Extremely rare. Favours Cley.
.... **Ring-billed Gull**	*L. delawarensis*	Rare.
.... **Common Gull**	*L. canus*	Relatively common resident.
.... **Lesser Black-backed Gull**	*L. fuscus*	Relatively common resident. All waters and marshes.
.... **Herring Gull**	*L. argentatus*	Common resident on coast.
.... **Yellow-legged Gull**	*L. michahellis*	Scarce summer visitor. Cley is best.
.... ***(Caspian Gull)***	*L. cachinnans*	Rare vagrant, usually summer.
.... **Iceland Gull**	*L. glaucoides*	Moderately rare winter visitor. Phone bird newslines for details.
.... **Glaucous Gull**	*L. hyperboreus*	Moderately rare, usually winter, visitor. Favours King's Lynn Docks.
.... **Great Black-backed Gull**	*L. marinus*	Common on all waters and coast.
.... **Ross's Gull**	*Rhodostethia rosea*	Extremely rare.
.... **Kittiwake**	*Rissa tridactyla*	Relatively common seabird at all watchpoints. From late July to October best.
.... **Ivory Gull**	*Pagophila eburnea*	Extremely rare.
.... **Sooty Tern**	*Onychopion fuscata*	Extremely rare.
.... **Little Tern**	*Sternula albifrons*	Common summer visitor. From May to September at all seawatching points. Colonies at Blakeney Point and Yarmouth Beach.
.... **Gull-billed Tern**	*Gelochelidon nilotica*	Rare.
.... **Caspian Tern**	*Hydroprogne caspia*	Moderately rare summer vagrant. Any tern colony/ roost.
.... **Whiskered Tern**	*Chlidonias hybrida*	Rare.
.... **Black Tern**	*C. niger*	Scarce on spring and autumn passage. Lakenheath is a favoured site, on the flashes, but watch all Broads.
.... **White-winged Tern**	*C. leucopterus*	Rare passage vagrant.
.... **Sandwich Tern**	*Sterna sandvicensis*	Common summer visitor. From April to September at all seawatching points. Colonies at Blakeney Point.
.... **Lesser Crested Tern**	*S. bengalensis*	Extremely rare.
.... **Common Tern**	*S. hirundo*	Common summer visitor. From April to September at all seawatching points. Colonies at Blakeney Point. Breed inland on platforms on some Broads.
.... **Roseate Tern**	*S. dougallii*	Moderately rare summer visitor. Cley scrapes are a favoured site but look out at Blakeney Point and Breydon Water
.... **Arctic Tern**	*S. paradisaea*	Moderately rare summer visitor. Breeds on Blakeney Point. Also on passage on any water, The Broads in April/May is best.

NORFOLK BIRD LIST

.... **Guillemot**	*Uria aalge*	Scarce at seawatching points.
.... **Razorbill**	*Alca torda*	Scarce at seawatching points.
.... **Black Guillemot**	*Cepphus grylle*	Moderately rare, winter.
.... **Little Auk**	*Alle alle*	Scarce during strong onshore winds in November. All seawatching points. Numbers vary from year to year.
.... **Puffin**	*Fratercula arctica*	Moderately rare. Pot luck at any seawatching point spring/autumn.
.... **Pallas' Sandgrouse**	*Syrrhaptes paradoxus*	Extremely rare.
.... **Rock Dove**	*Columba livia*	Descendant of Feral Pigeon. Pure birds now only found on Scottish islands
.... **Stock Dove**	*C. oenas*	Relatively common resident.
.... **Woodpigeon**	*Columba palumbus*	Very common everywhere.
.... **Collared Dove**	*Streptopelia decaocto*	Common in all villages.
.... **Turtle Dove**	*S. turtur*	Declining summer visitor. Still common in The Broads, The Brecks and Flitcham Abbey Farm.
.... **Rufous Turtle Dove**	*S. orientalis*	Extremely rare.
.... **Ring-necked Parakeet**	*Psittacula krameri*	Rare. Probably all escapes!
.... **Great Spotted Cuckoo**	*Clamator glandarius*	Rare.
.... **Cuckoo**	*Cuculus canorus*	Common summer visitor. Best seen in May when displaying. Foulden Common good to actually see, rather than hear Cuckoos.
.... **Barn Owl**	*Tyto alba*	Common resident. Any marsh or field at any time of day, but dawn and dusk preferred.
.... **Scops Owl**	*Otus scops*	Extremely rare.
.... **Snowy Owl**	*Nyctea scandiaca*	Extremely rare.
.... **Little Owl**	*Athene noctua*	Scarce resident. Best seen at Flitcham Abbey Farm or Weeting Heath
.... **Tawny Owl**	*Strix aluco*	Common resident. More often heard than seen, but a winter roost at Holkham Hall is a good bet to see one.
.... **Long-eared Owl**	*Asio otus*	Scarce resident. Breeds in extensive woodlands but rarely seen. Listen out for the squeaks of the young during April/May at Dersingham Bog, Thetford forest etc. Possible on passage at Holme or Winterton Dunes.
.... **Short-eared Owl**	*A. flammeus*	Scarce resident. Best seen in winter on any marsh but pot luck which one. Best places seem to be Breydon Water at dusk or Halvergate/Berney Marshes.
.... **Tengmalm's Owl**	*Aegolius funereus*	Extremely rare.
.... **Nightjar**	*Caprimulgus europaeus*	Common summer breeder. Mid May to the end of August at Salthouse Heath, Roydon Common, Dersingham Bog, Winterton, etc.
.... **Common Swift**	*Apus apus*	Common in summer. From May to August everywhere, but best at Titchwell where they often fly below you as you stand on the footpath.
.... **Pallid Swift**	*A. pallidus*	Rare.
.... **Pacific Swift**	*A. pacificus*	Extremely rare.
.... **Alpine Swift**	*A. melba*	Rare.
.... **Little Swift**	*A. affinis*	Extremely rare.
.... **Kingfisher**	*Alcedo atthis*	Scarce resident. Try Strumpshaw, Flitcham Abbey Farm.
.... **Bee-eater**	*Merops apiaster*	Moderately rare spring vagrant. Usually in flight.
.... **Roller**	*Coracias garrulus*	Rare.
.... **Hoopoe**	*Upupa epops*	Moderately rare. Can turn up at any time of year.
.... **Wryneck**	*Jynx torquilla*	Scarce passage vagrant. Winterton, Holkham and Holme dunes best bets, usually in autumn.
.... **Green Woodpecker**	*Picus viridis*	Common resident in most woods, parks etc. Listen out for its loud, laughing call.
.... **Gt Spotted Woodpecker**	*Dendrocopos major*	Common resident in all woodland.
.... **Lr Spotted Woodpecker**	*D. minor*	Hard-to-see resident. Supposedly Common but best at Holkham Park in March, where they display by drumming and fluttering like a butterfly!
.... **Calandra Lark**	*Melanocorypha calandra*	Extremely rare.

NORFOLK BIRD LIST

.... **White-winged Lark**	*M. leucoptera*	Extremely rare.
.... **Short-toed Lark**	*Calandrella brachydactyla*	Moderately rare passage vagrant.
.... **Woodlark**	*Lullula arborea*	Increasingly common in suitable areas. Weeting Heath best, but any clearing in Thetford Forest.
.... **Skylark**	*Alauda arvensis*	Common resident all marshes and fields.
.... **Shorelark**	*Eremophila alpestris*	Scarce winter visitor. Bird newslines will tell you the favoured areas but usually Titchwell, Salthouse Beach or Holkham Gap.
.... **Sand Martin**	*Riparia riparia*	Common summer visitor. On passage at all coastal sites plus all summer at Pentney Gravel Pits, Cley etc.
.... **Swallow**	*Hirundo rustica*	Common summer visitor, everywhere.
.... **Red-rumped Swallow**	*H. daurica*	Rare.
.... **House Martin**	*Delichon urbica*	Common summer visitor everywhere.
.... **Richard's Pipit**	*Anthus novaeseelandiae*	Moderately rare autumn passage migrant. Try Blakeney Point, Winterton or Holme.
.... **Blyth's Pipit**	*A. godlewskii*	Extremely rare.
.... **Tawny Pipit**	*A. campestris*	Moderately rare passage migrant. Declining records, try sites for Richard's Pipit.
.... **Olive-backed Pipit**	*A. hodgsoni*	Rare, autumn.
.... **Tree Pipit**	*A. trivialis*	Scarce summer breeder. Dersingham Bog, Roydon Common, Thetford Forest. Also on passage on coast.
.... **Meadow Pipit**	*A. pratensis*	Common resident, all marshes.
.... **Red-throated Pipit**	*A. cervinus*	Rare passage migrant.
.... **Rock Pipit**	*A. petrosus*	Localised winter resident. Breydon Water, Blakeney.
.... **Water Pipit**	*A. spinoletta*	Scarce winter resident. The Serpentine at Cley always holds a few up to March.
.... **Yellow Wagtail**	*Motacilla flava flavissima*	Scarce migrant plus summer breeder. Cley (east bank), Buckenham Marshes, Kelling Quags etc
.... ***(Blue-headed Wagtail)***	*M.f. flava*	Moderately rare spring migrant. Try Cley east bank.
.... ***(Black-headed Wagtail)***	*M.f. feldegg*	Rare.
.... ***(Grey-headed Wagtail)***	*M.F thunbergi*	Rare.
.... ***(Syke's Wagtail)***	*M.f. beema*	Rare.
.... **Citrine Wagtail**	*Motacilla citreola*	Rare.
.... **Grey Wagtail**	*M. cinerea*	Scarce resident. Best in harsh weather on ice-free waters. Try Sparham Pools.
.... **Pied Wagtail**	*M. yarellii*	Common resident everywhere. A large roost in Norwich city centre is a spectacular sight!
.... ***(White Wagtail)***	*M. alba*	Scarce spring migrant on coast.
.... **Bohemian Waxwing**	*Bombycilla garrulus*	Scarce winter visitor, not every year. Watch any berry bush carefully plus listen to bird newslines.
.... **Dipper**	*Cinclus cinclus*	A black-bellied race occasionally winters in the county. Listen to telephone newslines for details.
.... **Wren**	*Troglodytes troglodytes*	Common resident everywhere.
.... **Dunnock**	*Prunella modularis*	Common resident everywhere.
.... **Alpine Accentor**	*Prunella collaris*	Extremely rare.
.... **Robin**	*Erithacus rebecula*	Common resident everywhere.
.... **Thrush Nightingale**	*Luscinia luscinia*	Extremely rare.
.... **Nightingale**	*L. megarhynchos*	Scarce and declining. End of April to early June best at Salthouse Heath and Foulden. Very skulking, more often heard than seen.
.... **Bluethroat**	*L.a svecica*	Scarce on passage, usually spring. Blakeney Point, etc.
.... **Red-flanked Bluetail**	*Tarsiger cyanurus*	Extremely rare.
.... **Black Redstart**	*Phoenicurus ochruros*	Scarce on passage, usually spring. Usual migrant hotspots. Moderately rare breeder.
.... **Redstart**	*P. Phoenicurus*	Relatively common on passage: try Holme, Holkham Pines, Wells Woods, Yarmouth Cemetery. Scarce breeder.
.... **Whinchat**	*Saxicola rubetra*	Scarce passage migrant. Holme, Winterton, Holkham Pines, Wells Woods, etc.
.... **Stonechat**	*S. torquata*	Scarce Resident at Horsey Gap. Winter at Cley, Titchwell etc.

NORFOLK BIRD LIST

	Species	Scientific name	Status
....	***(Siberian Stonechat)***	*S. stejnegeri*	Moderately rare passage migrant.
....	**Isabelline Wheatear**	*Oenanthe isabellina*	Extremely rare.
....	**Wheatear**	*O. Oenanthe*	Common on passage at coastal sites.
....	**Pied Wheatear**	*O. pleschanka*	Rare.
....	**Black-eared Wheatear**	*O. hispanica*	Extremely rare.
....	**Desert Wheatear**	*O. deserti*	Rare.
....	**Rock Thrush**	*Monticola saxatilis*	Extremely rare.
....	**White's Thrush**	*Zoothera dauma*	Extremely rare.
....	**Siberian Thrush**	*Z. sibirica*	Extremely rare.
....	**Ring Ouzel**	*Turdus torquatus*	Scarce passage migrant. Coastal watchpoints plus Choseley Barns.
....	**Blackbird**	*T. merula*	Common resident everywhere.
....	**Black-throated Thrush**	*T. fuficollis*	Extremely rare.
....	**Fieldfare**	*T. pilaris*	Relatively common winter resident everywhere.
....	**Song Thrush**	*T. philomelos*	Relatively common resident everywhere.
....	**Redwing**	*T. iliacus*	Relatively common winter resident everywhere.
....	**Mistle Thrush**	*T. viscivorus*	Common resident, especially in coniferous woods.
....	**Cetti's Warbler**	*Cettia cetti*	Scarce resident. Very skulking, but sings very loudly from thick cover. Ted Ellis Reserve, Rockland Broad seem best to actually see one. Widespread around other Broads.
....	**Pallas' Grasshopper Warbler**	*Locustella certhiola*	Extremely rare.
....	**Lanceolated warbler**	*L. lanceolata*	Extremely rare.
....	**Grasshopper Warbler**	*L. naevia*	Heard more often than seen. Try Winterton, Horsey Gap, Upton Fen, Hickling, etc. Relatively scarce.
....	**River Warbler**	*L. fluviatilis*	Extremely rare.
....	**Savi's warbler**	*L. lusciniodes*	Moderately rare breeder. One or two pairs usually present in The Broads. Details not given at request of the RSPB. Can turn up in any reedbed.
....	**Aquatic Warbler**	*Acrocephalus paludicola*	Extremely rare.
....	**Sedge Warbler**	*A. schoenbaenus*	Common summer breeder. Any marsh or riverside vegetation.
....	**Paddyfield Warbler**	*A. agricola*	Extremely rare.
....	**Blyth's Reed Warbler**	*A. dumetorum*	Extremely rare.
....	**Marsh Warbler**	*A. palustris*	Moderately rare passage migrant. Sings from vegetation anywhere around water. Early June only. Listen to Bird newslines for any details.
....	**Reed Warbler**	*A. scirpaceus*	Common summer breeder. Any reedbed.
....	**Great Reed Warbler**	*Acrocephalus arundinaceus*	Rare.
....	**Booted Warbler**	*Hippolais caligata*	Extremely rare.
....	**Syke's Warbler**	*H. rama*	Extremely rare.
....	**Icterine Warbler**	*H. icterina*	Moderately rare passage migrant, any migration hotspot (Warham Greens, Winterton, Holkham Pines, Holme, Wells Woods, etc).
....	**Melodious Warbler**	*H. polyglotta*	Rare.
....	**Blackcap**	*Sylvia atricapilla*	Common summer breeder, increasingly seen in winter (try Titchwell). Breeds in all woods.
....	**Garden Warbler**	*S. borin*	Common summer visitor. Lynford Arboretum, The Broads, etc.
....	**Barred Warbler**	*S. nisoria*	Moderately rare autumn migrant. Warham Greens, Blakeney Point, Winterton Dunes, Wells Woods, etc.
....	**Lesser Whitethroat**	*S. curruca*	Relatively scarce summer visitor. Likes thick cover to sing from but not as skulking as Cetti's Warbler or Nightingale. Try Holme.
....	**Desert Warbler**	*S. nana*	Extremely rare.
....	**Whitethroat**	*S. communis*	Common summer visitor in hedgerows.
....	**Dartford Warbler**	*S. undata*	Rare.
....	**Ruppell's Warbler**	*S. rueppelli*	Extremely rare.
....	**Subalpine Warbler**	*S. cantillans*	Rare.
....	**Sardinian Warbler**	*S. melanocephala*	Rare.
....	**Greenish Warbler**	*Phylloscopus trochiloides*	Rare.

NORFOLK BIRD LIST

.... **Arctic Warbler**	*P. borealis*	Rare.
.... **Pallas' Warbler**	*P. proregulus*	Moderately rare autumn vagrant. Wells Woods, Winterton, Yarmouth Cemetery and Holkham Pines seem best. Newslines will have details, best in late Oct, early November.
.... **Yellow-browed Warbler**	*P. inornatus*	Annual but rare autumn vagrant. See Pallas' sites.
.... **Hume's Yellow-browed Warbler**	*P. humei*	Rare.
.... **Radde's Warbler**	*P. schwarzi*	Rare.
.... **Dusky Warbler**	*P. fuscatus*	Rare.
.... **Western Bonelli's Warbler**	*P. bonelli*	Extremely rare.
.... **Wood Warbler**	*P. sibilatrix*	Moderately rare breeder. Has bred at Kelling Triangle and Felbrigg Hall.
.... **Chiffchaff**	*P. collybita*	Common summer breeder, increasingly seen in winter (try Titchwell). Breeds in all woods.
.... **Willow Warbler**	*P. trochilus*	Common summer visitor, most woods.
.... **Goldcrest**	*Regulus regulus*	Common resident. Any woodland but especially coniferous.
.... **Firecrest**	*R. ignicapillus*	Scarce passage migrant, some may breed. Try Holkham Pines, Wells Woods, Yarmouth Cemetery, Holme, Winterton etc in October.
.... **Spotted Flycatcher**	*Muscicapa striata*	Localised breeder. Weeting Heath and East Wretham etc.
.... **Red-breasted Flycatcher**	*Ficedula parva*	Moderately rare autumn vagrant. Try Wells Woods, Holme, etc.
.... **Collared Flycatcher**	*F. albicollis*	Extremely rare.
.... **Pied Flycatcher**	*F. hypoleuca*	Passage migrant. Holme, Holkham, Winterton, Yarmouth Cemetery, etc.
.... **Bearded Tit**	*Panurus biarmicus*	Common resident. Most reedbeds, but pick a windless day for best results. Hickling, Cley, Titchwell, Gypsy Lane.
.... **Long-tailed Tit**	*Aegithalos caudatus*	Common and increasing resident everywhere.
.... **Blue Tit**	*Parus caeruleus*	Common resident everywhere.
.... **Great Tit**	*P. major*	Common resident everywhere.
.... **Coal Tit**	*P. ater*	Common resident. Coniferous forests best.
.... **Willow Tit**	*P. montanus*	Decreasing resident. Tottenhill Gravel Pits and Holkham Park.
.... **Marsh Tit**	*P. palustris*	Common resident around The Broads.
.... **Red-breasted Nuthatch**	`*Sitta canadensis*	Only one. Sorry, there won't be another one!
.... **Nuthatch**	*S. europaea*	Localised resident. Holkham Park best place, but also Ken Hill Wood, Wayland Wood, etc.
.... **Wallcreeper**	*Tichodroma muraria*	Extremely rare.
.... **Treecreeper**	*Certhia familiaris*	Localised resident. Secretive. See Nuthatch for sites.
.... **Penduline Tit**	*Remiz pendulinus*	Rare vagrant but Titchwell has produced regular January records so stay alert by the reedbed!
.... **Golden Oriole**	*Oriolus oriolus*	Moderately rare breeder. Fordham and Lakenheath. More often heard than seen.
.... **Isabelline Shrike**	*Lanius isabellinus*	Rare.
.... **Red-backed Shrike**	*L. collurio*	Moderately rare autumn vagrant. Usual migrant hotspots.
.... **Lesser Grey Shrike**	*L. minor*	Rare.
.... **Great Grey Shrike**	*L. excubitor*	Increasingly rare winter visitor: none in recent years. telephone newslines will have details of any in the county.
.... **Woodchat Shrike**	*L. senator*	Rare.
.... **Jay**	*Garrulus glandarius*	Increasingly common resident. Wayland Wood, Holkham Park, Hickling, etc.
.... **Magpie**	*Pica pica*	Increasingly common resident. Moving into all areas.
.... **Nutcracker**	*Nucifraga caryocatactes*	Extremely rare.
.... **Jackdaw**	*Corvus monedula*	Common resident everywhere.
.... **Rook**	*C. frugilegus*	Common resident everywhere.
.... **Carrion Crow**	*C. corone*	Common resident everywhere.

NORFOLK BIRD LIST

	Name	Scientific name	Notes
....	**Hooded Crow**	*C.c cornix*	Rare winter visitor to Horsey/Roydon Common.
....	**Raven**	*C. corax*	Rare winter visitor to the Horsey area.
....	**Starling**	*Sturnus vulgaris*	Common resident everywhere.
....	**Rose-coloured Starling**	*S. roseus*	Rare.
....	**House Sparrow**	*Passer domesticus*	Common resident everywhere, especially towns and villages.
....	**Tree Sparrow**	*P. montanus*	Moderately rare resident. Try Flitcham Abbey Farm or Welney.
....	**Rock Sparrow**	*Petronia petronia*	Extremely rare.
....	**Chaffinch**	*Fringilla coelebs*	Common resident everywhere.
....	**Brambling**	*F. montifringilla*	Scarce winter visitor. Try Holkham Park or Welney.
....	**Serin**	*Serinus serinus*	Moderately rare vagrant, any time of year.
....	**Greenfinch**	*Carduelis chloris*	Common resident everywhere.
....	**Goldfinch**	*C. C.*	Common resident everywhere.
....	**Siskin**	*C. spinus*	Localised resident. Usually coniferous forests.
....	**Linnet**	*C. cannabina*	Common resident everywhere.
....	**Twite**	*C. flavirostris*	Scarce winter resident. Best places include Holkham Gap and Titchwell.
....	**Common Redpoll**	*C. flammea*	Moderately rare winter visitor.
....	**Lesser Redpoll**	*C. cabaret*	Scarce resident. Numbers vary year to year. Try East Wretham Heath.
....	**Arctic Redpoll**	*C. hornemanni*	Moderately rare winter visitor.
....	**Two-barred Crossbill**	*Loxia leucoptera*	Rare, only in irruption years.
....	**Common Crossbill**	*L. curvirostra*	Scarce resident. Numbers vary year to year. Try Lynford Arboretum, Dersingham Bog, Holkham Pines, Wells Woods, etc. Learn their loud '*chip, chip*' call.
....	**Parrot Crossbill**	*L. pytyopsittacus*	Extremely rare.
....	**Common Rosefinch**	*Carpodacus erythrinus*	Passage vagrant. Winterton, Holme, Holkham Pines, Wells Woods, etc. Occasionally breeds.
....	**Bullfinch**	*Pyrrhula pyrrhula*	Scarce resident. Try Titchwell car park, Holme (Redwell Marsh hedges) Pentney Gravel Pits.
....	**Hawfinch**	*Coccothraustes*	Scarce and decreasing resident, best seen in winter. Barnhamcross Common, Lynford Arboretum, Holkham Park. Learn their '*tick, tick*' call.
....	**Black and White Warbler**	*Mniotilta varia*	Extremely rare.
....	**Lark Sparrow**	*Chondestes grammacus*	Extremely rare.
....	**White-throated Sparrow**	*Zonotrichia albicollis*	Extremely rare.
....	**Lapland Bunting**	*Calcarius lapponicus*	Moderately rare winter resident. No reliable sites any more, though Halvergate Marshes and Burnham Norton have held birds in the past. Salthouse Beach and Cley eye field are regularly visited by passage birds.
....	**Snow Bunting**	*Pletrophenax nivalis*	Localised winter visitor. Small flocks around Yarmouth Beach, Holkham Gap, and on the coast from Hunstanton to Brancaster. Very mobile!
....	**Pine Bunting**	*Emberiza leucocephalos*	Extremely rare.
....	**Yellowhammer**	*E. citrinella*	Relatively common resident. Flitcham Abbey Farm, Salthouse Heath, Kelling Heath, Choseley Barns, etc.
....	**Cirl Bunting**	*E. cirlus*	Extremely rare. Unlikely to be another one.
....	**Ortolan Bunting**	*E. hortulana*	Moderately rare autumn vagrant. Try Blakeney Point.
....	**Yellow-browed Bunting**	*E. chrysophrys*	Extremely rare.
....	**Rustic Bunting**	*E. rustica*	Rare.
....	**Little Bunting**	*E. pusilla*	Rare.
....	**Yellow-breasted Bunting**	*E. aureola*	Extremely rare.
....	**Reed Bunting**	*E. schoeniclus*	Common resident, all marshes and waterways.
....	**Black-headed Bunting**	*E. melanocephala*	Extremely rare.
....	**Corn Bunting**	*Miliaria calandra*	Scarce resident. Try Flitcham Abbey Farm, Welney or Choseley Barns all year round.
....	**Rose-breasted Grosbeak**	*Pheucticus ludovicianus*	Extremely rare.

DEFINITIONS OF BIRD GROUPS USED IN THIS BOOK

Some general terms have been used in the 'Target Birds' and 'Other possible bird species' sections, to save space. Here are the birds typically included in each group.

Common woodland birds
Woodpigeon, Tawny Owl, Great Spotted Woodpecker, Wren, Dunnock, Robin, Blackbird, Song Thrush, Mistle Thrush, migrant warblers, Goldcrest, Long-tailed Tit, Marsh Tit, Willow Tit, Coal Tit, Blue Tit, Great Tit, Nuthatch, Treecreeper, Jackdaw, Rook, Crow, Chaffinch, Greenfinch, Goldfinch.

Common wildfowl
Mute Swan, Greylag Goose, Canada Goose, Shelduck, Wigeon usually in winter, Gadwall, Teal, Mallard, Shoveler, Pochard, Tufted Duck, Goldeneye in winter.

Common waterbirds
Little Grebe, Great Crested Grebe, Cormorant, Grey Heron, common wildfowl, Moorhen, Coot.

Common finches
House Sparrow (not strictly a finch, of course), Chaffinch, Greenfinch, Goldfinch, Siskin, Linnet.

Winter thrushes
Blackbird, Fieldfare, Song Thrush, Redwing, Mistle Thrush.

Summer warblers
Lesser Whitethroat, Whitethroat, Garden Warbler, Blackcap, Chiffchaff, Willow Warbler. Sedge and Reed Warblers are also summer visitors, but these are specifically mentioned in Other Likely Species where they occur.

Winter raptors
Marsh Harrier usually seen in summer, though some over-winter, Hen Harrier, Sparrowhawk, Kestrel, Merlin, Peregrine, Barn Owl, Short-eared Owl included, though not strictly raptors.

Common waders
Oystercatcher, Ringed Plover, Golden Plover, Grey Plover, Lapwing, Knot, Sanderling, Dunlin, Snipe, Bar-tailed Godwit, Curlew, Redshank, Turnstone.

Passage waders
Little Ringed Plover, Ringed Plover, Little Stint, (not Temminck's Stint –which is scarce), Curlew Sandpiper, Dunlin, Ruff, Whimbrel, Spotted Redshank, Greenshank, Green Sandpiper, Wood Sandpiper, Common Sandpiper.

Common gull species
Black-headed Gull, Common Gull, Lesser Black-backed Gull, Herring Gull, Great Black-backed Gull.

Seaducks and winter seabirds
Red-throated Diver, Black-throated Diver, Great Northern Diver, Great Crested Grebe, Red-necked Grebe, Slavonian Grebe, Wigeon, Eider, Long-tailed Duck, Common Scoter, Velvet Scoter, Goldeneye, Red-breasted Merganser, Guillemot, Razorbill.

DEFINITIONS

Hirundines
Sand Martin, Swallow, House Martin, Swift (not a hirundine but included here to save space).

Passage migrants
Garganey, Little Gull, Black Tern, Hoopoe, Wryneck, Short-toed Lark, Woodlark, hirundines, Richard's Pipit, Tawny Pipit, Tree Pipit, Yellow Wagtail, Bluethroat, Black Redstart, Redstart, Whinchat, Wheatear, winter thrushes, Ring Ouzel, Icterine Warbler, Barred Warbler, summer warblers, Yellow-browed Warbler, Goldcrest, Firecrest, Spotted Flycatcher, Red-breasted Flycatcher, Pied Flycatcher, Red-backed Shrike, Great Grey Shrike, Brambling, Common Rosefinch, Ortolan Bunting, and many unmentioned rarities!

Passage seabirds
Divers, grebes, Sooty Shearwater, Manx Shearwater, Balearic Shearwater, Storm Petrel, Gannet, common wildfowl, common waders, Grey Phalarope, Pomarine Skua, Arctic Skua, Long-tailed Skua, Great Skua, Little Gull, Sabine's Gull, Kittiwake, terns, Guillemot, Razorbill, Little Auk.

Common scrub birds
Wren, Dunnock, Robin, Blackbird, Song Thrush, Mistle Thrush, summer warblers, Long-tailed Tit, Marsh Tit, Willow Tit, Blue Tit, Great Tit, common finches.

Terns
Sandwich Tern, Roseate Tern, Common Tern, Arctic Tern.

GLOSSARY/BIRDSPEAK

LIKE ALL OTHER activities, birdwatching has generated a language of its own and I've attempted to explain terms used in the book that may not be familiar to beginners and less experienced birdwatchers.

BIRDRACE: A competition, usually between teams of four people, to see how many species of birds can be seen and heard in a day.

BRECKLAND: A large area (400 square miles) of heathland and pine forest centred around Thetford, partly in Norfolk, the rest in Suffolk. Many scarce species of bird breed in the area.

BRECKS: Abbreviation for Breckland, see above.

BROADLAND: A popular holiday area for boat fanatics. Many broads, made up of former peat diggings, and rivers make up this area.

BROADS: See Broadland.

BTO: British Trust for Ornithology.

CATEGORY C: A category on the official British bird list containing species that have escaped from captivity in the past, but now have self-sustaining populations e.g. Canada Goose.

CHURRING: The distinctive sound made by Nightjars once dusk falls.

DIP: To go on a 'twitch' and not see the bird you went for.

GLOSSARY/BIRDSPEAK

DIPPER: One who 'dips' - a person who 'twitches' but misses the target bird. Not good!!

DUDE: A person who has all the top birdwatching equipment, but is a very poor birdwatcher – a bit like most politicians: style over content!

ECLIPSE: Male duck species moult out of breeding plumage in summer, and don a dowdy, female-type plumage known as eclipse.

FALL: A mass grounding of migrating passerines, usually as a result of fog or heavy rain.

FENCE-HOPPER: A bird that has escaped from captivity.

LIFER: A bird species you have never seen before – "that Desert Warbler at Salthouse was a lifer for me!".

LISTER: Someone who keeps a list of everything they see, everywhere they see it! Garden list, life list, world list, county list, year list, birds seen while undergoing open-heart surgery list, etc. My lists include 'birds seen at football matches'!

LOCAL PATCH: An area regularly covered by a birdwatcher, usually close to home. The feeling when something new turns up on your patch, rare or not, is pathetically exciting, particularly to a 'lister' such as me!

LOWLISTER: Someone who hasn't seen many species of bird.

LBJ: An affectionate term for Little Brown Job, any bird which has dowdy plumage – Dunnock, pipits, Garden Warbler, etc.

LRP: Shortened term for Little Ringed Plover.

NNR: National Nature Reserve.

NOA: Norfolk Ornithologists' Association.

NWT: Norfolk Wildlife Trust.

PLASTIC: Can refer to an escaped cage bird, or to a Category C species.

RAMSAR: A wetland site of international importance as defined at the convention in Ramsar, Iran.

RODING: The display flight of the Woodcock. Usually seen at dawn and dusk.

SSSI: Site of special scientific interest.

STRINGER: A person who misidentifies a bird and sticks to that identification. I have seen people 'string' a Collared Dove for a White's Thrush, a Little Tern for a Lesser Crested Tern, a Dunnock for a Black-faced Bunting and a tree stump for an Osprey. And one of those was me but thankfully only once!

TELESCOPE BRIGADE: A term sometimes used by beginners for a group of birdwatchers all huddled in one area peering through 'scopes, usually at a 'twitch'.

TICK OFF: To see a bird. Probably derived from 'listers' seeing a bird then ticking it off on one or more of their lists.

TWITCH: Travel to see a specific bird, usually a rare species, as soon as news of it breaks. Can involve a journey of many miles, or can just be to your 'local patch' to see something you have never seen there before. Has gained a bad name with beginners and birdwatchers who don't 'twitch', but is usually well organised, friendly and great fun if you don't 'dip'.

GLOSSARY/BIRDSPEAK

TWITCHER: Someone who goes on a twitch. Ardent 'twitchers' set off as soon as news breaks of a rare bird, anywhere in the country. Others go when they can, usually at the weekend after the target bird has flown on the Friday night!

WWT: Wildfowl and Wetlands Trust.

YEARLIST: A record of birds seen in Britain from January 1 to December 31.

YEARLISTER: Someone who tries to see as many species of bird in a year as possible. This has sometimes involved people seeing a rare bird on December 31, then travelling again to see it the next day to get it on two yearlists! The most famous example of this was in 1999/2000, when several birders turned up on January 1 2000 to 'yeartick' the Ivory Gull, present on Aldeburgh beach on December 31 1999. Unfortunately, the bird had been scared off the previous night by the Millennium fireworks display!

BIBLIOGRAPHY

Breckland Bird Reports (Edited by A. Wilson)
Available from A. Wilson, c/o BTO, The Nunnery, Thetford, Norfolk IP24 2PU

Norfolk Bird and Mammal Reports
Published yearly by the Norfolk and Norwich Naturalists' Society, Castle Museum, Norwich NR1 3JU.

The Birds of Cley (SJM Gantlett)
ISBN 0-9509903-0-2
Available from Sea Lawn, Coast Road, Cley-Next-The-Sea, Holt, Norfolk NR25 7RZ

The Birds Of Norfolk (Taylor, Seago, Allard, Dorling).
Published by Pica Press, ISBN 1-903206-02-2

Where To Watch Birds In East Anglia (Peter and Margaret Clarke)
Published by Helm.

USEFUL CONTACTS

BIRD NEWS, RECORDS AND INFORMATION

County Recorder
Dave and Jacquie Bridges. 01263 713 249; e-mail: dnjnorfolkrec@aol.com

Birdline East Anglia
09068 700 245.
Premium rate number.
Phone news to 0800 0830 803.

BROADS AUTHORITY VISITOR CENTRES

Beccles, The Quay, Fen Lane.
Tel/Fax 01502 713196.
Email: becclesinfo@broads-authority.gov.uk

Hoveton/Wroxham, Station Road.
Tel/Fax 01603 782 281.
Email: hovetoninfo@broads-authority.gov.uk

How Hill NNR, Ludham. Toad Hole Cottage Museum and 'Electric Eel' Wildlife Water Trail.
Tel/Fax 01692 678 763.
Email: toadholeinfo@broads-authority.gov.uk

Potter Heigham, The Staithe.
Tel/Fax 01692 670 779.
Email: potterinfo@broads-authority.gov.uk

Ranworth, The Staithe.
Tel/Fax 01603 270 453.
Email: ranworthinfo@broads-authority.gov.uk

For winter enquiries:
Broads Authority, 18 Colegate, Norwich NR3 1BQ. 01603 610 734, Fax 01603 765 710,
Email:broads@broads-authority.gov.uk

TOURIST INFORMATION CENTRES

Aylsham
Bure Valley Railway Station, Norwich Road, Aylsham, Norfolk NR11 6BW
Tel: 01263 733 903/01263 733 858
Fax: 01263 733 814
Email: aylsham.tic@broadland.gov.uk

Burnham Deepdale
Deepdale Farm, Burnham Deepdale Norfolk, PE31 8DD.
Tel: 01485 210 256
Fax: 01485 210 258
Email: info@deepdalefarm.co.uk

Cromer
Prince of Wales Road, Cromer, Norfolk NR27 9HS. Tel: 01263 512 497.
Fax: 01263 513613.
Email: cromertic@north-norfolk.gov.uk

Downham Market
The Priory Centre, 78 Priory Road, Downham Market, Norfolk PE38 9JS. Tel: 01366 383 287.
Fax: 01366 385 042.
Email: downham-market.tic@west-norfolk.gov.uk

Great Yarmouth
Maritime House, 25 Marine Parade Great Yarmouth, Norfolk NR30 2EN. Tel: 01493 846 345
Fax: 01493 858 588
Email: tourism@great-yarmouth.gov.uk

Holt
3 Pound House Market Place, Holt Norfolk NR25 6BW.
Tel: 01263 713 100
Fax: 01263 713 100
Email: holttic@north-norfolk.gov.uk

Hoveton
Station Road, Hoveton, Norfolk NR12 8UR. Tel: 01603 782 281
Fax: 01603 782281
Email: hovetoninfo@broads-authority.gov.uk

Hunstanton
Town Hall, The Green, Hunstanton Norfolk PE36 6BQ.
Tel: 01485 532 610
Fax: 01485 533 972
Email: hunstanton.tic@west-norfolk.gov.uk

King's Lynn
The Custom House, Purfleet Quay, King's Lynn, Norfolk PE30 1HP.
Tel: 01553 763 044
Fax: 01553 819 441
Email: kings-lynn.tic@west-norfolk.gov.uk

Loddon
Tourist Information Point, The Old Town Hall, 1 Bridge Street, Loddon Norfolk NR14 6ET. Tel: 01508 521 028.

Norwich
The Forum, Millennium Plain, Norwich, Norfolk NR2 1TF. Tel: 01603 727 927
Fax: 01603 765 389.
Email: tourism@norwich.gov.uk

Sheringham
Station Approach, Sheringham, Norfolk NR26 8RA. Tel: 01263 824 329 Fax: 01263 821 668
Email: sheringhamtic@north-norfolk.gov.uk

Swaffham
The Shambles, Market Place, Swaffham, Norfolk PE37 7AB.
Tel: 01760 722 255
Fax: 01760 723 410
Email: swaffham@eetb.info

Thetford
4 White Hart Street, Thetford, Norfolk IP24 2HA. Tel: 01842 820 689
Fax: 01842 820 986
Email: info@thetfordtourism.co.uk

Wells-Next-The-Sea
Staithe Street, Wells-next-the-Sea Norfolk NR23 1AN. Tel: 01328 710 885 Fax: 01328 711405
Email: wellstic@north-norfolk.gov.uk

Wymondham
The Market Cross, Market Place, Symondham, NR18 0AX.
Tel/fax 01953 604 721
Email: WymondhamTIC@btconnect.com
Web: www.wymondham-norfolk.co.uk

WILDLIFE GROUPS AND ORGANISATIONS

British Trust for Ornithology
The Nunnery, Thetford, Norfolk IP24 2PU. 01842 750 050. www.bto.org

Cley Bird Club
Peter Gooden, 45 Charles Road, Holt, Norfolk, NR25 6DA.

Disabled Birders Association
Bo Beolens, 18 St Mildreds Rd, Margate, Kent CT9 2LT.
www.disabledbirdersassociation.org.uk

Disabled toilets leaflet
RADAR, 12 City Forum, 250 City Road, London EC1V 8AF. 0207 125 03222

English Nature
Norfolk Office, 60 Bracondale, Norwich NR1 2BE. 01603 620 558.
www.english-nature.org.uk
Email: norfolk@english-nature.org.ok

Forest Enterprise
Santon Downham, Brandon, Suffolk IP27 0TJ. 01842 810 271

USEFUL CONTACTS

General Broads Authority
18 Colgate, Norwich, NR3 1BQ
01603 610734

High Lodge Forest Centre
01842 815434

How Hill Trust
How Hill, Ludham, Great Yarmouth NR29 5PG. Tel. 01692 6788555
www.how-hill.org.uk

The National Trust
East Anglia Regional Office, Blickling, Norwich NR11 6NF. 01263 733471.
www.nationaltrust.org.uk/regions/eastanglia/

Norfolk and Norwich Naturalists' Society
Membership Secretary: DL Paull, 8 Lindford Drive, Eaton, Norwich NR4 6LT

Norfolk Ornithologists' Association
Holme Observatory, Broadwater Road, Holme-Next-The-Sea, Norfolk PE36 6LQ. 01485 525406
www.noa.org.uk

Norfolk Wildlife Trust
Norfolk Wildlife Trust, Bewick House, 22 Thorpe Road, Norwich NR1 1RY
01603 625540
www.norfolkwildlifetrust.org.uk/

RSPB Eastern England Regional Office
Stalham House, 65 Thorpe Road, Norwich NR1 1UD. 01603 661662

RSPB Mid-Yare Reserves
Staithes Cottage, Low Road, Strumpshaw, Norwich NR13 4HF.
01603 715191.

RSPB Snettisham Reserve Office
Snettisham Business Centre, 43a Lynn Road, Snettisham PE31 7LR. 01485 542689

Ted Ellis Trust
Ted Ellis Trust at Wheatfen Nature Reserve, Surlingham, Norfolk NR13 5PT. www.tedellistrust.org.uk

PUBLIC TRANSPORT

Bus:
For local bus information contact Traveline 0870 6082608 www.travelineeastanglia.org.uk

Train:
One operates InterCity half-hourly services between Norwich and London Liverpool Street with local connecting services within East Anglia. Average journey time from London 1 hour 50 minutes. There are connecting services from the Midlands, the North of England and Scotland via Peterborough. Local Broads stations are located at: Acle, Beccles, Berney Arms, Brundall, Brundall Gardens, Buckenham, Cantley, Great Yarmouth, Haddiscoe, Hoveton and Wroxham, Lingwood, Lowestoft, Norwich, Oulton Broad, Reedham, Salhouse, Somerleyton and Worstead.

- National Rail Enquiries 08457 484950 www.nationalrail.co.uk www.thetrainline.com
- One 0845 600 7245 www.onerailway.com
- Central Trains 0870 6096060 www.centraltrains.co.uk
- www.bitternline.com for northern Broads and north Norfolk
- www.wherrylines.org.uk for central and southern Broads, Great Yarmouth and Lowestoft

Coach:
There are daily services from all major cities to Norwich operated by National Express, which also operates regular connections from Stansted, Heathrow and Gatwick airports.
National Express 08705 808080 www.nationalexpress.com

Cycle:
For the National Cycle Network contact Sustrans 0845 113 0065 www.sustrans.co.uk

Air:
Norwich is home to a major regional airport, Norwich International, with more than 300 worldwide connections via Manchester, Paris and Amsterdam. Journey time from Norwich to Amsterdam 40 minutes daily flights. London Stansted is within easy reach by road 85 miles.
Norwich International 01603 411923 www.norwichinternational.co.uk
Stansted 01279 680500 www.stanstedairport.com

Ferry:
Contact Stena Line 08705 707070 www.stenaline.co.uk or DFDS Seaways 0870 5333000 www.dfdseaways.co.uk

INDEX

INDEX

INDEX

INDEX

NORFOLK: MAP OF FEATURED SITES

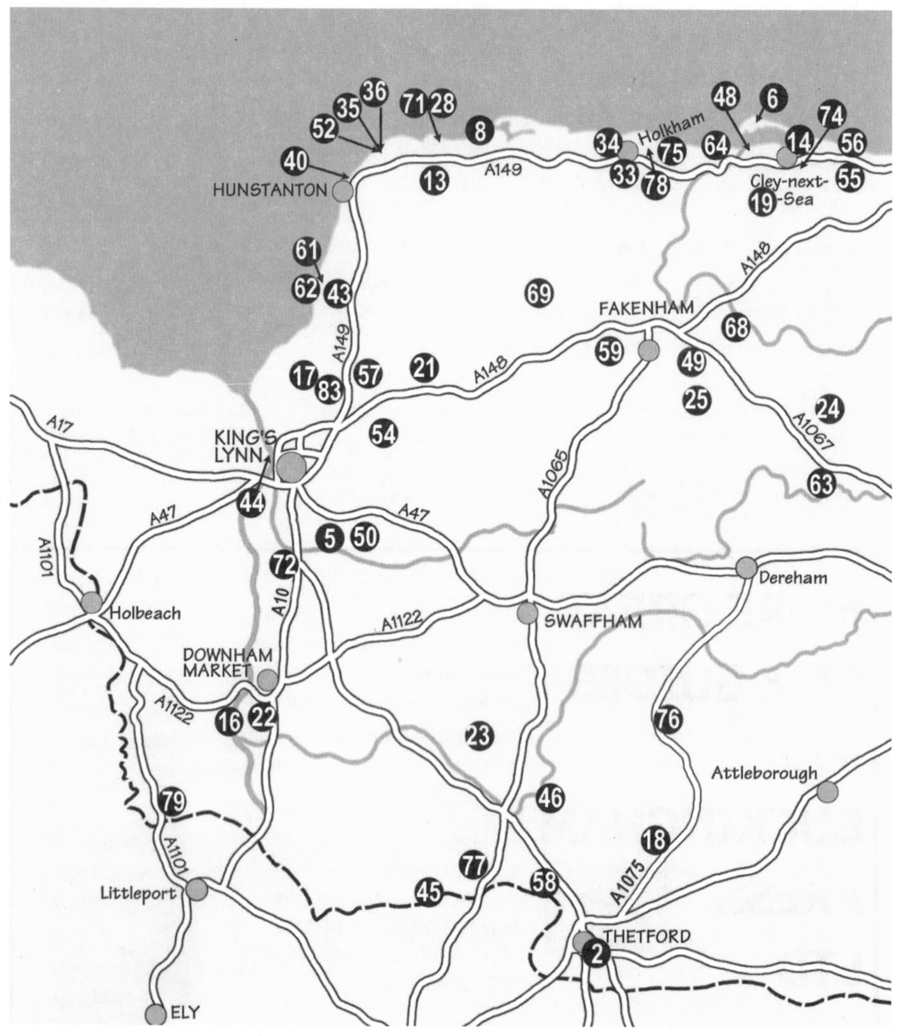

Key to sites

1 NWT Alderfen Broad
2 Barnham Cross Common
3 NWT Barton Broad
4 Berney Arms Marshes
5 Blackborough End Tip
6 Blakeney Point
7 Blickling Hall
8 Brancaster Marsh
9 Breydon Water
10 RSPB Buckenham Marshes
11 Burgh Castle
12 NWT Buxton Heath
13 Choseley Barns
14 NWT Cley Marshes
15 NWT Cockshoot Broad
16 Denver Sluice
17 Dersingham Bog
18 NWT East Wretham Heath
19 Farmland Bird Project
20 Felbrigg Hall
21 Flitcham Abbey Farm
22 Fordham
23 Foulden Common

Dear Julia,
with best wishes,
Eilidh Craster
x

LET'S MAKE A PLAN